THE RISE
OF THE ROMAN
JURISTS

THE RISE
OF THE ROMAN
JURISTS

Studies in Cicero's
pro Caecina

BY BRUCE W. FRIER

PRINCETON UNIVERSITY PRESS

Copyright © 1985 by Princeton University Press
Published by Princeton University Press, 41 William Street,
Princeton, New Jersey 08540
In the United Kingdom: Princeton University Press, Guildford, Surrey

Library of Congress Cataloging in Publication Data will be found
on the last printed page of this book

ISBN 0-691-03578-4

Publication of this book has been aided by a grant from The
Andrew W. Mellon Foundation.

This book has been composed in Linotron Janson

Clothbound editions of Princeton University Press books are printed
on acid-free paper, and binding materials are chosen for strength
and durability. Paperbacks, although satisfactory for personal collections,
are not usually suitable for library rebinding.

Printed in the United States of America by Princeton University
Press, Princeton, New Jersey

For John and Teresa D'Arms

More even than in Europe, here
The choice of patterns is made clear
Which the machine imposes, what
Is possible and what is not,
To what conditions we must bow
In building the Just City now.
   —W.H. Auden

Contents

vii

Contents

Tables and Figures

The map and the plan were both drawn by Jackie Royer; the plan of the late Republican Forum is after that in G. Lugli, *Itinerario di Roma Antica* (1975) 210. Theodore Peña took the photograph of the countryside around Castellum Axia, and the view of the Roman Forum today was provided courtesy of the Fototeca Unione at the American Academy in Rome.

Preface

I HAVE TWO stories to tell. The first is the story of a lawsuit brought more than two millennia ago, and of the remarkable speech delivered during it; the second is the story of how, in the decades preceding and following this lawsuit, the legal profession originated and first rose to influence. My conviction, upon which this book is based, is that these two stories are interlinked, though not in a direct causal way; they are interlinked because neither story is completely comprehensible without the other.

Cicero's speech *pro Caecina* was delivered during the third and final hearing of a lawsuit brought by Aulus Caecina probably in 69 B.C. Caecina, who had been named the principal heir of his late wife Caesennia, attempted to enter a farm allegedly within her estate. However, his way onto the farm was barred by Sextus Aebutius, who had organized a band of armed men to defend the farm's perimeter. Caecina then brought suit against Aebutius under the interdict *de vi armata*, in order to "recover" possession of the farm. Throughout the ensuing trial Cicero spoke on Caecina's behalf; and he later published, perhaps in a somewhat altered form, his final speech for his client.

I have long been interested in the *pro Caecina*. First of all, this speech, which is probably Cicero's last effort before the civil bar, is exceptionally fine; Cicero himself regarded it as a masterpiece of its kind, and later critics both ancient and modern have shared that judgment. It is therefore a pity that, because of its subject matter, the speech is so little known among most students of Roman literature. Further, the *pro Caecina* is the only one of Cicero's four surviving private orations that is also complete, and no private oration by any other Roman orator comes down in more than small fragments. This

Preface

fact alone gives the *pro Caecina* a considerable historical importance.

The speech is interesting in other respects. By the third hearing of Caecina's suit, the advocates for plaintiff and defendant had reached general agreement about events previous to the trial, the "facts of the case," or at least what could be proved. But they disagreed radically concerning the legal interpretation of these events. For this reason, the advocates mooted issues of great interest for a legal historian: the proper way to interpret the Praetor's Edict, the weight to be accorded to jurists' rulings on law, the role of *aequitas* in civil litigation, indeed the very nature and purpose of private law in Rome. The *pro Caecina* therefore provides an unusually good basis for discussing the social operation of late Republican law; and in the present book I use the *pro Caecina* for this purpose. On one level, my book reconstructs Caecina's lawsuit, from its origins to its decision, insofar as reconstruction is possible; on another level, I also treat the trial as "representative" in considering the Roman judicial system's effectiveness.

My decision to write a book on this subject was stimulated in part by the interesting chapter on the *pro Caecina* in Wilfried Stroh's *Taxis und Taktik* (1975). Stroh, who is mainly concerned with rhetorical technique and not with law, argues that in his speech Cicero deliberately falsifies the known sense of the interdict *de vi armata*, extravagantly misrepresents the argument of his opponent, and violently twists both facts and law in favor of his client. Although Stroh offers an especially well argued version of a view widespread in modern scholarship, I find that by and large I cannot agree with him. In particular, as to the central legal issue treated by Cicero, Stroh relies heavily on Giovanni Nicosia's *Studi sulla "Deiectio"* vol. I (1965), a justly praised book which, however, in treating the *pro Caecina* overlooks some important evidence that decisively refutes the central view Nicosia advances. If Nicosia is wrong, Stroh's arguments on this speech also founder; and to the extent that Stroh's position is today the prevailing view, it seems apparent that a reexamination of the speech is required. Further, in my opinion such a reexamination must reach not just the issues raised by Nicosia and Stroh, but also much deeper issues that touch on the operation of the Roman judicial system during the years when Cicero served as a private advocate (81-69 B.C.) and during the remainder of his life.

We know that in the late Republic, more or less during Cicero's lifetime, Roman legal science made important advances. During the second and early first century B.C., the stability of the Roman judicial system had been shaken by two important events: the introduction of important procedural reforms, mainly through the Praetor's Edict, and the emergence of rhetorical advocacy in pleadings. Both events tended to increase legal insecurity. The jurisconsults, Rome's unofficial legal experts, at first reacted slowly and rather tentatively to these challenges. At last, however, in the early first century B.C. a small group of jurisconsults (Q. Mucius Scaevola and his students) sought to counter disintegrative influences on law by reconstructing their ancient craft as a more autonomous and intellectual discipline. Their aim was evidently to secure for themselves and for law a more commanding presence within the Roman judicial system and Roman society generally. In essence, they ceased to be jurisconsults only, and became jurists as well, with major consequences for subsequent Western law. Through these men the legal profession walked for the first time onto the stage of history; the late Republican jurists were already "professionals" in that they possessed and exploited specific knowledge and skills which were inaccessible to laymen, and in that they also had at least rudimentary forms of regularized intercommunication, work autonomy, specialist literature, colleague "control," organized education, and even ethics.

In 69 B.C., as the *pro Caecina* shows (and much other evidence confirms), it was far from clear that the jurists' strategy would succeed. Yet by the early Empire the strategy had succeeded. The Roman jurists accomplished what earlier Mediterranean civilizations had not; they created an effective science of secular law. The crucial word is "effective." No one would deny the precociousness of late Republican jurispru-

Preface

dence; but the brilliance of the Roman jurists is not sufficient to explain their eventual success. In this book, I attempt to find further explanations in the external form of jurisprudence, the dynamics of the Roman judicial system, and the enormous changes in Roman society during the late Republic. My argument throughout this book, particularly in its later portion, is that in the late Republic the Roman judicial system was transformed from what we may call the "Ciceronian court" (still dominated by rhetorical advocacy) to the judicial system presupposed by classical Roman law, in which "questions of law" are settled mainly through reference to juristic *responsa*. I believe that this transition was largely complete even before the end of the Republic, and that it is not, save in some important details, an achievement of the Empire. In a general way, the *pro Caecina* serves to mark the transition; although in most respects it still partakes of the older era, in others it presages the impending change.

As has often been observed, substantive law is a system of rules, while procedural law is a system of roles. My book is organized in accordance with this sagacious observation. My first chapter is concerned with litigants and social sources of litigation. Chapter II discusses the Praetor's Edict and the opening (*in iure*) stage of trials. Chapter III is about the nature and effects of rhetorical advocacy within the second (*apud iudicem*) section of trials. The fourth chapter deals with the role of the jurists in the late Republican judicial system. Chapter V concerns the judge and the process of reaching a verdict. Chapter VI deals with popular attitudes toward law and with the shifting sources of judicial legitimacy during the late Republic. My conclusion sets out the main historical reasons for the rise of the Roman jurists in this period.

This is not, therefore, a general book about the law of the later Republic; indeed, such a book would be superfluous. Alan Watson's five books on the substantive law of the period already say most of what is worth saying; Franz Horak's *Rationes Decidendi* vol. I (1969) gives a good analysis of the characteristic modes of juristic reasoning in the late Republic; and Max Kaser's *Das Römische Zivilprozessrecht* (1966), now being

Preface

revised, remains the best modern treatment of procedure. The aims of my book are both more limited and more consciously sociological, and so I have dealt with details of substantive and procedural law only as they impinge rather directly on my central theme. It is my hope that the present book, for all the apparent complexity of its levels of argument, will none-theless help fill out the picture described by Watson, Horak, and Kaser, by setting the rise of the Roman jurists within its social context. My intent is to describe the internal and exter-nal conditions that made that rise possible, if not inevitable.

Finally, a word about "autonomous law." In a recent book, Sir Moses Finley has noted with repugnance "the survival of the old mystique about the law as something that stands above and outside society and its realities, with its own essence, its autonomous logic, its independent existence." Much of my own scholarly work (especially *Landlords and Tenants in Impe-rial Rome*, 1980) has been devoted to demonstrating the nu-merous lines of interrelationship between Roman private law and Roman society; that is clearly one purpose of the present book as well. But it is an error to consider the doctrine of "autonomous law" merely a frivolous "mystique." As I will try to show, "autonomous law" is an ideology central to the origin of the legal profession in the West. To such an extent is this true that we owe to "autonomous law" our very con-cept "lawyer"; for it is this doctrine that initially defines the legal profession's special competence as well as its claims with respect to society. The doctrine of "autonomous law," which appears for the first time in Cicero's *pro Caecina*, was to remain the guiding ideology of the legal profession for some two mil-lennia, through all vicissitudes of social and economic circum-stance.

In the twentieth century, to be sure, the doctrine of "au-tonomous law" is in shreds, the victim of relentless assaults upon it from numerous intellectual quarters. But caution is required before it is simply cast aside as a "mystique." First of all, for many centuries the doctrine was an article of faith among lawyers and non-lawyers alike, and as such it had pro-found influence both on how lawyers understood their work

Preface

and on how their work was perceived by others; historians who neglect the doctrine risk losing contact with the very reality they are seeking to explain. Second, as E.P. Thompson pointed out in *Whigs and Hunters* (1975), even today it is far from clear that the doctrine can be abandoned without endangering another fundamental tenet of the Western tradition, namely the rule of law. Indeed, the very capacity of modern legal systems to operate effectively without a doctrine of "autonomous law" is, at the least, still open to question; and some scholars, such as the sociologist Niklas Luhmann and the legal philosopher Bruce Ackerman, have called, in my opinion rightly, for the revival of "autonomous law" in a more sophisticated activist form. All of this is simply to say that "autonomous law" may not be quite so dead as it appears to be. The pendulum may swing back once more.

The doctrine of "autonomous law" serves also as a cornerstone for the venerable, if now increasingly inconvenient, division of labor between Roman historians and Roman legal historians. While I favor putting an end to this division of labor, I also favor doing so cautiously, lest the enormous independent achievements of Roman legal historians be submerged and rendered incomprehensible to future generations. At a minimum I would urge modern scholars to respect the values of pluralism in scholarly research.

The first two chapters of this book were written in Ann Arbor during the summer of 1980; the remaining chapters were written during the first seven months of 1983, partly in Ann Arbor and partly at the Institute for Advanced Study, Princeton. During the intervening period, thanks largely to an informal seminar with several graduate students in 1981, I revised my plan for the book; some slight inconcinnities in perspective may remain between the two portions of the book, though I have tried to remove them. Scholarship reaching my attention after August 1983 has been incorporated very sparingly.

Here at the University of Michigan I have been uncommonly lucky in my students and colleagues, both in the Department of Classical Studies and in the Law School; often

Preface

even the briefest conversation with one of them has clarified a nagging mystery. In particular, Professor Richard Lempert, a sociologist of law, has often discussed with me the intricacies of his field; although he may perhaps find much to disagree with in my approach and conclusions, he has deeply influenced this book. Professor James B. White also read my manuscript and offered many acute suggestions.

My stay at the Institute for Advanced Study was underwritten by the Institute and my home university, and proved amazingly helpful. I received much excellent advice from scholars in other historical and social fields, in particular some trenchant and salutary skepticism from Professor Gerhard Thür, a Greek legal historian from Munich.

Finally, I am grateful for this renewed opportunity to thank Princeton University Press and its Executive Editor, Joanna Hitchcock, who have encouraged and supported my work. Charles B. Purrenhage skillfully edited the manuscript for publication.

The debt I owe the dedicatees of this book is of a special kind. My friendship with John and Teresa D'Arms reaches back nearly two decades, and has meant very much to me. In a sense, John and Teresa also represent the poles about which I had intended this book to revolve: John with his deep and realistic understanding of Roman social life, Teresa with her keen practical grasp of what lawyering involves. For numerous reasons they were both much on my mind as I was completing this book, and I am glad now to offer it to them both.

July 1984

Abbreviations

THE FOLLOWING abbreviations are used in citations throughout my footnotes. I also abbreviate citations of legal and literary sources; the fuller forms can be found in in my index of passages cited.

ACIR	*Atti del Congresso Internazionale di Diritto Romano*, Rome 1933, 2 vols. (Pavia, 1934)
ACIV	*Atti del Congresso Internazionale di Diritto Romano e di Storia del Diritto*, Verona 1948, 4 vols. (Milan 1953)
AG	*Archivio Giuridico "Filippo Serafini"* (Milan)
AJPh	*American Journal of Philology* (Baltimore)
ANRW	*Aufstieg und Niedergang der Römischen Welt*, 3 vols., ed. H. Temporini (Berlin-New York, since 1972); cited by volume and fasicule
Bauman, R.A., *Lawyers*	Richard A. Bauman, *Lawyers in Roman Republican Politics: A Study of the Roman Jurists in Their Political Setting, 316-82 B.C.* (Münchener Beiträge zur Papyrusf. und Ant. Rechtsg. 75, 1983)
Bethmann-Hollweg, M.A., *Civilprozess*	M.A. von Bethmann-Hollweg, *Der Römische Civilprozess*, 3 vols. (Bonn 1864-1866; repr. Aalen 1959)
Bögli, H., *Beiträge*	Hans Bögli, *Beiträge zur Lehre vom Ius Gentium der Römer* (Bern 1913)
Bögli, H., *Rede*	Hans Bögli, *Ueber Ciceros Rede für A. Caecina* (Burgdorf 1906)
Boulanger, A., *Discours*	André Boulanger, *Cicéron, Discours* vol. VII (Paris 1929)
Bretone, M., *Tecniche*	Mario Bretone, *Tecniche e Ideologie dei Giuristi Romani* (Naples 1971)

Abbreviations

Bull.	*Bullettino dell' Istituto di Diritto Romano* (Rome, since 1940 Milan)
Costa, E., *Cicerone Giur.*	Emilio Costa, *Cicerone Giureconsulto* (Bologna 1916, 2d ed. 1927)
Costa, E., *Orazioni*	Emilio Costa, *Le Orazioni di Diritto Privato di M. Tullio Cicerone* (Bologna 1899)
CQ	*Classical Quarterly* (Oxford)
D'Ors, A., *Defensa*	Alvaro D'Ors Pérez-Peix, *Cicerón: Defensa de Aulo Cecina* (Madrid 1943)
FIRA	*Fontes Iuris Romani Anteiustiniani* 2d ed. vol. I (*Leges*; ed. S. Riccobono, 1941/1968), vol. II (*Auctores*; ed. I Baviera and I. Furlani, 1940/1964), vol. III (*Negotia*; ed. V. Arangio-Ruiz, new ed. with appendix 1968)
Frier, B.W., *LTIR*	Bruce W. Frier, *Landlords and Tenants in Imperial Rome* (Princeton 1980)
Fs. Flume	*Festschrift für Werner Flume*, 2 vols. (Cologne 1978)
Fs. Schulz	*Festschrift Fritz Schulz*, 2 vols. (Weimar 1951)
Fs. Schwind	*Festschrift Fritz Schwind* (Vienna 1978)
Fs. Steinwenter	*Festschrift Artur Steinwenter* (Graz-Cologne 1958)
Gruen, E., *Last Generation*	Erich S. Gruen, *The Last Generation of the Roman Republic* (Berkeley–Los Angeles–London 1974)
Harris, W.V., *Etruria*	William V. Harris, *Rome in Etruria and Umbria* (Oxford 1971)
Harris, W.V., *Imperialism*	William V. Harris, *War and Imperialism in Republican Rome* (Oxford 1979)
Horak, F., *Rationes*	Franz Horak, *Rationes Decidendi* vol. I (Aalen 1969)
IGRRP	R. Cagnat *et al.*, *Inscriptiones Graecae ad Res Romanas Pertinentes*, 4 vols. (Paris 1911-1927; repr. Chicago 1975)
ILLRP	Attilio Degrassi, *Inscriptiones Latinae Liberae Rei Publicae*, 2 vols. (2d ed.; Florence 1965 and 1963, respectively)

Abbreviations

ILS	Hermann Dessau, *Inscriptiones Latinae Selectae*, 3 vols. (Berlin 1892-1916; often reprinted)
Jordan, C.A., *Oratio*	Carolus Adolphus Jordan, *M. Tullii Ciceronis Oratio pro A. Caecina* (Leipzig 1847)
Jörs, P., *Rechtsw.*	Paul Jörs, *Römische Rechtswissenschaft zur Zeit der Republik* vol. I (Berlin 1888)
JRS	*Journal of Roman Studies* (London)
Kaser, M., *RPR*²	Max Kaser, *Das Römische Privatrecht*, 2 vols. (2d ed.; Munich 1971-1975)
Kaser, M., *RZ*	Max Kaser, *Das Römische Zivilprozessrecht* (Munich 1966)
Keller, F.L., *Sem.*	Friedrich Ludwig von Keller, *Semestrium ad M. Tullium Ciceronem* vol. I (Turici 1842-1850); paginated continuously
Kelly, J.M., *Judicature*	John Maurice Kelly, *Studies in the Civil Judicature of the Roman Republic* (Oxford 1976)
Kelly, J.M., *Litigation*	John Maurice Kelly, *Roman Litigation* (Oxford 1966)
Kunkel, W., *Herkunft*²	Wolfgang Kunkel, *Herkunft und Soziale Stellung der Römischen Juristen* (2d ed.; Graz-Vienna-Cologne 1967)
Lenel, O., *EP*³	Otto Lenel, *Das Edictum Perpetuum* (3d ed.; Leipzig 1927; repr. Graz 1960)
Lenel, O., *Pal.*	Otto Lenel, *Palingenesia Iuris Civilis*, 2 vols. (Leipzig 1889; repr. Graz 1960)
Lineam.	M. Talamanca *et al.*, *Lineamenti di Storia del Diritto Romano* (Milan 1979)
Lombardi, L., *Saggio*	Luigi Lombardi, *Saggio sul Diritto Giurisprudenziale* (Milan 1967)
MAL	*Memorie della Classe di Scienze Morali e Storiche dell' Accademia dei Lincei* (Rome)
MDAI(R)	*Mitteilungen des Deutschen Archäologischen Instituts, Röm. Abt.* (Mainz)
MEFR	*Mélanges d'Archéologie e d'Histoire de l'École Française de Rome* (Paris)

Abbreviations

Mél. de Visscher	*Mélanges Fernand de Visscher*, = *RIDA* 2-5 (1949-1950)
Mél. Girard	*Mélanges Paul Frédéric Girard*, 2 vols. (Paris 1912)
Mommsen, T., *Staatsrecht*	Theodor Mommsen, *Römisches Staatsrecht* vols. I-II (3d ed.; Leipzig 1887), III (Leipzig 1888); all repr. Darmstadt 1971
MRR	T. Robert S. Broughton, *The Magistrates of the Roman Republic*, 2 vols. (New York 1951), *Supplement* (New York 1960); cited usually by year and magistracy
Mus. Helv.	*Museum Helveticum: Revue Suisse pour l'Étude de l'Antiquité Classique* (Bale)
Nicolet, C., *Ordre*	Claude Nicolet, *L'Ordre Équestre a l'Époque Républicaine*, 2 vols. (Paris 1966-1974)
Nicosia, G., *Deiectio*	Giovanni Nicosia, *Studi sulla "Deiectio"* vol. I (Milan 1965)
Nörr, D., *Rechtskritik*	Dieter Nörr, *Rechtskritik in der Römischen Antike*, = *Bayerische Akad. der Wiss*, Phil.-Hist. Kl., Abh. 77 (Munich 1973)
Not. Scav.	*Notizie degli Scavi di Antichità* (Rome)
NRHD	*Nouvelle Revue Historique du Droit Français et Étranger* (Paris)
PBSR	*Papers of the British School at Rome* (London)
Pflüger, H.H., *Besitzklagen*	Heinrich Hackfeld Pflüger, *Die Sogennanten Besitzklagen des Römischen Rechts* (Leipzig 1890)
Pugliese, G., *Processo*	Giovanni Pugliese, *Il Processo Civile Romano*, 2 vols. (Rome 1961-1962 and Milan 1963, respectively)
RE	*Paulys Realencyclopädie der Classischen Altertumswissenschaft*, ed. G. Wissowa *et al.* (Stuttgart); cited by article and column number
Rec. F. Gény	*Recueil d'Études sur les Sources du Droit, en Honneur de François Gény* (Paris 1934)
RH	*Revue Historique du Droit Français et Étranger* (Paris; 4th series since 1922; succeeds *NRHD*)
Rh. Mus.	*Rheinisches Museum für Philologie* (Frankfurt)

Abbreviations

RIDA[3]	*Revue Internationale des Droits de l'Antiquité* (Brussels; 3d series since 1954)
RIL	*Rendiconti dell' Istituto Lombardo di Scienze e Lettere* (Milan)
Roby, H.J., *Private Law*	Henry John Roby, *Roman Private Law in the Times of Cicero and of the Antonines*, 2 vols. (Cambridge 1902)
Schiavone, A., *Nascita*	Aldo Schiavone, *Nascita della Giuriprudenza: Cultura Aristocratica e Pensiero Giuridico nella Roma Tardo-Repubblicana* (Rome-Bari 1976)
Schiller, A.A., *Mechanisms*	A. Arthur Schiller, *Roman Law: Mechanisms of Development* (The Hague–Paris–New York 1978)
Schmidlin, B., *Rechtsregeln*	Bruno Schmidlin, *Die Römischen Rechtsregeln* (Cologne-Vienna 1970)
Schmidlin, B., *Rek.*	Bruno Schmidlin, *Das Rekuperatorenverfahren* (Freiburg 1963)
Schulz, F., *Legal Science*	Fritz Schulz, *History of Roman Legal Science* (Oxford 1946)
Schulz, F. *Principles*	Fritz Schulz, *Principles of Roman Law* (Oxford 1936), trans. from *Prinzipien des Römischen Rechts* (Munich-Leipzig 1934)
Scr. Ferrini Mil.	*Scritti in Onore di Contardo Ferrini Pubblicati in Occasione della Sua Beatificazione*, 4 vols. (Milan 1947-1949)
SDHI	*Studia et Documenta Historiae et Iuris* (Rome)
St. Biondi	*Studi in Onore di Biondo Biondi*, 4 vols. (Milan, 1965)
St. Bonfante	*Studi in Onore di Pietro Bonfante*, 4 vols. (Milan 1930)
St. Grosso	*Studi in Onore di Giuseppe Grosso*, 6 vols. (Turin 1968-1974)
St. Volterra	*Studi in Onore di Edoardo Volterra*, 6 vols. (Milan 1971)
Stroh, W., *Taxis*	Wilfried Stroh, *Taxis und Taktik: Die Advokat. Dispositionskunst in Ciceros Gerichtsreden* (Stuttgart 1975)

Abbreviations

Synt. Arangio-Ruiz	*Synteleia Vincenzo Arangio-Ruiz*, 2 vols. (Naples 1964)
SZ	*Zeitschrift der Savigny-Stiftung für Rechtsgeschichte*, Romanist. Abt. (Weimar)
TAPhA	*Transactions and Proceedings of the American Philological Association* (Cleveland)
TR	*Tijdschrift voor Rechtsgeschiedenis* = *Revue d'Histoire du Droit* = *The Legal History Review* (Haarlem, since 1950 Groningen)
Vonglis, B., *Lettre*	Bernard Vonglis, *La Lettre et l'Esprit de la Loi dans la Jurisprudence Classique et la Rhétorique* (Paris 1968)
Watson, A., *Law Making*	Alan Watson, *Law Making in the Later Roman Republic* (Oxford 1974)
Watson, A., *Obligations*	Alan Watson, *The Law of Obligations in the Later Roman Republic* (Oxford 1965)
Watson, A., *Persons*	Alan Watson, *The Law of Persons in the Later Roman Republic* (Oxford 1967)
Watson, A., *Property*	Alan Watson, *The Law of Property in the Later Roman Republic* (Oxford 1968)
Watson, A., *Succession*	Alan Watson, *The Law of Succession in the Later Roman Republic* (Oxford 1971)
Watson, A., *XII Tables*	Alan Watson, *Rome of the XII Tables: Persons and Property* (Princeton 1975)
Wenger, L., *Quellen*	Leopold Wenger, *Die Quellen des Römischen Rechts* (Vienna 1953)
Wieacker, F., *Recht²*	Franz Wieacker, *Vom Römischen Recht* (2d ed.; Stuttgart 1961)
Wiseman, T.P., *New Men*	T.P. Wiseman, *New Men in the Roman Senate, 139 B.C.–A.D. 14* (London 1971)
WS	*Wiener Studien: Zeitschrift für Klassische Philologie und Patristik* (Vienna)

THE RISE
OF THE ROMAN
JURISTS

I

The Litigants:
Aulus Caecina and Sextus Aebutius

> magna . . . alea est, litem
> ad interdictum deducere
> —Frontinus

THE TRIAL began with the death of a wealthy matron named
Caesennia, from the city of Tarquinii in Etruria. She died
probably in late 70 B.C., or early in 69.[1] Her will divided her
estate into three very unequal shares:[2] 23/24 of the entirety
(or about 95.8%) to her second husband, Aulus Caecina; 1/36
(or about 2.8%) to Marcus Fulcinius, a freedman of her first
husband; and 1/72 (or about 1.4%) to a friend of hers named
Sextus Aebutius.

Within a few weeks or months of Caesennia's death, two of
her heirs were in court: the principal heir, A. Caecina, was
suing the minor heir, Sex. Aebutius, the ground for the suit
being that the defendant Aebutius had used a band of armed
men forcibly to prevent Caecina from entering a farm that
allegedly formed part of Caesennia's estate. The board of "recoverers" (*recuperatores*), who had been named by the Urban
Praetor P. Cornelius Dolabella to decide this case, required
three hearings before they could reach a verdict. Virtually our
only source for the case is Cicero's *pro Caecina*, the published

[1] Cicero's *pro Caecina* dates to 69 B.C.; for argument, see Chapter II, at
notes 9-15.
[2] Cicero, *Caec.* 17. Save as indicated, I cite the *pro Caecina* by section number only (e.g., 17) from A.C. Clark's Oxford text (1905).

3

version of an oration delivered on the plaintiff's behalf during the third and final hearing (*Caec.* 6).

In this chapter, I reconstruct the circumstances that led to Caecina's suit against Aebutius, and then discuss the historical and social background of this lawsuit.[3]

TARQUINII AND ROME

Most of the events leading up to the trial took place either at Rome or in Tarquinii (see Figure 1). The Fulcinian farm, the object of the dispute, was located *in agro Tarquiniensi* (11, 15), "in the territory of Tarquinii." This ancient Etruscan city, once one of the most powerful in Italy, was in Cicero's day becoming a small rural town of minor economic significance. Tarquinii lay on an eroded bluff of tufa, from which it looked out across a narrow alluvial plain to the Tyrrhenian Sea; Rome was less than a hundred kilometers to the south by the trunk road, the *via Aurelia*. Behind the city, the *ager Tarquiniensis* extended inland, within the watershed of the river Marta, as far as the Lago di Bolsena (Vitruv. 2.7.3; Pliny, *NH* 2.209) and the *via Cassia*, the consular highway bisecting the breadth of Etruria. Apparently ever since the settlement of 281/280 B.C., Tarquinii and its territory had been effectively subject to Roman rule, and in 90 B.C. its residents had become citizens of Rome, as had most other Italians.[4] By the later Roman Republic, Tarquinii's time in the sun was over.

Caesennia and her first husband, M. Fulcinius, were both members of the native upper classes in Tarquinii (10); the Caesennii and Fulcinii are attested among the numerous

---

[3] All modern recountings of the background to the *pro Caecina* ultimately derive from F.L. Keller's exhaustive *Semestrium ad M. Tullium Ciceronem* vol. I.2 (1841) 273-538 and stress legal above social aspects. H.J. Roby, *Private Law* vol. II 510-535, is exceptionally keen on the psychological interplay. W.L.F. Felstiner *et al.*, *Law and Society Review* 15 (1980/1981) 631-654, stress the importance of analyzing the early stages of legal disputes.

[4] On the status of Tarquinii, see M. Torelli, (cited below n.6) 187, preferable to E. Ruoff-Väänänen, in *Acta Inst. Rom. Finl.* 5: *Studies in the Romanization of Etruria* (1975) 52-55. The latter book is referred to in this chapter as *SRE*.

Tarquinii and Rome

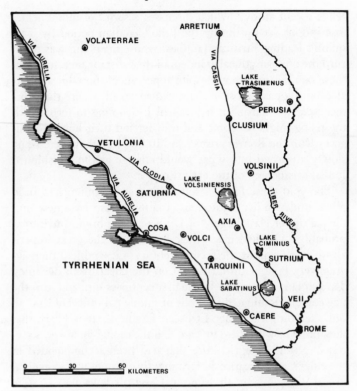

FIGURE 1. Southern Etruria during the late Republic. Most of the old Etruscan cities were linked to Rome by the great consular highways. The territory of Tarquinii ran inland, up to the Lago di Bolsena and the *via Cassia*, and included Castellum Axia, a fortlet near the site of the Fulcinian farm. The three lakes along the lower *via Cassia* are all in the craters of extinct volcanoes.

Etruscan-language funerary inscriptions from that city,[5] and M. Fulcinius still owned ancestral land there (11). The temper of this native aristocracy has been movingly depicted in To-

---

[5] Fulcinii: cf. the HVLXNIE (*Corpus Inscriptionum Etruscarum* 5357, 5358, 5388) with M. Cristofani, *MAL* 14.4 (1969) 253. The Caesennii are, of course, far better known: Cristofani, 251 (CEISINIE). The subsequent history of the Caesennii is discussed by R. Syme, *JRS* 67 (1977) 38-49, esp. 44-45, with other references.

5

The Litigants

relli's recent study,[6] which discusses a series of monumental inscriptions set up during the Julio-Claudian period by Tarquinii's leading Etruscan families, whose main aim was to record the quasi-mythical grandeur of their distant ancestors. But these families were not, despite appearances, nostalgically fixated on the past; most of them had survived, where their former peers at Tarquinii had failed, by coming to terms with the rising might of Rome and transferring their hopes to alliances with the Roman aristocracy. In this way they were being slowly absorbed into what would emerge as the refashioned Italian aristocracy of the early Empire.[7]

The void these families left behind at Tarquinii had been filled, under rather mysterious circumstances,[8] by a new municipal upper class largely of Latin or Italic origin: investors, probably, who had made their fortunes in the great imperialistic expansion of the second century B.C. and had then aggressively bought up farm land on the cheap from declining Tarquinian aristocrats.[9] In the first centuries B.C. and A.D. the newcomers dominated the rolls of municipal officeholders, all but excluding the older Etruscan families.[10] It is likely that they brought with them to Tarquinii the capital-intensive, slave-based system of agriculture that had been recommended in the elder Cato's treatise on farming; this system was in general use at Tarquinii by the time of Caecina's lawsuit.[11] Despite their differences from the native Etruscans in speech and manner, there is no evidence of serious social friction between

[6] M. Torelli, *Elogia Tarquiniensia* (1975), esp. 185-197. At pp. 137-142 and 192, Torelli discusses monuments of the Caesennii.

[7] On this, see M. Torelli, *Dialoghi di Archeologia* 3 (1969) 312 ff.

[8] The Gracchan colony at Tarquinii, referred to in the *Libri Coloniarum* 219.1 L, is very doubtful, cf. W.V. Harris, *Etruria* 205; E. Ruoff-Väänänen, in *SRE* (cited n.4) 38; M. Torelli, (cited n.6) 191.

[9] On the process, see W.V. Harris, *Imperialism* 93-104. For other "investors" at Tarquinii, see below, notes 32, 64; also M. Torelli, (cited n.6) 187-191. And note Q. Flavius, a Tarquinian who killed a slave (Cic. *Rosc. Com.* 32); also Q. Fulvius Lippinus, owner of a 40-*iugera* deer park (Varro, *RR* 3.12.1), who had senatorial relatives, cf. T.P. Wiseman, *New Men* 261.

[10] Cf. M. Torelli, (cited n.6) 187-189.

[11] See below, at notes 29-31.

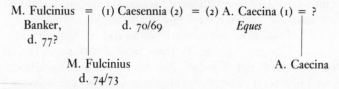

Table 1
The Relations of Caesennia

M. Fulcinius = (1) Caesennia (2) = (2) A. Caecina (1) = ?
Banker,   d. 70/69   *Eques*
d. 77?

M. Fulcinius   A. Caecina
d. 74/73

these two groups, whose interests were perhaps largely complementary: the surviving Etruscan families busied themselves with the society and politics of Rome, while the newcomers settled down to enjoying a privileged place in a municipal backwater. Yet as we shall see below, some latent hostility between them and the older families may have remained.

M. Fulcinius and Caesennia married within their class (see Table 1). Only one child, a son named for his father, seems to have survived to adulthood; since this son was capable of both marrying and writing his own will as of about 74 B.C. (12), and hence was 14 years or older by then,[12] his parents were presumably married by 89 B.C. at the latest, probably somewhat earlier. Caesennia came to the marriage with a substantial dowry, at least part of which was in cash (11). While this dowry was doubtless provided by her family, she was not under a father's *potestas* when her first husband died, since she then took back the dowry into her own hands (15).

Fulcinius is described by Cicero (10) as a man of the first rank at Tarquinii, who in Rome ran a "not dishonorable banking establishment" (*argentariam non ignobilem*); his wife, by contrast, "was born in the highest station and was of most upright character" (10: *summo loco natam et probatissimam feminam*). It is hard to recapture the social tone of these remarks,

[12] As to marriage, cf. A. Watson, *Persons* 39 (citing Servius in D. 12.4.8); as to wills, see Gaius 2.113 *et al.* The marriage between Fulcinius and Caesennia is likely to have been *cum manu*, since she later had the power to write a will (*Caec.* 17); on this, see A. Watson, *Persons* 152-154 and *Succession* 22-23, 73-75.

but Cicero appears to suggest that the match was a better one for Fulcinius than for his wife.[13] The Roman banking community, which mainly financed various kinds of loans, offered one standard profession for new men to make their way upward in Roman society;[14] but banking had an unsavory reputation. Cicero's scathing reference later in the speech (27) to the *argentarius* Sex. Clodius Phormio, a witness for the defense, is typical of negative comments on *argentarii* in ancient writings.[15] As it happens, yet another witness for the defense, the discreditable Senator C. Fidiculanius Falcula, who had twice narrowly escaped in trials for judicial corruption some years before (28-29), was also linked to Rome's banking community.[16] A gentleman did not willingly pursue banking as a profession.

The banking establishment run by Fulcinius perhaps came into existence before his marriage, in the turbulent years leading up to the outbreak of the Social War in 91 B.C. But Fulcinius' ancestors may well have been established at Rome even earlier; scholars have suggested a relationship with Fulcinia, the paternal grandmother of the great captain C. Marius[17]—if so, a valuable but politically risky connection. In any event, during the ensuing years Fulcinius, his son, and his wife appear fully at home with Roman legal rules and procedures,

[13] On terminology, see J. LeGall, in *Recherches sur les Structures Sociales* (ed. C. Nicolet, 1970) 275-286, at 279. Claude Nicolet, who considered Fulcinius an *eques* in *Ordre* vol. I 364, evidently thought better of the idea; Fulcinius is omitted from the prosopography in vol. II. On Caesennia, B. Rantz, *RIDA*[3] 29 (1982) 265-280, is highly inaccurate.

[14] See T.P. Wiseman, *New Men* 77-89. On the activities of *argentarii*, see G. Thielmann, *Die Römische Privatauktion* (1961); J. Andreau, *Les Affaires de Monsieur Jucundus* (1974); C.T. Barlow, *Bankers, Moneylenders, and Interest Rates in the Roman Republic* (Diss. North Carolina, 1978). All cite further bibliography. On ancient (esp. Greek) banking, see R. Bogaert, *Banques et Banquiers dans les Cités Grecques* (1968).

[15] Cf. C. Nicolet, *Ordre* vol. I 362-363.

[16] See *ILLRP* 1027, 1030: *tesserae nummulariae* of C. Fidiculanius (a freedman?), dating to 62 and 61 (?) B.C. On Fidiculanius, contrast Cicero's complete exoneration of him in *Cluent.* 103-104, 108, 112-113, during a trial in 66 B.C.; and see below, note 64.

[17] Plut. *Mar.* 6.3. Cf. T.P. Wiseman, *New Men* 55; at p. 189 he conjectures, less confidently, a connection with L. Fulcinius, a Quaestor in 148 B.C.

just as one might expect of a banker's family; no doubt they were even "more Romanized than most at Tarquinii."[18] Fulcinius must have moved his family to Rome almost at once after his marriage.

But the bank did not prosper. Cicero refers to "times when payment of debt was very difficult" (11: *temporibus illis difficillimis solutionis*). This is almost surely a reference to the collapse of credit which followed the invasion of the Roman province of Asia by the forces of Mithridates in 89.[19] The crisis was aggravated by the lingering effects of the Social War in Italy, and then prolonged by the civil wars between the partisans of Sulla, Marius, and Cinna from 88 to 81. The immediate consequence of the credit collapse was a general call-in of debts, which led to a riot in 89 during which an Urban Praetor who had been sympathetic to debtors was murdered by a mob of angry creditors led by a plebeian Tribune;[20] and then to a series of measures for debt relief undertaken during the next several years.[21] Outright debt relief could hardly have helped the stability of Rome's banking community. Fulcinius, impelled by his need for liquid assets, "sold" a farm he owned in Tarquinii to his wife, in exchange for part of her cash dowry (11), essentially trading his own land for her cash; Cicero praises the financial advantages of this transaction for both parties (since land prices were doubtless artificially depressed), but the "sale" was plainly a device of convenience for him.[22] The dowry *fundus* lay near the fortlet

[18] W.V. Harris, *Etruria* 284.

[19] Cic. *Leg. Man.* 19, with E.J. Jonkers, *Social and Economic Commentary on Cicero's* de Imperio Cn. Pompeii (1959) *ad loc.*; cf. Cic. *Leg. Ag.* 2.83. This great economic depression lies behind many of Cicero's early speeches, including the *pro Quinctio* and even the *pro Roscio Comoedo* (33, 37).

[20] The fullest sources are Val. Max. 9.7.4 and Appian, *BC* 1.54.232 ff.; cf. also Livy, *Per.* 74.

[21] T. Frank, *AJPh* 54 (1933) 54-58; C.T. Barlow, *AJPh* 101 (1980) 202-219. On lowered land prices caused by insecurity, see Cic. *Rosc. Com.* 33 (referring to Tarquinii, cf. 32).

[22] So most commentators. This transaction is not irregular in later law, provided that worth is given: Julian, D. 23.4.21; Scaev., D. 23.4.29 pr.; Modest., D. 23.3.26. However, Cicero's wording is ambiguous, and B. Kübler, in *Mél. Girard* vol. II 43-61, thought, with some justice, of a *fiducia* or

FIGURE 2. The countryside around Castellum Axia. The view is along a valley, at the end of which the site of Castellum Axia is marked by the remains of a square medieval tower. The landscape was formed primarily by beds of compacted ash laid down by surrounding volcanoes; in time these beds eroded to form steep bluffs interspersed with long and fertile alluvial valleys. In one of these valleys the Fulcinian farm will have lain.

Castellum Axia (20), in the extreme eastern part of the *ager Tarquiniensis.*[23] (See Figure 2.)

Eventually, perhaps in expectation of the chaos let loose by Sulla's invasion of 83 B.C. (and perhaps also in fear of Sulla

---

a sale with right of repurchase; H. Bögli, *Beiträge* 71-73, of a return of dowry through repurchase (cf. Paul, D. 23.3.73.1). In any case, I shall refer to this *fundus* as "the dotal farm."

[23] See G. Colonna, in *The Princeton Encyclopedia of Classical Sites* (1976) 132, with bibliography; M. Torelli, *Etruria* (Guide Archeologiche Laterza no. 3, 1980) 229-233. The site is today accessible only from Viterbo, about 8.5 km. distant; it contains substantial Etruscan remains, but little from after 50 B.C. In antiquity the *via Cassia* would have been used to reach it. See also note 64.

himself, if the Fulcinii were related to Marius), M. Fulcinius dissolved his Roman bank altogether and returned home to Tarquinii. With the money thus realized he purchased "some property" (*quaedam praedia*) adjacent to the farm now in his wife's dowry (11). The newly purchased property was what came to be called the Fulcinian farm (15: *fundum illum Fulcinianum*; cf. 82); the Fulcinian farm would much later be the object of the suit between Caecina and Aebutius.

There is much about Fulcinius' purchase of this farm that is interesting from an historical viewpoint. First, it is clear from the details of the story (and explicitly stated by Cicero in section 16) that this farm, like the dowry property beside it, was large enough to constitute a major financial asset; and this should mean that we are dealing with the capital-intensive, "Catonian" type of farm mentioned above.[24] Such *fundi* were normally between 50 and 250 *iugera* (12.6 and 63 hectares) in area, and usually cost upwards of HS 20,000; the Fulcinian farm was more expensive than most (16), and another farm mentioned by Cicero in this speech cost nearly HS 50,000 (28).[25] It may well be (if we can lay any stress on the

[24] On the Roman *fundus* system, see esp. T. Mommsen, *Hermes* 19 (1884) 393-416; W. Heitland, *Agricola* (1921) 203-212; K.D. White, *Farm Equipment of the Roman World* (1975) 214-222; J. Percival, *The Roman Villa* (1976), esp. 152 ff.; A.J.L. van Hooff, *Historia* 31 (1982) 126-128. On the *fundus* as a legal unit of production, see A. Steinwenter, *Fundus cum Instrumento* (1942) 10-22; and now P.W. de Neeve, *TR* 52 (1984) 3-19. On Cato's agricultural system, see A.E. Astin, *Cato the Censor* (1978) 240-266. I regret lacking access to *Societá Romana e Produzione Schiavistica* (ed. A. Giardina and A. Schiavone, 1981); but see D.W. Rathbone's review in *JRS* 73 (1983) 160-168, esp. 161-162.

[25] It is not easy to measure size, but see K.D. White, *Roman Farming* (1970) 280-284; also R. Duncan-Jones, in *Studies in Roman Property* (ed. M.I. Finley, 1976) 12-24, and *Economy of the Roman Empire* (1974) 323-326, on the size of larger estates. On value, cf. *ibid*, 210-215 and 229 n.645, 231 n.669 (HS 20-24,000); *Studies* 13 (average unit in estates costs ca. HS 50,000). Gaius, 3.161, gives a price for one *fundus* of HS 150,000; Pliny, *NH* 14.48, records HS 400,000 for an exceptionally expensive vineyard of 60 *iugera*. A *fundus* possibly at Tarquinii was worth HS 100,000 in ca. 75 B.C. (Cic. *Rosc. Com.* 32-33, by the most usual dating and manuscript reading). It is not easy to believe that thirteen *fundi* at Ameria could be worth HS 6,000,000, about HS 460,000 on average; cf. Cic. *Rosc. Am.* 6 and 20.

difference between *quaedam praedia* and *fundus Fulcinianus*) that Fulcinius himself converted the Fulcinian farm to the newer mode of production, by combining smaller units into a larger, better capitalized, and more efficient entity.[26] Like most such *fundi*, the Fulcinian farm specialized in one cash crop—in this case, apparently olive oil (22).

Second, the two adjacent *fundi* were almost certainly operated with slave labor.[27] To be sure, no slaves are mentioned in the earlier part of our story; during at least part of this time the Fulcinian farm was let to a tenant farmer (17, 94), who doubtless supplied his own slaves.[28] But the mob that resisted Caecina's entry onto the Fulcinian farm was mainly recruited from local slaves and freemen (20, cf. 30), and Aebutius' own slave Antiochus, possibly acting as his bailiff, was ordered to lead the charge (22, 25); Cicero also says that Aebutius' neighbors had brought along their own slaves (24, 26). Slave labor had clearly come to predominate in the Tarquinian countryside.

Third, part of the attractiveness of the Fulcinian farm was doubtless its contiguity to the dotal property. Fulcinius presumably anticipated that Caesennia would predecease him, thereby allowing him to take the dowry property as his own and join it with the adjacent farm. In the event, Fulcinius died first and the ownership of the two farms was divided; but Cicero uses the same rationale to supply a motive for Caesennia's alleged later desire to buy the Fulcinian farm (15-16). In short, there is abundant evidence from this speech that Tarquinii was experiencing a process familiar in Italian agriculture,[29] whereby capital-intensive mid-sized farms were cre-

[26] Note that *fundi* are normally named for their organizers: P. Veyne, *MEFR* 64 (1957) 112-114.

[27] So also P.A. Brunt, *Italian Manpower* (1971) 552; on slaves in southern Etruria, see pp. 350-353. On Plut. *Tib. Gr.* 8.7, see D.B. Nagle, *Historia* 25 (1976) 487-489, not wholly persuasive. Note Cicero's description of the Tarquinian countryside as "deserted" (*Caec.* 1: *desertis*); this refers to the depopulation of peasantry.

[28] See B.W. Frier, *SZ* 96 (1979) 217-218.

[29] On the Roman transformation of Etruscan agriculture, see now T.W. Potter, *The Changing Landscape of South Etruria* (1979) 120-137; cf. D.B. Nagle, *Athenaeum* 57 (1979) 411-436, on the area around the *via Cassia*.

ated by the use of slave labor and then assembled like building blocks into larger units sometimes called *latifundia*.[30] The use of tenants to operate individual farms within these larger units was an increasingly common practice in the late Republic.[31]

Fulcinius' return to Tarquinii removed him from the Roman maelstrom; but it brought him, perhaps, no lasting peace.[32] Sometime after his return Fulcinius died; Cicero is deliberately vague about the details: "I will pass over many pertinent facts which are irrelevant to the present case" (11). Much of the civil war of 83-81 was fought in Etruria, though generally to the north of Tarquinii and especially around Volaterrae, the home of Caesennia's second husband. The war was followed by resettlements of Sullan veterans in Etruria, the severe and lasting social effects of which precipitated an armed rebellion led by the Consul M. Aemilius Lepidus in 78 and 77 B.C. Lepidus' rebellion was taken up by much of Etruria, with major battles fought also in the south (one less than 40 km. north of Tarquinii).[33] Though Fulcinius may well have died in 77, it is hard to know what side (if any) this Romanized Etruscan would have favored. At his death her dowry (including the dowry farm) reverted to Caesennia (15), and she became wealthy in her own right; Cicero implies that her properties were extensive (94). By will Fulcinius left his property (including the Fulcinian farm) to his son and namesake M. Fulcinius; but the usufruct on all of it was evidently di-

[30] K.D. White, *Bull. Inst. Class. Stud.* 14 (1967) 62-79; see also F.G. de Pachterre, *La Table Hypothécaire de Veleia* (1920).

[31] Cf. in general P.A. Brunt, *JRS* 52 (1962) 71 nn.31-33; K.-P. Johne *et al.*, *Die Kolonen in Italien und den Westlichen Provinzen des Römischen Reiches* (1983), esp. 52-53 on the *pro Caecina*; P.W. de Neeve, *Colonus* (1984), esp. 85-86; and on legal sources, N. Brockmeyer, *Historia* 20 (1971) 732-742 (in part uncritical). Further bibliography in my article (cited n.28).

[32] On the complex political background in Etruria (which is vividly reflected in Cicero's *Second Catilinarian*), see W.V. Harris, *Etruria* 251-298; E. Rawson, *JRS* 68 (1978) 132-152. Tarquinii was not untouched by the civil wars; cf. Val. Max. 5.3.3 (murder there, on a farm owned by a Sextilius, of C. Caesar Strabo in 87 B.C.).

[33] At Cosa, cf. Sall. *Hist.* 1.82 M; Exuperant. 6.38; Rutilius 1.297-298. Lepidus' army must, at the very least, have passed close to Tarquinii. On Lepidus, see L. Labruna, *Il Console Sovversivo* (1976).

The Litigants

vided between his wife and son (11), which meant that during her lifetime she would receive half its revenues.[34]

Shortly thereafter the younger M. Fulcinius also died (12: *brevi tempore*); since there was a four-year interval between the ensuing sale of his estate and the death of Caesennia (19, 94), his death can probably be dated to 74 B.C., the year (as it happens) in which the infamous C. Verres was Urban Praetor. In his will the younger Fulcinius left his entire estate to P. Caesennius, presumably a Tarquinian relative of his mother; the Fulcinii themselves were probably now extinct, since they are not further attested at Tarquinii.[35] Out of his estate Fulcinius legated a large fixed sum of money (*grande pondus argenti*) to his wife, and the bulk of his estate (*partem maiorem bonorum*) to his mother, Caesennia (12).[36] The younger Fulcinius' will was probably designed to circumvent the *lex Voconia* of 169 B.C., whereby those registered in the first census class (an estate of HS 100,000 or more) were forbidden to make women their heirs; as it happens, Verres, in his Edict, had extended the *lex Voconia* to cover those who had not been registered in the census, doubtless because no census had been held since 86/85.[37] But Fulcinius' large legacies to his mother

[34] But later passages in the speech state that, at least after her son's death, Caesennia received "the usufruct" (19, 94), and there is no mention of rent sharing. The plaintiff may well have asserted this (Caesennia's accounts were missing, 17), since it would be one sign of her owning the farm. I wonder, however, whether Cicero, at 11, has not (deliberately?) made a mistake in reporting the will. See also A. D'Ors, *Anuar. de Derecho Civil* 1 (1952) 84; G. Crifò, *Studi sul Quasi-Usufrutto Romano* vol. I (1977) 68-70.

[35] Therefore M. Torelli's attempt, (article cited n.7) 313, to link them with the senatorial Fulcinii Triones at Rome should probably be rejected.

[36] Latin really allows no other interpretation of *partem maiorem bonorum*; but various interpreters, starting with C.A. Jordan, *Oratio* (1847) *ad loc.*, have taken the words to mean "a larger share [than his wife's *grande pondus argenti*]," in an unnecessary effort to avoid the problem discussed below at note 38.

[37] Cf. A. Watson, *Succession* 29-31, on the *lex Voconia*, and p. 129, on the *legatum partitionis* to women as a means to circumvent it. Cf. H. Stiegler, *RE* Suppb. XI s.v. "partitio legata" (1968) 1037-1043, with bibliography. On Verres' Edict, see Cic. 2 *Verr.* 1.104-114, with Chapter II, at notes 25-28. On the meaning of the adjective *census* in the *lex Voconia*, see Ps.-Asconius p. 247 St. (on Cic. 2 *Verr.* 1.104). On the law, see now R. Vigneron, *Labeo* 29 (1983) 140-153.

and wife must at least have come close to formal violation of
another provision of the *lex Voconia*, whereby no single legatee
could receive more than the heir received.[38] It is therefore
germane to note (from Cic. 2 *Verr.* 1.110) that Verres, allegedly for corrupt reasons, did not extend this provision of the
lex Voconia to include *incensi*. We should probably interpret
Caesennia's relative P. Caesennius as having more or less col-
luded with the younger Fulcinius in the arrangement,[39] whereby
Caesennia would receive the lion's share of her son's estate.

In order to carry out the will, P. Caesennius, together with
the legatees (12), decided to auction off the estate and thus
pay the large charges on it (13). At this point in the story the
defendant, Sex. Aebutius, makes his first appearance; but he
had been, for a long time previously (13: *iam diu*), a friend
and confidant of Caesennia, doubtless ever since she had been
widowed. He had probably met her in Rome, where she seems
to have lived.[40] Cicero's portrait of Aebutius (13-15) is of course
uncompromisingly hostile: Aebutius is little better than an
adventurer, making his living from defenseless women whom
he advises and represents in court.[41] Cicero's aversion is overtly
social. From Cicero's viewpoint, Aebutius was certainly not
wealthy—the orator jeers that Aebutius probably has no other
farm than the one he claims (94);[42] however, as events were
to show, Aebutius was not without certain other social resources. Why was it, then, that a wealthy Tarquinian lady
took up with such a man, in preference to her true friends
and relatives (15: *amici cognatique*) on whom Cicero implies she
should have relied (14), but whom she did not make her heirs
even to a fraction (17)? Why did she remain friends with him
even after her second marriage, to the extent of leaving him a

---

[38] Cf. A. Watson, *Succession* 167-170; the rule is not entirely clear in our
sources. Most commentators have interpreted *Caec.* 12 to make Fulcinius' will
conform with the *lex Voconia*; e.g., A. Metro, *Labeo* 9 (1963) 314-316. But the
results are very strained in view of Cic. *Leg.* 2.49.

[39] See esp. Cic. *Fin.* 2.55, 58.

[40] So W.V. Harris, *Etruria* 284.

[41] On Aebutius' experience as a *cognitor*, see Chapter II, at notes 73-78.

[42] The manuscript reading ("si quem habes") should be retained; D.R.
Shackleton Bailey emended to "habet," *Harv. Stud. Class. Phil.* 83 (1979) 240,
missing the joke, on which see H.H. Pflüger, *Besitzklagen* 41.

small portion of her estate (17)? Cicero, with deep contempt that may not be entirely feigned, argues that Aebutius had thrust himself forward as a "self-appointed friend" (*voluntarius amicus*), offering Caesennia sham solicitude and doing little services from which he himself in fact profited (14, 17). Caesennia had accepted his attentions owing to her lack of foresight and acumen (15).

Caesennia may have seen the matter differently. In the years after her first husband's death she became, doubtless for the first time in her life, personally and financially independent of family and husband; Aebutius may well have been a token of that independence.[43] Cicero does not imply any romantic relationship between the two; on the contrary, he suggests their friendship put business first, and he remarks in passing that Aebutius had access to her account books (17: he allegedly stole them after her death). Cicero does not refer to any scandal of misconduct by Aebutius toward Caesennia; and he had an excellent source for rumor in his client, her second husband. Even after her remarriage Aebutius may have served her as a counterweight against Caecina; her last will shows continued trust in him. The antipathy of the two men was very deep, as events would show; it may also have been of very long standing.

The piecemeal auction of her son's estate was arranged and advertised by the *argentarius* Sex. Clodius Phormio (27) and held in Rome (15-16).[44] P. Caesennius, as heir, was the seller of the estate (27: *auctor*). Cicero describes the auction rather cursorily (16-17). The Fulcinian farm was knocked down to Aebutius, and Phormio's bank books showed him as the purchaser of record (17).[45] But many other potential buyers had

[43] It is not unlikely that she had also placed reliance on M. Fulcinius, her husband's freedman (and procurator?), who received double Aebutius' portion in her will (17). Although she must have had a tutor (perhaps P. Caesennius?), she seems to operate quite independently; on her ability to write a will (which would require a tutor's authorization also), see note 12.

[44] Auctions in the late Republic are described by G. Thielmann, (cited n.14) 47-55; on this one, see also pp. 109-110. Cf. J. Andreau, (cited n.14) 73-116; R.M. Thilo, *Der Codex Accepti et Expensi* (1980) 232-235.

[45] Cf. A. Watson, *Obligations* 36-37. If this transaction was typical (bibliography in note 44), the amount which Aebutius bid (16: *licetur*), minus a

allegedly been deterred from bidding for the farm: some out of respect, because they assumed on the basis of rumor that Aebutius was acting for the dead man's mother, and some also because the price was high (16). Her friends and relatives had earlier urged Caesennia to buy the farm, as a good investment of her inheritance in land abutting her dowry property (15). For all of this Cicero could doubtless produce witnesses. But Cicero obviously had no hard evidence to back up his allegation that Caesennia had given Aebutius a mandate to buy the Fulcinian farm (15), nor could he prove that Caesennia had taken delivery of the farm from Aebutius and paid him for it (17). Her second husband, however, seems to have been unshakeably convinced that this was true; his later actions show the depth of his conviction. Caesennia may well have told him this. But after her death the only evidence was hearsay. It is at least as consistent with what we know of the transaction to suppose that Caesennia decided against buying the farm, but advised Aebutius to take advantage of the contrary rumor and buy the farm for himself relatively cheaply. Both P. Caesennius and the banker Phormio were willing to testify for the defense, in any case.

The ambiguity persisted after the sale mainly because the Romans lacked all methods of publicly registering changes in the ownership of land.[46] For if Caesennia did not buy the

commission and other charges, was paid at once by Phormio to Caesennius; Aebutius promised by stipulation to Phormio (16: *promittit*) that he would pay this amount plus interest in the future. Phormio's *tabulae* (17) witnessed this transaction in the form of "money expended" to Caesennius and "money received" from Aebutius (17: *expensa pecunia . . . acceptaque*). The Praetor forced *argentarii* to produce their records as evidence of sale: Lenel, *EP*[3] 62-64. (Note that there seems to have been no evidence of a mancipation to Aebutius, much less one from him to Caesennia.) On G. Sacconi, *Ricerche sulla Delegazione* (1971) 180-182, see F. Sturm, *Iura* 22 (1971) 263. On Aebutius' role as an alleged intermediary, see A. Corbino, in *Studi A. Biscardi* vol. III (1982) 278-287.

[46] Much of Cicero's speech presupposes this point; cf. note 45 on proving transfer. Although census returns required respondents to list land owned (e.g., *FIRA* vol. I, no. 16 sec. 4), these returns were not cross-checked and had only evidentiary value even in the Empire, cf. Papinian, D. 10.1.11 (as emended by Mommsen); and there had been no census from 86/85 to 70/69. Cicero, in any case, does not refer to the census.

Fulcinian farm, she would nonetheless have retained at least
the half-usufruct entitling her to half its revenues for her lifetime. The farm had probably been managed directly hitherto,
by her first husband and then by his son; Caesennia now altered the farm's management by leasing it to a tenant farmer
(17, 94). To those who thought she had purchased it, she
appeared to be taking possession, and of course Cicero says
that she did so (17, 19, 94); but this is not the only construction that could be placed on her actions. The disposition during the next four years of the rent from the farm seems to
have been entirely unclear, and not even the tenant would
have been a very good source as to whether Aebutius (as owner)
had ultimately received half the rent. The tenant's lease would
have run, to judge from parallels, for five years,[47] and so was
drawing to its end when Caesennia died four years later. Cicero is unclear as to whether the tenant was produced as a
witness at the trial (cf. 94).

It was not long after the auction (17: *neque ita multo post*)
that Caesennia, now a double beneficiary of wills, married her
second husband, the plaintiff Aulus Caecina;[48] the marriage
dates to 73, perhaps, or 72. The alliance was of two powerful
families, both "on the threshold of the Senate (if not already
represented)."[49] Caecina's family came from the North Etruscan city of Volaterrae; Cicero claims, and seems honestly to
have believed,[50] that his client bore the most esteemed family
name in Etruria (104, as emended). Their fortunes apparently
unscathed, the Caecinae had survived the Sullan siege and

[47] See, e.g., Pliny, *Ep.* 9.37.2; Marcellus, D. 19.2.9.1; Ulpian, D. 12.1.4.1,
19.2.13.11; Paul, D. 19.2.24.2, 4; etc.

[48] I take A. Caecina, the plaintiff, to be the father of Cicero's homonymous
correspondent in 46; so rightly E. Rawson, (cited n.32) 137 n.43, against C.
Nicolet, *Ordre* vol. II 812-814, and P. Hohti, in *SRE* (cited n.4) 418-419, who
identify the two men for inadequate reasons. These authors all cite further
bibliography.

[49] T.P. Wiseman, *New Men* 60-61.

[50] Cf., e.g., *Fam.* 6.6.3 and 9. This A. Caecina is probably the Roman
eques referred to by Pliny, *NH* 10.71; C. Nicolet, *Ordre* vol. II 813-814, comes
to the same conclusion about his status by using *Caec.* 103. On the Pliny
passage, see E. Rawson, (cited n.32) 138 n.50.

Tarquinii and Rome

capture of Volaterrae in 81; perhaps they had collaborated,[51] although Caecina himself, like the ancient Etruscan families at Tarquinii, had a deep interest in Etruscan antiquities, an interest he transmitted to his son.[52] While Caecina's wealth no doubt derived mainly from the Volaterran estates of his family,[53] he nonetheless lived in Rome (19), and his family was sponsored in society by the powerful Servilii Isaurici.[54]

It was doubtless at Rome that Caecina met and married Caesennia. If this was in fact a marriage of convenience for them and their families, it achieved its purpose; when Caesennia died a few years later, she left the great bulk of her estate to her husband (17). Once again Cicero skips ahead, omitting details of the period between Caesennia's marriage and death "so as to get on with my story" (17: *ut in pauca conferam*). Despite her marriage, Caesennia did not give up her friendship with Aebutius. While Cicero stresses the ties of affection that bound Caesennia to her first husband and her son (12), he does not say anything similar about her second husband,

[51] Cicero refers to Caecina's bravery (*Fam.* 13.66.1) and loyalty (*Caec.* 104), which might imply pro-Roman military activity. E. Rawson, (cited n.32) 137 n.45, suggests that his client relationship to the Servilii (cf. n.54) dates from his assistance to Servilius Vatia during the siege of Volaterrae (on the role of Vatia there, Gran. Lic. 36.8). On the Sullan treatment of Volaterrae, see Chapter III, at notes 11 ff.

[52] Cic. *Fam.* 6.6.3. The son was from boyhood a close friend of Cicero (*Fam.* 6.9.1) and had a rhetorical education (Sen. *NQ* 52.1). He became an expert on Etruscan religion, as well as a sometime participant in politics; cf. P. Hohti, in *SRE* (cited n.4) 427-432, with E. Rawson, (cited n.32) 137-138. He is presumably the father (cf. Cic. *Fam.* 6.5.1, 6.13, 7.1 and 4-6) of A. Caecina Severus (*suff.* 1 B.C.) and A. Caecina Largus (*suff.* A.D. 13), and the grandfather of C. Caecina Largus (cos. 42); cf. R. Syme, *JRS* 56 (1966) 58-59. There were, however, other members of the Volaterran family, cf. e.g. Cic. *Att.* 16.8.2 and E. Fiumi, *Not. Scav.* (1955) 123; and the family was spread throughout Etruria, cf. E. Rawson, 137 n.46. On the family tombs at Volaterrae, see J.P. Oleson, *Latomus* 33 (1974) 870-873; on their vast estates, Rawson, 138. See also O. Luchi, *Prospettiva* 8 (1977) 37-41.

[53] He exploited his racing horses in Rome; cf. Pliny, *NH* 10.71, with note 50 above. Caecina's son also had business connections in Asia: Cic. *Fam.* 6.6.2 (referring to 58 B.C.), 8.2.

[54] Cic. *Fam.* 13.66.1 (written in 45 B.C. to P. Servilius Vatia Isauricus, cos. 79 B.C.); see above, note 51.

The Litigants

nor does he describe Caecina's later pursuit of the Fulcinian farm as being motivated by anything other than a wholly commendable desire to lay hold on what was his. This was, of course, in large measure the reality of family life in the late Republican upper classes, among whom Caesennia, at the end of her life, had virtually arrived.

CAESENNIA'S HEIRS

When she died, Caesennia left behind an estate that was partially ambiguous as to its assets, plus a potential conflict between two heirs, her widower and her friend. This was, to be sure, a volatile situation, but not one necessarily destined to end in litigation. The picture Cicero paints is a fascinating one of thrust and counter-thrust, stratagems of feint and parry, while each side maneuvered to achieve a position of strength over the opponent. Caecina's goal was plain: to consolidate his grasp on the handsome estate he had inherited practically intact. Sex. Aebutius may have been motivated by different concerns, above all by disappointment and resentment at the smallness of his share;[55] surely he had hoped for more than 1/72 from his late female friend. Further, he doubtless felt himself handicapped by his social inferiority to Caecina. Aebutius' aim was to increase the portion allotted by Caesennia; he was at first obliged to pursue this goal with cunning rather than force.

Aebutius struck first, by challenging, apparently in conversation with others, Caecina's right to inherit under a Roman will (18); Aebutius argued that Caecina was barred from inheriting because of a Sullan law imposing civil restrictions on Volaterrans (102). If this were true, then Aebutius and the other heir would have their portions increased *pro rata*, and Aebutius would thus inherit a third, which is presumably what Cicero means when he says that Aebutius "exaggerated" his

[55] So H.J. Roby, *Private Law* vol. II 532; cf. G. Nicosia, *Deiectio* 53 n.128.

share (19: *exaggeraret*).[56] Cicero devotes to this question a lively
appendix of his speech as preserved (95-102), in which he flails
away at the issue without ever quite coming to grips with it;
but, as we shall see later, this portion of the speech appears
to have been added on to the version for publication because
the matter was an important talking point at the time.[57] In
fact there is no sign that Aebutius seriously pressed the argument except in the early stages of the dispute. By raising
the Volaterran matter he sought to put Caecina on the defen-
sive, in hopes of eliciting an offer of a favorable settlement,
as Cicero observes (18); in this he failed. Indeed, his move
may well have backfired, by bringing into the dispute political
issues and forces whose power far exceeded the bounds of the
immediate quarrel.

Caecina's response, according to Cicero, was a show of prudence and resolve (18). Caecina took the "high road." He began touring Caesennia's properties (including the dotal properties, 21) and taking possession of them as the principal heir;
in the course of this tour he visited the Fulcinian farm and
inspected the accounts of the tenant farmer (94). At this point
Caecina may not yet have realized that the Fulcinian farm was
to be a bone of contention; probably he knew little of the
doubtful transaction whereby his late wife, before her second
marriage, had allegedly acquired the farm, and he may simply
have assumed that the farm belonged to Caesennia. It is hard
to be sure, but later he seems never to have wavered in his
belief about the farm's ownership, and he even claimed surprise when Aebutius called it into question (20: *hoc novae litis
genus*). If Caecina was initially in any doubt, then Aebutius'
high-handed and aggressive conduct later on may well have
induced in him a resolve to crush the upstart. Even Caecina
may not have remembered his own actions rightly. His inspection of the tenant's accounts is not proof positive as to his
intentions, since it could be that he was only checking to de-

[56] The manuscripts have *ipse* (*scil*. Caecina) doing the exaggerating; the text
was emended by F.L. Keller, *Sem*. 276-292, to *iste* (*scil*. Aebutius). See note
58.

[57] See Chapter III, at notes 17-18.

The Litigants

termine if the rent, of which Caesennia had taken at least half, had been duly paid. The ambiguity of the farm's status thus continued for a while longer.

Upon his return to Rome, Caecina applied to the Urban Praetor for an arbiter to divide the estate, now mostly in his possession, among the various heirs (19).[58] Caecina thereby gave clear signal of several things: his rejection of an out-of-court settlement with Aebutius; his confidence in his own civil status as a Volaterran; and his willingness to pursue the matter at law if necessary. His application to the Praetor involved civil authorities for the first time in the settlement of Caesennia's estate. There can be little doubt that by this time, at least, Caecina had begun to seek legal advice on his position. But if he was intending to frighten off Aebutius by this display of firmness, he very much underestimated his man.

Aebutius' reply was a few days in coming (19: *illis paucis diebus*), no doubt signifying its careful calculation. Aebutius formally notified Caecina, in the Roman Forum, that the Fulcinian farm belonged not to the inheritance but to him (19, 95); and more or less simultaneously Aebutius occupied the farm in his own name (cf. 20). Cicero stresses this sequence of events, which he understandably found suspicious: Aebutius' hopes of a settlement had been dashed, and only now he raised the issue of the Fulcinian farm, seeking in effect to subtract from the estate an asset undoubtedly much larger than his share. On the other side of the case, however, were some weighty considerations: Caecina's visit to the farm had alerted Aebutius that Caecina might consider it part of the inheritance, so that Aebutius was now obliged to reply; Caecina's rejection of an informal compromise favoring Aebutius may have dissuaded the latter from simply forgoing a poten-

[58] Caecina asked for a *iudicium familiae eriscundae*; cf. Lenel, *EP*[3] 206-210. The passage was extensively analyzed by F.L. Keller, *Sem.* 276-292, who showed that it was Caecina who sought the suit; for the legal background, see esp. Gaius, D. 10.2.1.1. The manuscript reading *ipse* (emended to *iste*, cf. n.56) meant that Aebutius brought the suit. *Ipse* was defended by H. Bögli, *Rede* 10-23. But see P. Koschaker, *SZ* 28 (1907) 450-452; E. Balogh, *ACIR* vol. II (1934) 323 n.1; G. Nicosia, *Deiectio* 33 n.72, with further bibliography.

tially disputed claim to the farm's ownership; and Aebutius' entry forthwith into a suit on dividing the inheritance would have weakened his legal position, in that he might have seemed not only to concede Caecina's right to inherit, but also to abandon prematurely a claim that the Fulcinian farm was not part of the inheritance.[59]

Questions of ownership, as between a testator and a heir, could not be settled in a suit to divide an inheritance.[60] Caecina turned at once to handle the question of the Fulcinian farm; in doing so, he relied on the opinion of a *consilium* (20: *de amicorum sententia*; cf. 95), a further sign of his increasing concern about an upcoming lawsuit. He decided to request from Aebutius that, on a mutually agreeable day, Caecina enter the farm and "be led off in the time-honored way" (20: *de fundo Caecina moribus deduceretur*), by an act of formalized violence (cf. 2, 22, 32, 95). From the legal standpoint there is much about this request that remains hotly controverted, and I will consider the matter at length in a later chapter;[61] let me here summarize that discussion by saying that such a *deductio* appears to have been customary rather than legal in the strict sense, and that by Cicero's time the relationship of the *deductio* to ensuing actions at law was probably very ambiguous. In principle, however, all that the *deductio* accomplished was to show up clearly, in a formalized way, that both parties acknowledged the existence of a dispute between them over property rights.

The two parties met and talked, apparently for the first time since Caesennia's death; a date for the *deductio* was agreed (20). Aebutius later went back on this agreement, and it is not

[59] The last reason was given by F. Keller, *Sem.* 283-287, based on Scaevola, (12 *Quaest.*) D. 10.2.37: "Qui familiae eriscundae iudicio agit, confitetur adversarium sibi esse coheredem"; but the text is emended from "non confitetur," using the *Basilika*. See also H.H. Pflüger, *Besitzklagen* 29-32. On the private nature of *denuntiatio*, see E. Balogh, (cited n.58) 320-329; it was not necessarily an unfriendly act, cf. Cic. *Tull.* 54.

[60] So, at any rate, Pomponius, D. 10.2.45 pr. (and Paul/Pomp., D. 10.2.25.7); cf. Africanus, D. 44.1.18. The legal situation was exhaustively discussed by F.L. Keller, *Sem.* 359-366; but note also H.H. Pflüger, *Besitzklagen* 30-33.

[61] Chapter II, under subhead "Law and Custom."

The Litigants

clear why he initially assented; perhaps at first he saw no
danger for himself in the customary procedure. Upon reflection, however, he changed his mind; why? It is farfetched to
suppose that he feared Caecina would seize the farm and then
refuse to be voluntarily expelled;[62] but it should not be forgotten that Caecina had a claim to previous possession on the
basis of his inspection of the tenant's accounts. The question
is hard to judge; Cicero was not privy to Aebutius' deliberations. Perhaps Aebutius was influenced by a sense of social
inferiority to Caecina, which led him to believe that it was
unwise to admit, even in a formalized way, the existence of a
dispute about property rights in the farm.[63]

Cicero's narrative of the resulting debacle is not easily sur-
passed for vividness (20-22). On the appointed day Caecina
and a group of his friends (20), who would act as his advisors
and witnesses, arrived at the fortlet called Castellum Axia,
close to the farm. There they learned that Aebutius was ru-
mored to have raised and armed the countryside, both freemen and slaves, so as to resist Caecina's entry. Aebutius himself then arrived to confirm the rumor in person, threatening
deadly violence if they persisted (20). Caecina consulted his
consilium and on their advice (21) left Castellum Axia and approached the farm. He was met on the road by a large band
of armed men who stood barring his way not only to the
Fulcinian farm, but also to the dotal farm adjoining it; present
as an observer was Aebutius' *amicus*, the infamous Senator C.
Fidiculanius Falcula, later a witness at the trial (28-30).[64] Cae-

[62] So H.J. Roby, *Private Law* vol. II 516. Cf. also Chapter II, note 134.

[63] Aebutius' turnabout and its significance are further discussed in Chapter
II, at notes 121-125.

[64] Falcula undoubtedly became a Senator thanks to Sulla, cf. R. Syme,
Papers Brit. Sch. Rome 14 (1938) 23; his main property, allegedly acquired with
bribe money, was nearly 50 Roman miles from Rome (*Caec.* 28), hence possibly in the vicinity of Tarquinii (Castellum Axia lay 50 miles from Rome,
Steph. Byz. s.v. "Axia"; cf. note 23). The nomen is very rare; E. Rawson,
(cited n.32) 150, notes a freedman Fidicolanius from the Poggi Alti region to
the north. The nomen is also obviously Italic, cf. W. Schulze, *Zur Geschichte
Lateinischer Eigennamen* (1900) 553; but P. Hohti, in *SRE* (cited n.4) 426-427,
and E. Rawson make him an Etruscan, improbably. On Fidiculanius, see
also C. Nicolet, *Ordre* vol. II 877-878.

cina's party was first turned back from the dotal farm (21), through which they had doubtless hoped to enter the Fulcinian farm. The group then attempted direct entry to the Fulcinian farm. Here Aebutius and his band once more confronted them. Antiochus, Aebutius' slave, was ordered to kill anyone crossing the row of olive trees that marked the farm's boundary; Cicero says that Aebutius himself gave the order in a loud voice (22), but one of Aebutius' neighbors also claimed to have given it (25). When Caecina persisted toward the olive trees, he was met by a shower of missiles and even a bit of swordplay; he and his friends and witnesses (22: *amici advocatique eius*) fled in terror and confusion (2, 22).

Two points can be made about this incident. First of all, Aebutius' defense of the Fulcinian farm is a rather spectacular example of Roman reliance on self-help,[65] which was in general very widely tolerated by Roman law.[66] But Aebutius did not act alone; he was also successful in obtaining help from neighboring landowners, a large number of whom testified for the defendant at the trial (24-27). The opinion of the neighborhood ought to count for something, since these men were willing to believe not only that Aebutius owned the farm, but also that he was so indisputably the owner that he was justified in resorting to great violence in defending his claim. But the matter is not quite so simple. Cicero, in discussing the defense's witnesses, lists seven of these neighbors. Not only do they all bear Italic (i.e., non-Etruscan) family names, but most of their families are also represented either in the list of local magistrates for this period at Tarquinii or in Latin funerary inscriptions of the prominent dead.[67]

The comparison is illuminating:

P. Vetilius (24)   C. Vetilius Q.f. IIII vir i.d., II quin.:
                     CIL 11.3384-3385

[65] See Chapter III, at notes 72-73.

[66] G. Wesener, in *Fs. Steinwenter* 113-114; T. Mayer-Maly, *RE* s.v. "vis" (1960) 319.

[67] Most of the information in this list comes from M. Torelli's *Elogia Tarquiniensia* (1975) 188-190, here abbreviated *ET*. While Torelli makes no use of the *pro Caecina*, it seems to reinforce many of his conclusions.

The Litigants

A. Terentius (25)   cf. Terentilius, *ET* pp. 170-171
L. Caelius (26)   cf. C. Coelius C.f. Valens (aed.?):
                      CIL 11.3384
P. Memmius (26)   *CIL* 11.3457
P., L. Atilius (27)   *CIL* 11.3407-3408
P. Rutilius (27)   *CIL* 11.3473

In other words, these landowners, who had come with their slaves[68] to help Aebutius, were like Aebutius himself relative newcomers to the territory of Tarquinii; Caecina's claim to the farm rested on ownership traced back through his late wife and her first husband, both members of the ancient Etruscan aristocracy at Tarquinii. There is thus a hint in Cicero's narrative of more or less overt social conflict at Tarquinii, and it is not hard to amplify on this theme: Caecina, a Romanized Volaterran backed by powerful Roman friends, stood in opposition to a grouping of local Italic landowners. In this respect, Caecina's advantage in having the dispute litigated at Rome deserves emphasis, especially when reading the scornful remarks Cicero heaps on Aebutius' municipal witnesses. One of these witnesses, P. Memmius, had however helped Caecina to escape through a farm owned by his brother (26), which suggests that there were some cooler heads in the crowd.

Second, Caecina, in entering the fray against Aebutius' little army, had acted deliberately. Throughout the narrative portion of his speech Cicero stresses that Caecina relied on advice from his friends (*amici*) in arranging and attempting to carry out the *deductio*; the word *amici* occurs four times in the passage 20-22. Caecina's conduct is characterized above all by prudent deliberation, though even Cicero thinks he was rash to approach the farm (21); however, only in his final rush to the olive trees does Cicero think Caecina to have shown more determination than judgment (22), presumably because Caecina thereby neglected his earlier insistence on avoiding danger to life and limb (20: *salvo capite*). Cicero, of course, blames all the ensuing violence on the defendant Aebutius. But Cae-

[68] See above, at note 28.

cina's persistence is still worth comment. Perhaps, as Cicero argues (20, 21), Caecina failed to believe that Aebutius was serious in his threats; Caecina may not have understood the man very well. But there is another possible reason for Caecina's odd mixture of prudence and rashness, namely that his rashness was not uncalculated. In referring to this incident later in the speech, Cicero notes, almost in passing (95), that among Caecina's *amici* who advised him in Rome about the *deductio* was C. Aquilius Gallus, the eminent jurist who played a large role in shaping Caecina's case.[69] As we shall see in the next chapter, it is not inconceivable that Caecina's persistence resulted in part from Aquilius' advice.

In the aftermath of the incident at Tarquinii, the two parties returned to Rome. Caecina obtained from the Urban Praetor an interdict *de vi hominibus armatis*, whereby Aebutius was ordered to restore the plaintiff to the place whence he had been forcibly expelled by a band of armed men. The defendant replied that he was already in technical compliance with the interdict. A wager of law was made on the truth of this statement, and a panel of *recuperatores* was appointed to decide the issue (23). The question at law was thus to be not the inheritance directly, nor even the ownership of the Fulcinian farm, but rather the possession of the farm and the legal consequences of the armed confrontation. At the outset of their quarrel neither of the parties could possibly have foreseen such an outcome.

THE PROBLEM OF LITIGIOUSNESS

In the preceding pages I have tried to reconstruct "the making of a lawsuit," mainly by reading between the lines of Cicero's narrative and, wherever possible, bringing to bear supplemental information from other sources. There is obviously a certain danger in this method. The danger, however, does not

[69] On the text of *Caec.* 95, see Chapter IV, at notes 1-3. On Cicero's use of Aquilius, cf. Chapter III, at note 107; Chapter IV, at note 48. On Aquilius and *deductio*, see Chapter II, at notes 135-137.

The Litigants

seem to me to lie so much in the fact that Cicero's speech is inevitably biased toward his client; the bias is largely correctable, and in any case the "facts" were not really at issue by this point in the trial. We would undoubtedly profit from knowing more, especially about Aebutius' background; but the fundamental lines of the dispute seem clear enough. Rather, the real danger lies in even implicitly acceding to the view that this sequence of events somehow led necessarily to Caecina's seeking an interdict. Of course this is untrue. If Caecina, upon hearing at Castellum Axia of Aebutius' threats, had been persuaded by his *consilium* that it was no longer worthwhile to pursue his claim to the Fulcinian farm (and Caecina may well have felt afterward that this decision might have been the wiser one), then Caecina's suit would never have been; but every detail up to that point, and every motive of every character, would still have been in place. Everything would still be exactly the same, except of course that we would never have heard of the episode.

To be sure, certain considerations were already impelling Caecina forward into a suit. A suit between Caecina and Aebutius was already long since "in the air"; both sides had invested time and resources in their quarrel, they had begun to muster their allies, and in the process they had raised expectations (which craved fulfillment) in themselves, their adversaries, and third parties. This is an important point deserving of further comment. In my narrative above concerning the origins of Caecina's suit, Roman citizens were pictured as pursuing their ambitions for economic and social status; many of their actions had legal implications of one kind or another. The characters in this story had married and formed dowries, created and managed and dissolved banks, transferred property by private sale and auction, leased farms, written wills disposing of their estates to heirs and legatees, and so on—transactions involving every major branch of Roman private law, but never involving, so far as we know, even the hint of a *possible* lawsuit.[70] During this time these actors had used

[70] Note the many ambiguities: the elder Fulcinius' will (cf. note 34), his

28

private law mainly as a means to an end that was predominantly non-legal in character; though they doubtless gave at least passing consideration to the legal implications of their conduct, law was kept more or less to the "back region" of their interactions, while the "front region" was dominated by their social and economic purposes.[71] In such interactions there was room for a considerable tolerance of legal ambiguity; the actors did not have to concern themselves continuously with the possibility of lawsuits and how they might fare in them. The ambiguous status of the Fulcinian farm, at least in the minds of some of them, sufficiently displays the limits of their attentiveness.

All of this changed rather abruptly when Caecina and Aebutius began to feud about Caesennia's will. Now the frame of reference for their interactions was inverted: private law became not only the means to an end, but also a large part of the end itself, in the sense that both parties consciously and overtly prepared their positions in lawsuits, without necessarily committing themselves thereby to carrying one out; while their normal, more purely social ambitions were ostensibly retired into the "back region" of their interactions. Each party began to think, both of himself and of his opponent, no longer as "ordinary" Romans, but rather as potential adversaries in a court of law. In essence, they began behaving less as "ordinary" Romans, and more as incumbents of a special social role or position. A social position can be defined as "a social identity that carries with it a certain range (however diffusely specified) of prerogatives and obligations that an actor who is accorded that identity (or is an 'incumbent' of that position) may activate or carry out: these prerogatives and obligations

handling of his wife's dowry (cf. note 22), Caesennia's lease of the Fulcinian farm (cf. at notes 46-47). By contrast, the drafting of the younger Fulcinius' will shows real concern for currently prevailing law; see above, at notes 36-38.

[71] Cf. A. Giddens, *Central Problems in Social Theory* (1979) 207-209. See esp. E. Goffman, *The Presentation of Self in Everyday Life* (1959) 106-140; also *Frame Analysis* (1974) 74-77. Cf. Cic. *de Or.* 1.248-251. But matters of inheritance tended to provoke litigation; see below, at note 94.

constitute the role prescriptions associated with that position."[72]

Caecina and Aebutius of course did not cease to occupy the social positions they had previously held; indeed, these previous positions helped to shape their strategies as potential litigants and would continue to have great importance within the subsequent trial. It is just that they now assumed, in relation to each other and to the third parties they involved in their quarrel, a new social position. They accordingly began to behave differently: they served formal notice on one another (*denuntiat* in 19, 20), they "demanded" suits (*postulavit*, 19), they held formal colloquies with set agenda (20), they clarified positions (19), they paid formal visits and inspected books (94), they gave orders to their slaves in loud voices meant to be overheard (22), they summoned their "friends" into *consilia* (20, 22, cf. 28-30), and so on.

Even as "potential litigants," Caecina and Aebutius had already crossed the boundary into the judicial system of Rome; they had assumed roles (in which they would persist as actual litigants) that were properly a part of that system. Because a judicial system is formalistic and rule-oriented, and because its procedures often appear to pit adversaries against one another, the interactions associated with it frequently have a game-like quality.[73] Caecina and Aebutius could seem to have been engaged in playing an elaborate game, continually testing one another for strong and weak points, moving from issue to issue in the search for tactical advantage. Such games

---

[72] A. Giddens, (cited n.71) 117; cf. 115-120. On the importance of roles in judicial procedure, see N. Luhmann, *Legitimation durch Verfahren* (2d ed. 1975) 82-90; also C.H. Sheldon, *The American Judicial Process* (1974) 73-98.

[73] Cf. J. Huizinga, *Homo Ludens* (Engl. trans. 1950) 76-88 ("Play and Law"). There are also many insights into this question in R. Callois, *Les Jeux et les Hommes* (1958), trans. as *Man, Play, and Games* (1961). E. Goffman, *Encounters* (1961) 17-81 ("Fun in Games"), has some useful comments; and cf. *idem*, *Strategic Interaction* (1969) 115-119, on the crucial difference when a specialized social office (such as a court) is invested with enforcement power in games. On game theory in general, see esp. M.D. Davis, *Game Theory: A Nontechnical Introduction* (2d ed. 1983). Much of this bibliography is also relevant in my other "adversary" chapters: III and IV.

The Problem of Litigiousness

are quite common in the preparatory phases of lawsuits; similar episodes are referred to in the other private orations of Cicero.[74] The point about games, of course, is that they have an impetus of their own; normally it is personally distressing to have to retire without having won the game, and this becomes even more true after one has committed resources. In the stage preparatory to their trial, Caecina and Aebutius had each striven either to force the other out of the game altogether (and into abandoning claims or offering unfavorable compromises) or to make the other assume an awkward posture in a resulting trial.

With regard to Caecina, we are therefore left with two questions: why did he initially assume the position of a "potential litigant" vis-à-vis Aebutius, and why did he then end the preliminary game where he did, by bringing an interdict against Aebutius? To answer the second question first: a "rational" man, deciding whether or not to pursue a private claim through a lawsuit, will proceed if he calculates, on the basis of the most accurate possible assessment of all available evidence, that "the expected benefits of doing so will exceed the expected costs."[75] This equation is in theory perfectly straightforward: expected benefits are equal to the value of the predicted award, multiplied by the probability (from 0 to 1) of establishing one's claim against the defendant; expected costs are the value of what one will have to forgo in time, money, and lost opportunities in order to conduct the case.[76]

---

[74] See *Quinct.* 19 ff.; *Rosc. Com.* 56 (consulting a jurist); *Tull.* 13 ff. This type of confrontation, in which parties seek through discussion an outcome preferred by both, is called a "negotiated game": A. Rapaport, *Two-Person Game Theory* (1966) 94 ff. Unlike the typical trial, it is not a zero-sum game; both parties may conceivably gain a better position.

[75] S.S. Nagle and M.G. Neef, *Decision Theory and the Legal Process* (1979) 145, cf. 141-146, whom I follow in this paragraph. These matters are, however, much more complicated than may appear; see now G. Tullock, *Trials on Trial* (1980), a far more comprehensive treatment, as well as R. Lempert and J. Sanders, *Desert, Disputes, and Distribution: A Social Science Perspective on Law and the Legal System* (forthcoming) chap. 5.

[76] I omit consideration of time discounting, whereby future payments of

31

The Litigants

This calculation is made, of course, in measures that are theoretically monetary and objective; even someone who does not know its exact terms can make it intuitively.

In practice, however, human beings generally find it difficult to make such "rational" decisions;[77] and the process of "rational" decision making was probably even more difficult for a potential Roman litigant such as Caecina. In the first place, the equation described above takes account only of monetary values. As such it is bound to be more appealing in a modern context than in an ancient one, where *Homo oeconomicus* had a narrower foothold.[78] Caecina was undoubtedly torn by considerations often observed elsewhere in late Republican society: e.g., a general reluctance to become involved in lawsuits,[79] on the one hand; a sense of outrage generated by his contempt for Aebutius and by his humiliating flight from the olive trees, on the other. Any of these social considerations might well have impaired his "rational" judgment; and even Caecina's constant reliance on a *consilium* of *amici* may not have restored the balance completely.

Second, it would not have been easy for Caecina to calculate the "expected benefits" of bringing a suit against Aebutius. Private law in the late Republic was characterized by a high degree of legal insecurity surrounding the outcome of

---

money are given a lower present value; and I assume that the prospective defendant is ready and able to pay any judgment.

[77] For a psychological discussion, see R. Nisbet and L. Ross, *Human Inferences: Strategies and Shortcomings of Social Judgment* (1980). I might observe that the theory of Economic Man has recently undergone significant modifications, mainly owing to Herbert Simon and his collaborators; see, e.g., A. Newell and H.A. Simon, *Human Problem Solving* (1972) 787 ff., where the shaping of human behavior by the "task environment" is stressed. M.D. Davis, (cited n.73) 57-74 and 123-135, cites much psychological evidence for nonrational performance in game playing. See also W.Z. Hirsch, *Law and Economics* (1979) 2-8, on "the interface between law and economics."

[78] So M.I. Finley, *The Ancient Economy* (1974), in part following Karl Polanyi. The references in Cicero's speech to bookkeeping (17, 94) do not imply modern attitudes; on ancient bookkeeping, which essentially tracked income and expenditure, see esp. G.E.M. de Ste. Croix, in *Studies in the History of Accounting* (ed. A.C. Littleton and B.S. Yamey, 1956) 14-74.

[79] See, e.g., J.M. Kelly, *Judicature* 97-102.

The Problem of Litigiousness

cases. Now a measure of indefiniteness is bound to be present in any system of law; litigants, in planning their strategies, must rely on probabilistic judgments about such matters as disputed rules of law or the availability and admissibility of evidence. In Rome, however, such areas of uncertainty were considerably greater both in number and extent.[80] This subject lies very close to the central theme of the present book, for it has many important sociological aspects; at present it is enough to say that Roman litigants would often have found it both hard to know when claims were actionable and hard to predict the outcome of suits. A lawsuit therefore represented for them a much greater gamble.

Third, many of the "expected costs" of trials were difficult to evaluate in monetary terms. For instance, Caecina did not directly pay Aquilius for his legal advice, nor Cicero for his three speeches on the plaintiff's behalf;[81] but he did incur thereby, in each case, a social obligation which he could be called upon to repay eventually. Decades after this trial, Caecina's son, in writing to Cicero, still refers to himself as "your old client" (*Fam.* 6.7.4: *veterem tuum . . . clientem*), the word *cliens* evoking a rich social history at Rome.[82] How was one to place a monetary value on such relationships?

[80] I have dealt below with the following topics: the instability and partial inaccessibility of praetorian courts (Chapter II); the indifference of rhetorical advocacy to positive law (Chapter III); the indefiniteness and partial inaccessibility of juristic law (Chapter IV); the lack of justification, the non-publication, and the unappealability of judicial decisions (Chapter V); and the pressure of public opinion in shaping law (Chapter VI). V. Aubert, *Journal of Conflict Resolution* 11 (1967) 43-46, has an interesting discussion of why people go to court.

[81] On jurists: W. Kunkel, *Herkunft*[2] 286-287 (the idea of pay was unheard of). On advocates: G. Kennedy, *The Art of Rhetoric in the Roman World* (1972) 12-14, with literature; the *lex Cincia* of 204 B.C. forbade pay for advocates, though this statute was often violated (cf. Dio, 54.18.2). See also I. Shatzman, *Senatorial Wealth and Roman Politics* (1975) 70-73.

[82] There is a vast literature. See the classic discussions of A. von Premerstein, *RE* s.v. "clientes" (1900) 23-55; M. Gelzer, *Die Nobilität der Römischen Republik* (1912), repr. in his *Kleine Schriften* vol. I (1964) 17-135, esp. 75-89 ("Gerichtspatronat"). Also W. Neuhauser, *Patronus und Orator* (1958); N. Rouland, *Pouvoir Politique et Dépendance Personnelle* (1979) 275-296, 469-475; R.P. Saller, *Personal Patronage under the Early Empire* (1982) 7-39.

The Litigants

Caecina had other legal recourses than the interdict *de vi armata* against Aebutius; for example, he might have proceeded, as the defense indeed pointed out, with an action on outrage (35: *iniuriarum*). Quite likely Aebutius had anticipated such an action. The argument would then have turned on the propriety of Aebutius' armed defense of the Fulcinian farm. Probably Caecina was reluctant to bring such a suit while the issue of ownership was still unsettled. Cicero explains the matter a bit differently: in an *actio iniuriarum* Caecina would obtain money, but not possession of the farm (9, 35). By contrast, the interdict *de vi armata* was a relatively newfangled invention,[83] with little jurisprudence or case law surrounding it. Caecina, in bringing the interdict on the advice of his friends (doubtless including Aquilius), may have seriously overestimated the strength of his legal position. It is well to keep in mind the factors that may have misled him.

If Caecina's decision to bring the interdict was arguably a miscalculation resulting from his inability to assess "rationally" his prospects in court, then it is not unreasonable to suppose that similar miscalculations could also have marked the interactions of Caecina and Aebutius earlier on; and we have in fact seen evidence that both men made such mistakes.[84] Indeed, it is one part of gamesmanship to induce opponents to miscalculate by keeping them off-balance and uneasy; so both the parties had relied on surprise as a tactic, and sometimes they got back more than they bargained for. Anyone can miscalculate in human interaction; the situation is no different today than it was in antiquity. What I am stressing is that a Roman litigant (or "potential litigant") faced certain problems which his modern equivalent does not—although the insecurities of modern legal systems are still numerous and should not be minimized.

I come now to the other question raised above: why did Caecina begin to deal with Aebutius not in his normal way, but rather as adversary to adversary? It should be noticed that

[83] Its wording had recently been changed; see Chapter II, at notes 45-49.
[84] See above, at notes 57, 58, 62-63.

The Problem of Litigiousness

Aebutius himself initially indicated more interest in a settlement than in a lawsuit, as Cicero clearly implies (18-19); it
was Caecina who first approached the Praetor (19). Without
in any sense aiming to exhaust the subject, I want to point
out four factors in the relationship between Caecina and Aebutius, factors that probably contributed to precipitating a
lawsuit. All of them might be thought of as "factors of litigiousness" associated with normal behavioral patterns in law-
permeated societies.[85]

First, there is the fact that both Caecina and Aebutius were
men of some social standing. As for Caecina, the matter speaks
largely for itself: a distinguished and wealthy Volaterran, now
resident in Rome, he enjoyed both the patronage of a great
consular family[86] and access to the finest in Roman jurists and
orators. He was probably himself an *eques*.[87] With Aebutius
matters are naturally less clear; but Cicero notwithstanding
(13-14) he did not lack resources. His long friendship with
Caesennia (and with other wealthy matrons, 13) attests to that,
as do his relations with neighboring landowners at Tarquinii.
He had some access to the Senate through Fidiculanius Falcula, to be sure not one of its more creditable members, who
had witnessed the melee at the Fulcinian farm (28-30); Aebutius' access was sufficient to gain him advice from a jurist
(79-80, 95) and also advocacy from the extremely distinguished Senator C. Calpurnius Piso, who would be Consul in
67 B.C. It is a generally observed tendency that, other things
being equal, resort to law is likelier to occur in the upper
ranks of a society than in the lower.[88] This is presumably
because law itself is a form of social control, with which the

---

[85] It should not be forgotten, however, that the rate of litigiousness and the
consciousness of claims varies considerably in different cultures; cf., e.g.,
L.M. Friedman, *Law and Society* (1977) 15-16.

[86] The Servilii Isaurici, see notes 51, 54. W.V. Harris, *Etruria* 282-283,
suggests that Pompey also supported Caecina's claim to citizenship.

[87] See note 50.

[88] See D. Black, *The Behavior of Law* (1976) 16-21, citing other literature.
Black's views on law remain controversial, cf. *Law and Society Review* 17 (1983)
337-390.

The Litigants

upper orders, simply by virtue of their position, are more apt to be concerned; they have a stake in law that the lower orders do not.[89] Caecina and Aebutius are, in any case, typical of the litigants one meets with overwhelming frequency in the sources on Roman trials—neither so exalted as to be insulated by social influence from the nuisance of suits, nor so humble (as the vast majority of Romans were) that they were all but insignificant for purposes of private law.[90]

Second, there is the social position of Caecina and Aebutius, relative this time not to Roman society as a whole but to each other. Caecina and Aebutius, despite their general prosperity compared to the condition of most Romans, were not on equal footing; there is no reason to doubt Cicero's insistence on Caecina's social superiority to Aebutius. Caecina was lord of an aristocratic municipal family that produced a consular within two generations after this trial; Sex. Aebutius is never heard of anywhere except in Cicero's speech. (The other Aebutii prominent at Rome may be his kin, but the name is not uncommon and none of the others bears his praenomen.[91]) Once again, it has been observed that, other things being equal, resort to law tends to run in a direction from top to bottom within society; and evidence for this proposition has been collected also for Rome.[92] The reasons are no doubt similar to those already discussed under the first point above: law is part of the apparatus by which societies are governed. On the other hand, Aebutius' position was not so low that Caecina could simply overbear him by sheer social pressure. Thus, although Caecina had wished to avoid a quarrel "with such an unwor-

[89] Add that they enjoy superior resources for waging lawsuits, and that their disputes are more likely to involve substantial values (on the worth of a *fundus*, see note 25).

[90] See B.W. Frier, *LTIR* 48-51, for a discussion; also Chapter VII, at notes 11-12 and the succeeding paragraph. But a thorough study is needed.

[91] There is little point in observing that "Aebutius was a well-established Roman name by the early second century at least": W.V. Harris, *Etruria* 284 n.2. Late Republican Aebutii are canvassed in C. Nicolet, *Ordre* vol. II 757-760.

[92] D. Black, (cited n.88) 21-30. On Rome, see J.M. Kelly, *Litigation* 62-66; P. Garnsey, *Social Status and Legal Privilege* (1970) 181-218, esp. 216-218.

thy man" (23: *cum tam improbo homine*), in the end he had little choice.

Third, Aebutius and Caecina had from the outset an arm's-length relationship. They were joined together at first only by their mutual connection to Caesennia, and may have had hostile feelings toward one another even during her lifetime; after her death they remained in connection only through the inheritance and their dispute over the Fulcinian farm. Their relationship was essentially confined to one "zone" of inter-action, and was not likely to continue past the termination of their immediate dispute. This fact made it more likely that litigation would result.[93] The reason is that those involved in simple, short-term relationships are more prone to prefer the "zero-sum" outcome, with clear winners and losers, that liti-gation typically provides; while those involved in complex, long-term relationships prefer compromise and negotiated set-tlements with no absolute winners, since such settlements al-low the relationships to continue.

Indirectly, Roman private law may even have encouraged litigation in the type of situation that occurred after Caesen-nia's death. It has often been observed that the Romans were particularly litigious during estate settlements,[94] a fact that has an obvious explanation. Roman private law concentrated both power over dependents and wealth in the hands of a relatively few *sui iuris* persons. The death of a wealthy person had two immediate consequences: first, it created a rift in an established social scheme, disorienting especially the expec-tations upon which the deceased's dependents had hitherto patterned their lives; second, it set the stage for a redistribu-tion of the deceased's estate, an event upon which the future prosperity of those interested in the estate could quite literally depend. (One thinks, for instance, of a disinherited adult son.) This combination of social dislocation and financial jeopardy was an explosive one, productive both of suits and of law;

[93] See, for instance, L. Nader and H.F. Todd, *The Disputing Process* (ed. Nader and Todd, 1978) 12-19. The same point was made by Aristotle, *Nic. Eth.* 1162 b 16 ff. (8.13.4).

[94] See, e.g., J.M. Kelly, *Judicature* 81-92.

better than one-quarter of the *Digest* is devoted to the law of succession alone, and problems involving succession often stand behind cases on quite unrelated subjects. Romans learned to expect lawsuits in the aftermath of death, and their expectations were father to the fact.

Fourth, there is an additional psychological element that perhaps transcends, in its final importance, all those named above: some individuals are simply more apt to litigate than others. With regard to lawsuits, they are "accident prone": easily dissatisfied with their lot, always ready to take offense at real and imagined injustices, quick to press grievances, and hostile to compromise. If Cicero's view of him is even close to correct, Aebutius was probably such a man: too quarrelsome as an advocate (14: *defensoris nimium litigiosi*),[95] awkward and disagreeable in the company of males (14), given to exaggerating his rights (19) and to backing his claims with coarse threats (22). However, even Cicero admits (17) that Aebutius had initially aimed for compromise, not confrontation, with Caecina.

In Cicero's view, Caecina was entirely different: brave and resourceful (18), exceedingly cautious (22), well-mannered and valorous and loyal (104), most decidedly not quarrelsome (23); it is not Caecina, but his opponent, who is acting "fanatically" in this suit (10, 65: *summo iure*).[96] One may well wonder if this is all quite accurate. On Cicero's own account, Caecina had pursued his "rights" undeviatingly from the outset, never deigning to answer Aebutius' initial offer of compromise (18). Even his advocate wondered at Caecina's stubborn determination outside the Fulcinian farm (21-22). As a man, Caecina was perhaps not utterly unlike Aebutius, except that his background gave him the saving grace of greater social ease and his biography shows nothing in the way of personal frustration to his career. Cicero asserts with confidence that the *recuperatores* had twice postponed judgment in hopes that Ae-

[95] It was, however, normal to accuse one's opponent of litigiousness: Cic. *de Or.* 2.182.

[96] On this phrase, see Chapter III, at notes 88-89. Many psychological insights into Aebutius' conduct can be had from E. Goffman, *Stigma* (1963).

butius would surrender the farm and avoid an embarrassing adverse verdict (6-8); perhaps, however, the judges' hopes had run in quite the opposite direction, but Caecina would not budge.[97] Caecina hoped through this trial to prove himself to the jurors and to their class (103).

The quarrelsome are not pleasant people; they lead lives of inner anger and unrest, and they are a burden to others, often entirely without relation to their apparent success in life. Yet in two senses they have a greater importance than their peers for those interested in law's progress within society. On the one hand, their more or less permanent discontent leads them willy-nilly into disputes with their acquaintances, and some few of these disputes inevitably end up in courts. Because they are more willing than others to take up quarrels, they act as bearers of law outward, into society. As I observed above,[98] normally most individuals place law in the "back region" of their action; but the presence of the quarrelsome within society compels everyone, at least for self-protection, to be more prudent in acting than would otherwise be required, and hence more conscious of law and legal rules. The quarrelsome force law upon those who might otherwise be indifferent or hostile to it. To the extent that attentiveness to law is a source of benefit to a society (and that extent may vary, of course), everyone else is the third-party beneficiary of the litigious.

On the other hand, the litigious do not confine their discontent to their fellows; they are apt to regard with a jaundiced eye the very legal systems they employ. They are querulous, continuously demanding the creation of new legal rules or the alteration of old ones; and because they relentlessly pursue their grievances with argument and emotion, they force legal systems to take account of their complaints. They at least make legal systems reconsider and justify old positions, and often they also provoke law into doing new things. In this they are indispensable agents of legal change, and yet

[97] See Chapter V, at notes 55-56, 69-70, 86-89.
[98] At note 71.

39

they are often ungrateful even for changes designed to appease them.[99] Any practicing attorney will recognize the type of person I am describing.

All four of these "factors of litigiousness" helped make a trial between Caecina and Aebutius more rather than less likely to occur. These factors are pertinent in explicating particular situations, in that they show how a social system can contain within itself stimuli to the use of law, and hence to law's propagation. The first two factors (the social standing of the potential litigants in relation to society as a whole and to each other) involve the social stratification characterizing all known societies, and its character and degree in specific historical circumstances. The third factor (the nature of the relationship between the potential litigants) is a function of the development of impersonal interactions within societies, including above all, one would suppose, the prevalence of a money-based economy.[100] Even the fourth factor (psychological "proneness" to litigation) is at least in part fostered by the degree of social resentment and anomie to which societies give rise by promoting individual aspirations that, for whatever reason, cannot be fulfilled;[101] and this, in turn, is a function of social evolution toward the production of surplus and the creation of systemic complexity. In all these ways, therefore, a social system enters into and informs the process of law.

Caecina's suit against Aebutius ostensibly concerned only the possession of one farm near Tarquinii. It was not an "im-

[99] A similar point is nicely made in Theophrastus' description of the Querulous Man (Char. 17.9); compare the vivid portrayal of the type in Plautus, Men. 571 ff. (esp. 582-583: litium pleni, rapaces viri). For some bizarre examples of overtly litigious behavior in the late Republic, see Cic. de Or. 1.179 and Gell. 20.1.13. The issue of quarrelsomeness is well examined in B. Moore, Injustice (1978) 462-468 ("Individual Personality"). On litigiousness, see S. Vago, Law and Society (1981) 213-218, with literature, esp. M. Galanter, Law and Society Review 9 (1974) 95-160; J.K. Lieberman, The Litigious Society (1981).

[100] See now D. Daube, SZ 96 (1979) 1-16; but also A. Bürge, SZ 99 (1982) 128-157.

[101] I refer, of course, to Durkheim's theories in Le Suicide (1897); cf. A. Giddens, Émile Durkheim (1978) 113-114. Compare the concept of "relative deprivation" in T.R. Gurr's Why Men Rebel (1970) 24-44.

portant" suit from the viewpoint of late Republican Rome; there was here no sense of genuine legal crisis, notwithstanding Cicero's palaver to the contrary. But Caecina's suit did not therefore come to the Urban Praetor as a purely intellectual problem in the application of positive law, a problem divorced from its social roots in time and place. The events that gave rise to this suit cut across a great many important contemporary issues of political, social, and economic life; these events presuppose a setting, along with characters who were made by and who made that setting.[102] The two litigants, in their persons, bore with them all this history like baggage into the Praetor's court. Caecina's lawsuit is probably only marginally different in significance from the many hundred thousands of lawsuits out of which classical Roman law was forged. How would that system deal with Caecina and Aebutius?

[102] Cf. A. Giddens, (cited n.71) 53-59, esp. 54: "Social Activity is always constituted in three intersecting moments of difference: temporally, paradigmatically (involving structure which is present only in its instantiation) and spatially. All social practices are *situated* activities in each of these senses." Modern legal anthropology also favors an approach that "treats disputes as but one event in a series of events linking persons and groups over time and possibly involving other disputes. Disputes are social processes embedded in social relations." So L. Nader and H.F. Todd, (cited n.93) 16; see also S.F. Moore, *Law as Process: An Anthropological Approach* (1978).

II

The Urban Praetor:
P. Cornelius Dolabella

non ergo a Praetoris Edicto, ut plerique
nunc, . . . hauriendam iuris disciplinam putas?
—Cicero

To LEGAL historians, the Edict of the Urban Praetor is the perfectly familiar stuff of scholarship; its numerous rubrics and headings constitute the major procedural framework within which the classical jurists operated, and so historians have had to become intimately acquainted with its convoluted phraseology. Yet probably few scholars have seriously considered what the Edict must have looked like, and perhaps even fewer have seen the attempted recreation of it in the Museo della Civiltà Romana in the Roman suburb of EUR.[1]

The visual display at the Museo brings out one important feature of the Edict: it cannot be read as a continuous document. The modern lawyer, at home with the austere draftsmanship of the great codes, will find in the Edict only a bewildering conglomeration of causes and forms of action—on the standard count, nearly three hundred separate rubrics, many with multiple headings. They are arranged in a seemingly haphazard order that reflects the casual accretion of centuries; for instance, the fundamental negligence action *ad legem Aquiliam* is lodged obscurely between an action for damage

---

[1] For a brief description of this reconstruction, see the *Catalogo* (undated) 536, on Room XLVI, no. 20. The wording of the reconstruction is based on Otto Lenel's monumental assemblage of the Hadrianic redaction: *Das Edictum Perpetuum* (1st ed. 1883, 3d ed. 1927); cf. L. Wenger, *Quellen* 408-410, and notes 6 and 101 below.

caused by defendant's cattle grazing on plaintiff's land and an *actio in factum* against shipowners and innkeepers for damage done to the property of guests.[2] The Edict's syntax and vocabulary, furthermore, are dense and at times obscure. The use of such a document obviously required expert guidance.

The Romans, however, saw the Edict quite differently. As Pomponius puts it (D. 1.2.2.10), the Edict was set up so that citizens could know about, and take precautions concerning, the law that each magistrate would maintain on every subject.[3] In its essence, the Edict was an emphatically public document: a great whitewashed board (*album*) with bold red letters (*rubricae*) set up in the Forum for all to read.[4] Indeed, "the very word Edictum still recalled the original form of oral statement, even at a time when the written record had long since eclipsed in significance the oral statement."[5] Even in an age when the Edict had acquired permanent and predictable form through the Hadrianic redaction (ca. A.D. 125), still it retained this curiously ambiguous nature: on the one hand, emphatic publicity and access for all; on the other hand, language so crabbed and technical that no layman could comprehend it.

In this chapter I examine some aspects of the Edict and its procedural law during a much earlier time, when its wording was still quite fluid and its contents still changed almost yearly. In the late Republic the Urban Praetor had considerable freedom to define his own *iurisdictio*, the causes of action he would or would not accept during his year in office;[6] the Edict was,

---

[2] Lenel, *EP*[3] 198-206.

[3] This statement reflects the constitutional principle expressed in the *lex Cornelia* of 67 B.C.; earlier, enforcement had been rather freer, cf. below at notes 91-101.

[4] See Kipp, *RE* s.v. "edictum" (1905) 1941, for sources. It is not known exactly where the Edict was posted. The existence of a single Edict is unconvincingly denied by G. Mancuso, *Praetoris Edicta* (Ann. Sem. Giurid. Palermo, 1983).

[5] Cf. L. Wenger, *Quellen* 408 n.5 *in fine* (my translation).

[6] See M. Kaser, *RZ* 28-30. On the late Republican development of the Edict, see A. Watson, *Law Making* 31-62, with O. Behrends, *SZ* 93 (1976) 299-305, and M. Kaser, *TR* 45 (1977) 161-166 (both reviews); also the assess-

The Urban Praetor

as Cicero puts it (2 *Verr.* 1.109), his "annual statute," *lex annua*. Praetors controlled substantive law only indirectly, through manipulation of procedure; and accordingly they compensated by developing a highly intricate procedural law, in much the same way that classical Athens or medieval England did.

The first section of this chapter looks at the ways in which the Edict was shaped by the political nature of the urban praetorship. The second section considers the Urban Praetor's administration of judicial procedure, especially the standards he employed in granting or denying lawsuits. The third section discusses a difficult technical problem raised by the *pro Caecina*: the relation of *deductio quae moribus fit* to contemporary judicial procedure. The reader should be forewarned that, because of the subject matter, parts of this chapter are difficult. The issues I will be treating, however, are essential to understanding how the late Republican judicial system operated.

THE PRAETOR AND HIS LAW

When Caecina demanded an arbiter to divide Caesennia's estate (*Caec.* 19), and later when he obtained the interdict *de vi hominibus armatis*, he appeared before the Urban Praetor P. Cornelius Dolabella (*Caec.* 23), a man of the highest nobility. The Cornelii Dolabellae (the cognomen means "hatchet") were a cadet line of the great patrician family. By Cicero's time the Dolabellae had two main branches: a more eminent and violent branch, characterized by the praenomen Gnaeus, and a lesser branch using the praenomens Lucius and Publius. The Praetor who granted the interdict to Caecina belonged to this lesser line; he is quite probably the son of L. Cornelius P.f. L.n. Dolabella, who celebrated a triumph from Further Spain in 98 B.C.[7] Like his father, P. Dolabella obtained no higher office than the praetorship.

---

ment by F. Wieacker, *Recht*[2] 83-127, and M. Talamanca and M. Bretone, in *Lineam.* 151-171, 377-380.

[7] *Acta Triumphalia*. He is presumably the grandson of the L. Dolabella mentioned by Livy (40.42.8-11: 180 B.C.).

P. Dolabella is an obscure figure, known to history mainly from an anecdote about his term as Propraetor in the Roman province of Asia. The story shows him to have possessed considerable common sense. A woman from Smyrna, accused of poisoning her husband and son, urged in mitigation that she had acted because they had earlier killed her son by a previous marriage. Dolabella referred the case to the Athenian Areopagus, who reached the Solomonic outcome of adjourning the trial for one hundred years.[8]

Dolabella's governorship provides the chief basis for dating the *pro Caecina*. The speech must date after 74 (since it refers to a trial in that year, *Caec.* 28-29), but before 66, since at *Orator* 102 Cicero clearly implies that the speech was delivered before the *pro lege Manilia* in 66, and the Urban Praetor for 66 is known.[9] The year 67 is ruled out because C. Piso, advocate for the defense, was Consul in 67; it is scarcely credible that as Consul he would have argued a civil case. On the other hand, all the Roman governors of Asia are known from 76 down to 69,[10] the year in which L. Licinius Lucullus was relieved of command and the province "returned" to ex-Praetors (Dio 36.2.2).

There are thus three possible dates for Piso's praetorship: in 70, with a governorship during what of 69 was left from Lucullus' term;[11] in 69, with a governorship in 68; or in 68, with a governorship in 67. Of these dates, the middle one is preferable, on admittedly shaky grounds: this dating allows

---

[8] Val. Max. 8.1 *amb.* 2; Gell. *NA* 12.7; Amm. Marc. 29.2.19. Cf. *IGRRP* 4.422, a perfunctory dedication from Pergamum. My attempt below to date the *pro Caecina* recapitulates my article in *TAPhA* 113 (1983) 222-231. G. Nicosia, *Deiectio* 149-152, dated Dolabella's praetorship to before 71. Although this view found wide acceptance, e.g. W. Stroh, *Taxis* 100, and G. Crifò, *Studi sul Quasi-Usufrutto Romano* vol. I (1977) 68 n.7, it is impossible on prosopographic grounds.

[9] C. Antonius Hibrida: cf. Cic. *Mur.* 40, discussing the political advantage to Antonius of the games given by Urban Praetors. For other sources on his praetorship, see *MRR*. C. Piso was also Proconsul in Gaul during 66-65.

[10] M. Junius Silanus in 76; M. (Junius?) Juncus in 75; and Lucullus from 74-69. See *MRR*.

[11] W.V. Harris, *Etruria* 281, raises this possibility.

The Urban Praetor

the politically powerful L. Manlius Torquatus to be Praetor in 68 and Propraetor of Asia in 67 (he was Consul in 65, and it is unlikely that his career was delayed);[12] and there is already a probable candidate for the urban praetorship of 70.[13] Therefore Dolabella's praetorship should be tentatively assigned to 69. Two further considerations support this chronology. First, Sex. Aebutius' challenge to Caecina's civil status as a Volaterran (*Caec.* 18, 95-102) is appropriate in 69 because this political issue had almost undoubtedly surfaced in the census of 70/69.[14] Second, if the trial was in 69, then Caesennia's son must have died in late 74 or early 73, four years before (*Caec.* 19, 94); and the younger Fulcinius' will appears to reflect provisions that were contained in Verres' Edict of 74, but in no other Edict before or after.[15]

The Praetor of 69 probably survived his Asian propraetorship by no more than a few years. He is not referred to during the well-documented period of the late 60's, nor in any of Cicero's letters and other works from that time onward. Cicero is not likely to have known him well, although two decades later his daughter Tullia was briefly married to Dolabella's debauched son Publius.

Dolabella is fairly typical of Urban Praetors in the late Republic. During the twenty-one years from 81 to 60 B.C., some nineteen names of Urban Praetors are known (some very tentatively).[16] They are a rough cross-section of the late Republican aristocracy:[17] six patricians (in 81, 78, 69, 64, 63, and 60), of whom only two later became Consuls (those of 64 and 60); five plebeians of consular families (in 79, 73, 72, 71, and

[12] So *MRR* vol. II 142 n.9. On Torquatus' political connections, see E. Gruen, *Last Generation* 133-134.

[13] M. Mummius, who as Praetor received letters from the Governor of Sicily on the letting of vectigal contracts: Cic. 2 *Verr.* 3.123. He was probably an Urban Praetor, addressed in his capacity as sometime president of the Senate.

[14] See W.V. Harris, *Etruria* 282-284.

[15] See Chapter I, at notes 35-39.

[16] See the appendix to this chapter.

[17] Compare the statistics for the praetorship as a whole: E. Gruen, *Last Generation* 163-167.

The Praetor and His Law

66) and two of praetorian families (in 77 and 65), all of whom later became Consuls; and one plebeian of a senatorial family (in 75) and five *novi homines* (in 76, 74, 70, 67, and 62), none of whom obtained the consulate. A high proportion of these Urban Praetors (nine out of nineteen, or 47%) became Consuls, a fact that supports Cicero's remark (*Mur.* 41) about the political advantages of the urban praetorship.[18] These advantages were closely correlated, however, with the previous status of each Praetor's family. The right background made the urban praetorship a political plum.

Sulla's reforms of 81[19] had raised the number of Praetors to eight and instituted a process of sortition whereby the incumbents were distributed to the two "civil" courts (the urban and peregrine praetorships, occasionally combined as in 78[20]) and the various criminal *quaestiones*. Under normal conditions their term of office coincided with the calendar year; however, by Sulla's rules they were elected in the cumbersome Centuriate Assembly during late July of the year preceding. Only after election did they learn what court or courts they would head. This electoral system therefore laid no stress on obtaining Urban Praetors with expertise in civil law; indeed, the system worked to thwart this possibility. In 65 two jurists, Servius Sulpicius Rufus[21] and P. Orbius (Cic. *Flacc.* 76, 79), served as Praetors; but the urban praetorship for that year was occupied by L. Licinius Murena, a *vir militaris* with no previous experience in law (Cic. *Mur.* 35-42). Likewise, in 66 C. Aquilius Gallus headed the *quaestio de ambitu* (Cic. *Cluent.* 147), while C. Antonius Hibrida, of discreditable background, was Urban Praetor. As Cicero explains in the *pro Plancio* (62), the

---

[18] Cicero gives two reasons: the games given by the Urban Praetor (*Mur.* 38-40) and the chance to earn a reputation for fairness (41). On the second reason, see below at notes 91-101.

[19] On what follows, see E. Vagiglio, *Silla e la Crisi Repubblicana* (1956) 87-94; also F. Càssola and L. Lombardi, in *Lineam.* 372.

[20] Cf. *CIL* 1².2.589 (= *ILLRP* 512).

[21] Cic. *Mur.* 35, 41-42; his friends had "hoped" that Servius would obtain the urban praetorship (41). On the Urban Praetor's usual ignorance of law, see F. Wieacker, *Recht²* 86-88, 107-108.

47

Roman electoral system was designed not to secure experts, but men of a certain general character who, in carrying out their offices, would rely not on professional knowledge, but rather on common sense and on experience both social and governmental. None of the Urban Praetors in the late Republic is known to have had more than a layman's comprehension of Roman law.

Praetorian courts were allotted soon after the election (Cic. 2 *Verr*. 1.104). The designated Urban Praetor therefore had nearly five months to prepare his Edict. The current Edict served him as a ready model. Innovations presented more of a problem; because the Urban Praetor normally lacked legal expertise, drafting of changes would have to be left to jurists[22] or to the small staff attached to his office.[23] No doubt suggestions for change also often came from these quarters, as well as from other parties interested in the content of private law; it may be, for instance, that Urban Praetors took advice from their colleagues.[24] Nonetheless, the Urban Praetor was ultimately responsible for his own Edict, and it was he alone who was praised or criticized for his innovations.

In 70, one year before Caecina's suit, the infamous C. Verres was tried for extortion during his propraetorship in Sicily, 73-71. Cicero prosecuted, and he later published the extended orations that he would have delivered had Verres not fled to avoid condemnation. The first of this sprawling and brilliant set of speeches is concerned with Verres' career up to 73, and especially with his urban praetorship in 74 (2 *Verr*. 1.103-

[22] See, e.g., F. Schulz, *Legal Science* 50-51; cf. L. Lombardi, *Saggio* 60-61. But we need not assume, and lack all evidence to prove, major juristic influence on the content of the Edict prior to the late Republic; so already O. Karlowa, *Römische Rechtsgeschichte* vol. I (1885) 479. It is exaggerated to claim that the Praetor "reigned but did not rule" as the "spokesman for jurisprudence"; *contra*: O. Carrelli, *La Genesi del Procedimento Formulare* (1946) 280-281.

[23] Cf. R. Düll, *SZ* 63 (1943) 393-396, who exaggerates their influence; see now W. Eder, *Servitus Publica* (1980) 71-75.

[24] A. Watson, *Law Making* 64-82, argues that the Urban Praetor's Edict was in effect a collegiate effort; but see the reviews of O. Behrends, (cited n.6) 303-305, and M. Kaser, (cited n.6) 165-166. For influence on the Urban Praetor's Edict from that of the Peregrine Praetor, see below, at notes 38-40.

The Praetor and His Law

158). According to Cicero, Verres composed his entire Edict
to accommodate those who had bribed him (119). Cicero lists
three changes introduced by Verres:

1) The Voconian law of 169 forbade those registered in
the first census class from making women their heirs; Verres
retroactively extended this prohibition to cover those not
registered in the census but of sufficient wealth. Doubtless
he justified his position by the fact that no census had been
held since 86/85.[25]

2) Hitherto, when a dead man had apparently left no
will, Urban Praetors had awarded *possessio bonorum* to the
intestate heirs; those claiming inheritance under a will not
yet produced were left to sue the intestate heirs. Verres
reversed this rule. He also declined to disturb the earliest
possessor of a disputed inheritance, and instead he forced
the rival claimant to bring an action on ownership (2 *Verr.*
1.114-118).

3) Verres awarded a share *contra tabulas* to the daughter
of the patron of a testate freedman (presumably only if he
died without natural children), and enforced this rule retroactively (2 *Verr.* 1.125-127).[26]

Cicero produces little direct evidence that these changes were
induced by bribery. Instead, he develops a sustained indict-
ment of the innovations themselves, on three basic counts.
First, he employs extensive legal analysis; he criticizes the excess verbiage in Verres' innovations (111), their inconsistency
with other provisions or with themselves (110, 116-117), and
above all their perverse retroactive application of novel standards to past transactions (107-109, 125).[27] This leads on to
Cicero's second criterion, that even in their prospective work-

[25] Cic. 2 *Verr.* 1.104-114, 118; 2.21. This change is reflected in the will of
the younger Fulcinius; see Chapter I, at notes 35-39. See also M. Bartosek,
in *St. Scherillo* vol. II 649-679. On the change in *possessio bonorum* discussed
below, see *idem*, in *Fg. von Lübtow* (1970) 255-266.
[26] On this innovation, which did not survive into classical law, see A. Watson, *Persons* 231-233 and *Succession* 186-187.
[27] Cicero's remarks on retroactivity are critically discussed by G. Broggini,
Coniectanea (1966) 343-412.

ing Verres' innovations violate fundamental equity (112-114,
116); Cicero disapproves of their implications for public policy. The third criterion is rather different: Cicero measures
Verres' Edict against the standard set by other Edicts before
and after his. Cicero regards novelty as *prima facie* suspect,
since it violates long-standing *consuetudo iuris*, the usage of the
Praetor's court (105, 114-115, 125); and he draws further inferences from the failure of later Praetors to retain the innovations (111-112, 117-118). While Cicero uses these observations to strengthen his charge of bribery, they are in fact the
sort of criteria that could be used to evaluate almost any change
in the Edict. Bribery or no, Cicero does not even hint that
Verres' changes were not law, not fully valid as law; only that
they were "bad" law.[28]

Praetorian law had arisen, in Papinian's famous phrase, "to
assist or supplement or correct the *ius civile*."[29] There is no
need to dwell on the vagueness of this formulation; suffice it
to say that in the late Republic Urban Praetors had little shy-
ness about reshaping their Edicts on an annual basis. The
process of election and sortition guaranteed a wide diversity
of incumbents: bad Praetors (like Verres) balanced by good
ones, men of nobility by those of somewhat humbler station,
all with different understandings and interests. Praetorian law
necessarily reflected this mélange of social types; its most
prominent characteristic was its breadth.[30]

[28] Cicero's attitude (a common one in antiquity) has affinities with modern
legal positivism; cf. D. Nörr, *Rechtskritik* 19-43 (42-43 on Cicero). T. Mayer-
Maly, *Gnomon* 49 (1977) 174, in reviewing Nörr, explains the evidence differently.

[29] D. 1.1.7.1: "adiuvandi vel supplendi vel corrigendi iuris civilis gratia."
I do not intend to trace the Edict's history; there is a summary of modern
scholarly views in A.A. Schiller, *Mechanisms* 402-441. The legal achievement
of the Urban Praetors is fairly assessed by C. Gioffredi, *SDHI* 13/14 (1947/
1948) 102-122; F. Wieacker, *Recht*[2] 112-120. See now the important article of
M. Kaser, *SZ* 101 (1984) 1-114, esp. 65-73.

[30] Unfortunately, it is rarely possible to identify the Praetors responsible
for named innovations: A. Watson, *Law Making* 31-33. Thus we cannot know
whether the Salvius who introduced the *interdictum Salvianum* (governing pledges
by tenant farmers) was a member of the Salvian family from rural Feren-

Praetors who were vigorous of intellect even helped to create public policy.[31] In 79 B.C. the Urban Praetor was Cn. Octavius, a well-connected aristocrat who was crippled by severe gout and yet retained a slow and gentle manner.[32] His exemplary praetorship is sympathetically described by Cicero nearly two decades later (*Q. Fr.* 1.1.21-22). According to Cicero, Octavius made two major changes in the Edict. The first established that when magistrates "issued wrongful decrees" (*iniuriose decreverant*), these same decrees were then to be enforced on them as private citizens; the provision, which in somewhat altered form entered the permanent Edict,[33] obviously deals with much the same concerns as those motivating the *lex Cornelia* of 67.[34] The second innovation was even more startling: the *formula Octaviana* (Cic. 2 *Verr.* 3.152), designed to force followers of Sulla to return what they had extorted through force or fear.[35] This action also entered the

---

tinum, cf. T.P. Wiseman, *New Men* 259 (citing *ILLRP* 588-590). Likewise, the Praetor Publicius who introduced the commercially useful *actio Publiciana* (Just. *Inst.* 4.6.4) may be the Q. Publicius who was Praetor in 67 (Cic. *Cluent.* 126), and also the influential benefactor of Asia mentioned by Cicero (*Q. Fr.* 1.2.14). On the man and his family (apparently from Verona), cf. T.P. Wiseman, *New Men* 8 n.6, 20, 255, drawing on his article in *CQ* 15 (1965) 158-159; *contra*: E. Gruen, *Last Generation* 166. F. Serrao, *La "Iurisdictio" del Pretore Peregrino* (1954) 110-111, argues, perhaps rightly, that the Publicius of 67 was Peregrine Praetor.

[31] I have dealt with the Edict in the 70's and 60's in my article (cited n.8) 231-237. Here I merely summarize my views.

[32] Cf. Sall. *Hist.* 2.26 M; Cic. *Brut.* 217, *Fin.* 2.93; Quintil. 11.3.129. On his ties to the Sullan aristocracy, see E. Gruen, *Last Generation* 124-125; like all Urban Praetors who during this period made edictal innovations concerning *vis*, he was a conservative supporter of the Senate. The identification of Octavius and the dating of his praetorship may now be considered certain: A.W. Lintott, *Violence in Republican Rome* (1968) 129-130; A. Metro, *Iura* 20 (1969) 520-521.

[33] Lenel, *EP*³ 58-59.

[34] See below, at notes 92-93.

[35] It suffices to refer to B. Kupisch, *In Integrum Restitutio und Vindicatio Utilis* (1974) 158-167, and the review of M. Kaser, *SZ* 94 (1977) 124-126, with which I substantially agree. Kaser also discusses the relation of this formula to the later *actio quod metus causa* (pp. 126-132). Both authors cite much further bibliography.

permanent Edict;[36] on the public law side, it directly foreshadows the establishment of a permanent criminal *quaestio de
vi*, through the *lex Lutatia* (probably of 78) and the *lex Plautia*
(probably of 70).[37]

The social turbulence of the 70's made violence a recurring
edictal theme. In 76 the Peregrine Praetor[38] M. Terentius Varro
Lucullus introduced a new *iudicium*, the nature and background of which is discussed by Cicero in a private oration
pro Tullio, delivered five years later (*Tull.* 7-12).[39] Owing to
the continual internal war, armed violence in the countryside
had become commonplace, particularly by gangs of slaves (10:
familiae); Cicero refers to the chaos unleashed by the long cycle
of civil wars ending in Lepidus' rebellion in 78/77. The new
action was directed against owners of *familiae*, and empowered a panel of *recuperatores* to estimate the amount of damages
done to the plaintiff (up to a maximum set by him); adverse
judgment was for quadruple this amount. The new action
passed almost at once into the Urban Praetor's Edict.[40] In 71

[36] Lenel, *EP³* 111-114.

[37] See now the convincing reconstruction by R.A. Bauman, *Labeo* 24 (1978)
60-74, reviewing L. Labruna, *Il Console Sovversivo* (1976).

[38] For his office, see Ascon. p. 84 C. It seems doubtful that, as some scholars have supposed, the Peregrine Praetor had jurisdiction over suits between
Roman citizens. See the summary of the dispute by L. Labruna, *Vim Fieri
Veto* (1971) 19 n.41; and now A. Watson, *Law Making* 65-67, on whose arguments M. Kaser, (cited n.6) 165-166. The census of 86/85 apparently left
many new citizens unregistered: P. Brunt, *Italian Manpower* (1971) 90-94;
perhaps the Peregrine Pretor retained jurisdiction over them.

[39] The date of the *pro Tullio* was established by F. Münzer, *RE* s.v. "Fa-
bius" (1909) 1747-1748, who observed that *Tull.* 14 and 18-19 must refer to
the aftermath of Spartacus' occupation of Thurii in 72 (App. *BC* 1.117.547;
Flor. 2.8.5). See also J. Annequin, in *Actes du Colloque sur l'Esclavage* (Ann.
Litt. Univ. Besançon, 163; 1970) 215-223, and my article (cited n.8) 225. L.
Quinctius, advocate for the defense, also served in this year as a legate to
Crassus (*MRR*), but would have been demobilized after Crassus' ovation early
in the year. Legal historians still waver in dating the speech; cf. M. Balzarini,
St. Grosso vol. I 323 n.2, summarizing modern views.

[40] So A. Watson, *Law Making* 65-67. Certainly Cicero, in the *pro Tullio*,
does not suggest its importation was recent. The development of this *iudicium*, and its putative relationship to the later *actio vi bonorum raptorum*, are
hotly debated; bibliography in M. Kaser, *RPR²* vol. I 626-627; vol. II 435-

Cicero's client M. Tullius brought suit against P. Fabius under the Lucullan *iudicium*. At *Tull.* 7 and 31, Cicero quotes part of the *formula* for this action; it reveals the emergence of a new legal phrase and category, which also gave the *iudicium* its name (*Tull.* 9): *vis hominibus coactis armatisve*, "violence done through men assembled or armed."

The new *iudicium* soon affected the possessory interdicts allowing plaintiffs to recover possession of land taken by violence (the interdicts *unde vi*), with consequences that were to have a considerable impact on Caecina's lawsuit. L. Caecilius Metellus, Urban Praetor in 71, inherited an Edict containing at least two such interdicts. By far the oldest had existed "among our ancestors" (*Tull.* 44), probably since at least the early second century B.C.[41] As Cicero remarks, its wording had changed over the years;[42] in 71 (*Tull.* 44) it ran as follows:

> Unde tu aut familia aut procurator tuus illum aut familiam aut procuratorem illius in hoc anno vi deiecisti, cum ille possideret, quod nec vi nec clam nec precario a te possideret, <eo restituas>.

This is the classical interdict *de vi*. In 69 it appears to have had identical wording;[43] Cicero refers to it as "the everyday interdict" (*Caec.* 91: *illud cotidianum interdictum*). In English:

> Whence you or your household or procurator have within this year thrust out [*deiecisti*] by force this man or his household or procurator, at a time when he possessed what he

---

436. On the *iudicium*, see recently L. Solidoro, *Atti. Acc. Naz. di Sci. Mor. e Pol. Napoli* 92 (1981) 197-229.

41 The exact date is unknown; but the *exceptio vitiosae possessionis*, first attested in 161 (Ter. *Eun.* 319-320), probably originated in this interdict.

42 Cf. Lenel, *EP*³ 462. Note the rather different wording in the *lex agraria* of 111 B.C. (*FIRA* vol. I no. 8, line 18): "[Sei quis . . .] . . . ex possessione vi eiectus est, . . ." By contrast, *Rhet. ad Herenn.* 4.40 (". . . ut me vi de meo fundo deieceris . . .") indicates that the later wording was in place by the mid-80's. See Chapter IV, at notes 152-154.

43 Cic. *Caec.* 91, and in general 86-93. So also in 63 B.C.: Cic. *Leg. Ag.* 3.11.

possessed neither by force nor by stealth nor on grant from you, thereto shall you restore him.

The interdict remained virtually unchanged, except for the elimination of some words later deemed superfluous, until its inclusion in the final Hadrianic redaction of the Edict.[44]

Alongside this "everyday" interdict there was another, with somewhat harsher form;[45] Cicero gives a hypothetical wording (*Tull.* 29):

Unde dolo malo tuo, M. Tulli, M. Claudius aut familia aut procurator eius vi detrusus est, <eo restituas>.

In English:

Whence M. Claudius or his household or procurator has been driven out [*detrusus est*] by force owing to your malice aforethought, M. Tullius, thereto shall you restore him.

This interdict differed from the interdict *de vi* in four significant ways: 1) it used the verb *detrudere* instead of *deicere* (the two are almost synonymous,[46] but *detrudere* connotes greater force and physical directness, cf. *Caec.* 49); 2) it eliminated the requirement that the thrusting out need have occurred "within this year"; 3) it required that the defendant's "malice aforethought" (*dolus malus*) lie behind the thrusting out (cf. *Tull.* 29-30), but did not specify the defendant's vicarious liability for his own *familia* and procurator;[47] and 4) it omitted

[44] See Ulpian, D. 43.16.1 pr., with Lenel, *EP*[3] 461-465, and M. Kaser, *RPR*[2] vol. I 399.

[45] Whether this interdict was in fact harsher has been the subject of protracted (and largely pointless) debate; cf. G. Nicosia, *Deiectio* 98-99. Cicero, in any case, construes it as such; at a minimum, this must indicate its use in the late 70's. The *detrudere* interdict, like the later interdict *de vi armata*, probably led to a trial before *recuperatores*; see B. Schmidlin, *Rekup.* 47-50. The *detrudere* interdict was plainly quite old, since its wording is referred to by Lucilius (frg. 825 Marx, = 902 Krenkel, with Marx's commentary); *contra*: Nicosia, pp. 103-104.

[46] So Cicero, *Tull.* 44-45. See also note 47.

[47] G. Nicosia, *Deiectio* 97-109, sees here the fundamental characteristic of the *detrudere* interdict, and thinks that this interdict became outmoded as interpretation expanded the ambit of the interdict *de vi*; Nicosia thus inclines

the entire *exceptio vitiosae possessionis* which in effect directed a verdict for the defendant if the plaintiff, prior to being thrust out, had possessed "by force or by stealth or on grant" from the defendant.

Metellus evidently removed the *detrudere* interdict from his Edict (cf. *Tull.* 29; *Caec.* 49) and replaced it with another interdict, which, so Cicero says (*Tull.* 46), was directed against the same domestic turbulence that the Lucullan *iudicium* handled (cf. *Tull.* 8). This new interdict was the interdict *de vi armata*,[48] under which Caecina brought suit against Aebutius two years later. In 69 its wording (*Caec.* 37, 41, 55, 59, 87-88) ran:

> Unde tu aut familia aut procurator tuus illum[49] vi hominibus coactis armatisve deiecisti, eo restituas.

In English:

> Whence you or your household or procurator thrust out this man by force with men assembled or armed, thereto shall you restore him.

This new interdict resembled the older *detrudere* interdict in some respects: it lacked the restriction "within one year" and the *exceptio vitiosae possessionis*. But it altered the defendant's vicarious liability by eliminating the requirement of *dolus malus*

---

to exaggerate the novelty of the interdict *de vi armata*. Significantly, Nicosia scarcely deals with Cic. *Caec.* 49, where the interdict *de vi armata* is described as a successor to the *detrudere* interdict. The reference to the defendant's *dolus malus* in the *detrudere* interdict was plainly responsible, as Cicero saw, for the similar reference in the Lucullan *iudicium*.

[48] Or *de vi hominibus armatis*, Cic. *Caec.* 23; see also G. Nicosia, *Deiectio* 103 n.39 and 140 n.126. The historical reconstruction given here is not certain; as I note in my article, (cited n.8) 237, the two interdicts may have remained together in the Edict for a year or two. See also G. Nicosia, pp. 97-101 and 152-153.

[49] G. Nicosia, *Deiectio* 154-157, attempts to insert at this point the words *aut familiam aut procuratorem illius* (parallel to the interdict *de vi*). This is unpersuasive in view of Cic. *Caec.* 37, which Nicosia fails to explain away. There is no reason to assume that the two interdicts had entirely parallel wording; the interdict *de vi armata* appears to reflect later developments in edictal interpretation.

and instead listing the subordinates for whose conduct he was responsible. The general form and wording of the new interdict *de vi armata* derived directly from the interdict *de vi*, of which it explicitly presented itself as a special case; and that case was largely determined by the phrase *vi hominibus coactis armatisve*, borrowed from the Lucullan *iudicium*.

By the third hearing of Caecina's lawsuit (the hearing in which the *pro Caecina* was delivered), it had become clear that the two parties differed radically in their interpretation of the interdict *de vi armata*. I will discuss their debate in later chapters; but it is evident in any case that the new interdict raised substantial legal questions, especially as to the manner in which its use of the category *deiectio* was to be interpreted: by reference to the older legal category of *detrusio* (cf. *detrusus est* in the *detrudere* interdict) or by reference to the probably wider concept of *deiectio* in the interdict *de vi*? Was the change from the *detrudere* interdict to the interdict *de vi armata* merely the replacement of one set of words by another and more "modern" set, or did it involve a change in substantive law as well, and if so, what change? What inferences could be drawn from the absence in the interdict *de vi armata* of the *exceptio vitiosae possessionis* and other features of the interdict *de vi*? What was the legal significance of the borrowings from the Lucullan *iudicium*? These were (and are) very difficult questions, on which the verdict in Caecina's lawsuit came to depend.

When Caecina brought suit under the new interdict, the great era of praetorian creativity was (for reasons we shall presently examine) drawing to an end. The motives for edictal innovation had been, in the main, political: the Edict served as a means whereby lucky members of the aristocracy could win for themselves repute and advancement. Cicero might, in a flight of juvenile imagination, class "most" of the Edict as *consuetudo*, "custom";[50] this is true only if *consuetudo* is used, as it is in the Verrines (2 *Verr.* 1.105, 116) and in the *pro Caecina*

---

[50] On Cic. *Inv.* 2.65-67, 160-162 (an immature statement), see D. Nörr, *Divisio und Partitio* (1972) 11-12. Recent literature on the Roman theories of legal sources is discussed by M. Kaser, *Fs. Flume* vol. I 101-123.

(23), to mean the "regular usage of the Praetor's court." But in the later Republic Praetors do not seem to have felt themselves unduly constrained by *consuetudo*. Rather, to a remarkable extent, they still thought themselves free to shape their Edicts on a yearly basis, in accord with the developing "needs" of community and class. Judgment on their changes was swift in coming; the next year's Praetor expressed his opinion by retaining or deleting the innovations of his predecessor.

The "annual statute" must have produced, in many instances, an instability and insecurity resulting from constantly shifting procedural forms: not just new actions, but new versions of old ones.[51] To those timid souls who had hoped to find in law a kind of certainty that the world in general did not provide, such continual change posed a threat; but the more venturesome (including, one would suppose, the more litigious) will have observed such changes carefully, and then turned their minds toward exploiting law's new resources. As I argued in Chapter I, Caecina's lawsuit was probably one instance of the resulting litigation.

ACCESSIBILITY: THE CAPABILITIES OF LAW (1)

As with the Edict, so with the court: in form, great emphasis on the open and public nature of law; but in substance, the same penetration of legal procedure by social and political motives.

At the time of the *pro Caecina*, the Urban Praetor's court was set up in the open air at the southeastern end of the Forum, most probably in the relatively small, flat area (about 20 m. on a side) lying between the Regia and the Temples of Vesta and Castor, adjacent to the *Sacra Via*.[52] (See Figures 3 and 4.)

[51] On this, A. Watson, *Law Making* 33-34 (though it need not follow that form analysis is futile).

[52] This area, though also occupied by the *lacus Juturnae*, has room for the Urban Praetor's tribunal. See above all C. Gioffredi, *SDHI* 9 (1943) 262-267; cf. J. Paoli, in *Mél. de Visscher* vol. IV 302 n.54; P. Romanelli, *Gnomon* 17 (1954) 258-260. A different view is taken by L. Richardson, *MDAI(R)* 80 (1973) 222-223, 232, who does not cite Gioffredi. These topographical ques-

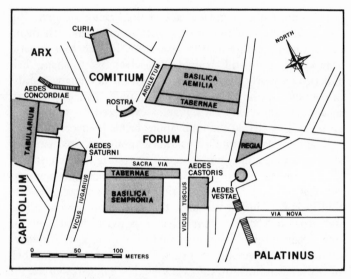

FIGURE 3. The late Republican Forum, before its imperial monumentalization. About 80 B.C. the Urban Praetor's tribunal was moved from the Comitium to the southeastern end of the Forum, probably to the area between the Temples of Vesta and Castor. Most private trials were heard in the Forum itself or in the large basilicas flanking it. This simplified reconstruction of the Forum (after Lugli) omits many details.

The court had been relocated there from its ancient seat in the Comitium at the opposite end of the Forum; this relocation, complete by 74 B.C. (Cic. 2 *Verr.* 1.129, 5.186), probably was caused by Sulla's extensive rebuilding of the Comitium area in 80.[53] Cicero alludes to the new location when he describes Aebutius, "the overly quarrelsome advocate," as an "habitué at the Regia" (*Caec.* 14: *defensoris nimium litigiosi, contriti ad Regiam*). Porphyrion, commenting on Horace (*Epist.*

tions are hotly disputed, and I simply follow the likeliest view; for further bibliography, see E. Nash, *Pictorial Dictionary of Ancient Rome* (2d ed. 1968) s.v. "Tribunal Praetorium"; also F. Coarelli, *Il Foro Romano* (1983) 158-159.

[53] On the architectural development of the Forum, see P. Zanker, *Forum Romanum* (1972).

1.19.8), asserts that the Praetor's tribunal and benches were first set up in this area *a Libone*; presumably he has in mind the same Libo who erected the small monument called the *puteal Libonis* (or *puteal Scribonianum*) next to the Regia. The *puteal* is depicted on a denarius of 62 B.C.; to judge from this schematic representation, it was erected no more than a few decades earlier.[54] It is quite likely that the moneyer's father, L. Scribonius Libo,[55] had the *puteal* constructed; and if we may credit the scholiast's testimony that Libo also moved the Praetor's tribunal, he was surely acting as Urban Praetor to organize the court in its new location. An appropriate and possible year is 80,[56] the last year of Sulla's *dominatio*. In time the *puteal Libonis* became virtually a symbol of the Praetor's court.

In the shadow of the tall temples surrounding this area, each Urban Praetor had constructed a wooden podium to serve

[54] For the coin, M. Crawford, *Roman Republican Coinage* vol. I (1974) 441-442. On the date of the *puteal*, see G. Fuchs, *Architekturdarstellungen auf Römischen Münzen* (1969) 23-26 and 124-125; E. Welin, *Studien zur Topographie des Forum Romanum* (1953) 33, who suggests that the moneyer's father constructed the *puteal*.

[55] He is known from *ILLRP* 411, and perhaps also from *ILLRP* 567-568 (dedications from Caudium); he may be the Proquaestor pro Praetore from Further Spain, cf. *MRR* vol. II p. 481.

[56] The date is appropriate also because in 80 the Senate let contracts for refurbishing the Temple of Castor next to the Urban Praetor's tribunal; the duty of enforcing these contracts devolved (at least eventually) on the Urban Praetor, cf. Cic. 2 *Verr.* 1.130. Festus, p. 448 L, though badly mutilated, makes clear that the Senate authorized the *puteal* as well.

FIGURE 4 (on the overleaf). The Roman Forum in its present state, seen from the Capitoline Hill. Most visible remains are of imperial constructions. On the left, behind the Arch of Septimius Severus, is the Curia in its location after Julius Caesar. The Forum remains flanked by large basilicas. Although in the Empire private trials were heard mainly in the imperial forums to the north, the centumviral court sat in the Basilica Julia on the right. At the far end of the Forum, the three columns of the Temple of Castor and a reconstructed part of the circular temple of Vesta are visible; the Regia is obscured by the substructions of the Temple of Julius Caesar.

as his tribunal;[57] the podium was about 1 m. high, and large enough to accommodate the Praetor's chair of office (*sella curulis*) and the seats of his staff and *consilium*. Beside the tribunal stood the Urban Praetor's two lictors, their axes shrouded in rods, as symbols of his authority.[58] Before the tribunal at ground level, from which they were obliged to look upward in order to see or address the court, were grouped the litigants and their friends and representatives, seated (when they were not speaking) on bench-like wooden chairs called *subsellia*. Beyond them stood the gallery (*corona*) of interested onlookers. The court's furnishings were extremely spartan, as was also its stark spatial symbolism.

No walls or railings defined the limits of the court, which instead lay exposed on its perimeter to the bustling life of the Forum;[59] yet the "lofty tribunal" (as it was called: *excelsum suggestum*, *sublime tribunal*, or the like) had about it a sense of "apartness" and dignity that sufficed to enrage Romans when its space was invaded by the profane, whether or not they were entitled to be there. The tribunal was a place alien to violent or undignified conduct (so Cicero, *Vat.* 34), where advocates should always appear in togas and speak proper Latin.[60] Magistrates obeyed a similar protocol; it was unbecoming to appear dressed in a Greek *pallium*, or to give any overt display of anger or partiality, or to vomit from drunkenness, or to be

[57] For descriptions and sources, see H.D. Johnson, *The Roman Tribunal* (1927), esp. 26-36. Also C. Gioffredi, (cited n.52) 228-244; L. Richardson, (cited n.52) 220-221.

[58] On the number, see Mommsen, *Staatsrecht* vol. I 384; Samter, *RE* s.v. "fasces" (1909) 2003-2004; and on the *lex Plaetoria*, which defined the Praetor's jurisdiction, Censor. *Die Nat.* 24.3, with E. Weiss, *RE* Suppb. V s.v. "lex Plaetoria" (1931) 582.

[59] For instance, we know that tribunals were still made of wood mainly because mobs from the Forum often used them to construct bonfires (e.g., Ascon. p. 33 C; Suet. *Caes.* 84.3; cf. Cic. *Vat.* 21). The Catilinarian conspirators lurked suspiciously around the Urban Praetor's tribunal (Cic. *Cat.* 1.32). The "principle of publicity" is applied to the Praetor's court by A. Checchini, *Scritti Giuridici e Storico-Giuridici* vol. II (1958) 119-127.

[60] See H.D. Johnson, (cited n.57) 23-24. Advocates in togas: Mommsen, *Staatsrecht* vol. III 221. Proper Latin: Gell. *NA* 1.22.1-6.

smothered in kisses by an ardent admirer.[61] The tribunal was a place "apart," both in the spatial sense and in the figurative sense that Romans felt themselves to be departing from the ordinary when they came before it. This "apartness" was crucial in establishing the legitimacy of what was transacted there.[62]

After narrating the events that led up to Caecina's lawsuit, Cicero describes, with a terseness commended by rhetorical handbooks,[63] the procedure Caecina had used in obtaining the interdict *de vi armata* (*Caec.* 23): "As a result of these events, the Praetor P. Dolabella, following normal usage [*consuetudo*], granted an interdict *de vi hominibus armatis* ordering Aebutius, with no defense [*exceptio*], to restore Caecina whereto he had been thrust out. Aebutius replied that he had already restored him.[64] A wager at law [*sponsio*] was arranged. It is your task to judge the outcome of this wager." The stylized simplicity of Cicero's account would mislead, however, if it were taken to mean that this sequence of events was somehow automatic and inevitable. In fact, the opposite was true.[65] Potential liti-

---

[61] See, respectively, Sen. *Ep.* 114.6; Sen. *Dial.* 3.16.5; Cic. *Phil.* 2.63; Martial, 11.98.14-19. Compare Cicero's censure of Verres' conduct on his tribunal: 2 *Verr.* 1.124; 2.94; 3.23, 28, 77; 4.86.

[62] See N. Luhmann, *Legitimation durch Verfahren* (2d ed. 1975) 59-68 ("Ausdifferenzierung") and 69-74 ("Autonomie"). I return to this topic in Chapter VI.

[63] See Quintilian, 4.2.132, who quotes this passage of the *pro Caecina* as exemplary; also Jul. Vict. p. 76 G-C. The transmitted text of the speech is defective and has been supplemented from Quintilian. Cic. *Caec.* 23: "His rebus ita gestis P. Dolabella Praetor interdixit, ut est consuetudo, de vi hominibus armatis sine ulla exceptione, tantum ut unde deiecisset restitueret. Restituisse se dixit. Sponsio facta est. Hac de sponsione vobis iudicandum est."

[64] That is, he claimed not to be bound by the interdict (cf. *Caec.* 41: "hoc interdicto Aebutius non tenetur"). Only in this sense had he already carried out the interdict (cf. *Caec.* 55, 60, 80, 82, 92). Cf. G. Gandolfi, *Contributo allo Studio del Processo Interdittale Romano* (1955) 94-95. In effect, the person to whom the interdict is directed is bound only to the extent that the state of affairs presumed in the interdict actually exists: M. Kaser, *RZ* 324.

[65] I have dealt with this subject in more general terms in *LTIR* 48-55; there I emphasized that Roman private law tended to be directed toward the socially privileged, a fact with important consequences for legal history. The

The Urban Praetor

gants faced many obstacles: first, they had to know how to approach the Praetor; second, they had to be willing to undergo the procedure required for initiating suits; and third, they had to accept the risk that their claims, even though formally acceptable, might be arbitrarily rejected by the Praetor.

In the first place, the Urban Praetor was not obliged to make himself continuously available to plaintiffs. Round about the simple architecture of his court there had grown up an elaborate etiquette. Court was held only on certain days and during certain hours; some actions were performable only from the tribunal (*pro tribunali*), others while the Praetor stood in the flat area before it (*de plano*), and still others wherever he happened to be, even outside the court (*in transitu*).[66] Most legal historians believe that interdicts were an exception to this etiquette, because they proceeded mainly from the Praetor's *imperium* rather than his *iurisdictio*.[67] For this reason they might be granted at any time (even on *dies nefasti*[68]), and therefore, presumably, in any place. In point of judicial principle this is doubtless true; Praetors must have reserved the capacity to issue interdicts in emergencies.[69] Cicero, at one point in the *pro Caecina* (36), describes the Praetor "for whole days" (*totos dies*) issuing interdicts to forbid the use of force, to order restoration, to regulate controversies on ditches and drains,

---

analysis below is intended to bring out some additional points relevant to the *pro Caecina*. See also Chapter I, at notes 86-90.

[66] M. Kaser, *RZ* 146, with bibliography, esp. M.A. von Bethmann-Hollweg, *Civilprozess* vol. II 161-178. See also D. Nörr, in *St. C. Sanfilippo* vol. III (1983) 523, 525-532. Cicero, *Part. Orat.* 99-100, comments on the intricacy of pre-trial proceedings, and urges that participants have expert knowledge. On the volume of late Republican litigation, see Chapter VII, note 14.

[67] See Julian, D. 43.8.7, with M. Kaser, *RZ* 318 n.2. It is, however, formalistic to insist on this idea too narrowly.

[68] Gaius 4.29; cf. A. Berger, *RE* s.v. "interdictum" (1916) 1687 (but there is no evidence that special days were reserved for giving interdicts). Also G. Pugliese, *Processo* vol. II.1 184-185. On *dies nefasti* (about one-third of the year), see A.K. Michels, *The Calendar of the Roman Republic* (1967) 35 and 61-83.

[69] This is clear in Gaius, D. 11.7.9 pr.: a person, if prohibited by another from burying a dead body, may seek an interdict "at once" (*statim*).

on water rights and roads. This passage, though hyperbolic, clearly shows that interdicts were issued frequently.

However, in the late Republic interdictal procedure was being rapidly absorbed into the structure of *iurisdictio*. In form, the interdict remained an order to do or not do something, but this order was not backed up by an immediate sanction; when a defendant (like Aebutius) declined to amend his conduct in conformance with the plaintiff's wishes, what followed was simply a trial on the merits of the case. (Its form is described directly.) Praetors seem to have been generally reluctant to grant interdicts on the basis of *ex parte* communications; before seeking the interdict, the plaintiff was expected to contact the defendant and notify him as to the hearing, so that both sides could present their versions of the case.[70] It is clear from *Caec.* 23 that both Caecina and Aebutius were present when Dolabella granted the interdict *de vi armata* to Caecina. The Praetor's hearing of both sides came to be known as a *cognitio*—not a full-dress investigation of the affair, but rather mainly a determination that the plaintiff had a *prima facie* case for demanding an interdict.[71] As interdictal procedure became more elaborate, it seems reasonable to suppose that it increasingly occurred within the regular judicial calendar, and that interdicts were normally issued *pro tribunali*.[72] Unfortunately, the state of our sources makes it impossible to confirm this assumption.

[70] How the plaintiff was to do this is not exactly clear; cf. G. Gandolfi, (cited n.64) 49-55. Ulpian, D. 43.29.3.14, allows issuance of an interdict also against someone who does not respond to a summons.

[71] See M. Kaser, *RZ* 318 and 323-324. *Cognitio* involved not only the *prima facie* adequacy of the plaintiff's case, but also questions of jurisdiction and litigative capacity: *ibid.* 176-178. There is still debate about the extensiveness of such hearings; G. Gandolfi, (cited n.64) 66-76, argued they could be rather detailed, while A. Biscardi, *Iura* 7 (1956) 357-360, in reviewing Gandolfi, was more cautious. See also M. Lemosse, *Cognitio* (1944) 192-195.

[72] See A. Pernice, *SZ* 14 (1893) 145. As was observed by A. Biscardi, *La Protezione Interdittale nel Processo Romano* (1938) 33-34, many intricacies of interdictal procedure might well have required advice from a *consilium*. On the presence of jurists in the *consilia* of Republican Praetors, see O. Behrends, *SZ* 86 (1969) 192-193, with bibliography. Verres ignored the jurists: Cic. 2 *Verr.* 1.120.

Procedural complexity places a considerable burden on prospective litigants. Either they themselves must understand the intricate procedures (and know how to locate the correct ones) or they must have access to someone who can assist them; if as a result they make it rewarding (financially or otherwise) for others to master the requisite skills, there can emerge a class of legal "paraprofessionals" operating at a level just below that of the judicial system. Aebutius was a *cognitor* (*Caec.* 14), one who held himself ready to act for others (mainly helpless women, says Cicero) before courts of law.[73] No special legal education was required for this "profession," only a thorough familiarity with the judicial ambiance. Another of Cicero's private orations involved a *cognitor*: the actor Q. Roscius was being sued by Fannius, who had allegedly acted as his *cognitor* in a previous trial (Cic. *Rosc. Com* 32, 38, 53-55). This speech shows that Pseudo-Asconius (p. 190 St.) is wrong in claiming that *cognitores* represented only clients who were present in court;[74] but the underlying point is doubtless correct: *cognitores* were an incipient class of lawyers. Their skills were mainly technical, and therefore confined in principle to the *in iure* portion of the trial before the magistrate;[75] the second portion of the trial "before the judge" (*apud iudicem*) was the normal domain of the rhetorically trained advocate.

In any case, what is interesting about these *cognitores* is that, for all their usefulness in facilitating legal procedure, they were

[73] Compare *Rhet. ad Herenn.* 2.20: the aged and the infirm appoint *cognitores* (an example of law based on equity). This is the earliest reference to *cognitores*; cf. M. Kaser, *RZ* 47. On *cognitores*, see M. Kaser, *RZ* 153-156, with bibliography. They are distinct from *procuratores*, and were appointed by formal words: Gaius 4.83, 97; *Vat. Frg.* 318, 319. Aebutius was also a *defensor* (*Caec.* 14); this means that he undertook the interests of absent defendants, cf. M. Kaser, *RZ* 157, 164-165. See also N. Roland, *Pouvoir Politique et Dépendance Personelle* (1979) 277-280.

[74] This was untrue also in later classical law: Ulpian, D. 3.3.10. On Cicero's speech *pro Roscio Comoedo*, see C. Wirbel, *Le Cognitor* (1911) 36-53. Fannius was of course not a professional *cognitor*; *contra*: W. Stroh, *Taxis* 152-154.

[75] See Paul, D. 3.3.16; Gaius, D. 46.7.7. Cf. Lenel, *EP*[3] 94-95: edictal restrictions on changing *cognitores* after *litis contestatio*. In the two fragments cited, *procurator* was substituted for *cognitor* by the compilers, as often elsewhere.

of relatively low social standing,[76] presumably because their "profession" was considered banausic when exercised on a regular basis. The Praetor, to protect his court from unsavory influences, excluded certain classes of people from acting as *cognitores*.[77] The *cognitores* functioned at the margin of the late Republican judicial system. Only slowly did the notion take hold at Rome that a professionally trained class of legal advocates was not only convenient, but also instrumental, to law's operation.[78]

Nonetheless, despite Cicero's sneers at Aebutius, the defendant's prior familiarity with judicial usage (*consuetudo*) undoubtedly gave him some initial edge in his dealings with Caecina. Caecina had sought to counter this advantage by consulting a jurist (*Caec.* 95). Perhaps he used a *cognitor* as well. It was vitally important to be exact on procedure; Cicero (*de Or.* 1.168-169) recounts an anecdote about a defendant whose representative demanded from the Urban Praetor of 91 a procedural device designed only for plaintiffs, and thereby transformed himself and his client into figures of pity or ridicule. When Cicero stresses that Caecina received an interdict "without any built-in defense" (*Caec.* 23: *sine ulla exceptione*), he may imply that Caecina had succeeded in thwarting Aebutius' attempt to insert one into the interdict.[79]

---

[76] See, e.g., Hor. *Sat.* 2.5.32-38; Ovid, *Am.* 1.12.23-24; Suet. *Vit.* 2.1. See W. Kunkel, *Herkunft*[2] 330-331, who discusses the process whereby *cognitores* gradually merged with *advocati*. Cicero, *de Or.* 1.166-169 (discussed just below), shows that advocates also sometimes represented clients before the Praetor.

[77] Lenel, *EP*[3] 91-93: those forbidden include soldiers, women, and people afflicted with judicial *infamia*.

[78] On the use of professional lawyers, see G. Sawyer, *Law in Society* (1965) 109-125. Cf. R.D. Schwarz and J.C. Miller, *Amer. Journ. Sociol.* 70 (1964) 159-169; L.M. Friedman, *Law and Society* (1977) 20-34. D. Rueschemeyer, *Lawyers and Their Society* (1973) 1, gives three "core characteristics" of lawyers: "(1) specialized knowledge of legal rules, (2) partisan advice to clients not related by kinship, and (3) representation of clients in relation both to other parties and to legal authorities." I would tentatively add: (4) rationalized payment by clients for services rendered, and (5) formal independence from the judicial system. It must be stressed (against some of the authors cited above) that the Roman jurists were not "lawyers" in this sense.

[79] This is of course not certain, since Cicero probably refers to the *exceptio vitiosae possessionis* (cf. *Caec.* 63, 90-93); see Chapter IV, at notes 135-137. But

Getting into court was only the first step; being effective in court was also required. The Edict contained numerous actions. The plaintiff had to choose one of them, and it was not always obvious which was best. As Cicero remarks (*Caec.* 8), the Praetor allowed litigants to solve such questions for themselves; he did not steer them into the "correct" action. Caecina's suit coupled two issues: his claim of the Fulcinian farm and the outrage of the armed encounter outside the farm. If he had focused on the first issue, Caecina might have brought suit to recover the property for the estate (e.g., through a *hereditatis petitio*[80]); if he had focused on the second issue, he might have brought, as his opponents pointed out (*Caec.* 9, 35), either a criminal charge or an *actio iniuriarum*. Caecina's use of the interdict *de vi armata* appears at first like a good way to preserve the relevance of both issues, a course that was desirable if a suit on just one issue would be more likely to fail. On this reasoning, Caecina's legitimate claim to the Fulcinian farm made Aebutius' defense of it the more outrageous; while the desperate nature of Aebutius' actions at the farm suggested in turn that he at least considered Caecina's claim to have merit.

Whatever the strength of this reasoning (we shall examine it in subsequent chapters), the decision to use the interdict was not without certain risks, quite apart from its novelty and uncertain interpretation. These risks derived from the peculiarity of interdictal procedures, for which virtually our sole source is Gaius (4.138-170).[81] Gaius defines the interdict *de vi armata* as an interdict "for recovery of possession" (4.154-155: *reciperandae possessionis causa*); Cicero twice states virtually the

---

it may not be inconceivable that Aebutius sought the *exceptio* mentioned by Cic. *Fam.* 7.13.2 ("quod tu prior vi hominibus armatis non veneris"). Cf. F.L. Keller, *Sem.* 330-336; G. Nicosia, *Deiectio* 69-85, with bibliography.

[80] Essentially, this is just a specialized form of vindication; cf. A. Berger, *Encyclopedic Dictionary of Roman Law* (1953) s.v. Caecina would sue for the portion of the *fundus* owed him under the will. Cf. Chapter I, note 60.

[81] See M. Kaser, *RZ* 329-330. The interdictal system fell into disuse in the later Empire, and most references to procedure have been eliminated from *Digest* texts.

same (*Caec.* 9, 75). After a restitutory interdict was issued, the defendant had the opportunity to demand an *arbiter* who would decide the merits of the case under a so-called *formula arbitraria* (Gaius 4.163);[82] however, the defendant was obliged to exercise this option immediately, and if he failed to do so, he could not seek it later (164). The *formula arbitraria* avoided the *sponsio* procedure described below; if the defendant was condemned, he was ordered simply to pay the value of the object if he failed to restore it. If the plaintiff lost, he too incurred no further penalty, except that he might be counter-sued on a *iudicium calumniae* if his suit had been vexatious; liability was for one-tenth of the value at stake in the original suit.[83]

However, if (like Aebutius) the defendant did not demand an *arbiter* forthwith, there ensued a more elaborate procedure. Each side made a judicial wager (*sponsio*) with the other. The defendant promised that he would pay the plaintiff a certain amount if he had contravened the Edict by not restoring the property in question; and the plaintiff in turn promised to pay the defendant the same amount if the defendant had not contravened the Edict (Gaius 4.165). The amount of the wagers was apparently set by the plaintiff on oath, and it was limited only by the value of the property in question.[84] The parties then constructed three *formulae* for simultaneous decision by the judge (or judges): two of them ordered the judge to decide who owed what under the reciprocal *sponsiones*, and a third

---

[82] For the Republic this procedure is attested only for the interdict *quod vi aut clam* (cf. Cic. *Tull.* 53), but its generalization can be presumed. A more difficult question is whether the option was available even for the interdict *de vi armata*, which used *recuperatores* as judges; the question is unanswerable, but Gaius does not indicate any exception. See also Y. Bongert, in *Varia* (Publ. Inst. Droit Rom. 9, 1952) 179-182.

[83] Gaius 4.163, cf. 175-176; M. Kaser, *RZ* 214, with bibliography. There is admittedly no evidence that *calumnia* was actionable in the Republic.

[84] See Lenel, *EP*³ 450. Lenel's account is to be sure rather hypothetical; he assumes that the *sponsio* was set by the plaintiff in the same way as with a *vadimonium* (Gaius 4.186), and derives the limit on its value from Ulpian, D. 43.17.1 pr. (highly reworked). No source indicates that a plaintiff could not set a value lower than the object's real worth.

ordered the judge to award the plaintiff the value of the property if he won his suit and the defendant did not restore the object (165). It is plain from *Caec.* 23 that Caecina's lawsuit followed this second procedure, since the parties arrived at a *sponsio*.

This two-stage interdictal procedure unquestionably represents two stages of historical development; the procedure *per formulam arbitrariam*, without *sponsiones*, was designed so that the defendant could avoid the penal wagers.[85] But why did the new procedure persist alongside the old one even late into the classical period? The answer, I think, is to be found in game theory. The defendant who requested an *arbiter* immediately, and thereby declined to undergo the *sponsiones*, revealed a certain lack of confidence in his own case; indeed, one early imperial jurist was even prepared to assert that the defendant thereby tacitly conceded a duty to restore the property.[86] This view was rejected by subsequent jurists, but it is an interesting attempt to draw legal consequences from the use or non-use of procedural forms; it plainly reflects the evaluation generally given to the defendant's use of the *formula arbitraria*.

I can illustrate the point still more clearly with regard to the *sponsiones*. Suppose (purely hypothetically) that the Fulcinian farm is worth HS 50,000 to Caecina, and that he estimates his chances of winning the lawsuit at about three in ten; but it will cost him, both in direct and indirect outlays, HS 5,000 in order to complete the lawsuit. According to the equation given above in Chapter I,[87] Caecina will bring his suit if he is rational; his expected benefits are HS 15,000 (= .3 x 50,000), while his expected costs are only HS 5,000. But now suppose that Caecina must make an additional wager with

[85] M. Kaser, *RZ* 329-330.

[86] Gaius 4.163: for this reason, Proculus denied the *iudicium calumniae* (see note 83) to a defendant who requested an *arbiter*.

[87] At notes 75-76. Let me stress that the values in this example are only illustrative. Note the ambiguity of the equations given below if (e.g.) Caecina could estimate his likelihood of winning only at "somewhere between 1 in 10 and 5 in 10"; cf. Chapter I, at note 80, on the effects of legal insecurity.

the defendant for the full value of the farm. The expected benefits of the lawsuit rise to HS 30,000 (= .3 x [50,000 + 50,000]); but the expected costs rise to HS 40,000 (= 5,000 + [.7 x 50,000]).[88] In other words, it is now no longer in Caecina's interests to continue the suit. Caecina is thus faced with an agonizing choice: if he wagers the full value of the farm, he risks making his expected costs higher than his expected gains; but if he wagers less than the full value, he risks communicating to all the world that he considers his position a weak one.

I suggest that it was precisely this gaming aspect which made the cumbersome and antique interdictal procedure attractive to the Romans. Roman courts were notoriously lacking in methods of discovery; the parties, who were responsible for preparing their own cases, had few ways to learn, in advance of trial, the nature and strength of each other's case, and courts were similarly handicapped because they saw the cases only through the highly rhetorical presentation of advocates. Procedural risks, such as the defendant's decision on whether to wager and the plaintiff's decision on how much to wager, helped to convey additional information both between the parties and to the court. Admittedly, this information still had to be interpreted; a rational man will quickly learn how to bluff when his case is weak,[89] and despite his best efforts he may often err in estimating the strength of his own case.[90] Nonetheless, procedure will shed limited light on what the parties think of their own evidence. When Caecina requested the interdict from Dolabella, he ran some risk that in the en-

[88] We should perhaps add to his expected costs the risk of a *iudicium calumniae* (cf. note 83); and this risk is directly related to the odds of his losing. It is important to note that the plaintiff could probably set a *sponsio* lower than the object's worth (see note 84).

[89] On bluffing, see J. von Neumann and O. Morgenstern, *Theory of Games and Economic Behavior* (1944) 186-219. Bluffing takes place for two reasons: "to give a (false) impression of strength in (real) weakness; . . . to give a (false) impression of weakness in (real) strength" (p. 189). The former variety is more common in judicial settings.

[90] See Chapter I, at notes 77-82.

suing procedure he would be forced to expose his hand prematurely.

Up to this point I have described two complicating factors in the use of legal procedure: the degree of expertise required from litigants and the risks inherent in procedural forms. The Praetor's court, however, made matters still more complex through the person of the Praetor himself. The Praetor made the ultimate decision about whether or not to award Caecina an interdict; he enforced his own Edict. As Cicero explains in the *pro Murena* (41), Urban Praetors won both renown (*gloria*) through the the importance of their duties, and influence (*gratia*) through their dispensation of justice. A "wise" Praetor, thinks Cicero, will be uniform in his judgments so as to avoid giving offense, and yet courteous in hearing cases so as to win good will. This is the essence of the "role model" constructed by Cicero: evenhandedness (*aequitas*), character (*integritas*), and affability (*facilitas*).

No doubt the man often rose to the model; but it goes without saying that not all Praetors were "wise" in Cicero's sense. Ignorance of the law, and even outright corruption, were not rare.[91] Furthermore, it is easy to overlook the extent to which Cicero's standards were shaped by his own background; the *novus homo* inevitably preferred a rigorous (if affably administered) "formal justice." Cicero could illustrate his views with two Praetors from the 70's. In 79 Cn. Octavius, in enforcing the *formula Octaviana*, had tempered his austere harshness (*severitas acerba*) with a gentleness of manner (*lenitas*) and much seasoning of human sympathy (*multis condimentis humanitatis*)—a highly pleasing combination, so Cicero observes, amid the general arrogance and license at Rome (*Q. Fr.* 1.1.21-22). The contrasting example is C. Verres, who in 74 had frequently ruled in contravention of his own Edict (2 *Verr.* 1.119-121), had not been uniform in his decisions (120), and had

[91] At any rate, not in the Empire: J.M. Kelly, *Litigation* 89-101; but Kelly's picture of the Republic (pp. 85-89) is probably too rosy. On juristic advice to Praetors, see H. Lévy-Bruhl, *RH* 5 (1926) 5-39. Cic. *Quinct.* 33 is a good example of a Praetor brought into line by a jurist; but contrast 2 *Verr.* 1.120.

Accessibility

behaved toward litigants of lower status than his own with "haughtiness" and "savagery" (122: *superbiam, crudelitatem*); Cicero adduces illustrative examples (122-127), and asserts that Verres' fellow Praetor L. Piso filled several notebooks with intercessions against Verres' decrees (119).

Inevitably, perception of such events turned on social standing. The privileged generally inclined to regard the letter of the law as harsh and unfeeling; a magistrate's use of his discretion gave leeway for influence and generosity, for distinction between friend and foe, and for leniency when preset standards were "unwittingly" contravened.[92] Others saw the question differently. In 67 B.C. the Tribune C. Cornelius secured passage of legislation requiring Praetors to announce at the outset of their term what law they would use, and then not to deviate from that standard.[93] Our sources inform us that Praetors had hitherto been accustomed to awarding suits much more freely, according to their friendship or enmity with litigants (Dio 36.40.1-2); though no one from the Senate dared speak against the proposed law, it was generally disliked since it removed a source of popularity or influence (*studium aut gratia*) from Praetors who were seeking higher office (*ambitiosis Praetoribus*: Ascon. p. 59 C). These aristocrats agreed with Cicero that it was perfectly proper for Urban Praetors to use their jurisdiction as a steppingstone to the consulate; but while Cicero thought that a Praetor should above all aim to secure a reputation for evenhandedness, the aristocrats believed he should seek more direct and tangible political rewards from the handling of his office.

[92] I paraphrase Livy 2.3.3-4 (complaints of conservative aristocrats against the Republic). This ancient *topos* (cf., e.g., Plato, *Politicus* 294 a-c) is recently revived by J. Noonan, *Persons and Masks of the Law* (1976). On the political nature of the urban praetorship, see Cic. *Flacc.* 6 ("Praeturae iuris dictio, res varia et multiplex ad suspiciones et simultates"), with 100.

[93] See A. Metro, *Iura* 20 (1969) 500-524 and La *"Denegatio Actionis"* (1972) 145-150. Differently: A. Guarino, in *ANRW* vol. II.13 (1980) 70-72. On Cornelius' legislation, see M. Griffin, *JRS* 63 (1973) 196-213 (esp. 208); A.M. Giomaro, *St. Urbinati* ser. A (Sci. Giur.) 43 (1974/1975) 269-325; and, with further literature, M. Kaser, *RPR*[2] vol. I 206 n.6. See also Chapter VI, at notes 87-96.

The problem, therefore, was not merely one of praetorian incompetence or venality;[94] the whole standard for administering private law was subject to ongoing debate. Cicero's first private oration had involved him in criticism of allegedly unfair decisions by two Urban Praetors, Burrienus in 83 (*Quinct.* 69) and Cn. Dolabella in 81 (30-31). Valerius Maximus (7.7.5, 7) recalls two other Praetors of this era, Q. Metellus probably in 73 and C. Piso probably in 72, who had exercised free discretion in refusing to apply their Edict. Indeed, such use of discretion was expected of Praetors and enjoyed considerable popularity; thus when in 77 the Urban Praetor granted *possessio bonorum secundum tabulas* to an otherwise fully qualified man who happened to be a eunuch, he was stripped of his *iurisdictio* by the Consul and reprimanded by the Senate (Val. Max. 7.7.6). By contrast, Q. Pompeius Rufus, Urban Praetor in 91, refused to enforce the will of Q. Fabius Maximus Allobrogicus because his son and heir was reputed to be a wastrel; Pompeius' defense of moral standards won universal praise (Val. Max. 3.5.2). But compare the extraordinary episode in 89, when the Urban Praetor Sempronius Asellio was killed by a mob of creditors; some sources claim he had been administering law in favor of debtors (Livy, *Per.* 74; Val. Max. 9.7.4), but another suggests that he simply had failed to uphold the traditional, though non-statutory, rights of creditors (App. *BC* 1.54.235-236). The Senate offered a reward for information on the assassins, says Appian (239), but no takers were forthcoming.

The problem with praetorian justice was far more pervasive than scholars have generally realized. At the time of the *pro Caecina*, upper-class Romans were divided into two groups: the status elite who thought of the Praetor's court as an extension of the existing social order, so that the Edict was to serve only as a guideline from which departure was easily justified through perceived social needs or even personal convenience;

---

[94] J.M. Kelly, *Litigation*, perhaps confines his attention too closely. See also the rather frenetic remarks on Verres by M. Bartosek, in *St. Grosso* vol. III 319-358. I lack access to this author's *"Verrinae," Die Bedeutung der Reden gegen Verres* (1977).

Accessibility

and the "outsiders," who like Cicero saw the court as a source
of law that was constant and abiding, at least relatively autonomous from social contingency, and not to be upset except
perhaps in extraordinary circumstances.[95] The *lex Cornelia de
iurisdictione* upheld this second view, in the teeth of substantial
opposition. The statute contained little to restrain a truly rapacious Praetor such as Verres (indeed, it does not even seem
to have borne a sanction); instead, the *lex Cornelia* more nearly
resembled a statement of constitutional principle.[96] In 65 Cornelius was tried for *maiestas*, and the law was inevitably brought
up once again by his accusers. Cicero defended Cornelius in
a speech that is now lost, but on which Asconius' commentary is preserved. The fragments of the speech (Ascon. p. 74
C) show that Cicero gathered up instances in which honorable
men had been denied their rights by capricious Praetors (those
of 81 and 78 are named); Cicero must surely have argued that
the indiscriminate violation of formal justice is a threat to all,
whatever their station or background.[97] It is a threat to the
very rule of law, because it undermines law's promise of long-
term predictability.

Cicero's argument may seem irresistible; certainly it is deeply

[95] At *Caec.* 65-75, Cicero puts forward his view of *ius* as the mainstay of
the social order, "uniform among all and identical for everyone" (70: *aequabile
inter omnes atque unum omnibus*). On this passage, which reflects contemporary
polemics, see Chapter IV, at notes 168-175.

[96] See, for a summary of recent scholarship on the law, A.A. Schiller,
Mechanisms 412-413. Add A. Guarino, (cited n.93) 70-72; M. Talamanca, in
Lineam. 165-166. Note the interesting remarks on praetorian *fides* in H. Hüb-
ner, *Gedächtnisschrift Hans Peters* (1961) 104-106. See also F. Schulz, *Principles*
229-230; B. Vonglis, *Lettre* 187-190. On the legal consequences of non-suiting
by the Praetor, see recently W.J. Zwalve, *Proeve ener Theorie der Denegatio
Actionis* (Diss. Groningen, 1981), with further literature. It is doubtful that
ex-Praetors were liable at criminal or civil law for their rulings: cf. M. Kaser,
RZ 171 and n.4; J.M. Kelly, *Litigation* 98-99. At any rate, no case is known.

[97] See Ascon. p. 74 C (quoting Cicero in defense of the *lex Cornelia*): the
Urban Praetor of 81 deprived C. Volcacius of "his normal and everyday
rights" (*communi et cotidiano iure*), and the one of 78 was too free "in making
a gift of the law" (*in gratificando iure*). So also, in essence, A.W. Lintott, *CQ*
27 (1977) 184-186. This is certainly the thought in Cic. 2 *Verr.* 2.30. See also
Chapter VI, at notes 69-77, and Chapter VII.

The Urban Praetor

embedded in the Western legal tradition. But one further consideration should be kept in mind. If Praetors were to continue adjusting the Edict on an almost yearly basis, it was the inevitable concomitant that they exercise discretion in enforcing the Edict; for only thereby could they provide for unforeseen inequities. A Roman Praetor was not like a modern judge; the Praetor shaped substantive law indirectly, by expanding or limiting access to the courts. Each new year brought a new Praetor with new ideas and often a new Edict. And Praetors might honestly disagree; the rhetorical treatise *ad Herennium*, written about 85 B.C., even constructs a rhetorical figure around such disagreements, citing as an example contradictory rulings on the admissibility of the *actio mandati* against heirs (2.19).[98] The Praetor's law was a rough-and-tumble affair, still not entirely free from *kadi*-like standards of substantive irrationality.[99] The *lex Cornelia de iurisdictione* dealt this system a serious blow. Even though the statute apparently did nothing to limit the power of edictal innovation at the outset of a term, and even though it left substantial room for *in iure* review of claims,[100] nonetheless it was surely a step in the process that led to the decline of praetorian creativity and the fossilization of the Edict.[101]

Caecina, in bringing an interdict against Aebutius, had to keep simultaneously in mind a great variety of practical con-

[98] See A. Watson, *Obligations* 151-152. The nature of this disagreement is unclear; the Praetors were Sex. Julius Caesar (123 B.C.) and M. Livius Drusus (115 B.C.). See also L. Vacca, *Contributo allo Studio del Metodo Casuistico* (1976) 67-92, esp. 82 ff.; and below, Chapter III, at notes 105-108.

[99] See Max Weber, *Wirtschaft und Gesellschaft* (4th ed. 1956) 572: "Die römische Rechtsfindung ihrerseits war in der Zeit der Republik eine eigentümliche Mischung von rationalen, empirischen und selbst von Kadijustizelementen." See A.T. Kronman, *Max Weber* (1983) 73-80, esp. 76-77. On the nature of discretion, see K.C. Davis, *Discretionary Justice* (1971).

[100] See A. Metro, in the works cited above (note 93).

[101] On the decline of the Edict, see M. Kaser, *RPR*[2] vol. I 207-208; A. Watson, *Law Making* 40-41 and 56-58. On the role of the *lex Cornelia*, see F. Wieacker, *Recht*[2] 122. Associated with this decline is the emergence of juristic commentaries on the Edict; see Chapter IV, at notes 84, 132. And see now M. Kaser, (cited n.30) 102-111.

siderations stemming from the institutional structure of Roman law: the intricacy of its procedures, the implications of procedures for his claim, even the character and malleability of the current Praetor. These considerations surely played a large role in Caecina's decision to use the Praetor's court. Potential litigants are bound to ask themselves questions of three different types.[102] They will inquire, first, about substantive law (i.e., about their likelihood of winning under existing substantive rules); second, about institutional structures (their convenience, accessibility, and swiftness); and third, more generally, about what we might call the "legal culture": "is going to court a thing that people do (or do not do)? What would their neighbors think about the lawsuit? Could they expect to get justice in court? Do they consider judges corrupt or stupid, or honest and impartial? Would they feel uncomfortable in court, embarrassed or exposed? What do they know about law, lawyers, and courts? What has been their prior experience with law?"[103]

What I want to emphasize is this: while in the short run, for any particular litigant, questions about substantive law and institutional structure are formally independent from questions about legal culture, in the long run legal culture is certain to be heavily influenced, if not actually determined, by general experiences in courts; law is, in this sense, more than the simple conglomeration of rules and institutions. "Social forces do not 'make' law directly. First they pass through the screen of legal culture. This is the vital screen of ideologies, beliefs, values, and opinions that takes interests and desires and determines their fate: whether to be turned onto the legal system in the form of demands, or to be shunted off onto another track, or to dribble off into oblivion."[104] Those Romans who were professionally concerned with the process of

---

[102] On what follows, see L.M. Friedman, (cited n.78) 7.

[103] *Ibid.* See also L.M. Friedman, *The Legal System: A Social Science Perspective* (1975) 193-222. Roman legal culture has never been systematically studied, though various books by J.M. Kelly have it as a subsidiary theme.

[104] L.M. Friedman, (cited n.78) 7.

law (the jurists and to a large extent also the advocates) had therefore an abiding interest in the legal culture of Rome.

Ultimately at issue in this discussion is one crucial aspect of the "capability" of law: the extent to which it can be used as an instrument of social control. A legal system is informed by the generality or narrowness of the lawsuits it handles, and by the quality of its decision making; in turn, its effectiveness in guiding conduct is limited by popular perceptions of its "reach." The pattern is circular and dynamic; its essence is capability. Capability designates "the cluster of problems which impede and distort efforts to further preferred values through a legal system. If values are the quiet engines of our legal system, the capability problems are the frictions, the ruts and the biases of the road. The machinery of Justice responds as much to the road as to the engine."[105]

In this section I have dealt with a group of such problems arising from the nature of the Praetor's court in the late Republic. These problems affect access to the threshold of the judicial system, and they produce incapacity that is institutional even though it is not institutionalized.[106] The incapacity to litigate has important ramifications for the capability of law: "Litigative incapacity makes it certain . . . that the join between law and society will be imperfect; that, as Karl Llewellyn once put it, the law in action will be different from the law on the books."[107]

LAW AND CUSTOM: *Deductio Quae Moribus Fit*

An episode in the *pro Caecina* illustrates the "imperfect join" between law and society. At a certain point in their conflict Aebutius suddenly gave formal notice to Caecina that the Fulcinian farm was not part of Caesennia's estate; Aebutius claimed

[105] R. Danzig, *The Capability Problem in Contract Law* (1978) 1-2. Anthropologists remain skeptical of law on this point; see, e.g., A. Allott, *The Limits of Law* (1980).

[106] Formal incapacity to litigate is also characteristic of the Praetor's court: M. Kaser, *RZ* 147-152.

[107] R. Danzig, (cited n.105) 2.

that he had purchased this farm for himself at the auction of
the younger Fulcinius' estate, and that while Caesennia had
appeared to possess it during the four years since then, in fact
she had only been exercising the usufruct left her in her first
husband's will (*Caec.* 19). Caecina then consulted his *consilium*,
and on their advice arranged with Aebutius that they meet at
the farm on a given day; Caecina would then be expelled by
Aebutius "in the customary way" (*moribus*) from the farm.
However, between this conference and the predetermined day
Aebutius allegedly changed his mind and decided that, if possible, Caecina was to be prevented from entering the farm
(20). I have already described the resulting melee.

Two years earlier a somewhat similar set of events had occurred prior to a lawsuit in which Cicero also delivered an
oration, the *pro Tullio*.[108] M. Tullius owned an ancestral farm
in the region of Thurii. A neighboring farm was purchased
by the defendant P. Fabius (*Tull.* 14) in partnership with a
certain Cn. Acerronius (16). In time Fabius regretted his purchase, and eventually he arranged to sell his share to Acerronius;[109] but in advertising the sale, Fabius included as part of
his holdings a plot of land called the *centuria Populiana*, which,
so Cicero claims, had always belonged to Tullius (16). Warned
of Fabius' intentions, Tullius wrote to his procurator and his
bailiff (17), who apparently arranged to station a guard on the
land for Tullius; doubtless as a consequence of Tullius' action, Fabius was unable to hand over the *centuria Populiana* to
Acerronius (17). In response, Fabius gathered a band of armed
ruffians and began to size up the forces defending the *centuria*
(18-20). Fabius then went with Acerronius to see Tullius, and
offered him a choice: either Tullius should expel him from
the plot or vice versa. Tullius replied that he would expel
Fabius and arrange formal bond (*vadimonium*) for a court appearance in Rome; Fabius agreed to this (20). However, during the following night Fabius' armed gang seized the con-

[108] The *narratio* of the *pro Tullio* (13-23) is lacunose, and not every detail of
the story is certain. On the date of the speech, see note 39.

[109] This is the usual interpretation, cf. F.L. Keller, *Sem.* 605-608; but cf.
H.H. Pflüger, *Besitzklagen* 48 n.128.

tested plot, killing all but one of Tullius' slaves on the property
(21-22). Tullius then brought suit under the *iudicium* that had
been introduced by Lucullus in 76 (see above at n. 38).

The similarity between the case of 71 B.C. and Caecina's
case is evident. In both cases, the two parties personally arranged for one of them to be formally expelled from a piece
of property, the ownership of which they were contesting;
and in both cases one of the two parties then went back on
the arrangement. In Caecina's case, the current possessor, who
was to do the expelling, refused to carry out the ceremony
and used armed violence to prevent the other party from entering; in Tullius' case, the current possessor, who was to do
the expelling, was violently dislodged from the property by
armed men of the other party. Two difficult questions arise
from these narratives: what was it that the parties were seeking to accomplish through their arrangement for the formal
expulsion of one of them, and why did this arrangement ultimately fail in each case? Since we have almost no evidence
except for the two speeches of Cicero, it is likely that we will
never be entirely sure of the answer to either question; the
pages below describe only a tentative solution.

Cicero refers to the arrangement in various ways: as "force
stemming from agreement" (*vis ex conventu*, cf. *Caec.* 22), or as
"expulsion in the customary way" (*deductio moribus*, cf. *Caec.*
20, 27), or as "force committed in the customary way" (*vis
facta moribus*, cf. *Caec.* 2), or as "force and expulsion in the
customary way" (*vis ac deductio moribus*, cf. *Caec.* 32), or simply
as "expulsion" (*deductio*, cf. *Tull.* 20). The arrangement therefore contains four elements: force, expulsion, agreement, and
a customary framework.[110] It takes place outside of court and

[110] Clearly, this is a single unified ceremony; see G. Nicosia, *Deiectio* 35
n.78, 38 n.84 (*in fine*). P. Krüger, *Kritische Versuche im Gebiete des Römischen
Rechts* (1870) 87, attempted to divide *deductio* from *vis ex conventu*; this is quite
unconvincing, cf. H.H. Pflüger, *Besitzklagen* 24-25. With the phrase *ex conventu*, compare *Rhet. ad Herenn.* 2.20: "sunt item pacta quae sine legibus ob-
servantur ex convento." The phrase is glossed as *ex utriusque commodo* in *Caec.*
20. However, *conventus* for *conventum* is very rare (but cf. the manuscripts of
Cic. *Att.* 6.3.1), and emendation is more than tempting. See also N. Du-
mont-Kisliakoff, *La Simulation en Droit Romain* (1970) 69-72.

before the initiation of a legal action, but it is meant to prepare the way for a subsequent suit. The prospective litigants repair to the contested property (*Caec.* 20: *in rem praesentem*), where, in accord with their previous agreement (*ex conventu*), one of them uses "force" (*vis*) against the other; this "force" is ceremonial and customary, and consists in one party "leading out" or expelling (*deducere*) the other from the property in question. The ceremony serves to identify the two parties to the quarrel, the piece of property for which they are contesting, and even, to some extent, the nature of their dispute.

If we had only Cicero's description of the facts in either case, plus a description of the ceremony itself, I doubt scholars would have hesitated in identifying *deductio* as a formal prelude to a suit on ownership. The ceremony itself bears a close resemblance to other rituals used in the ancient world to initiate suits on the equivalent of ownership.[111] Furthermore, in both orations Cicero emphasizes ownership as the underlying issue. Caecina claimed the Fulcinian farm for his wife's estate, while Aebutius alleged that he had purchased it for himself at the auction; Tullius asserted that the *centuria Populiana* was part of his ancestral property, while Fabius asserted that he had purchased it in partnership with Acerronius. The formal ceremony of *deductio* served to encapsulate each dispute. In the nineteenth century it was therefore commonly asserted, with some justice, that *deductio* prepared the way for a suit on ownership—either the archaic *legis actio sacramento in rem*[112] or the slightly more modern *actio in rem per*

---

[111] See above all L. Mitteis, *SZ* 23 (1902) 274-300, on *exagogé*. This article has been heavily (and in part rightly) criticized through the years: see E. Rabel, *SZ* 38 (1917) 313; A. D'Ors, *Defensa* 32-33, with bibliography; M. Kaser, *SZ* 64 (1944) 193-195 and *Eigentum und Besitz* (2d ed. 1956) 257 n.17. In my opinion, however, the central point remains unscathed: the temptation is irresistible to suppose that *exagogé* was voluntarily arranged; cf. Demoth. (*Zenoth.*) 32.17-20. See also A. Kränzlein, *Eigentum und Besitz im Griechischen Recht* (1963) 140-142; A.R.W. Harrison, *The Law of Athens* vol. I (1968) 219. Recently G. Thür, *SZ* 94 (1977) 293-305, has offered a rather different view of *deductio* and its relation to *exagogé*; but his view, while ingenious, seems irreconcilable with the *deductio* described in Cicero's two speeches.

[112] This was the view of Savigny, in *Vermischte Schriften* vol. I (1850) 292-307 (published 1817), with a "Nachtrag" of 1849 (pp. 308-314) evaluating

The Urban Praetor

sponsionem.[113] Admittedly, the Ciceronian *deductio* does not figure in ancient descriptions of the procedure in these two actions.

In the *pro Caecina*, however, Cicero presents the matter quite differently. That Aebutius did not carry out the *deductio*, argues Cicero, reflects Aebutius' belief that, if he had carried it out, he would not have succeeded "in retaining possession" (*Caec.* 2: *in possessione retinenda*); the very fact that Caecina sought a *deductio* is evidence that Caecina had possessed the farm (95); the dispute between Caecina and Aebutius is a "controversy about possession" (33: *possessionis controversiam*); and so on (41, 46-47). In the *pro Tullio* the matter is admittedly less clear. The *centuria Populiana* appears to have been standing vacant at the time when Fabius advertised it for sale,[114] but it may be that Fabius had also made some other move to possess it; in any case, Tullius evidently then directed his procurator and bailiff to seize it (*Tull.* 16-17). On the strength of this evidence, twentieth-century scholars have gradually swung round to the view that *deductio* prepared for an interdictal suit on possession—either the interdict *uti possidetis*[115] or the interdict *de vi.*[116] Once again, however, none of our sources for the

---

Keller's criticism; see further G. Nicosia, *Deiectio* 35 n.80. There seem to be no modern spokesmen for this view. On the procedure, see M. Kaser, *RZ* 66-76 (based esp. on Gaius 4.16-17).

[113] So esp. F.L. Keller, in *Zeitschr. f. Gesch. Rechtswiss.* 11 (1842) 287-332. For other bibliography, see G. Nicosia, *Deiectio* 35 n.79: esp. A. Exner, *SZ* 8 (1887) 167-195; E. Jobbé-Duval, *Etudes sur l'Histoire de la Procédure Civile* vol. I (1896) 463-472. This view seems to me essentially correct. On the procedure, M. Kaser, *RZ* 76-77; and below, at note 123.

[114] In any case, there is no clear sign of prior occupation; the former staff had probably been driven off during Spartacus' occupation (cf. *Tull.* 14 and note 39).

[115] There is an extensive bibliography in G. Nicosia, *Deiectio* 36 n.81. Scholars have proposed many ways, none very persuasive, to match *vis ac deductio moribus* with the interdictal *vis* mentioned by Gaius 4.170 (cf. Cic. *Caec.* 45; *Fam.* 7.13.2). This view is recently rejected by G. Nicosia, 36-37 (esp. 37 n.84), and L. Labruna, (cited n.38) 158-168; but it is revived by C. Bellu, *Studi Economici-Giuridici Univ. Cagliari* 48 (1973/1974) 37-68, whose argument seems very forced (esp. pp. 59-63).

[116] For bibliography, G. Nicosia, *Deiectio* 36 n.81; see esp. H. Bögli, *Rede*

82

two interdicts describes anything closely resembling Ciceronian *deductio*. The closest analogue, one which is actually
drawn by Cicero (*Caec.* 45), is the formalistic, two-sided *vis*
that was enacted after issuance of the interdict *uti possidetis* (cf.
Gaius 4.170); but this ceremony apparently did not have an
accompanying *deductio*, involved "force" committed by both
sides rather than by just one, and in any case had to follow
issuance of an interdict, for which there is no evidence in
either of Cicero's speeches.[117]

Granted the enormous quantities of ink that have been spent
in debating *deductio*, there simply may be no answer to the
riddle.[118] Some lines of analysis do, however, remain probable. First of all, Cicero (at least in the *pro Caecina*) lays great
weight on the "customary" side of *deductio*. To be sure, the
custom was very widespread; Thurii and Tarquinii are at virtually opposite ends of peninsular Italy, yet Fabius and Caecina do not appear to have proposed anything strange to their
counterparts. Furthermore, Caecina offered a *deductio* on the
advice of his *consilium*, including the jurist Aquilius Gallus (cf.
Caec. 95), which shows that the legal establishment in Rome
was not unaware of *deductio*. Nonetheless, it may be ingenuous to anticipate finding an exact replica of *deductio* among
the many procedural devices of the Praetor's court;[119] indeed,
surely one cardinal feature of *deductio* was that two landowners far away from Rome (like Fabius and Tullius) could carry
out a *deductio* on their own and then head off to Rome secure
in the knowledge that the outline of the impending suit was
clear (*Tull.* 20). There is no obvious reason why the Praetor's
court should have attached procedural significance to *deductio*,

---

29-36; C. Chabrun, *NRHD* 32 (1908) 5-27. So also A. D'Ors, *Defensa* 38 ff.;
G. Thür, (cited n.111) 305. I propose below that the eventual applicability
of the interdict *de vi* led to the decline of *deductio*.

[117] Cf. R. Saleilles, *NRHD* 16 (1892) 291-297. To be sure, one might suppose, as Saleilles does, that the procedure for the interdict *uti possidetis* changed
over time; so too C. Bellu, (cited n. 115) 63-66.

[118] G. Nicosia, *Deiectio* 37, finally opts for the view that *deductio* is part of
a procedure unknown to us; while not impossible, this is a counsel of despair.

[119] So also L. Labruna, (cited n.38) 161, 168; the point was made already
by E. Jobbé-Duval, (cited n.113) 386.

rather than regarding it as (at best) mere evidence of the parties' intentions—just as in sales law the customary bestowal of a ring might signify the intended agreement on sale, without itself being conclusive evidence of a sale's existence.[120] And, for the rest, if *vis ac deductio moribus* could be linked to any known legal procedure at Rome, a degree of scholarly consensus on this point would surely have emerged by now.

Second, it is also clear that *deductio* was radically flawed in the late Republic. When a customary mechanism, in general use around 70 B.C., is never definitely alluded to even once during the Empire, there can be little doubt of its emerging disutility. In the *pro Tullio*, the *deductio* failed to occur because, so it appears, Fabius decided his best hope for securing the *centuria Populiana* was if he himself possessed it; accordingly, when Fabius put the choice and Tullius preferred to retain possession for himself (thereby declining the role of expellee), Fabius sent armed men to seize the land. In the *pro Caecina*, the *deductio* failed to occur because Aebutius, the current holder of the land, allegedly had refused to go through with the ceremony and had shut the farm's borders to Caecina; Cicero gives no motivation (except sheer bloodymindedness) for Aebutius' change of heart, and we will have to return to the problem below. Perhaps it is wrong to draw conclusions from two highly contingent sets of events; but it seems evident that some Romans found it no longer in their interest to pursue a customary *deductio*, even if this meant going back on their word, and that their dissatisfaction was somehow linked with the importance they attached to holding possession of disputed property.

What I want to argue, therefore, is that *deductio* was a purely customary ceremony that somehow fell between the cracks of developing praetorian procedure; as a consequence, it slipped rapidly into disuse. The historical scenario I describe below is admittedly hypothetical, but has nonetheless the major ad-

---

[120] Cf. Ulpian, D. 19.1.11.6; comparable is the handshake used to "seal" contracts in the modern world.

vantage of providing a clear explanation for the events described in Cicero's two speeches.

What was it that Aebutius thought he had agreed to when he arranged for a *deductio* with Caecina? Aebutius at first probably considered *deductio* solely as a direct prelude to a suit on ownership.[121] In such a suit, his claim to the farm, based on the auction, would be tested against that of Caecina, based on the inheritance from his wife; the burden of proof would be on Caecina. This was comfortable ground for Aebutius. Doubtless, as many scholars have supposed,[122] the projected action was the *actio in rem per sponsionem* described by Gaius (4.91, 93-94); this judicial procedure was familiar in the Ciceronian period and may well date back to the third century B.C.[123] In this procedure, the plaintiff extracted from the defendant a judicial promise (*sponsio*) to pay a trivial sum of money if the object in question belonged to the plaintiff; this promise then became the basis for a judicial *formula* ordering the judge to decide whether the defendant owed the sum. In order to secure that the defendant would return the property if the judge ruled against him, the defendant was also obliged to undertake a stipulation to that effect (*stipulatio pro praede litis vindiciarum*). *Deductio* symbolically established in advance, before the parties repaired to the Praetor's court, which of them

[121] Aebutius had, of course, just given formal notice to Caecina on this point (*Caec.* 19), and Caecina's offer of a *deductio* was a direct response (20).

[122] See above, note 113. F. Bozza, *St. Bonfante* vol. II 611-613, argues that *deductio* could not have been a prelude to this *actio* because it is not mentioned in the description of the *sponsio* procedure at Cic. 2 *Verr.* 1.115-116 (concerning the taking of possession by presumptive heirs; cf. Ps.-Ascon. p. 249 St., on 2 *Verr.* 1.115). However, this misses the point of *deductio*, which parties used when they agreed on possession; in the case discussed in the *Verrines*, the Praetor normally favored one party's claim.

[123] It suffices to cite G. Pugliese, (cited n.68) vol. I 359. Modern scholarship has tended to follow M. Kaser, *Eigentum* (cited n.111) 282 ff., who lays great stress on the plaintiff's one-sided burden of proving ownership, the defendant's right to title being technically irrelevant; cf., e.g., K. Hackl, *Praeiudicium im Klassischem Römischen Recht* (1976) 189-192, with further bibliography. In practice, however, it was doubtless impossible to keep the defendant's right from being discussed in court, since often, as in the *pro Caecina*, the two were intertwined.

would act as plaintiff, and which as defendant, during the impending lawsuit. It was therefore especially useful if any doubt was possible as to possession,[124] and I suggest that it was invented for this purpose.

For Aebutius, so far so good. The *deductio* would confirm him in possession and give him the favored position of defendant in an *actio in rem*. Why, then, did Aebutius change his mind? The answer may lie in his belated recognition that *deductio* opened the door not just to a suit on ownership, but also to one on possession; in other words, he came to realize or learned from others that *deductio* raised the very issue it was supposed to settle.[125] This is, at any rate, most emphatically the line taken by Cicero, who even maintains that Caecina's very proposal of a *deductio* was evidence of his earlier possession (*Caec.* 95). In fact a good deal of Cicero's speech is devoted to expounding the steady increase in the legal concept of *vis*: it includes not only direct physical force, but also indirect and psychological force (41-44); it embraces "anything which, owing to risk of danger, either compels us to leave a place or prevents us from entering" (46); when the word "force" is used at law, even "very slight force" is designated (47: *pertenuis vis*). It seems hard to deny that Cicero would group the *vis* used in *deductio* under the category of *pertenuis vis*, especially since *deductio* did not involve prior resort to a court or magistrate.

Why is it that Aebutius might fear a suit on possession? Most legal historians have agreed that he was rather secure on this point, since Cicero's arguments in favor of Caecina's possession (*Caec.* 94-95) are perfunctory and legally weak. I shall argue in the next chapter, however, that the difficulties with Caecina's claim to possession probably emerged only in the

[124] In this view, the parties committed themselves to an understanding of the controversy between them. The contempt once expressed for this view (e.g., H.H. Pflüger, *Besitzklagen* 24-25) stemmed from the positivist conviction that *deductio* had to be of legal, not customary, origin.

[125] It is perhaps slightly more probable that he learned this was the interpretation given to *deductio* by Caecina. On the Ciceronian view of *vis*, see Chapter III, at notes 71-78.

course of the first two hearings of the case; initially, before the case was heard, Caecina's claim might have seemed much stronger.[126] In any event, the four-year interval between the death of the younger Fulcinius and the death of his mother Caesennia presented that rarest of situations in which a third party (the *colonus*) had physical control of the property, but it was at least objectively uncertain for whose benefit this physical control was being maintained.[127] Aebutius himself may never have visited the farm before Caesennia's death; Cicero says nothing on this point. Initially Aebutius could not be sure what evidence Caecina might have as to his late wife's alleged mandate to buy the farm; only in the trial did it emerge that he had nothing but hearsay and circumstantial evidence. After Caesennia's death, the ambiguity had briefly continued; Caecina's inspection of the tenant's accounts might or might not have been an attempt to take possession (cf. *Caec.* 94). If Aebutius feared an immediate test of possession, it can hardly be said that he was suffering from an excess of prudence.

Finally, what action on possession did Aebutius fear? The answer must be the interdict *de vi*, since Cicero himself appears to rule out the interdict *uti possidetis* (*Caec.* 45).[128] Under an interdict *de vi* (the wording of which is given above at notes 42-43), Caecina would have sought to recover possession after having been ejected from possession by force (Gaius 4.154: *ex possessione vi deiectus*); and Cicero at several points in his speech emphasizes that Caecina's aim was "to re-seek possession" (*Caec.* 9: *possessionem . . . repetitam*) or to "be restored to possession" (75: *in possessionem . . . restituetur*). In short, Cicero is apparently arguing that ceremonial *deductio* could be an act preparatory to obtaining the interdict *de vi*, and that an interdict *de vi* could then serve in turn as a basis for establishing posses-

---

[126] Chapter III, at notes 48-49.

[127] See Chapter I, at notes 46-47; also R. Saleilles, (cited n. 117) 282-283.

[128] I understand Cicero to be drawing an analogy between the *vis* used by Aebutius and the *vis* used after issuance of the interdict *uti possidetis*. The manner in which Cicero here introduces the interdict *uti possidetis* is hardly consistent with it being in the hearer's mind as a result of the discussion of *deductio*.

sion prior to a suit *in rem* on ownership;[129] the evolution in
the interdict's function would be rather similar to that which
had occurred earlier in the interdict *uti possidetis*.[130] Aebutius,
on becoming aware of this possibility, declined to undergo
the ceremony and refused Caecina admission to the Fulcinian
farm, so as to stave off an apparent admission that possession
was disputed.

The procedural structure of "classical" Roman property law
is outlined in Ulpian's famous commentary on the interdict
uti possidetis (D. 43.17.1.1-4), the general authenticity of which
has recently been defended.[131] Ulpian says (1-3) that when a
dispute arises about ownership, the parties will either agree
or disagree as to who is the possessor and who is, by consequence, the plaintiff (*petitor*). If they agree (*convenit*), then the
possessor is accorded the privilege (*commodum*) of defending
the suit on ownership, while the other party has the burden
(*onus*) of being plaintiff. But if they disagree, the interdict *uti
possidetis* is used to establish which party is the "stronger possessor" (*potior possessor*). Ulpian goes on (4) to compare the interdict *uti possidetis*, used for retaining possession, with the
interdict *de vi*, used for recovering possession after it has been
wrested away by force.

In sum, my suggestion is that *deductio* was devised and became customary as a means for making evident, in a formalistic fashion, an agreement concerning which party was the
possessor, so that the two parties could get on with an action
in rem. Fabius' offer to let Tullius choose who would be the
possessor (*Tull.* 20) probably shows that by custom the parties
could and did negotiate the issue of possession. The disutility
of *deductio* emerged only as the ambit of the interdict *de vi*
increased, so that *deductio* no longer served to confirm agreement on possession—that which had been its primary original

[129] A view quite similar to mine was suggested by A. Exner, (cited n.113)
192-193; despite the contempt for this position in P. Koschaker, *SZ* 28 (1907)
453 ("eine reine Hypothese"), I think it explains evidence that is otherwise
incomprehensible.
[130] This is the view of L. Labruna, (cited n.38) 240-286.
[131] L. Labruna, (cited n.38) 143-194.

Law and Custom

function. The consequence was that traditional *deductio* rapidly dropped from use, and the interdict *de vi* never became an important procedural preliminary to suits on ownership.[132] The interdict *uti possidetis* was thereby left as the principal method for initiating disputes on ownership where the parties were not agreed on possession; but if they were agreed on this issue (and simple informal agreement, *conventio*, eventually sufficed), then they proceeded directly to an action *in rem*. This is the procedural structure of "classical" Roman property law.

Scholarly interpretations of *vis ac deductio moribus* have, it seems to me, usually presupposed too static a view of Roman law; they have assumed not only that this law remained essentially unchanged throughout the classical period, but also that the Romans generally agreed on the meaning of various procedures. In the case of the *pro Caecina*, this has led to the acceptance at face value of Cicero's partisan views on the interpretation of *deductio* (Piso's rebuttal does not survive[133]); the consequence has been that Aebutius' change of mind has remained virtually inexplicable.[134] However, if we assume that Roman law in Cicero's day was still highly fluid (the state of the Edict almost enjoins this belief), then we can probably discern, in the events leading up to Caecina's lawsuit, the confusion resulting from such fluidity: on the one hand, Aebutius, confidently agreeing to a traditional ceremony, only to learn that the meaning of the ceremony was no longer certain;

[132] See H.H. Pflüger, *Besitzklagen* 59-67, who in attacking Exner's views raises further objections against this use of the interdict *de vi*. On the other hand, the interdict *uti possidetis* had the abiding defect that the parties had to appear before the Praetor, then return to the disputed property, and then return back to the Praetor; it was tempting to discover a shortcut. See also H. Siber, *Scr. Ferrini Mil.* vol. IV 105-106.

[133] What might that rebuttal have been? Perhaps, that courts should accept the objective meaning the parties attach to *deductio*.

[134] A good example of the fumbling on this point is Keller's suggestion, *Sem.* 392, that Aebutius feared Caecina would seize possession. This fantasy (inspired by the *pro Tullio*) is richly embroidered by H.H. Pflüger, *Besitzklagen* 33-37; cf. H.J. Roby, *Private Law* vol. II 516. But Aebutius may have asserted something like this; see above, note 79.

The Urban Praetor

on the other hand, Caecina, playing on his opponent's ignorance in order to shift the dispute onto ground apparently
more favorable to himself.

We come now to the jurist, C. Aquilius Gallus. For many
years he had been a central figure in the judicial system of
Rome;[135] more than a decade before he was the *iudex* in Cicero's earliest private lawsuit (*Quinct.* 1, *et al.*). During the
70's he had the opportunity to observe, and perhaps to help
shape, the substantial edictal changes in the handling of *vis*.[136]
When Aebutius notified Caecina that he owned the Fulcinian
farm, Caecina consulted his friends, and on their advice he
proposed a ceremonial *deductio* (*Caec.* 20); of these *amici*, only
one is named, and he is Aquilius (95).[137] If *deductio* had, by
the late 70's, assumed an arguably ambiguous character,
Aquilius would surely have known that fact. The trap was
beautifully baited; for once Aebutius had invited Caecina onto
the Fulcinian farm, he found it hard to "disinvite" him. Aebutius' use of armed force to prevent Caecina from entering
the farm brought the whole dispute into the still more problematic domain of the recently introduced interdict *de vi armata*. Here little experience guided the judges, and hence there
was little that was judicially impossible.

Those who are reflective will find much food for thought
in these events. The "imperfect join" between law and society
is plain. Caecina's lawsuit occurred against the backdrop of a
rapidly changing legal system, in which new rules and procedures led to a dissonance between popular perceptions of
law (such as the traditional understanding of *deductio*) and what
law had become "in fact." No doubt dissonance is common

[135] See *Caec.* 78 (esp. *tot annos*). For more on Aquilius' career, see Chapter
IV, at notes 6-10, 28-47.

[136] In this respect, as L. Labruna, (cited n.38) 13-27, observes, Cicero's
repeated contraposition of *vis* and *ius* (e.g., *Caec.* 5, 33; *Sest.* 91; *Leg.* 3.42)
appears to reflect an "ideology," perhaps of juristic origin, guiding the Praetor's court in the post-Sullan years; cf. *Caec.* 104 and Chapter III, at notes
71-78. As to Aquilius' influence on the Edict in the 70's, see Chapter IV,
note 39.

[137] On the text, see Chapter IV, at notes 1-3.

even under the most favorable conditions; individuals find it difficult to alter conduct in swift response to stimuli, and attitudes often die hard.[138] But at Rome a variety of conditions (including the "capability problems" discussed above) made it unusually difficult for law to influence conduct. If a Roman was intimidated by the intricate yet crucially important procedures of law, and if he could not be sure of getting formal justice even should he succeed in mastering these procedures, his lack of understanding necessarily lowered his incentive to stay abreast of legal change. He might react with aversion to law, hoping that he would never be dragged into court.[139]

This response too was a considerable gamble, for he risked being taken advantage of by those who were more skilled. A judicial system like Rome's, which communicated information about rules in a confused and haphazard manner, also tended to lavish favors upon those who had access to good information on current law. The jurists often harp on the evils of not knowing the law (*imperitia* or *ignorantia iuris*).[140] The court itself became a classroom, where the more knowledgeable were allowed to instruct the less so. From this standpoint, Aquilius could view Caecina's lawsuit with considerable equanimity, and even with some satisfaction if the publicity surrounding the trial finally brought attention to the ambiguities of *vis ac deductio moribus*; for in that event Aquilius would have helped drive from use this strange but time-honored practice occurring far outside the Praetor's control. On the other hand, Caecina might see the matter in a more personal light; for it was he who would pay if Aquilius' stratagem failed.

Custom confronts law with some of its most difficult problems.[141] In the first place, the growth of normative custom

---

[138] Cf. W.K. Muir, *Law and Attitude Change* (pb. ed. 1973) 132-138.

[139] On this attitude in the late Republic, see J.M. Kelly, *Judicature* 97-98.

[140] On the maxim *ignorantia iuris non excusat*, see B. Schmidlin, *Rechtsregeln* 35-39; and now T. Mayer-Maly, *Iura* 27 (1976) 1-16. The problem is discussed from a rhetorical viewpoint by *Rhet. ad Herenn.* 2.24 and Cic. *Inv.* 2.95; orators obviously would not accept a narrow doctrine.

[141] On what follows, see esp. D. Nörr, in *Fs. Felgentraeger* (1969) 353-366. On "Gewohnheitsrecht," see now M. Kaser, in *Fs. Flume* vol. I 110-118; W.

itself often represents the failure of law to provide for situations in a fashion perceived as adequate by the participants; and when a social system strongly determines conduct (as was true in the late Republic), individuals, even though they are antagonists on some specific issue, may still place far more confidence in socially accepted (customary) modes of conduct than they do in legal rules and practice.[142] Second, the development of law often impels law finders to take custom into account in devising rules. But this process rarely results in the continued coexistence of law and custom; for, depending on the case, law finders will tend either to disapprove of custom (and hence to restrict its use through sanctions) or to approve it (and hence to absorb it within the legal system). The rise and decline of *vis ac deductio moribus* seem to illustrate these historical patterns perfectly, and also the kinds of individual frustration resulting from them.

Appendix
URBAN PRAETORS FROM 81 TO 60 B.C.

The following list is derived from my article, "Urban Praetors and Rural Violence: The Legal Background of Cicero's *pro Caecina*," in *TAPhA* 113 (1983) 221-241. All evidence for dating is discussed there. Here I only list names and all activities associated with the Urban Praetor's judicial functions. In addition, I have indicated known events in Cicero's career as a private advocate.

81—Cn. Cornelius Dolabella. Criticized by Cicero for depriving C. Volcacius of his rights: (Ascon. p. 74 C, quoting Cicero) and for granting an irregular *sponsio* to Sex. Naevius against P. Quinctius (Cic. *Quinct.* 30-31).

80—L. Scribonius Libo (?). Perhaps the Libo who moved the Urban Praetor's tribunal from the Comitium to the area near the *puteal Libonis*: Porphyr. on Hor. *Epist.* 1.19.8.

Waldstein, in *Fg. von Lübtow* (1980) 105-126; and in general A.A. Schiller, *Mechanisms* 253-269. On custom as a source of positive law, see H.L.A. Hart, *The Concept of Law* (1961) 44-47.

[142] See D. Black, *The Behavior of Law* (1976) 107-111, 126-130.

Appendix

79—Cn. Octavius M.f. Cn.n., Consul in 76. Introduced the *formula Octaviana* regulating extortion, and also a provision enforcing on private citizens any legal innovations they themselves made as magistrates: Cic. 2 *Verr.* 3.152, *Q. Fr.* 1.1.21. Praised for firmness and fairness in handling defendants: Cic. *Q. Fr.* 1.1.21-22. The Urban Praetor of 79 probably granted a *vindicatio in libertatem* on behalf of an Arretine woman: Cic. *Caec.* 97. At about this date Cicero delivered a private oration on behalf of Titinia, wife of C. Aurelius Cotta (Cos. 75), against Ser. Naevius represented by C. Scribonius Curio (Cos. 76): Cic. *Brut.* 217.

78—L. Cornelius Sisenna. Also Peregrine Praetor: *CIL* 1².2.589 (= *ILLRP* 512). Criticized for not giving P. Cornelius Scipio *possessio bonorum* of Cn. Cornelius, probably a freedman: Ascon. p. 74 C (quoting Cicero).

77—Cn. Aufidius Cn.f. Orestes, Consul in 71. Granted *possessio bonorum* to a eunuch, as a result of which his *iurisdictio* was revoked by the Consul and he was reprimanded by the Senate: Val. Max. 7.7.6.

76—Salvius (?). The Urban Praetor who introduced the *interdictum Salvianum* may date to this year. An Urban Praetor in 76 or shortly thereafter received into the Edict the *iudicium de vi coactis armatisque hominibus* (cf. Cic. *Tull.* 9). The *actio de dolo*, devised by Aquilius Gallus, is first attested in this year (Cic. *Nat. Deor.* 3.74, dramatic date; cf. *Off.* 3.60).

75—C. Licinius C.f. Sacerdos. Verres' predecessor, of good reputation: Cic. 2 *Verr.* 1.130; Ascon. p. 82 C.

74—C. Verres. Made substantial changes in his Edict: Cic. 2 *Verr.* 1.104-119, 125; 2.21. Also frequently departed from his Edict: 2 *Verr.* 1.119-127. For other sources, see *MRR*.

73—Q. Caecilius C.f. Q.n. Metellus (Creticus), Consul in 69. (Urban Praetor either in 73 or 72.) Denied *possessio bonorum secundum tabulas* to a pimp: Val. Max. 7.7.7. The Urban Praetor of 73 removed all edictal changes made by Verres: Cic. 2 *Verr.* 1.111, 117. At about this date an Urban Praetor granted a *condictio certae pecuniae* to C. Fannius Chaerea against Q. Roscius (cf. Cic. *Rosc. Com.* 33 for the date).

72—C. Calpurnius Piso, Consul in 67. (Urban Praetor in

73, 72, or 70.) Granted *possessio bonorum contra tabulas* to a man ignored in the will of his natural son: Val. Max. 7.7.5.

71—L. Caecilius C.f. Q.n. Metellus, Consul in 68. Had the *formula Octaviana* in his Edict: Cic. 2 *Verr.* 3.152; also probably introduced the interdict *de vi armata*: Cic. *Tull.* 46. He or his immediate successor eliminated the *detrudere* interdict (compare Cic. *Tull.* 29 with *Caec.* 49). L. Metellus granted an *actio de vi coactis armatisque hominibus* to M. Tullius (Cic. *Tull.* 9, 39).

70—M. Mummius (?). (The urban praetorship is unsure; cf. Cic. 2 *Verr.* 3.123.) At about this date Cicero considered defending Q. Mucius Orestinus (Tr. Pl. 64) in an *actio furti* brought by L. Fufius Calenus (probably brother of the moneyer in 70): Ascon. p. 86 C (quoting Cicero); Fufius was also a witness against Verres in 70 (Cic. 2 *Verr.* 2.23).

69—P. Cornelius (L.f. P.n.?) Dolabella. Granted the interdict *de vi hominibus armatis* to Caecina (Cic. *Caec.* 23) and, earlier, probably also the *iudicium familiae erciscundae* (19).

68—Unknown.

67—Q. Publicius (?). The date is reasonably secure (cf. Cic. *Cluent.* 126). Publicius may be the Praetor who introduced the *actio Publiciana* (Just. *Inst.* 4.6.4); but cf. note 30 above. In this year the *lex Cornelia* forbade Praetors to depart from their Edicts (Ascon. p. 59 C; Dio 36.40.1).

66—C. Antonius Hibrida, Consul in 63. (Cf. Cic. *Mur.* 40). On the *actio de dolo*, see above under 76 B.C.

65—L. Licinius Murena, Consul in 62. (Cic. *Mur.* 41; cf. *Mur.* 35-41 and Pliny, *NH* 33.53.) Ser. Sulpicius Rufus was also Praetor in this year; the *actio Serviana*, probably named for him, may have been introduced in 65.

64—M. Valerius Messalla Niger, Consul in 61. (Cf. *Inscr. Ital.* 13.3.77, = *ILS* 46; this date is likely.)

63—L. Valerius Flaccus. (Cic. *Flacc.* 6, 100.)

62—Q. Tullius M.f. M.n. Cicero (?). (Cf. *Schol. Bob.* p. 175 St.)

61—Unknown.

60—P. Cornelius P.f. Lentulus Spinther, Consul in 57. (Cf. Pliny, *NH* 19.23; Val. Max. 2.4.6.).

III

The Advocates:
M. Tullius Cicero and C. Calpurnius Piso

omnes enim illae causarum ac temporum sunt,
non hominum ipsorum aut patronorum
—Cicero

CAECINA's appearance before the Praetor Dolabella was undoubtedly a brief one (*Caec.* 23). In short order Caecina requested the interdict *de vi armata*; then Dolabella, perhaps
after a brief *cognitio*, followed "custom" by issuing the interdict *sine ulla exceptione*. Aebutius replied that he was already
in compliance; Caecina demanded and received an action on
the interdict;[1] Caecina estimated the farm's value, and the reciprocal *sponsiones* were made; a panel of *recuperatores* was selected to hear the case; and the three *formulae* were devised
for the panel's simultaneous decision. It appears that these
events transpired without a hitch, neither side raising the grave
legal issues that would later come to dominate the trial.[2] All
told, the proceedings before Dolabella need have lasted no
more than thirty minutes, probably rather less if the routine
(*consuetudo*) was familiar and the preparations had been careful.

In the early classical period, Roman civil trials, even those
based on interdicts, were characterized by an historically dis-

[1] For *agere ex interdicto*, see Gaius 4.141.
[2] In Chapter II, at note 79, I suggest that Aebutius may have sought an
exceptio but was refused. Cicero does not indicate whether Aebutius also raised
the citizenship issue discussed below.

95

The Advocates

tinctive two-part format. The first part of the trial took place "at law" (*in iure*) before a presiding magistrate, typically the Urban Praetor. Here an actionable issue was isolated and framed for decision through appropriate *formula* or *formulae*, and (depending on the precise action brought) one or more private individuals were named judges and ordered to decide the issue; the parties participated actively in the process, but the magistrate guided it to a reasonably swift conclusion.

The proceedings *in iure* created a kind of scenario for the second stage of the trial "before the judge" (*apud iudicem*). This stage transpired outside the Praetor's presence and was presided over by the judge(s) who had been named in the first part of the trial. In a later chapter, I will discuss in more detail the formal aspects of the *apud iudicem* stage.[3] Here it suffices to stress two points. First, the normal judge in a Roman civil case was emphatically not a legal professional, nor even a magistrate, but instead a layman with no special training in the law. His task was to hear both sides and then determine the outcome of the issue presented to him in the *formula*.

Second, the physical ambiance of the judicial hearing was not very much different from that of the Praetor's court. But the *apud iudicem* portion nonetheless contrasted markedly with the brusque and business-like atmosphere *in iure*. Here there was far more room for expansiveness of exposition, and details of cases could be examined on a more than superficial basis. If the verdict was still unclear, it was even possible for the judge to re-hear the whole case[4] and then (as with Caecina's lawsuit) to re-hear it yet again, until he felt certain of his decision. At the outset of his published speech *pro Caecina*, Cicero complains about how frequent and even customary such adjournments had become, especially in cases where judgment for the plaintiff involved disgrace or dishonor for the defendant (*Caec.* 6-7).

---

[3] Chapter V, under subhead "The Court of the *Recuperatores*."

[4] Thus, Tullius' lawsuit was heard twice (*Tull.* 5), as was that concerning the Arretine woman (*Caec.* 97); Quinctius' trial was heard several times (*Quinct.* 3: *aliquotiens*). On such re-hearings, see Chapter V, at notes 86-89.

The Political Issue

Within the judicial hearing the talents of the trained orator had latitude for full display, for this was the domain of the advocate.[5] In the first section of this chapter, I discuss the issue of Caecina's citizenship, which may have determined the alignment of orators on either side. In the next two sections I reconstruct the course of the debate between Cicero and his opponent Calpurnius Piso during the three hearings of Caecina's lawsuit. Finally, in the last section, I evaluate the attitudes of orators toward positive law and their effect upon its administration in the late Republic.

The Political Issue: Volaterrae and Arretium

At an early stage in his dispute with Caecina, Aebutius proposed that Caecina could not inherit from his wife, owing to the civil disabilities that Sulla had imposed on Volaterrans (*Caec.* 18, 102). He thereby touched, perhaps unwittingly, on a most sensitive nerve.

About one-tenth of the argument in Cicero's published speech (*Caec.* 95-102) is devoted to refuting Aebutius' charge. Yet there is no sign when Cicero first mentions the issue that it had played any major role in the trial; Cicero does not mention it in his *partitio* of the argument at 32, nor does he refer to it in the *peroratio* (103-104).[6] The section on Caecina's citizenship is introduced entirely without preparation, through an extraordinarily abrupt change of subject (95: *At enim Sulla legem tulit*); the transition is so sudden that some scholars have supposed, unnecessarily, a lacuna in the text.[7] But while the

[5] On the rise of rhetorical advocacy in late Republican Rome, it suffices to refer to G. Kennedy, *The Art of Rhetoric in the Roman World* (1972), esp. chap. I ("Early Roman Rhetoric"). For the effects on private law, see G. Pugliese, *Jus* 11 (1960) 390-395.

[6] See also Cic. *Orat.* 102: "Tota mihi causa pro Caecina de verbis interdicti fuit. . . ."

[7] See, e.g., M.A. von Bethmann-Hollweg, *Der Römische Civilprozess* vol. II (1865) 838; A. Gasquy, *Cicéron Jurisconsulte* (1887) 137-138; R. Rau, in *Silvae: Festschrift E. Zinn* (1970) 178 and n.7, who traces the view back to the Renaissance; and W. Stroh, *Taxis* 99 n.59.

The Advocates

text is slightly disturbed at this point,[8] it is unlikely that anything has been lost.[9]

In fact, the awkward change of subject appears to be deliberate, introducing an issue that was, by the time of the third hearing, no longer germane to the trial's development. Cicero himself admits that the citizenship question has little to do with the "logic of the hearing" (101: *ratio vestri iudicii*) and that the *recuperatores* are not supposed to rule on it (102). Much of the reasoning in this section is rushed and sketchy; yet Cicero concedes that even so it will probably be considered too long (101). If we suppose that Aebutius had pressed this issue in the trial itself, it is still not easy to see how it related to judgment under the interdict *de vi armata*.

It is therefore not unreasonable to hypothesize that, during the trial's third hearing, Cicero did not deliver the argument on citizenship, but that he later inserted *Caec.* 95-102 when editing the speech for publication.[10] Why? Cicero himself states that he dwells on the issue because of its great contemporary significance (101). While, as we shall see, this is indeed true, there may be more to the remark than first appears. The citizenship issue may have played an important role in shaping the early stages of Caecina's lawsuit, even though it was of small significance in the outcome.

Sulla, after defeating his opponents in 82/81, dealt harshly with the vanquished. Northern Etruria was singled out for punishment. Volaterrae, Caecina's native city, had forced Sulla's army into a protracted siege. As a consequence, Volaterrae, together with Arretium and possibly some other cit-

---

[8] See Chapter IV, at notes 1-3.

[9] See E. Ruhstrat, *Jb. f. Dogmatik* 19 (1881) 137-138; A. Boulanger, *Discours* vol. VII 73 n.3. Little weight attaches to Cicero's claim in the *conclusio* (104) that he has proven Caecina's ownership of the Fulcinian farm, since Cicero probably refers to his earlier speeches (so Boulanger). As E. Ruhstrat, 137-138, observes, Cicero seems to refer back to this proof already at *Caec.* 19. See also below, at note 31.

[10] On later editing of the *pro Caecina*, see note 67. W. Stroh, *Taxis* 99-100, regards *Caec.* 95-102 as part of the original speech, but as not responsive to Piso's argument.

ies, suffered an alteration in civil status.[11] We know little about
Sulla's law except what we learn in Cicero's speeches *pro Caecina* and *de Domo Sua* (79). The law removed full Roman citizenship from the populations of Volaterrae and Arretium, and reduced both cities to the civil status of Ariminium (*Caec.* 102); therefore Aebutius could allege that Caecina, as a resident of Volaterrae, "had worse rights than other citizens" (18: *deteriore iure esset quam ceteri cives*). Unfortunately, we cannot exactly define the civil status of Ariminium, except to say that it was a Latin colony founded in 268 B.C. and that Cicero (102) names it one of the "Twelve Colonies"—whatever that may mean.[12]

While Sulla was still alive (therefore in 79 or early 78), his law was subjected to an unusual kind of test for constitutionality, in a case described by Cicero (*Caec.* 97).[13] A woman from Arretium was being held by another person as a slave. A third party brought suit to establish her liberty (a *vindicatio in libertatem*). The plaintiff was represented in the trial by Cicero, and the defendant by the distinguished orator C. Aurelius Cotta; the case was heard before the archaic magistral court of the *decemviri stlitibus iudicandis*.[14] The formal procedure for this trial obliged the plaintiff to take an oath (*sacramentum*) in the following words: "I aver that this woman is free by citizen right" (*aio hanc mulierem esse liberam ex iure Quiritium*). Perhaps because the remainder of his case was weak,

[11] See W.V. Harris, *Etruria* 259-267, esp. 264 ff. Volaterran land was also confiscated: E. Gabba, *Republican Rome: The Army, and the Allies* (trans. P.J. Cuff, 1976) 45-46, 69. A.J. Pfiffig, *Grazer Beitr.* 8 (1979) 141-152, surveys Sulla's anti-Etruscan measures and Cicero's lifelong resistance to them; L. Zambianchi, *RIL* 112 (1978) 119-129, concentrates on the social problems caused at Volaterrae by Sulla's measures.

[12] The evidence is reviewed by A.N. Sherwin-White, *The Roman Citizenship* (2d ed. 1973) 102-104. Cf. esp. A. Bernardi, *St. Ciapessoni* (1948) 237-259.

[13] The best reconstruction of this case is by F. Dessertaux, in *Mélanges Gérardin* vol. I (1907) 181-196, whom I follow; summarized: *idem, Études sur la Formation Historique de la Capitis Deminutio* vol. I (1909) 195-211. See also G. Franciosi, *Il Processo di Libertà* (1961) 40-43, 146-147; W.V. Harris, *Etruria* 274-276.

[14] See, with bibliography, M. Kaser, *RZ* 40-41; J.M. Kelly, *Judicature* 66-69. On Cotta as an orator: Cic. *Brut.* 201-205.

Cotta resorted to a technicality; he asserted that in any case the plaintiff's oath could not be valid (*iustum*) "because Roman citizenship had been removed from the Arretines" (*quod Arretinis adempta civitas esset*). Therefore, so Cotta reasoned, while the woman might perhaps be free, she could not be free "by citizen right." The court hesitated on this point; two hearings were required before they rendered judgment for the plaintiff (*Caec.* 97).

Cicero apparently never published the speeches he delivered on behalf of the Arretine woman. But there can be little doubt that the substance of his argument on citizenship is reproduced summarily in *Caec.* 95-102. His logic runs as follows: Sulla's law, like most Republican legislation, contained the catchall proviso that "if any of these proposals is made contrary to our legal order, it is not proposed in this statute" (95: *Si quid ius non esset rogarier, eius ea lege nihilum rogatum*). This proviso presumes the existence of a category of things the proposal of which is "contrary to our legal order." What is included in this category? At a minimum, says Cicero, a person's liberty cannot be involuntarily removed, that is, he cannot be made a slave to another; therefore, *a fortiori* and also by tradition, his citizenship cannot be involuntarily removed (96), a principle allegedly established in the case of the Arretine woman (97). Apparent exceptions to this rule are illusory. One by one Cicero examines them: citizens who join Latin colonies, or who are surrendered by the state to enemies,[15] or who are sold by their *paterfamilias*, or who are sold by the state for avoidance of military service or the census, or who go into exile. In all these cases, so Cicero claims, the loss of liberty or citizenship is in some sense voluntary, occurring through the will or deliberate act either of the subject or of his *paterfamilias* (98-100). Cicero further argues that this traditional list of exceptions by its nature cannot be extended (99), and in particular cannot be extended to include removal

---

[15] Here, at least, Cicero's argument is based on outmoded jurisprudence: A. Watson, *Persons* 244-249; R.A. Baumann, *RIDA*³ 25 (1978) 225-226.

of citizenship or liberty by statute (100),[16] since such a practice would threaten all citizens, both old and new (101).

This piece of constitutional interpretation comes to us in highly abbreviated form; but Cicero was so impressed by its force that he repeats portions of it almost word for word twelve years later (*de Domo Sua* 77-79; cf. *Balb.* 31). Whatever one may think of the argument's plausibility,[17] in 79 Cicero won his case, and claimed thereby to have established that Sulla's law was unconstitutional and void. Cicero asserts that no one thereafter doubted the legal rights of those affected by Sulla's law (*Caec.* 97); but more probably he just hoped that the law would slip into desuetude through non-enforcement. Yet the issue refused to die. In 78/77 Aemilius Lepidus apparently used the injustice of Sulla's law in order to rally Etruscan support (Sall. *Hist.* 1.77.14 M); plainly there was still some sentiment for the law's enforcement. Finally, in 70/69 the censors were obliged to confront the matter once again, since they had to decide whether to enroll as citizens the residents of Volaterrae and Arretium.[18] In this emotionally charged atmosphere, Aebutius' raising of the issue against Caecina had considerable political significance.

The case of the Arretine woman, which began as a simple *vindicatio in libertatem*, eventually went off on the much narrower issue of Sulla's law. It is not unlikely that a decade later

[16] But Mommsen compares the statutory removal of citizen rights from Capuans in 210, as a consequence of their rebellion: *Staatsr.* vol. III 139-141. In any case, Aebutius himself had not asserted that Caecina was not a citizen (cf. *Caec.* 18).

[17] There is a good discussion, with bibliography, in J. Bleicken, *Lex Publica* (1975) 339-347; see also F. Serrao, *Classi, Partiti, e Legge* (1974) 89-92. Cicero's argument involves some sophistry; cf. E. Levy, *SZ* 78 (1961) 152-154. Some scholars have thought it wholly bogus: e.g., Mommsen, *Staatsr.* vol. III 335 n.2 (cf. 335-336); C. Gioffredi, *SDHI* 13/14 (1947/1948) 67-72. On the relation of this provision to the *ius civile*, see G. Pugliese, *ACIV* vol. II 63-84; further bibliography in S. di Paola, *Synt. Arangio-Ruiz* vol. II 1075 n.2. See also G. Nocera, *Il Potere dei Comizi e i Suoi Limiti* (1940); M. Kaser, *Iura* 3 (1952) 65-75; F. de Martino, *Storia della Costituzione Romana* vol. I (1958) 395-401; E. Ferenczy, in *Fg. von Lübtow* (1970) 267-280.

[18] See W.V. Harris, *Etruria* 282-284; but it is less clear that Caecina's lawsuit finally disposed of the issue (*contra* pp. 276-281).

Cicero at first believed Caecina's lawsuit would develop similarly: Caecina's formal claims to ownership and subsequent possession of the Fulcinian farm would be quickly established, and the trial would then go off on the "technicality" of Sulla's law. When the conflict between Caecina and Aebutius erupted into a lawsuit, Cicero had already reached the very apex of the Roman bar. His vigorous prosecution of Verres in 70 had resulted in a humiliating defeat for the defendant's illustrious advocate Q. Hortensius Hortalus.[19] Now in 69 Cicero's advocacy for Caecina would earn him the gratitude of a wealthy and powerful Etruscan family, as well as political loyalty from the city of Volaterrae.[20] The cause of Volaterran rights was in itself an attractive one for Cicero, since it offered him the opportunity to defend a sympathetic issue from familiar ground; and his orations *pro Tullio* in 71 gave him a firm understanding of recent legal developments in the possessory interdicts and the law governing violence.[21] Cicero, though uncommonly busy with other things during 69,[22] was too shrewd to ignore this chance for doing well by doing good.

If Caecina sought out an orator known to have views on Sulla's legislation, so too, as it seems, did Aebutius. Nearly a quarter century after Caecina's lawsuit, Cicero describes C. Calpurnius Piso as a stalwart and facile orator, not a bit slow in thinking, but who in countenance and demeanor seemed more acute than he was (*Brut.* 239).[23] However, apart from

[19] See Vonder Mühll, *RE* s.v. "Hortensius" (1913) 2474-2475, based on Cic. *Brut.* 320, 323-324. See also, e.g., D. Stockton, *Cicero: A Political Biography* (1971) 41-49. On the trial, see P. Brunt, *Chiron* 10 (1980) 273-289.

[20] See Chapter I, at notes 81-82; W.V. Harris, *Etruria* 283-284, noting esp. Cic. *Fam.* 13.4.1 (Volaterrae gives political support to Cicero, apparently in his election to consulate, see D.R. Shackleton Bailey *ad loc.*); T.N. Mitchell, *Cicero: The Ascending Years* (1979) 102-103.

[21] The *pro Tullio* is notable for its long historical analyses of these subjects (7-12, 29-34, 38-46).

[22] As Curule Aedile, he gave three games (*Mur.* 40), and also defended M. Fonteius and P. Oppius in trials *de repetundis*. See M. Gelzer, *Cicero* (1969) 51-52.

[23] "C. deinde Piso statarius et sermonis plenus orator, minime ille quidem tardus in excogitando, verum tamen vultu et simulatione multo etiam acutior

the lawsuit in 69, Piso is not known to have served as an advocate; and since Cicero's attacks on Piso's weaknesses in the *pro Caecina* (e.g., 67, 98) resemble his condescending remarks in the *Brutus*, Cicero may generalize from his one face-to-face encounter. But what Cicero does not mention in either work is Piso's most salient trait; namely, a redoubtable conservatism that at times verged on the fanatic. Piso has been called the most conservative member of the Senate; certainly he was a diehard defender of the Sullan restoration,[24] and his defense doubtless extended to Sulla's law on the civil status of Volaterrae and Arretium.

Had the trial in fact developed in the way Cicero may have anticipated, he could have been confident of relatively easy victory. Within the *pro Caecina*, the argument on citizenship has a curiously anticlimactic structure. Cicero first establishes at length that Caecina has full citizenship because Sulla's law is unconstitutional (95-101). But he then observes that this question is not actually at stake in the present trial; and that, even if it were, Volaterrans would nonetheless be able to inherit from Roman citizens, since the residents of Ariminium and the other Twelve Colonies could do so (102).[25] While Cicero treats this as a matter of common knowledge, it may be that his view was disputed, since otherwise Aebutius' original objection to Caecina's inheritance would have been extraordinarily captious. Cicero, in any case, prefers to rest his refutation on the broader ground of unconstitutionality; nor does he leave the subject before dilating on why law should be interpreted in such a way as to preserve the citizenship of so upright a person as Caecina (102).[26]

---

quam erat videbatur." Compare the lavish praise of C. Piso when he served as *iudex* in the lawsuit against Q. Roscius: "Tu, C. Piso, tali fide, virtute, gravitate, auctoritate ornatus . . ." (Cic. *Rosc. Com.* 7).

[24] Cf. F. Münzer, *RE* s.v. "Calpurnius" (1899) 1376-1377; E. Gruen, *Last Generation* 38 ("one of the most conservative figures in the Roman senate").

[25] See also A.N. Sherwin-White, (cited n.12) 102-104, 303-304; W.V. Harris, *Etruria* 280-281.

[26] This *topos* was normal in cases concerning citizenship, as the *pro Archia* and *pro Balbo* show.

The Advocates

If at an early stage in Caecina's lawsuit the "political issue" helped determine the alignment of advocates on either side, this issue was also probably aired during the trial itself—perhaps during the first hearing of the case. At this time Cicero doubtless delivered an argument drawn loosely from his speech for the Arretine woman. However, by the trial's third hearing the issue, and indeed the entire question of Caecina's ownership, had obviously receded into the background; in summarizing his third speech, Cicero alludes only in passing to his formal proof of ownership (*Caec.* 104). Nonetheless, Cicero's insertion of the argument into the published version of the speech suggests the orator's deep feelings on the issue and also how important it had been in shaping the trial. Republican advocacy knew no sharp division of private law from its political ambiance; political issues frequently intrude in Cicero's private orations.[27] Admittedly, open reference to politics required some tact and strategic skill, lest judges be unnecessarily offended; thus, Cicero declines to dwell at any length on Sulla's *dominatio*, "that disaster for the state" (95: *calamitate rei publicae*; cf. 18).[28] On the other hand, if the opportunity presented itself, Cicero had no inclination to avoid the wider context of private lawsuits.

THE EARLIER SPEECHES

The *pro Caecina*, as we have it, purports to be Cicero's speech during the third hearing before the *recuperatores*. At the speech's outset, Cicero admits that his plan for conducting the case will be far different from what it had been at the first hearing (*Caec.* 3). As Cicero puts it, he had then expected to rely on his own argument (*in defensione mea*) and his own witnesses;

[27] This is clearest in the *pro Quinctio* (where the events leading up to the trial are set against the background of Sulla's invasion, and involve a threatened tribunician veto, 29, 65) and in the *pro Tullio* (with its descriptions of rural unrest in the wake of Spartacus' revolt; note also the defendant's appeal to tribunes, 39); less clear in the *pro Roscio Comoedo*.

[28] On this issue, however, he and Piso held sharply different views; cf. note 24.

now he has reconstructed his case so as to base it on his opponent's "confession" (*in confessione adversarii*) and on the defense witnesses.[29] Cicero goes on to argue that Aebutius has in effect convicted himself by openly admitting what the plaintiff contended and then trying to shift discussion to a legal quibble (4). This defense strategy has produced two adjournments and a wholly unwarranted delay in deciding the case (5-9).

These remarks clearly point to a change in Cicero's strategy, a recasting of the plaintiff's case in order to meet roadblocks that had been put in its way by the defense. With some effort the earlier strategy can be pieced together, and an account given of Cicero's reasons for abandoning it.[30] Cicero's earlier speeches had rested more on his own argument and witnesses (*Caec.* 3). The plaintiff's witnesses are mentioned only once, in section 94, as attesting the fact that Caecina had come to the Fulcinian farm and inspected the tenant's accounts. The original argument for the plaintiff seems to have gone as follows.

P1: Ownership

Cicero claims to have shown that Caecina owned the Fulcinian farm (104); this demonstration must have been made in an earlier speech, since the existing speech omits the issue.[31] Cicero's argument can be deduced from the *narratio* of the *pro Caecina*. Caecina's title was traced back to the auction of the younger Fulcinius' estate; Aebutius, as the purchaser of record, had acted on mandate from Caesennia, who subsequently paid him for the farm and became its owner by taking possession of it and leasing it to a tenant (13-17, 94). Caecina was her principal heir (17), and notwithstanding Aebutius'

[29] At *Caec.* 24, Cicero states he will discuss the defendant's *confessio et testes* before his own argument and witnesses; this more accurately summarizes the *argumentum*, see below at note 65.

[30] The reconstruction of the earlier hearings in W. Stroh, *Taxis* 90-91, differs in some respects from mine. The best discussion of the various issues in the *pro Caecina* is still H.J. Roby, *Private Law* vol. II 510-535.

[31] On the supposed lacuna in *Caec.* 95, see above at notes 7-9.

objections was capable of inheriting (18, 95-102). While the issue of ownership was not strictly relevant in an interdictal procedure (104), Caecina's firm claim to title did provide a necessary background for evaluating the defendant's actions.[32]

P2: Possession

The argument[33] is briefly summarized in 94-95, which is probably an epitome of Cicero's original argument (modified in light of Piso's objections). Even before her son's death, says Cicero, Caesennia's usufruct gave her a sort of possession of the farm, as indeed the defense admits.[34] After the son's death and the auction of his estate, she took full possession and leased the farm (17: *Caesennia fundum possedit locavitque*), and subsequently she held possession through her tenant (94); Cicero's juxtaposition of her possession with the lease suggests that he saw the lease itself as the act of a possessor.[35] When Caesennia died, Caecina, as her principal heir, held possession *eodem iure*; that is, through the tenant (94).[36] Caecina then entered the farm and inspected the tenant's accounts, as part of the process of going round his late wife's property (94);[37] in consequence, he was *in possessione bonorum* (19). Finally, Aebutius' own subsequent actions confirm this account.[38] Aebutius gave

---

[32] Quintilian, 7.5.3, explains that ownership should be discussed even in interdictal suits, in order to win the judge's favor.

[33] On this argument, see in general F.L. Keller, *Sem.* 342-375.

[34] *Caec.* 94: "Caesenniam possedisse propter usufructum non negas." Why didn't Piso deny this? In juristic sources, *possidere* is sometimes used non-technically of usufructuaries: cf. G. Nicosia, *St. Zingali* vol. III (1965) 497 ff.; M. Kaser, *RPR²* vol. I 389 n.39. Piso doubtless pointed out this non-technical sense of *possidere* (cf. 19); but Cicero sees a sort of possessory continuity between the earlier usufruct and her possession after the auction. On the legal situation, see below, note 48.

[35] See F.L. Keller, *Sem.* 343-345.

[36] This is contrary to classical law: cf. Javolenus, D. 41.2.23 pr.; Paul, D. 41.2.30.5. See F.L. Keller, *Sem.* 345-346.

[37] W. Stroh, *Taxis* 91, is therefore incorrect in holding that Caecina had never set foot on the farm. For a good discussion, see F.L. Keller, *Sem.* 352-353; H.J. Roby, *Private Law* vol. II 528-529.

[38] On the argument, see F.L. Keller, *Sem.* 354-375.

formal notice that he owned the farm (19), an action that makes little sense unless he felt Caecina had previously taken possession (95). And that is how Caecina interpreted the *denuntiatio* when he then offered to be led out from the farm by formal violence (20, 95). Although in his third speech Cicero argues that the question of possession is irrelevant and *extra causam* (94), his earlier production of witnesses on the question (94)[39] indicates that possession played a much larger role in his first two speeches.

P3: Applicability of the Interdict

Here Cicero's argument can be reconstructed by conjecture. Caecina had possessed the farm; but then, before the day of the attempted *deductio*, Aebutius had seized it. Caecina subsequently tried to reenter property that rightfully belonged to him; but Aebutius used *vis armata* to drive him back from the farm. Cicero is certain to have produced his own witnesses to this fracas (cf. 3, 24). The interdict *de vi armata* requires a defendant to restore property to one whom he has "thrust out" by force; and because of Caecina's previous possession, it does not matter that Caecina was not still in possession at the time armed force was used (64-66, 75-77). Aebutius' actions nonetheless constitute ejectment, and these actions clearly involve armed force (41-63).[40] Most of Cicero's interpretation of the interdict is presumably ascribable to the jurist C. Aquilius, who had frequently been present among Cicero's supporters in earlier hearings (77); in particular, it is clearly Aquilius' liberal interpretation of *deiectio* that Piso rejected when he attacked the jurists' authority (65).

On the basis of these three points, Cicero argued that his client should prevail in the interdictal procedure. *Prima facie*, Cicero's argument was very strong. It may even have been truth. All that it wanted was evidence.[41]

[39] What witnesses? Probably the *colonus*.

[40] The legal aspects of this question are considered in Chapter IV, at notes 134 ff.

[41] So also H.J. Roby, *Private Law* vol. II 531-532; cf. also G. Nicosia, *Deiectio* 53 n.128.

The Advocates

In his reply to Cicero's case, Piso provided witnesses and a "confession" (*Caec.* 3, 24, 104).[42] There were in fact ten witnesses,[43] and their names clearly reveal Piso's strategy, even if we did not have Cicero's further allusions to Piso's argument. Two witnesses certified Aebutius' title to the Fulcinian farm: P. Caesennius, the *auctor fundi* who had arranged the auction, and Sex. Clodius Phormio, the banker who had financed the sale (27). The banker's account books, in which the transaction was recorded, were also offered in evidence (16-17). For the rest, fully eight witnesses described the encounter at the farm itself. Four admitted having come with their own slaves (24, 27); one recounted the disproportion between the numbers of the two sides (26); three had heard Aebutius' threats against Caecina, and two attested Caecina's reply that he still wished to be formally expelled (24, 27); one stated that he himself had ordered Aebutius' slave to attack Caecina if the latter persisted (25),[44] and one related his efforts to assist Caecina in his flight (26, 44). Only the last defense witness, the disreputable Senator Fidiculanius Falcula, wavered as to the essential details, and his confused and contradictory testimony was highly embarrassing to the defense (28-30).

Cicero regards these witnesses as broadly confirming his client's version of the encounter (*Caec.* 24, 31).[45] But Piso used these same witnesses to construct an impressive argument in

[42] By and large, I assume in what follows that Cicero's report of Aebutius' argument, though distorted, is basically accurate. Many modern commentators disagree. In particular they assert, without apparent evidence, that Piso's linkage of *deiectio* with possession was his original (and only) position. See, e.g., H.J. Roby, *Private Law* 518-519; G. Nicosia, *Deiectio* 43-45; W. Stroh, *Taxis* 91-93. For contrary arguments, see note 58. On the proper methods for interpreting Ciceronian speeches, see esp. P.A. Brunt, *CQ* 32 (1982) 146.

[43] On the number, see Chapter V, at notes 21-23.

[44] This testimony appears to contradict Cicero's account in *Caec.* 22.

[45] The same technique of alleging a confession is used in *Tull.* 1-2 and is recommended by *Rhet. ad Herenn.* 2.46. Such supposed "confessions" are taken too literally by N. Scapini, *La Confessione nel Diritto Romano* vol. I (1973) 139-146.

108

defense of Aebutius; this defense isolated and undermined the weakest points in Cicero's initial position.

D1: Ownership

Both documents and witnesses clearly establish that Aebutius acquired the farm at the time of the auction (*Caec.* 16-17, 19, 27). By contrast, Cicero has only hearsay evidence that Caesennia had intended to purchase the farm (15-16), and no proof that she paid for it (17); nor is there firm evidence that Caesennia ever considered herself the farm's owner. Cicero's highly abusive attack on P. Caesennius ("greater in girth than in authority"[46]) and Sex. Clodius Phormio ("as shady and untrustworthy as Terence's Phormio"[47]) suggests how damaging their testimony was to his view that at the time of the auction "everyone knew" of Caesennia's mandate to Aebutius. Finally, Caecina's sole claim to ownership is based upon his inheritance from Caesennia; but he could not inherit because of the civil disability Sulla had imposed on Volaterrans (cf. 18, 95-102).

D2: Possession

Until her son's death, Caesennia had only a usufruct in the Fulcinian farm, and this usufruct, so Piso contended, simply continued during the four years between her son's death and her own (19). Piso evidently interpreted the lease of the farm as part of the exercise of this usufruct, and not as a sign of possession;[48] he is also likely to have asserted that Aebutius

[46] *Caec.* 27: "non tam auctoritate gravi quam corpore." The play is on the word *auctoritas*, which in private law has a technical meaning: the alienor of a *res mancipi* (e.g., land) by mancipation is obliged as *auctor* to defend the alienee against claims of ownership by third parties. This is not, to be sure, Caesennius' role as witness in the present lawsuit, since the plaintiff alleges that Caesennia then received title from Aebutius.

[47] *Caec.* 27: "nec minus niger nec minus confidens quam ille Terentianus est Phormio." Cicero refers to Terence's *Phormio* (161 B.C.), whose title character is an unscrupulous parasite. Quintilian, 6.3.56, admires this passage of Cicero.

[48] Thus he rejected Cicero's argument at 94, on the basis of reasons given at 19. The legal situation of the usufructuary in classical law is succinctly

had himself taken possession of the farm directly after the auction, during the four-year interval that passed "without controversy" between Caesennia and Aebutius (19: *sine ulla controversia*). In any case, the full force of Piso's argument on ownership becomes evident at this point: for if Caesennia was in fact owner, then her leasing of the farm (which presumably involved a visit to it) could well be interpreted as an exercise of her possession; but if she was not owner, then her actions are not germane to the issue of possession. It is not clear how Piso treated Caecina's visit to the farm after Caesennia's death. Cicero's *narratio* argues that Aebutius saw the visit as a threat to his own property rights (19, cf. 95); but Piso may also have argued that Caecina's trip did not necessarily imply intent to take possession and was merely an effort to settle past accounts with the tenant.[49] In any event, Piso undoubtedly emphasized Aebutius' subsequent possession of the farm, prior to the incident complained of.

D3: Applicability of the Interdict

It is this portion of Piso's case that Cicero describes as a *confessio* (3, 24, 104), and on which he proposes to concentrate his own third speech. At various points in the *pro Caecina*, Cicero presents extended paraphrases of this supposed *confessio*. His summaries are of course not neutral in tone; but they apparently do bring out the main lines of Piso's case. The first three summaries are put in the first person, as though Aebutius himself were speaking: "I summoned together, gathered, and armed these men; I obstructed your approach through fear of death and threat to your life; with a sword I thrust you back *reieci* and terrified you."[50] "I did not thrust you out

---

stated by Gaius 2.93: "usufructuarius . . . non possidet, sed habet ius utendi et fruendi. . . ."

[49] So U. Wesel, *TR* 38 (1970) 355: "Es ist jedoch mehr als fraglich, ob er [*scil.* Caecina] dadurch Besitzer geworden war. Denn die Abrechnung erfolgte offensichtlich für die Vergangenheit, bis zum Tode der Caesennia, nicht für die Zukunft." And so already C. von Savigny, *Das Recht der Besitzes* (7th ed. 1865) 425 n.4. Is Caecina's intent unimportant?

[50] *Caec.* 24: "convocavi homines, coegi, armavi, terrore mortis ac periculo

deieci, but only obstructed you. For I did not allow you to enter the farm; instead, I placed armed men in the way to make you realize that if you set foot on the farm, it would mean your instant death."[51] "I did everything that you allege, actions at once disorderly and rash and dangerous. But what of it? I acted with impunity, since you have no grounds to sue me in civil or praetorian law."[52]

Piso therefore freely admitted that Aebutius had used armed men in order to prevent Caecina from entering the Fulcinian farm; indeed, testimony from eight of his ten witnesses tended to support this "confession." But Piso gave the incident an interpretation entirely different from Cicero's. In the first place he minimized the violence by arguing that no one had in fact been killed or wounded in the incident (*Caec.* 41); Aebutius' use of force had not been excessive. In the second place he argued that Aebutius' use of violence was not actionable (34).

Piso's argument rested on his interpretation of the verb *deicere* in the interdict. The interdict required that the defendant need have "thrust out" the plaintiff (*deiecisti*).[53] Piso argued that, in a literal sense, Aebutius had not "thrust out" Caecina, but had merely "thrust him away" and prevented him from entering the farm. Cicero, again using verbs in the first person, repeats Piso's argument over and over in progressively sharper form: *non deieci, sed obstitui* (31); *eieci ego te armatis hominibus, non deieci* (38); *non deieci, non enim sivi accedere* (64); *non deieci, sed eieci* (84).[54] In *Caec.* 66 the argument is paraphrased

---

capìtis ne accederes obstiti; ferro . . . te reieci atque proterrui." Here, and in succeeding quotations, I have omitted parenthetical comments by Cicero.

[51] *Caec.* 31: "Non deieci, sed obstiti; non enim sum passus in fundum ingredi, sed armatos homines opposui, ut intellegeres, si in fundo pedem posuisses, statim tibi esse pereundum."

[52] *Caec.* 34: "Feci equidem quae dicis omnia, et ea sunt et turbulenta et temeraria et periculosa. Quid ergo est? impune feci; nam quid agas mecum ex iure civili ac praetorio non habes."

[53] Cf. Chapter II, at notes 48-49.

[54] In sections 38 and 84, the manuscripts have *eieci* rather than the *reieci* of most modern editions. Likewise 66 (quoted below): *eiectus* instead of *reiectus*. F.L. Keller, *Sem.* 393-400, emended all three passages; but the manuscript reading is defended by W. Stroh, *Taxis* 94 n.48. Cicero uses *reicio* at 24

The Advocates

more fully and sarcastically: "Whence were you thrust out? From a place which you were prohibited from reaching? You were thrust away, not out [*eiectus es, non deiectus*]. I admit having gathered men, I admit having armed them, I admit having threatened you with death, I admit liability under the Praetor's interdict if its intent and fairness should prevail. But I discover in the interdict one word behind which I may hide. I did not thrust you out [*deieci*] of a place to which I prohibited you from coming."[55]

Piso had obtained this interpretation from a jurist he did not name, but whom Cicero believes to know (79).[56] This jurist, when approached by Cicero, allegedly maintained that "it cannot be shown that a person was thrust out except from a place in which he was" (79: *non posse probari quemquam esse deiectum nisi ex eo loco in quo fuisset*).[57] This jurist therefore supported the main line of Piso's argument. Since Caecina had not been on the farm, he could not have been "thrust out" of it.

But Piso also had a "fallback position," one less extreme in its literalism. It is likely that this fallback position emerged not in Piso's first speech (where he had presumably relied on the anonymous *responsum*), but only in the second, in reaction to Cicero's criticism of the initial position;[58] for Cicero de-

---

(paraphrasing Aebutius) and 88, but *eiectus* in contrast to *deiectus* in 50. The question is close, but I would keep the manuscript reading, since it can also be defended by the fact that the interdict may previously have used *eicere* (cf. Chapter IV, at notes 152-154)—a fact that Piso may have exploited.

[55] *Caec.* 66: "Unde deiectus es? an inde quo prohibitus es accedere? eiectus es, non deiectus. . . . Fateor me homines coegisse, fateor armasse, fateor tibi mortem esse minitatam, fateor hoc interdicto Praetoris vindicari, si voluntas et aequitas valeat; sed invenio in interdicto verbum unum ubi delitiscam: non deieci te ex eo loco quem in locum prohibui ne venires."

[56] On the text, see Chapter IV, at notes 49 ff., where I also attempt to deduce the jurist's name. There I also dissent from W. Stroh, *Taxis* 98 (with n.56), who argues that Cicero's conversation with this jurist is a fiction.

[57] As the text goes on to show, the jurist meant this view quite literally.

[58] So already E. Costa, *Orazioni* 97-100; *Cicerone Giur.* 127-128. Did Piso actually advance two distinct interpretations of *deiectio*? Cicero clearly states that he did (90). Most modern commentators believe that he did not, and that Cicero is deliberately misrepresenting Piso's argument (cf. note 42). Against

scribes the fallback position as having emerged out of the wreckage of Piso's defense (90), thus indicating that Piso had at first clung to the narrower view. Cicero describes the fallback position in the following way: "But first note that you have been forced to give up the reasoning whereby you denied that anyone can be thrust out *deieci* except from a place where he then was. You admit this is possible. But you deny he can be thrust out if he does not possess."[59] This final sentence is twice repeated in *Caec.* 91 as well, with a slightly more epigrammatic wording.[60]

This "fallback position" (which substantially duplicates the view later taken by the classical jurists[61]) will be further discussed in Chapter IV. For now it suffices to make two points. First, the "fallback position" differs from Piso's initial view in that it allows the "thrusting out" not only of someone who is physically expelled from a place where he is, but also of one who possesses something that he is then prevented from reaching. In retreating to this "fallback position," Piso must therefore have argued that Caecina did not successfully take possession of the farm when he entered it to inspect the ten-

---

this view, it should be observed: the two positions are in fact distinct; each is defensible from the wording of the interdict; Piso's view plainly corresponds with that of the unnamed jurist (79-80), while the second view does not; Piso's first view better corresponds with a point in the trial when he was not sure he could prove Caecina's lack of possession, while his second position reflects his confidence on this point; and in the end there is no clear reason to suppose that Cicero is lying, especially before such an audience. In any case, nothing supports Nicosia's view that the "fallback position" was in fact the "bulwark" of Piso's defense: *Deiectio* 44.

[59] *Caec.* 90: "Ac primum illud attende, te iam ex illa ratione esse depulsum, quod negabas quemquam deici posse nisi inde ubi tum esset; iam posse concedis; eum qui non possideat negas deici posse."

[60] *Caec.* 91: "Negas deieci, nisi qui possideat." The same argument is also quoted in indirect discourse in 90 ("eum deieci posse qui tum possideat; qui non possideat, nullo modo posse") and in direct discourse in 91 ("deici nemo potest qui non possidet"). Cicero is careful to repeat the argument frequently, obviously for the benefit of the *recuperatores*. These careful repetitions are hardly reconcilable with the view that Piso took no other position on *deiectio*; cf. note 58.

[61] Chapter IV, note 143, for sources.

ant's books (94). Presumably he asserted that the farm was in Aebutius' possession before Caecina's visit, and had remained in it thereafter (cf. above, D2). Therefore Caecina could not use the interdict.

Second, within the context of the trial Piso's "fallback position" had, at least in Cicero's view, the clear characteristics of a desperate retreat (90). Cicero can assert this because Piso is modifying a position that has been shown to be too extreme. The procedural context of Piso's modification must be kept in mind, for an orator does not always find it easy to explain to his audience the distinction between a tactical withdrawal and a retreat; Cicero himself would face the same problem shortly. Since Piso's "fallback position" was far more defensible than his original position, he might have carried the day had he adopted it sooner. However, as it seems, Piso continued to waver, not fully committing himself to the new position.[62]

It is reasonably clear that Piso devoted much more time to the interdict's interpretation than Cicero had anticipated. In his opening remarks, Cicero expresses his annoyance that the trial is coming to concern not Aebutius' wickedness, but rather a point of law (4); it is plain he had not previously discussed the legal question in so much detail. The *recuperatores* likewise seem to have found themselves in a quandary, uncertain how to interpret the interdict and apply it to this case. Cicero states that they had two reasons for twice adjourning the trial: their uncertainty about the law and their unwillingness to injure the defendant's reputation through a adverse verdict (6). While Cicero's explanation is clearly partisan,[63] it may well be that the *recuperatores* did hesitate in reaching a verdict until the legal question had been clarified through debate.

By the time of the third hearing, Cicero's original argument had been seriously undermined by Piso's determined assault. Caecina's ownership of the Fulcinian farm could not be satisfactorily proved; his possession of the farm was questiona-

---

[62] For his possible reason see Chapter IV, after note 142.
[63] See Chapter I, at note 97.

ble; and the interdict itself had been shown to be ambiguous and uncertain. But Piso's position had also altered with regard to the correct interpretation of the interdict; he had been driven to abandon his original view (which at least had some juristic support) in favor of a new and less literal one. The stage was set for the third and final hearing of the case.

Cicero's Strategy in the *pro Caecina*

Cicero's private orations are generally characterized by their formal organization, which was prescribed in rhetorical teaching.[64] Cicero's maturest explication of this organization is in the *de Oratore*, a three-book treatise finished in late 55 B.C.; there he considers the organization as enjoined by the very nature of public speech (2.307). Speeches comprise the following: preliminary remarks designed to catch the hearer's attention (the *exordium*); a description of the facts of the case (the *narratio*); a proof that settles both contested facts and doubtful points of law (the *argumentum*); and a final appeal that the hearers judge in one's favor (the *peroratio*). The names of these segments of a speech vary considerably in rhetorical handbooks; and other, lesser divisions can readily be added to the list. But the central point is that this organization not only gave the advocate a rational preliminary structure for organizing his speech, but also produced certain formal expectations in the minds of his rhetorically educated listeners.

The *pro Caecina* is generally unexceptional in its organization. The *exordium* (1-9) lays heavy stress both on the defendant's effrontery in past and present actions (1-3) and on the unwarranted timidity of the *recuperatores* in not reaching a verdict (4-9). The *narratio* proceeds to set out the facts of the case as Cicero wants them to be understood (10-23).

The long *argumentum* (23-102) is unusual only in that Cicero deals with the defendant's "confession" and witnesses (23-31) before passing on to his own argument. In section 31, the

---

[64] See in general K.Z. Méhész, *Advocatus Romanus* (1971) 132-140; W. Stroh, *Taxis* 7-30.

The Advocates

defendant's legal argument is used as a bridge into the plaintiff's case. At the start of 32, Cicero formally divides his own argument into two sections: *de re* and *de verbo*.[65] The section *de re* (32-85) begins by insisting that there must be a specific legal remedy for the harm that has been done to Caecina (32-40). Cicero goes on to contend that Aebutius' actions constitute *vis* within the meaning of the interdict (41-48); that the term *deiectio* is applicable to Aebutius' actions because the word must be liberally construed (49-64); that the jurist Aquilius' interpretation of the interdict, which favors Cicero, demands deference both because of his position as a jurist and in the interest of protecting property rights (65-79); and, finally, that the view of the unnamed jurist whose *responsum* had been cited by Piso is patently absurd even though it ultimately favors the plaintiff (79-85). In this portion of his speech Cicero deals exclusively with Piso's initial view on the meaning of *deiectio*.

The second section of the *argumentum* concerns the *verba* of the interdict (86-95). Cicero begins by showing that *unde deiecisti* must embrace not only literal thrusting out from a place, but also preventing someone from reaching it (86-89). But then he turns to Piso's "fallback position" on the meaning of *deiectio*, and argues that the difference in wording between the interdict *de vi* and the interdict *de vi armata* proves that possession is not required for the latter (90-93). Cicero concludes by briefly arguing *extra causam* that in any event Caecina had possession (94-95).

At this point is interposed a digression on the problem of Volaterran citizenship (95-102). The speech ends with a brief but confident *peroratio* in which Cicero praises the steadfastness of his client and rehearses the main points he has made in his speeches against Aebutius (103-104).[66]

[65] W. Stroh, *Taxis* 93 (with n.44), argues that the speech deliberately avoids a formal *partitio*; but the division is in fact reasonably obvious, and it is echoed at 86 and 90. Cicero's placement of the argument based on equity before that based on law may indicate that he thought his case weak on law; cf. Quintil. 7.5.3.

[66] Many commentators confine the *peroratio* to 104; but the exalted tone is already established in 103, where also themes from earlier sections are re-

The published version of the speech is likely to differ from the actual speech only slightly.[67] The *narratio* seems too long, as Cicero himself concedes (10); much of it has relatively small connection with the issues raised in the *argumentum*, and the facts were already long since before the *recuperatores*. Presumably Cicero published a more extended version of the *narratio* in order to provide readers with an adequate understanding of the case. The digression on Volaterran citizenship (95-102) is almost surely a later addition to the speech; it concerns an issue of great public interest that was indeed raised by the trial but in the end had little relevance to the trial's final hearing.[68] The rest of the speech seems authentic.

The most cursory comparison of the *pro Caecina* with what appears to have been the argument of Cicero's earlier speeches[69] reveals how deeply Cicero had re-thought his case. The argument on ownership is now reduced to a fleeting assertion in the *peroratio*, together with an observation that ownership is irrelevant (95). Caecina's possession is argued briefly and *extra causam* (94-95), and in the *peroratio* Cicero states that this question is also not germane (104). Everything has come to center on the legal implications of Aebutius' act against Caecina and, above all, on the interpretation of the interdict.[70]

Of the seventy-three chapters in the original *argumentum* (23-95), a full sixty-seven chapters (23-89), or almost 92%, are in one way or another concerned with refuting Piso's initial

---

prised: Aebutius' *audacia petulentiaque* and Caecina's steadfastness (cf. 1 ff.), Caecina's fear of seeming to win by trickery (cf. 10), his defense of law against a common threat (cf. 75-76). Cicero's direct address to the *recuperatores* in 103 is further evidence.

[67] There is no evidence that the speech was heavily rewritten for publication: *contra* J. Hombert, *Les Plaidoyers Écrits et les Plaidoires Réelles de Cicéron* (1925) 251; A. Boulanger, (cited n.9) 73 n.3. The question of later editing is closely examined by W. Stroh, *Taxis* 31-54, who discounts its importance. Little depends on the issue.

[68] See at note 10.

[69] Above, at notes 31-41.

[70] See Cicero, *Orat.* 102, quoted in note 6. Cicero precisely describes such a tactical withdrawal in *de Or.* 2.294 (cf. 303).

The Advocates

interpretation of the interdict, particularly as regards the word *deiecisti*. Only four chapters (90-93), nearly 6%, deal with Piso's "fallback position"; while the remainder (94-95) is consigned to the "proof" of Caecina's possession. Cicero's refutation of Piso's initial position is one of the most devastating pieces of rhetoric and reasoning that Cicero ever produced; in a sustained series of brilliant arguments, Cicero utterly annihilates Piso's position on every conceivable ground of law and equity. In the process, Cicero clearly seeks to build up for his client, whose case is in great peril, a reservoir of sympathy and understanding. By contrast, Cicero's refutation of Piso's "fallback position" is curt, highly legalistic, and almost dismissive of Piso's second thoughts. What explains the difference?

We may begin with the refutation of Piso's first position. Cicero's argument rests on two recurrent themes. The first of these themes is the dichotomy between violence and law, *vis* and *ius*. The theme is already sounded in the *exordium*: "this violence which is especially opposed to law" (5: *vis ea quae iuri maxime est adversaria*). In section 33 Cicero asserts that "nothing is so inimical to law as violence" (*nec iuri quicquam tam inimicum quam vis*). This dichotomy, while it perfectly suits the context of the speech, is also a deeply held conviction of Cicero, one that returns in later speeches and philosophical works.[71] On a broader level, it echoes the Praetor's ancient command *vim fieri veto* ("I forbid the use of force"), and more especially it reflects the recent praetorian campaign against random violence.[72] The dichotomy Cicero draws between *ius* and *vis* may be properly designated an ideology, since it hardly begins to describe the complex role played by *vis* within Roman law.[73]

As the speech progresses, Cicero makes clear what he means

[71] E.g., *Sest.* 91-92 (an especially important passage); *Leg.* 3.42.
[72] Cf. L. Labruna, *Vim Fieri Veto* (1971) 10-27; J. Annequin, in *Actes du Colloque sur l'Esclavage* (Ann. Litt. Univ. Besançon, 163; 1974) 214-234.
[73] On *vis* and *ius* in general, see T. Mayer-Maly, *RE* s.v. "vis" (1961) 311-315. On self-help, see *ibid.* 315-323; G. Wesener, in *Fs. Steinwenter* 113-114, 119-120.

118

Cicero's Strategy

by *ius* and *vis*. His great eulogy of the *ius civile* (65-75), which Cicero himself later recognized as one of the most important sections of this speech,[74] describes private law as the unshakeable basis of secure property relationships and an enduring social order (74-75), a view that foreshadows a famous passage in the *de Officiis* (2.72-84).[75] Law arises out of *utilitas communis*, the general welfare; Cicero employs this phrase repeatedly (49, 50, 70).[76] Yet in a curious way it is also divorced from social strife, as a superstratum of enduring principles, institutions, and rules that remain valid despite personal influence or power (71-73). The jurists are the custodians of this law, and to undermine their authority is to weaken law itself (70). By contrast, Cicero understands *vis* as the use of terror for personal advantage; and this terror is not just physical violence itself, but also the psychological threat of physical harm (42-44, 76). The term *vis*, as used in law, means even slight force (47: *pertenuis vis*).[77] Any other interpretation means carnage if men must be physically injured before they can obtain their rights under the interdicts *unde vi* (46-47).

[74] Cic. *Orat.* 102: "ius civile laudavimus." R. Rau, (cited n.7) 181, wrongly emends *laudavimus* to *enodavimus*. On this very important section, see also Chapter IV, at notes 168 ff.

[75] See H.P. Kohns, *Gymnasium* 81 (1974) 494-498. Cf. esp. Cic. *de Or.* 1.188: "Sit ergo in iure civili finis hic: legitimae atque usitatae in rebus causisque civium aequibilitatis conservatio." Similar themes are frequent also in Cicero's speeches; see the numerous passages cited by C.J. Classen, *Latomus* 37 (1978) 614 nn. 54 and 56.

[76] See also 50 ("utilitatem . . . huius interdicti"). The phrase derives from Cicero's rhetorical definition of justice (*Inv.* 2.161): "Justitia est habitus animi communi utilitate conservata suam cuique tribuens dignitatem." Here *utilitas communis* acts as a restraint on formal justice, a common Ciceronian theme. Later writings tend rather to stress *utilitas publica*: T. Mayer-Maly, in *Das Neue Cicerobild* (ed. K. Büchner, 1971) 371-387; H.P. Kohns, (cited n.75) 485-494. On this concept in legal sources, see G. Longo, *Labeo* 18 (1972) 7-71 (esp. 11-15).

[77] Cf. Ulpian, (26 *ad Ed.*) D. 43.16.1.3 ("ad solam atrocem vim pertinet hoc interdictum"); *idem*, D. 43.16.1.29; Paul, *Sent.* 5.6.4. In general, the jurists require more than just "psychological" violence (contrast Cic. *Caec.* 46, 49). See A. Berger, *RE* s.v. "interdictum" (1916) 1677-1678; T. Mayer-Maly, *RE* s.v. "vis" (1961) 327.

The Advocates

Ostensibly, Cicero uses this argument only to rebut Aebutius' observation that no physical harm had in fact come to Caecina (41). But the argument has a larger purpose: to suggest that Caecina and Aebutius are, in their persons, representatives of the two contending forces. From the first sentence of the *exordium* (1) to the last sentences of the *peroratio* (103-104), Caecina is presented as a man quietly pursuing his rights, a man who has no choice but to invoke the interdict (8, 36); while Aebutius is a creature of *audacia, impudentia*, and *petulantia*. The "voice of law" (*vox iuris*) urges Caecina's case, while the "voice of unbridled desire" (*vox libidinis*) favors the view of Aebutius (76-77).[78] Aebutius, who is introduced in the *narratio* simply as an unscrupulous parasite (14), emerges in the argument as a sinister figure whose actions are opposed to *ius* and *aequitas* (33); he is, so to speak, the willful individual, whose deeds, from a social perspective, are disruptive and anarchic.

The argument's second theme, closely related to the first, is the connection between "law on the books" and society. Here the central concept is *aequitas*, a word Cicero uses twenty times in the *pro Caecina*.[79] *Aequitas* has a wide variety of meanings in Latin; but in this speech it is used in a very particular sense, to build a concept of "internal or immanent fairness" that mediates between an abstract, general rule and the concrete, specific case. Through interpretation, it seeks to make possible just decisions that accord with the "sense" of existing legal rules.[80] Cicero summarizes his position at 63: "In these

[78] On the role of law as a curber of unbridled anarchic desire, see also Cic. *de Or.* 1.194. For the contrast between law and *libido* or *cupiditas*: 2 *Verr.* 3.16; *Cluent.* 159; *Pis.* 37, 94.

[79] In the *peroratio* (104), Cicero even refers to "nostra disputatio de aequitate." The manuscripts have *decisio* for *disputatio*; the text was emended by D.R. Shackleton Bailey, *Harv. St. Class. Phil.* 83 (1979) 241 (and cf. *Caec.* 79).

[80] I roughly paraphrase M. Fuhrmann, in *St. Volterra* vol. II 71 (cf. 69-72), who bases his interpretation on F. Pringsheim, *Gesammelte Abhandlungen* vol. I (1961) 160-161. A similar position is taken by G. Ciulei, *L'Équité chez Cicéron* (1972) 53-61. Less useful is P.P. Parpaglia, *Aequitas in Libera Republica* (1973) 124-170. While Cicero normally uses *aequitas* in relation to substantive justice,

Cicero's Strategy

cases, the court is concerned not with mere words, but rather with the situation which these words were placed in the interdict to handle. The intent of their authors was that the consequences of deadly force be undone, and that the doer have no defense."[81]

Cicero's concept of *aequitas* is closely linked to one of the more important rhetorical commonplaces, the *controversia ex scripto et sententia*.[82] This commonplace involves a severe juxtaposition between the actual words of a writing and the orator's sense of what the author meant by his words (Cic. *Inv.* 2.121); rhetorical handbooks offered contrasting arguments in favor of upholding the strict words or preferring the intent.

Cicero's speech draws heavily on the vocabulary, forms of argument, and tactical maneuvers associated with the latter group of arguments.[83] The *verba* and even *litterae*[84] of the interdict provide only "nets" and "snares" (65: *aucupia verborum et litterarum tendiculas*), a "noose" (83: *verbi laqueo*), a "narrow and crooked path" (84: *verborum angustias . . . litterarum angulos*); against such traps, Cicero upholds the "essence" of the

---

he also sometimes employs the word for formal justice: e.g., *Top.* 23 ("valeat aequitas, quae in paribus causis paria iura desiderat"), with B. Riposati, *St. Biondi* vol. II 447-465; M. Herberger, *Dogmatik* (1981) 53-54.

[81] *Caec.* 63: "Verum in his causis non verba veniunt in iudicium, sed ea res cuius causa verba haec in interdictum coniecta sunt. Vim quae ad caput ac vitam pertineret restitui sine ulla exceptione voluerunt."

[82] Cf. Cic. *Inv.* 2.136: "semper is, qui contra scriptum dicet, aequitatis aliquid afferat oportet." See in general Cic. *Inv.* 2.121-143; the arguments *contra scriptum* are given at 2.138-143. The *Rhetor. ad Herenn.*, though its author used similar sources, bases the argument *contra scriptum* on the *aequum et bonum*, a less lofty concept (2.14). The history of the commonplace is obscure, but it appears to have expanded over time, from an original restrictive rule-and-exception framework to a later extensive writing-and-intent framework. Cf. B. Vonglis, *Lettre* 119-133; W. Stroh, *Taxis* 86 n.21, commenting on U. Wesel, (cited n.49) 343-366. Also J. Martin, *Antike Rhetorik* (1974) 46-48; T. Giaro, *Excusatio Necessitatis nel Diritto Romano* (1982) 38-40. The description of the pettifogging *calumniator* in *Caec.* 65 comes from *Rhet. ad Herenn.* 2.14 (or a similar source).

[83] On what follows, see esp. M. Fuhrmann, (cited n.80) 66-70.

[84] Cicero holds that the defendant's whole case "has hidden behind a single letter" (38: "in una littera latuisse"; i.e., *eieci* vs. *deieci*), or behind "a single word" (66: "verbum unum").

law (*res*: 49, 54, etc.), its "sense" (*ratio iuris*: seven times, cf. esp. 78), the "cause of fairness" (*causa aequitatis*: 57, 59, 81), the law's *voluntas* or *consilium* or *sententia* or *auctoritas*. He argues: words are inherently incapable of expressing the entirety of one's intent (esp. 51-52); statutes above all require an extended interpretation (esp. 54-55); it is both *utile* and *honestum* to give them such an interpretation (esp. 76-77); and adherence to the intent of words actually tends to confirm the wisdom and foresight of their authors (34, 40, 86). In accord with handbook recommendations, Cicero demolishes the contrary argument through craftily constructed "analogous cases" (35-39, 89), through attempts to carry literal interpretation *ad absurdum* (51-52), and even through an effort to show that literal interpretation would in fact favor his own side (79-89).

It is plain that Cicero enjoys the high ground of *aequitas* and the spirit of the law. He uses this vantage point in order to launch devastating attacks on a number of Piso's arguments: his theory that there is no legal remedy for the wrong done Caecina (32-40); his argument that Aebutius' act did not constitute *vis* (41-48); his narrow understanding of the concept *deiectio* (49-50, 64-67, 75-77). The final argument in particular is interlarded with lengthy digressions, including a word-by-word examination of the ambiguities in the interdict (55-61),[85] and a general discussion of the jurists and the nature of the *ius civile* (65-75). It slowly becomes plain that Cicero associates Piso's literal interpretations with the violent conduct of Aebutius, and that he regards Aebutius' *vis* as masked and protected by Piso's pedantic insistence on *verba*.[86] By the end of the *argumentum*, the voice of law is heard proclaiming that violence is not only physical but mental, that a person who is prevented from entering is "thrust out" (*deiectus*), and that *res* and *sententia* and *aequitas* ought to prevail. But the voice of unbridled desire (*libido*) states that there is no violence without bloodshed, that there is no *deiectio* unless a person has set foot

[85] This digression is in any case interesting for its extensive interpretations; cf. M. Balzarini, *St. Grosso* vol. I 358-364.
[86] Thus, Cicero's emphasis on "hiding" (see note 84).

Cicero's Strategy

on a place, and that all law should be twisted *verbo ac littera* (76-77). Thus Cicero attempts to link together his two main themes.

Much of this is paralleled in the treatment given to the two jurists in sections 77-81. C. Aquilius Gallus (77-78) is seen as the examplar of a hard-working, public-spirited jurist, "who never separates the *ratio* of the civil law from *aequitas*" (77: *qui iuris civilis rationem numquam ab aequitate seiunxerit*). The other jurist (79-81) takes refuge in legalistic phrases even though he freely admits that the sense of the interdict and *aequitas* are on Cicero's side and that these have usually prevailed in the past. The jurist even goes on to propose that since Caecina was at least "thrust out" from the place where he was then standing (the neighboring farm, or the public way), and since Aebutius has admitted "having restored" Caecina to this place,[87] Aebutius must lose his judicial wager (80). Cicero, while openly protesting the absurdity of this view (81, 85), triumphantly turns it against Piso (82-84). This last flurry forms a bridge to the second portion of Cicero's *argumentum*.

If the defendant is a man of violence and the defendant's advocate a proponent of literalism, Caecina is by contrast a representative of peace and compromise. At the end of his *exordium*, Cicero describes his client as not wishing to seem to have pressed his rights to their limit (10: *laborat A. Caecina ne summo iure egisse . . . videatur*).[88] The phrase *summo iure* suggests extreme insistence on one's legal rights, and recalls Terence's famous line that "extreme law is also often extreme pestilence" (*Heaut.* 796: *ius summum saepe summa est et malitia*).[89] As Cicero's withering attack continues, he makes it increasingly evident that it is Aebutius and Piso who, through their literalism, are guilty of this offense; and finally he states this outright (66).

[87] Cf. 23: "Restituisse se dixit [*scil.* Aebutius]." On this answer see Chapter II, note 64.
[88] This point is reexpressed in the *peroratio* (103).
[89] On the historical development of this ambiguous proverb, see A. Carcaterra, in *St. Volterra* vol. IV 627-666; also M. Fuhrmann, (cited n.80) 72-78.

The Advocates

On the other hand, in a marvelously lucid passage Cicero asserts that Caecina will bear an adverse verdict with equanimity—and that, in such an event, it is the interests of the Roman people, the rights of citizenship, and the property, fortunes, and possessions of everyone which will be cast in doubt (75-76, cf. 103).

By contrast with the impassioned oratory of the first portion of his *argumentum*, Cicero's section *de verbis* (86-95) is calm and collected. Cicero first argues that the word *unde* at the start of the interdict is sufficient to cover not only *deiectio* in the narrow sense preferred by Piso, but also *eiectio* (86-89).[90] Cicero then turns, at long last, to Piso's "fallback position," that *deiectio* demands at a minimum that the person who is "thrust out" must possess at the time (90-93). Cicero answers this argument by observing a lack of parallelism in the interdict *de vi* and the interdict *de vi armata*.[91] The former interdict contains a phrase expressly requiring that the plaintiff have possessed at the time when he was thrust out; while the latter interdict omits this phrase (91). Further, in the former interdict the text goes on to require that the plaintiff's possession be faultless as against the defendant (92). The omission of both requirements from the interdict *de vi armata* must be intentional, intended to strip away possible defenses from a defendant who has used armed violence (93). Therefore Caecina does not need to have possessed in order to use the interdict *de vi armata*; but in any case he had possessed (94-95).

Cicero's brief argument *de verbis* broadly conforms to the handbook recommendations for upholding the letter of the law,[92] though they are reproduced in abbreviated form so as

[90] The argument that *unde* means not only *ex quo* but also *a quo* is rather perfunctory filler.

[91] Cf. Chapter II, at notes 48-49. The interdict *de vi* contains the words "cum ille possideret quod nec vi nec clam nec precario a te possideret"; they are omitted in the interdict *de vi armata*. At 91 and 93, Cicero quotes (in slightly different form) only the words *cum ille possideret*; the remaining words are considered at 92 (*in fine*). Cicero's argument is evaluated in Chapter IV, under subhead "The 'Correct' Interpretation of the Interdict *de Vi Armata*."

[92] See Cic. *Inv.* 2.138-143. Stroh's elaborate argument that Cicero contradicts his earlier position on *verba* (*Taxis* 84-90) strikes me as a bit ingenuous.

Cicero's Strategy

not to detract from his own earlier arguments. Cicero lavishes
praise on the foresight of those who wrote the interdict (86,
93), and shows that they were fully capable of understanding
when to use exceptions (92-93). He even calls upon Piso as
his witness (89), using an analogous case drawn from the first
section of the *argumentum* (35-39).

Curiously, it is only in these final paragraphs of the *argumentum* that Cicero's own interpretation of the interdict finally
emerges. Cicero believes that the interdict applies when a defendant uses armed force either to expel someone from property or to prevent him from entering it; through this interdict,
the defendant, presuming of course that he now possesses the
property, is enjoined to restore it to the aggrieved plaintiff,
the validity of whose own prior claim to possession is not
germane. The defendant's misconduct lies in his reliance on
arms rather than on law in order to determine a question of
possession; owing to this misconduct, he is compelled to forgo
the normal defenses that would be available to him (93). Cicero does not defend this interpretation at any length, nor
does he explore the difficulties it creates.

Cicero's broader strategy in the *pro Caecina* is evidently designed with two main goals. First, he uses Piso's alleged
confession in order to force Piso to undertake the "burden of
proof" (a theme sounded already in section 4): granted that
Aebutius admits having used armed violence to impede Caecina, it is the defendant who must prove that this force was
justified and legal. Second, Cicero wishes to focus on Piso's
initial interpretation of *deiectio*, and to minimize the importance of Piso's "fallback position."[93] For most of the speech,
Cicero essentially treats Piso's initial position as if it were his
only view. Cicero builds around it his great dichotomies of *ius*
and *vis*, *aequitas* and *verba*; he exposes its essentially fallacious
nature and holds it up to ridicule. Piso's "fallback position" is
by contrast treated as if it were just an attempt to sidetrack

[93] This does not mean, however, that Cicero does not have confidence in
his argument against the "fallback position." See Chapter IV, under subhead
"The 'Correct' Interpretation. . . ."

The Advocates

the case, an afterthought born out of desperation (90). Cicero
states: "Count all the flaws in that argument, Piso!" (90: *Nu-
mera quam multa in ista defensione falsa sunt, Piso*). He thereby
suggests that this position is, if anything, even weaker than
Piso's initial one; and that, given time, he could produce arguments against the "fallback position" that are every bit as
devastating as those against Piso's initial view.

Cicero seems to have hoped that the scathing character of
his attack on Piso's initial position would force Piso to spend
time defending both it and himself, and that the *recuperatores*
would bring in a verdict on the basis of Piso's original position, while ignoring the "fallback position." Were Cicero to
fail in both these objectives, he could at least hope for a further adjournment while he summoned up new arguments
against the "fallback position." This strategy was undeniably
a gamble; but Cicero obviously preferred to gamble, rather
than to continue the inconclusive debate about Caecina's alleged property rights.

Cicero later considered his third speech for Caecina a masterpiece of its genre (*Orat.* 102).[94] Ancient critics agreed.
Quintilian refers to or cites the speech some fourteen times,
more than all Cicero's other private orations combined; Julius
Victor, in his *Ars Rhetorica*, cites it nine times, more often
than any other private or public speech. Tacitus names this
speech, along with the *pro Tullio*, as the archetype of Republican judicial oratory (*Dial.* 20.1). Indeed, the *pro Caecina* has
some claim to be considered the most brilliant speech ever
delivered in a private lawsuit, either in the ancient world or
since. As if he could not better his performance, Cicero apparently spoke no more before the private bar.[95]

[94] See L. Laurand, *Études sur le Style des Discours de Cicéron* vol. III (2d ed.
1927) 284-302; A. D'Ors, *Defensa* 10-12. Particularly acute is G.L. Hendrick-
son, *AJPh* 26 (1905) 274: ". . . in fact no one who reads the speech will call
the style simple. Objective it is and pragmatic, but intricate and hard." See
also J.C. Davies, in *Ciceros Literarische Leistung* (ed. B. Kytzler, 1973) 185-188.

[95] W. Stroh, *Taxis* 149-156, tries to date the *pro Roscio Comoedo* to 66, but
he ignores the fact that C. Piso, the *iudex* in that case, was governor of Gaul
in 66-65 (*MRR*). (Stroh's other argument is also wrong: Chapter II, note 74.)

Advocates View the Law: Agonistic Law

Caecina's lawsuit came to center on a disputed question of law: namely, how was the recently introduced interdict *de vi armata* to be interpreted? Cicero and Piso were both willing to submit this question for decision by the *recuperatores*. But how was it possible to be sure what the words of the interdict meant?

The answer is clear and undebatable. Piso and Cicero both recognized the words of the interdict as binding law,[96] but they did not recognize any certain method for determining what this law amounted to. They had no fixed "canons of interpretation." All that rhetoric offered was a loose framework of alternatives for interpretation.

Settled Law vs. Uncertain Law

Cicero is willing to concede that some legal propositions are incontestable; for example, that the birth of a son invalidates a previous will, or that a *sui iuris* woman cannot make a binding stipulation without her tutor's authorization (72).[97] These propositions constitute "the bonds of general welfare and life" (70: *vincula . . . utilitatis vitaeque communis*), and to question them is in effect to undermine law itself. But less clear is how these unassailable propositions can ever be recognized. In the *de Oratore*, a sort of answer is given: they are propositions about which no trial ever arises (1.241), i.e., they are rules of law that are generally observed without ever being contested;[98]

It is more likely that the speech dates to ca. 74 or 73; cf. Chapter I, note 19. On the date, see now J. Axer, *The Style and the Composition of Cicero's Speech 'Pro Roscio Comoedo'* (1979) 54-56.

[96] In Cicero's case, this point requires stress. The basic compatibility between legal positivism and *aequitas* is noted by D. Nörr, *Rechtskritik* 34-40.

[97] Compare the "time-honored" interpretation of *vis* in the interdict *uti possidetis* (*Caec.* 45).

[98] In Quintilian, 12.3.6-7, the *ius certum* is located in statutes and in usage (*aut scripto aut moribus constat*), and discerning it is a matter of cognition and not discovery (*cognitionis . . . non inventionis*) This *ius certum* is distinct from jurists' law, the *ius dubium* which must always be examined through *aequitas*.

The Advocates

and the example, obviously a stereotyped one, is invalidation
of a will owing to the birth of a son. This line of reasoning
suggests that the mere existence of a controversy suffices to
make legal propositions moot—a view adopted also by Quintilian (12.3.8). In any case, Cicero draws a sharp distinction
between the *ius non controversum* (*de Or.* 1.241) and the *ius varium* (*Caec.* 69); one major criterion that he advances for determining the latter category is that authority, especially juristic
authority, can easily be found on either side of the issue (*Caec.*
69; *Mur.* 28; *de Or.* 1.242). By this criterion, the interpretation
of the interdict *de vi armata* constituted *ius varium*, since juristic authority was divided. The reasonable inference is that
the judges therefore had considerable latitude in reaching a
decision.

The Interdict: Words vs. Intent

Despite the undeniable brilliance of Cicero's arguments in favor of the "spirit" of the law, there is not one of his arguments
that would not have been instantly recognizable to his rhetorically educated audience, nor one for which the rhetorical
handbooks did not provide a ready counter. Had Cicero been
obliged to compose an answer to his own speech, he would
have used such weapons without hesitation; he himself had
earlier described how to combat appeals to the higher moral
principle of *aequitas* (*Inv.* 2.135-137). It is wrong, therefore,
to argue that Cicero's arguments define a rhetorical mode of
interpretation set off against the supposedly narrower methods of the jurists.[99] What is more important to observe is that
when Cicero refers to the "will" of the interdict, or even to

On these and similar passages, see A.B. Schwarz, *Fs. Schulz* vol. II 204-211;
W. Kranz, *RbMus* 96 (1953) 190-191. Caecina's case allegedly rests on *ius
certum* (*Caec.* 10).

[99] This was the argument of Johannes Stroux, *Summum Ius Summa Iniura*
(1926), repr. in *Römische Rechtswissenschaft und Rhetorik* (1949) 7-66. See also
M. Gelzer, *Klein Schriften* vol. I (1962) 311: "Die Bedeutung von Ciceros Rede
[*pro Caecina*] für die Rechtsgeschichte liegt darin, dass sie gegenüber den alt-
mödischen *iuris consulti* und ihren Tifteleien über Buchstaben und Wörter die
moderne Lehre von *aequitas* entfaltete." (On the speech, see pp. 305-311; the
article dates from 1958). Most legal historians reject Stroux's extreme views;
see A. Bürge, *Die Juristenkomik in Ciceros Rede* Pro Murena (1974) 46-68.

the "will" of its author (*Caec.* 65: *voluntatem scriptoris*), he does not intend any specific historical "will"; for he adduces no historical information of any kind to back up his claims concerning the interdict's "intent."[100] Rather, he presumes a more general social purpose underlying the Praetor's Edict, a purpose that will not, for instance, leave the victim of armed aggression without legal recourse (36). As Piso argued (34, 41), this intuitive presumption is questionable at best. In any event, it is the sort of presumption that would tend to expand equitable application of law.

Previous Decisions

Cicero argues that a verdict adverse to his client will weaken the force of the interdict *de vi armata* (5, 38-40, 75-77).[101] In what sense is this true? Cicero argues that the verdict will be a signal to others in similar situations, that *deiectio* is to be narrowly interpreted (76); armed violence will in effect be sanctioned by the court's judgment (38), and the decision will become a sort of statute (40: *legem*). Rhetorical theory readily acknowledged previous judicial decisions as valid evidence for law;[102] indeed, Cicero himself uses such a previous decision in his argument on Volaterran citizenship (97). But this commonplace does not quite imply a theory of precedent;[103] for the citation of prior cases is purely informal, and the basic mode of argument seems to be that the previous decision was in fact correct.[104] In any case, evidently neither Cicero nor Piso could appeal to previous decisions on the interdict's interpretation.

[100] Contrast the *pro Tullio* on the *iudicium de vi coactis armatisque hominibus* (7-12) and the interdict *de vi armata* (46)—without concrete evidence, however.

[101] Cicero argues analogously at *Tull.* 36; see also the fragment of this speech in Julius Victor, p. 42 G-C, lines 6 ff. See the interesting discussion of "precedent" in sales law at Cic. *Off.* 3.66-67.

[102] *Rhet. ad Herenn.* 2.19-20, 46; Cic. *Inv.* 1.82-83 and 2.67, 68, 162; *de Or.* 2.116; *Top.* 28. So also *Caec.* 69: "id fuit ius quod iudicatum est." On the rhetorical theory, see L. Vacca, *Contributo allo Studio del Metodo Casuistico* (1976) 57-66.

[103] See M. Kaser, *Fs. Schwind* 115-130.

[104] So, at any rate, *Caec.* 69.

The Advocates

Juristic Decisions

Early Roman rhetorical theory, still heavily influenced by its Greek background, did not recognize juristic opinions as evidence for law.[105] Even developed rhetorical theory held that such *responsa* were mainly a means of proof, a type of evidence. Further, as Cicero maintains in the *de Oratore*, when law is ambiguous, the role played by the jurists is slight, since both sides can usually claim support from some jurist (1.242).[106] In Caecina's lawsuit both sides cited jurists to support their initial positions. But it is noteworthy that, as it seems, neither orator named the jurist he was using; Aquilius' name surfaced only because Piso attacked him by name,[107] doubtless drawing the logical inference from Aquilius' frequent presence at earlier hearings (77). Piso went on to argue that the *recuperatores* need not defer to the jurists' authority, an argument that Cicero says he has frequently heard before in other cases (65, 67). Yet although Cicero rebuts Piso's argument, he also supports the view that an orator should not weaken the authority of the jurists as such, but should rather argue that what they are saying is not in fact the law (68-69).[108] Despite this fact, Cicero does not go out of his way to round up prior juristic authority for his arguments; for instance, he does not cite the

[105] They are not included either in the *Rhet. ad Herenn.* 2.19 or in Cicero, *Inv.* 2.160-162; they were perhaps considered part of custom (cf. *Inv.* 1.14, *de Or.* 1.212, *Part. Orat.* 100). By contrast, juristic opinions are evidence for law in the *de Or.* 2.116 and in the *Top.* 28. Cf. D. Nörr, *Divisio und Partitio* (1972) 10-13; P. Stein, in *Ciceroniana* vol. III (1978) 26-27. Of course, Cicero concedes the general competence of jurists in law even in the *de Inv.* (1.14); but, as Quintilian observes (3.6.57-60), this competence led him to confuse Greek rhetorical theory.

[106] Cf. A. Watson, *Law Making* 103-104, who notes the tendency to "shop" for favorable opinions (Cic. *Fam.* 7.21; Javolenus, D. 28.6.39.2; Alfenus, D. 33.7.16.1). The role of jurists in buttressing orators' cases is described in Cic. *Top.* 65-66. See also A.B. Schwarz, *Fs. Schulz* vol. II 201-225; L. Lombardi, *Saggio* 70; A.A. Schiller. *Mechanisms* 287-288.

[107] *Caec.* 79: "meum auctorem vos pro me appellatis." (On the text see Chapter IV, note 49.) As W. Stroh, *Taxis* 87-88, observes, *vos pro me* should mean "you, not I"; but the rest of Stroh's argument seems wrong.

[108] On this argument see Chapter IV, at notes 168-172.

very expansive definition of *vis* given by Q. Mucius a generation earlier (D. 50.17.73.2, cf. 43.24.1.5), even though this
definition would have supported his position at *Caec.* 47.

The relativistic framework of rhetorical argument had only
marginal room for the notion of an uncontested positive law;[109]
indeed, it tended, within the context of specific cases, to expand the room for controversy, since its arguments and coun-
terarguments could be used to pry apart any notion of legal
fixity. Much of the modern criticism of Cicero's oration for
Caecina involves an appeal to a fixed framework that, for Cicero, virtually did not exist; Cicero simply would not have
understood what was meant by the allegation that he "falsified
the sense of the interdict."[110] The arguments against Cicero's
interpretation of the interdict are, as we shall see in the next
chapter, not entirely unpersuasive; but they are only persuasive, and do not constitute a conclusive proof that the words
of the interdict had a generally recognized "sense" in Cicero's
time, much less that Cicero "falsified" that sense.

In the pleading of cases, Republican private law was dominated by a "strong" form of adversary procedure—the sharp
clash of two competing orators, each of whom strives to advance his client's case at all costs. Yet in Cicero's many works
on oratory there is little trace of an "ideology of advocacy"[111]
that attempts to explain and justify the delicate ethical relationship between an orator, his client, his client's interests,

[109] Cf. P. Stein, (cited n.105) 29: "Thus the advocate can found his argument on any element which is recognized as evidencing what the law is, in
the knowledge that he may be met by a counterargument based perhaps on
a different ground."

[110] W. Stroh, *Taxis* 83: "Es ist offenkundig: Cicero verfälscht den Sinn des
Interdikts *de vi armata*, um von der Frage, ob Caecina *possessor* gewesen sie,
abzulenken." Rather more cautious is G. Nicosia, *Deiectio* 58-59, who argues
that *deiectio* was already a technical concept of dispossession, but that it also
had a more generic meaning not requiring possession; see Chapter IV, at
notes 147 ff.

[111] See W.H. Simon, "The Ideology of Advocacy: Procedural Justice and
Professional Ethics," *Wisconsin Law Review* 29 (1978) 30-144, esp. 34-39. See
also A.H. Goldman, *The Moral Foundations of Professional Ethics* (1980) 90-155;
M. Frankel, *Partisan Justice* (1980).

and the larger aims of the judicial system.[112] Clearly the pursuit of a case did often require an orator to advance well beyond the bounds of everyday morality.[113] But how far beyond? In *Caec.* 28-30 (cf. 73), Cicero subjects Fidiculanius Falcula, a defense witness, to a withering attack because, five years before, he had allegedly taken a bribe in deciding the poisoning trial of Oppianicus; Cicero had previously deplored this notoriously corrupt trial during his prosecution of Verres in 70.[114] But in 66 the exigencies of a different case forced Cicero to defend the verdict in the trial of Oppianicus. On this occasion Cicero takes an entirely different view of Falcula's "guilt" (*Cluent.* 103-104, 112-115). Cicero tries to explain the contradiction. He argues that each of his orations merely reflects its own time, not his beliefs as an orator. "For if cases could speak for themselves, no one would make use of an orator. But we orators are asked to state not what is established by our own authority, but rather what arises out of the situation and the case."[115] For the orator, the case should be everything.

To be sure, Cicero's attitudes on this subject are more than a little ambiguous. At times he advances a higher vision of the orator defending truth above all, while at other times he takes a more cynical (or realistic) stance.[116] His higher vision may perhaps be defended through reference to Aristotle's view that a kind of truth can emerge from contrary argument;[117]

[112] See, e.g., C. Neumeister, *Grundsätze der Forensischen Rhetorik* (1964) 15-17. The main source is Cic. *Off.* 2.51; on unworthy clients, see also *Cluent.* 57 and *Sull.* 81.

[113] Cf. Cicero, *de Or.* 1.227-233 and 2.30; also *Off.* 2.51. Compare Gellius, *NA* 1.6.4 (lawyers must even lie in their clients' defense), with Quintil. 2.17.21 (Cicero's boast that he had confused the judges in his speech *pro Cluentio*). Quintilian (12.1) has a protracted discussion of "good men" and "bad men" as orators; see esp. 33-45 on defending guilty clients.

[114] Cicero, 1 *Verr.* 38-40.

[115] *Cluent.* 139: "Nam si causae ipsae pro se loqui possent, nemo adhiberet oratorem. Nunc adhibemur ut ea dicamus, non quae auctoritate nostra constituantur sed quae ex re ipsa causaque ducantur." Cf. 140-142.

[116] See in general A. Michel, *Rhétorique et Philosophie chez Cicéron* (1960), esp. 158 ff.

[117] See for instance Aristotle, *Rhet.* 1.1 (1355 a 37), 1.2 (1355 b 25); *Top.* 1.2 (101 a 34). Cicero hints at this idea in *Off.* 2.51. The Aristotelian "prin-

nor would Cicero want to overlook the duty of the eloquent to defend their friends from peril.[118] But Cicero's more cynical view is not substantially different from the modern "principle of partisanship," which requires that a "lawyer work aggressively to advance his client's ends. The lawyer will employ means on behalf of his client which he would not consider proper in a non-professional context even to advance his own ends. These means may involve deception, obfuscation, or delay."[119]

As Cicero remarks at the outset of his earliest study of rhetoric, we cannot know for certain whether eloquence has brought more good or evil to the world (*Inv.* 1.1); and the relationship between *eloquentia* and *sapientia* would continue to trouble him the rest of his life.[120] Nor is it easy to assess accurately the effects of rhetorical advocacy upon the Roman judicial system.[121] Within trials themselves, the art of rhetoric tended to consider the issues raised by cases not from a narrowly defined legalistic perspective, but rather on a broader "agonistic" plane.[122] Rhetoric used the case only as a starting point for its expansive techniques. Cicero's *pro Caecina*, with its lofty dichotomies of *ius* and *vis*, *verba* and *voluntas*, shows this tech-

---

ciple of procedural justice" is normally used to defend modern American advocacy: W.H. Simon, (cited n.111) 38.

[118] See Cic. *Off.* 2.65-66; and in general W. Neuhauser, *Patronus und Orator* (1958). For the advocate as *amicus*, see Cic. *Tull.* 5. Similar ideas are still floated today: C. Fried, *Yale Law Journal* 85 (1976) 1060-1089, with the critique by E.A. Dauer and A.A. Leff, *Yale Law Journal* 86 (1977) 573-584.

[119] W.H. Simon, (cited n.111) 36. A canon of ethics, usually originating from the profession, tries to set limits on the modern lawyer's partisanship. Cf. Valentinian, C. 2.6.6.1 (A.D. 368), who states that advocates should do what the case demands, but avoid defamation. See also Quintil. 12.9.8 ff.

[120] See, e.g., E. Gilson, *Phoenix* 7 (1953) 1-19; G. Pugliese, in *Scr. Iemolo* (1963) 561-587.

[121] In particular, one must suppose that at least the rhetorically educated audience (including the judges) knew how to discount rhetorical argument even as they enjoyed it. Modern readers perhaps tend to take Roman rhetoric too seriously.

[122] See D. Nörr, in *Fs. Felgentraeger* (1969) 353-366. This observation is commonly made of Greek private trials; see the references in G. Thür, *Beweisführung vor den Schwurgerichtshöfen Athens* (1977) 315 n.1. For Rome, see esp. Cic. *de Or.* 2.178, 182-187.

nique clearly; Caecina's lawsuit has become, by the end of the speech, the "common cause and right of the Roman people" (*Caec.* 103: *communem causam populique Romani ius*).[123] The process continues even in points of detail: Caecina is personally a finer man than Aebutius (e.g., 23, 104); Aebutius' witnesses are contemptible scum even though they support Caecina's case (24-31); Aquilius Gallus is a wiser jurist than the pettifogger used by Piso (77-80); Piso himself is slow-witted in argument (67, 98); and so on. Piso's speech will have inverted Cicero's framework on a point-by-point basis. In this global duel of irreconcilable social forces, the narrower legal issue (the proper interpretation of the interdict) is all but swallowed up in a host of larger issues. Cicero seeks to establish his position as a coherent whole to be thrown up against his opponent's position as a coherent whole.[124]

Such an "agonistic" view of legal cases undeniably tended to obscure, corrode, and weaken the independent force of law within the late Republican judicial system. It was a matter of some controversy just how much law orators had to know—enough at any rate not to appear foolish in court or jeopardize their cases, but little more seems to have been normal.[125] Even orators who favored more detailed knowledge of law (and Cicero, who had studied with two well-known jurists, was among them[126]) nevertheless tended to regard the jurists and their legal science as largely an epiphenomenon to the judicial sys-

---

[123] In this text, *Romani* was rightly inserted by early editors on the strength of the parallel passage in 76.

[124] See G. Pugliese, (cited n.5) 398-399; M. Kaser, *RZ* 277.

[125] Compare Cic. *de Or.* 1.165-200, with 234-250; on the aporetic structure of *de Or.* 1, see A.D. Leeman, *Hom. K. Kumaniecki* (1975) 140-149. See now F. Bona, *SDHI* 46 (1980) 296-332. The *locus classicus* for rhetorical criticism of legal science is Cicero's *pro Murena*, 19-30, on which see A. Bürge, (cited n.99), with the review by D. Nörr, *SZ* 92 (1975) 290-293; also D. Nörr, *Rechtskritik* 84-87.

[126] Cicero studied with Q. Mucius Scaevola, the Augur, from ca. 90 until his death in 88 (Cic. *Lael.* 1, *Leg.* 1.13, *Brut.* 306, *Phil.* 8.31); and then with his homonymous cousin the Pontifex, killed in 82 (Cic. *Leg.* 2.47, 49; *Lael.* 1). On Cicero's own, not inconsiderable knowledge of law, see A. Bürge, (cited n.99) 31-45; on his continuing interest in it, *Leg.* 1.13. On the need for an orator to know some law, see esp. Cic. *de Or.* 1.173; *Brut.* 322; *Orat.* 120.

tem. Faced already with the task of mastering a formidable body of rhetorical lore, Republican orators regarded legal science as a late-formed and poorly organized field[127] that did not repay the effort, slight though it might be, of closer examination. When a particular case demanded special knowledge of some highly technical question, it was enough to ask a jurist for help.[128] To this extent, the corps of orators remained somewhat insulated from the developing legal science, and as yet did not constitute a profession of lawyers in the modern sense. Thus, juristic opinions filtered into trials through non-professional (and generally unsympathetic) channels.

As a youth, Cicero was deeply impressed by a famous lawsuit that almost perfectly embodied the problems faced by developing legal science in its conflict with rhetorical advocacy. This was the *causa Curiana*, argued before the centumviral court in the late 90's. Coponius had died, leaving a will in which he had written: "If one or more offspring be born to me, let him be my heir. . . . If my offspring dies before reaching the age of majority, let M.' Curius be my heir."[129] Coponius left no posthumous offspring. Curius claimed his estate as the substitute heir; but M. Coponius, the heir upon intestacy, argued that the institution of Curius was invalid because no

[127] Cic. *Mur.* 25: "tenuis scientia"; cf. *de Or.* 1.246. The jurists make large claims, but spend their time on trivial matters: *Leg.* 1.14. At his most extreme (e.g., *de Or.* 1.236), Cicero reduces jurists to little more than notaries; and he usually links them closely with cautelary activity (e.g., *de Or.* 1.212). Cicero had strong (and not uninteresting) views on the need for systematically organizing law; see Chapter IV, at notes 129-133.

[128] Cicero, *Part. Orat.* 99-100, suggests that orators should at least have (though most did not) a knowledge of procedural technicalities; but he sees these issues as separable from the main business of trials. Contrast the views of the Augur Scaevola in Cic. *de Or.* 1.167; of Q. Mucius in Pompon. D. 1.2.2.43; and even of Cicero (in the guise of Crassus), *de Or.* 1.173, 184.

[129] Cic. *Inv.* 2.122: "Si mihi filius genitur unus pluresve, is mihi heres esto. . . . Si filius ante moritur, quam in suam tutelam venerit, tum mihi . . . <scil. M.' Curius> heres esto." Somewhat differently, *de Or.* 2.141. The major sources are Cicero's *rhetorica*: *Inv.* 2.122; *de Or.* 1.180, 238, 242-244 and 2.24, 140-141, 220-222; *Brut.* 144-145, 194-198, 256; *Top.* 44. For recent accounts of the trial, see F. Wieacker, *Irish Jurist* 2 (1967) 151-164; R.A. Bauman, *Lawyers* 341-351 (too speculative); and bibliography cited below. See also now J.W. Tellegen, *RIDA³* 30 (1983) 293-311, unconvincing.

child had been born and, hence, the will's condition had not been met. Curius was represented by the famous orator L. Licinius Crassus, who relied on citations from the writings of his father-in-law, the jurist Q. Mucius Scaevola (the Augur);[130] but Crassus' main argument was built on his defense of the testator's presumed, but poorly expressed, intent. On behalf of the intestate heir, the written word was defended by the eminent jurist Q. Mucius Scaevola (the Pontifex, a cousin of the Augur). Curius prevailed.

The trial was famous, but its implications were shrouded in ambiguity.[131] Both sides cited the verdict in Caecina's lawsuit. Cicero used the trial as an example of interpretation based upon intent prevailing over a narrowly literal reading of the will (*Caec.* 53, 67, 69); Piso adduced it as evidence that the opinion of a jurist had no binding power on a court (67). Either view can be maintained. But perhaps more crucial is Cicero's observation in the *de Oratore* (1.244) that Scaevola's argument in this case was essentially only a handbook rehash of the rhetorical defense of *scriptum*, and not an exercise in abstract jurisprudence.[132] Certainly there is no reason to regard this trial as a victory of oratory over jurisprudence.[133]

[130] Cic. *de Or.* 1.242 (cf. 1.180); *Caec.* 69. It is doubtful that these citations concerned the issue at hand, rather than the general role of a testator's *voluntas*. Crassus also seems to have attacked the pretensions of the jurist: *de Or.* 2.24; *Brut.* 198.

[131] The technical legal question raised by this case is this: does a pupillary substitution (provision for a second heir in the event the first heir dies before puberty) include by implication a "vulgar" substitution (provision for a second heir in case the first cannot inherit)? The point continued to be disputed and was ultimately settled by a constitution of M. Aurelius: Modestinus, D. 28.6.4 pr. Cf. M. Kaser, *RPR*² vol. I 690; vol. II 494 n.35. G.L. Falchi, *SDHI* 46 (1980) 383-430, is certainly wrong to suppose that the *causa Curiana* turned entirely on jurisprudential issues and did not involve topical argumentation; see, by way of contrast, H.J. Wieling, *Testamentsauslegung in Römischem Recht* (1972) 9-15.

[132] See A. Watson, *Law Making* (1974) 122-133, esp. 129-131; but also R.A. Bauman, *Lawyers* 349-351. Q. Mucius also produced *responsa*, from his father (Cic. *Brut.* 197).

[133] For instance, Crassus also argued in favor of a narrow interpretation of law in the case described by Cicero, *Off.* 3.67. J. Stroux's notorious interpre-

The *causa Curiana* does, however, suggest one way in which the rhetorical advocacy of Roman courts did positively influence a developing legal science, at least in the long run. Rhetorical advocacy should probably not be thought of primarily as a direct source of law or of legal method (for law and rhetoric were fundamentally irreconcilable), but rather as an obstacle that nevertheless necessitated deep changes in law if it was to be overcome.[134] In this sense rhetoric became an indirect source of law. The jurists, in wrestling with the materials of law, could not wholly neglect the context within which law would be applied. The orator's duty was to persuade; and in order to persuade, he founded his case on generally prevailing or appealing social values.[135] But one of these values was also "legal security"—certainty as to the content of law, its recognizability, and its predictability.[136] Cicero himself understood the persuasiveness of this value and its close relation to the work of the jurists (*Caec.* 70-75). But juristic opinions, if they were to be judicially acceptable, could not *simply* emanate from the *auctoritas* of their creators. They had to be not only "right" from a formal viewpoint, but also (at least in general) defensible against objections from non-formal viewpoints (Cic. *Mur.* 29). Even Q. Mucius Scaevola could not bring it about that a testator's words be strictly followed, if such a result seemed blatantly to contradict a socially defined "common sense." Legal science must rest on broader foundations.[137]

The Ciceronian court, with its shameless tattoo of *loci communes*, formed nonetheless an indispensable laboratory where Rome's fledgling legal scientists could create and test their

---

tation of the *causa Curiana* (above, note 99) has been generally rejected; cf. F. Serrao, (cited n.17) 142-148.

[134] On the interrelationship between law and rhetoric, see A. Bürge, (cited n.99) 46-48.

[135] See Cic. *Part. Orat.* 90: "non ad veritatem solam, sed etiam ad opiniones eorum qui audiunt accommodanda est oratio. . . . "

[136] F. Schulz, *Principles* 239.

[137] This point underlies the famous story of the farmer who obtained from the jurist P. Crassus (cos. 131) a "responsum . . . verum magis quam ad suam rem accommodatum"; Crassus was talked out of his view by the orator Galba (Cic. *de Or.* 1.239-240). On the story, see F. Bona, *SDHI* 39 (1973) 426-449.

abstract rules in relation both to specific cases and community values.[138] Within the judicial system, jurists could witness new legal problems constantly arising and new legal ideas being struck off in the heat of controversy. Simultaneously, they were allowed to see something of their rules at work. It seems reasonable to discover, within the intensely competitive arena of forensic discussion, many of the impulses toward breadth and equity which gave to Roman private law its vitality as a living system and its vast influence as a dead one.

[138] See G. Broggini, *Coniectanea* (1966) 305-329, esp. 315-318; B.W. Frier, *LTIR* 203.

IV

The Jurists:
C. Aquilius Gallus and *Ignotus*

nihil hoc ad ius; ad Ciceronem
—Aquilius Gallus

AQUILIUS' NAME turns up twice in the *pro Caecina*. The first
time is at 77-79, where he is eulogized by Cicero for his juristic qualities and described as the "authority" for Cicero's
argument (79: *auctorem nostrae defensionis*). The second time is
in a troubled passage in the middle of 95, as Cicero concludes
his "proof" of Caecina's possession (94-95). The text reads:

> Ipse porro Caecina cur se moribus deduci volebat idque tibi
> de amicorum †de his de Aquilii† sententia responderat.[1]

Caecina proposed a *deductio* after consulting with a *consilium*
of his *amici* (20: *de amicorum sententia*). In Cicero's second report of the consultation, the manuscript archetype evidently
preserved some words between *amicorum* and *sententia*. For the
obelized words, one family of manuscripts has the nonsensical
reading *de his de quibus*; the other has either *de his de Aquilii* or
de his qui de Aquilii. While the archetype was obviously difficult to read at this point, the original manuscript may have
had something like *de huius quidem Aquili*.[2] In any case, nothing warrants deleting Aquilius' name from the text of section

---

[1] To this sentence the manuscripts add either *esse equum, et aequum, et acu*
or *et ad eum*. Most editors delete the words as dittography of *at enim* directly
following.

[2] So F.L. Keller, *Sem.* 524 n.405 (at 525).

The Jurists

95.[3] So Aquilius not only participated on Cicero's side in the trial, but he had also advised Caecina from an early point in his dispute with Aebutius.

In this chapter I explore the changing role of "legal experts" in the judicial system of the late Republic. The first section is devoted to more traditional "cautelary jurisprudence," while the second examines the new legal science of Q. Mucius and his followers. The third section discusses the "correct" solution to the major legal problem raised by Cicero's *pro Caecina*. A final section deals with the doctrine of "autonomous law," which to our knowledge is first enunciated in the *pro Caecina* and which became the guiding ideology of the classical Roman jurists.

C. Aquilius Gallus: *Illud Suum Regnum Iudiciale*

Late Republican jurisprudence has two sharply different aspects.[4] The first might be thought of as its "external" aspect—cautelary jurisprudence,[5] the communication of informed pronouncements or advice on law to petitioners who are ignorant or uncertain about legal rules. This "external" aspect, the subject of the present section, was traditionally associated with the desire of upper-class jurists to win friends and secure for

[3] As do the editions of A. Boulanger and A. D'Ors. C.A. Jordan, *Oratio* 280-281, argues that if Aquilius had in fact been advising Caecina so early, Cicero would have mentioned this fact at *Caec.* 20; but this need not follow, since it would be awkward to introduce Aquilius' name before the eulogy of him in 77-79. See also Chapter III, at notes 67-68, where I argue that the *narratio* was added to the published speech.

[4] On the general activities of late Republican jurists, it suffices to refer to A. Watson, *Law Making* 101-110.

[5] The nature of cautelary jurisprudence is discussed by F. Cancelli, *St. Volterra* vol. V 611-645, esp. 644-645; see also M. Bretone, in *Lineam.* 336-339. R.A. Bauman, *Lawyers*, discusses the major cautelary jurists up to Q. Mucius at length. Cic. *de Or.* 3.133-135 gives an especially vivid picture of the practice in the second century B.C.; and see Horace, *Sat.* 2.1, with E. Fraenkel, *Horace* (1957) 147-153; Macrob. *Sat.* 2.6.1-2. Note that *responsa* were often given in public (e.g., Ovid, *Ars Am.* 1.83-84); this is the *disputatio fori* of Pomponius, D. 1.2.2.5, cf. Cic. *Top.* 56, 66, 72. Second-century *iurisconsulti* often acted as advocates also.

themselves elective office; as a form of patronage, it first appeared in Rome during the third century B.C.

The second aspect is "internal," the development of methods for working with legal materials—what comes to be called the science (*scientia*) or art (*ars*) of law. This "internal" aspect of jurisprudence originated at a much later date, especially as a result of the writing and teaching of Q. Mucius Scaevola (cos. 95); I will deal with it at length in the second section of this chapter. My general contention is that during the late Republic the "internal" aspect of legal science steadily gained strength at the expense of the "external" aspect, until the communication of law came to be thought of as only an ancillary part of a jurist's duties, while legal science was increasingly looked upon as a study of value in itself.

C. Aquilius Gallus' family derived from southern Latium[6] but had very early established itself at Rome. In 176 L. Aquilius Gallus was Praetor in Sicily (Livy, 41.14.5, 15.5). But the jurist's branch of the family emerges only in his own generation, unless indeed it was the jurist's father who testified against a rapacious governor in the late second century.[7] The jurist was Praetor with Cicero in 66 and so was probably born ca. 110. Pliny (*NH* 17.2) notes the jurist's elaborate house on the Viminal, and in passing calls Gallus an *eques Romanus*.[8] The origin of his wealth is unknown,[9] but Cicero (*Quinct.* 17) at-

[6] R. Syme, *Historia* 13 (1964) 111-112, arguing from the family's probable enrollment in the Pomptine tribe, suggests Ulubrae as the hometown, and also notes links with Lanuvium; but Circeii is not impossible, cf. note 45. The relation of the Aquilii Galli to C. Aquilius Florus (cos. 259) and the M.' Aquilii (coss. 129, 101) is unknown.

[7] See Cicero, *de Or.* 2.265 (*Gallus*), with E. Badian, *Gnomon* 33 (1961) 495-496; E. Gruen, *Roman Politics and the Criminal Courts* (1968) 133-134. The witness may have been an equestrian merchant.

[8] C. Nicolet, *Ordre* vol. II 783-784.

[9] C. Gallus, a Senator and *vir primarius*, turns up as one of Verres' victims in Sicily (Cic. 2 *Verr.* 3.152-153). Some have thought he was the jurist: e.g., E. Badian, (cited n.7) 496; T.P. Wiseman, *New Men* 281. But against this are both the nomenclature (Cicero elsewhere hardly ever omits the nomen) and the circumstances of Cicero's anecdote. C. Gallus is more probably a relative, perhaps the father of P. Aquilius Gallus trib. in 55.

tests a link of *necessitudo* between the jurist and another equestrian family from southern Latium, the Quinctii Scapulae;[10]
in fact, a certain P. Quinctius Scapula had dropped dead while
seated at Aquilius' dining table (Pliny, *NH* 7.183). The date
of the jurist's death is uncertain, but must be after 56 (Cic.
Att. 4.12; *Balb.* 45) and before 44, when he is referred to as
deceased (Cic. *Top.* 51). In 44 Cicero's brother was contem-
plating marriage to a wealthy heiress named Aquilia (Cic. *Att.*
14.13.5).

Longstanding tradition held that a young man in search of
advancement should excel in at least one of three fields: law,
oratory, or the military.[11] In Rome of the 90's, an ambitious
youth, if he was disinclined to command legions, might nonetheless hesitate between law and oratory. During the century
from 201 to 95 B.C., some fifteen known *iurisconsulti* had reached
the consulate, and four the censorship.[12] Most of these men
had also the advantage of noble descent; but in 104 the *novus
homo* C. Flavius Fimbria, whose abilities both in oratory and
civil law were not negligible (Cic. *Brut.* 129), finally fought
his way through to the consulate, and C. Billienus, another
novus homo with legal knowledge, might well have made it had
Marius not monopolized the consulate for several years (*ibid.*
175).[13] The close relationship between the giving of legal *responsa* and the hope of political advancement is confirmed in a
curious anecdote about the late second-century jurisconsult C.

[10] Equestrian according to Dio 43.29.3; see C. Nicolet, *Ordre* vol. II 998-
999.
[11] This triad is found in Livy 39.40.5. Also in Ovid, *Am.* 1.15.3-6; Tac.
Dial. 28.6 and *Ann.* 4.6.2. Cf. Hor. *Ep.* 1.3.23-25. The three careers are
expressly contrasted in Cic. *Mur.* 24 ff. On the giving of legal *responsa* as a
means to increase one's wealth and influence, and on the eminence of second-
century jurisconsults, see Cic. *de Or.* 1.198 and *Off.* 2.65. As R. Syme, *The
Roman Revolution* (1939) 374, remarks, excellence in the favored fields rarely
sufficed in itself, absent noble birth or chance.
[12] W. Kunkel, *Herkunft*[2] 41.
[13] On Fimbria and Billienus, see W. Kunkel, *Herkunft*[2] 16-18; T.P. Wiseman, *New Men* 119.

C. Aquilius Gallus

Marcius Figulus, who brusquely ceased giving *responsa* after his bid for the consulate failed (Val. Max. 9.3.2).[14]

In the 90's, two Mucii Scaevolae largely dominated Roman jurisprudence, as if by family tradition (Cic. *de Or.* 1.39, 244).[15] The older of the two, Q. Mucius Q.f. Scaevola, was Consul in 117 and an Augur.[16] Cicero, after assuming the *toga virilis* in 90, studied with this Scaevola until his death in 88. Cicero often recalls him in later writings, particularly in book 1 of the *de Oratore*, where he is made to present his views on both rhetoric and law.[17] The Augur was in many ways typical of an older generation of jurists; gruff and plain-spoken, he regarded legal science as a simple discipline (*de Or.* 1.185),[18] and he confined his legal work to the giving of *responsa*.[19] His son-in-law, L. Licinius Crassus (cos. 95), was a distinguished orator whose considerable legal expertise (Cic. *Brut.* 145; Pompon., D. 1.2.2.40) was limited to the pleading of cases.[20] The young Cicero was dazzled by the constant stream of distinguished visitors in Scaevola's home (*de Or.* 1.200; cf. Plut. *Cic.* 3.2). The Augur gave no formal lessons, but simply allowed young men to attend as he responded to petitioners (Cic. *Brut.*

[14] Compare the *responsum* that P. Crassus gave during his campaign for the aedileship (Cic. *de Or.* 1.239-240).

[15] To the Mucii Scaevolae discussed below must be added P. Licinius Crassus Mucianus, born a brother of the Consul in 133. On his legal expertise: Cic. *de Or.* 1.170, 216, 239-240 and *Brut.* 98, 127; Pompon. D. 1.2.2.40. Note Mucianus' definition of an ideal citizen, in Gell. *NA* 1.13.10: "ditissimus, nobilissimus, eloquentissimus, iuris consultissimus, pontifex maximus." On the family, see R.A. Bauman, *Lawyers* 225-423.

[16] Sources for his life in F. Münzer, *RE* s.v. "Mucius" (1933) 430-436; see also R.A. Bauman, *Lawyers* 312-340.

[17] See F. Bona, *SDHI* 46 (1980) 332-351.

[18] See Cic. *Balb.* 45, whence Val. Max. 8.12.1. Cf. Cic. *Mur.* 28.

[19] Cic. *de Or.* 1.200; *Brut.* 306; *Balb.* 45; *Phil.* 8.31; *et al.* No fragments survive.

[20] In the *de Oratore* (1.165-200), Crassus strongly defends the view that an orator must know the law, though he also believes that law is largely the handmaiden of oratory (cf. 1.66 with 1.75). Note that Crassus was self-taught in law (*Off.* 2.47) and declined to give *responsa* (*Brut.* 155).

The Jurists

306);[21] his "students" were similar to Cicero, all destined for public affairs rather than for careers as jurists.[22]

Q. Mucius P.f. Scaevola,[23] Consul in 95 and a Pontifex, was the Augur's cousin, but a good deal younger. Son of the man who, it is claimed, had helped to found the *ius civile* as a coherent discipline (Pompon., D. 1.2.2.39), the Pontifex is the first in a rising generation that prized a far more deliberate mastery of legal materials, without at the same time abandoning pursuit of a political career. In the next section I will discuss Q. Mucius' writings in more detail, particularly his eighteen-book commentary on the *ius civile*. Although Q. Mucius was reputedly a far more gifted orator than his cousin the Augur, nonetheless he seems largely to have shied away from the civil bar—the *causa Curiana* being the only known exception (and an embarrassing one).[24] His famed personal temperance and rectitude also strongly marked his distinguished public career.[25] Only in his students was he perhaps

[21] This was normal for early legal education: Cic. *Orat.* 142-143; P. Jörs, *Rechtsw.* 231-238; F. Schulz, *Legal Science* 56-58. On the importance of such apprenticeship in Roman education, see esp. W. Steidle, *Mus. Helv.* 9 (1952) 11 ff. On Cicero and Scaevola, see K.A. Neuhausen, *WS* 13 (1979) 76-87. Servius is the earliest jurist to develop a more deliberate legal education; see note 116.

[22] Among them: M.' Acilius Glabrio, cos. 67 (Cic. *Brut.* 239; 2 *Verr.* 1.52); P. Sulpicius Rufus, trib. 88 (Cic. *de Or.* 1.66; *Brut.* 203), and perhaps his son Ser. Rufus, cos. 51 (cf. Cic. *Brut.* 150-151; *Fam.* 4.3.3), obviously before the latter had decided on jurisprudence (see below); and probably T. Pomponius Atticus (cf. Cic. *Leg.* 1.13). To this group should perhaps be added C. Visellius Aculeo, Cicero's relative and a close friend of L. Crassus (on his legal knowledge: Cic. *de Or.* 1.191, 2.2; *Brut.* 264), and perhaps also the civil advocate Q. Lucretius Vespillo (*Brut.* 178).

[23] See in general G. Lepointe, *Quintus Mucius Scaevola* vol. I (1926), rather superficial; F. Münzer and B. Kübler, *RE* s.v. "Mucius" (1933) 437-446; R.A. Bauman, *Lawyers* 340-421; and other bibliography cited below.

[24] His eloquence: Cic. *de Or.* 1.170, 180; *Brut.* 163 (which indicates that he published his speeches). On the *causa Curiana* see Chapter III, at notes 129-133. On his speech in defense of Rutilius Rufus *de repetundis*, see Cicero, *de Or.* 1.229 and *Brut.* 115.

[25] His reorganization of the provincial edict for Asia, probably in 94, deserves particular mention. For sources, see F. Münzer, (cited n.23) 438-439; E. Badian, *Publicans and Sinners* (1972) 89-91; R.A. Bauman, *Lawyers* 382-400.

C. Aquilius Gallus

unlucky; with one exception, they were somewhat dry and
bookish men who in the end made little impression either in
law or in public life.[26] The exception is C. Aquilius Gallus.
(See Table 2.)

While the differences between the dilettantish Augur and
the more systematic Pontifex do not quite amount to a dichotomy, the two Mucii Scaevolae are at least representative
of diverse streams in early-first-century jurisprudence.[27] C.
Aquilius' decision to attach himself to the Pontifex is not likely
to have been accidental; for Aquilius appears never to have
spoken in public,[28] and he built his reputation entirely around
cautelary jurisprudence. In 82 B.C. his teacher fell a tragic
victim to the murderous rampages of civil war.[29] In the following decade, during the Sullan restoration, Aquilius swiftly
emerged as the foremost jurist at Rome.[30] By the time of Caecina's lawsuit, his position was preeminent. Cicero's eulogy

His extreme rectitude often exceeded the legal minimum for conduct: Cic.
Off. 3.62-63; Val. Max. 4.1.11; *et al.*
[26] Besides Aquilius, Pomponius (D. 1.2.2.42) names L. Lucilius Balbus
(Stoic: Cic. *de Or.* 3.78; learned but slow: *Brut.* 154; Aquilius' *adsessor* in 81:
Quinct. 53-54); Sex. Papirius (otherwise unknown); and C. Juventius (probably in fact T. Juventius, a dry orator learned in law: Cic. *Brut.* 178). Pomponius indicates that their names were known only through Servius' writings;
none is cited in the *Digest.* To this list can be added Volcatius (or Volcacius,
cf. Chapter VI, note 55), Cascellius' teacher (Pliny, *NH* 8.40), on the strength
of Pompon. D. 1.2.2.45 (where Mommsen emended the text to read *Quinti
Mucii auditoris Volcatii auditor*). Cf. W. Kunkel, *Herkunft²* 20 n.39; but also P.
Jörs, *RE* s.v. "Cascellius" (1899) 1635-1636, who favors *Quinti Mucii et Volcatii
auditor*, probably rightly. Cicero also studied with the Pontifex after the death
of the Augur (*Lael.* 1; *et al.*).
[27] In any case, it seems wrong to call the Mucii Scaevolae a "school": *contra*
M. Bretone, in *Ciceroniana* 3 (1978) 48-52, see R.A. Bauman, *Lawyers* 421-
423.
[28] Thus, in the *Brutus* he is mentioned not as an orator, but as a jurist
(154).
[29] Of the numerous sources, the most moving is the earliest: Cic. *Rosc. Am.*
33. On his later years, see R.A. Bauman, *Lawyers* 400-421.
[30] As Pomponius, D. 1.2.2.49, observes, "ante tempora Augusti . . . qui
fiduciam studiorum suorum habebant, consulentibus respondebant." I.e.,
anyone could give *responsa* with no prior training. On legal quackery, cf. Cic.
Orat. 145 ("At ius profitentur etiam qui nesciunt") and *Planc.* 62.

Table 2
The Main Lines of the Late Republican Juristic Tradition

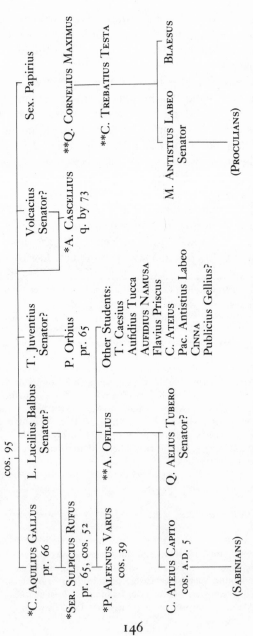

NOTE: This diagram describes the relationships between teachers and students during the late Republic; the main source is Pomponius, D. 1.2.2.41 ff. Names of jurists are capitalized if later sources attest their legal views. An asterisk before the name indicates that the jurist is known to have been equestrian or of equestrian origin; two asterisks mean that the jurist remained equestrian. A few jurists whose teachers and students are unknown have been omitted. The teacher of Q. Cornelius Maximus is unknown, but may have been Quintus Mucius or one of his students.

146

C. Aquilius Gallus

of Aquilius (*Caec.* 77-78) lays particular emphasis on his native justice, his strong belief in the relationship between the *iuris civilis ratio* and *aequitas*, and his accessibility.[31] Cicero's later remembrance in the *Brutus* (154) stresses his swiftness and sureness *in agendo et in respondendo*. Likewise, the jurist Ser. Sulpicius Rufus, his friend and student, attests Aquilius' immense influence *apud populum*.[32]

Aquilius left no systematic writings, or at any rate none that survived into the Empire; his holdings are only indirectly transmitted through juristic tradition.[33] As Cicero suggests, most of his work involved either *responsa* or more informal legal advice, such as that he gave to Caecina (*Caec.* 95); his role was in this respect already established by 81 (*Quinct.* 53; cf. *Balb.* 45). Aquilius, who plainly enjoyed the bustle of courts,[34] not only attended trials (*Caec.* 77), but also presided as a judge; in 81 he was the *iudex* in the lawsuit against Quinctius (Gell. *NA* 15.28.3),[35] and he also presided over a bizarre and poorly understood trial described by Valerius Maximus (8.2.2).[36] Both lawsuits hinged on highly technical procedural questions, with which Aquilius was obviously comfortable. His name is associated with a new method for novating debt

[31] This last was an important quality, since *responsa* were often given in the open Forum; cf. note 5.

[32] Pompon. D. 1.2.2.42. Too much is made of this phrase by F. D'Ippolito, *I Giuristi e la Città* (1978) 14-15. Servius' praise is perhaps slightly ironic; but Valerius Maximus (8.2.2) also names Aquilius a *vir magnae auctoritatis*.

[33] Pompon. D. 1.2.2.42. Of the twelve *Digest* fragments in Lenel, *Pal.* I 56, Aquilius' name is coupled with Servius' in three (nos. 7, 9, 10), with Ofilius' in three (nos. 5, 7, 9), and with Trebatius' in one (no. 5). Most of these decisions appear to be *responsa*.

[34] As did many jurists: Cic. *Top.* 65.

[35] There are also numerous references to him in Cicero's *pro Quinctio*. From *Quinct.* 3 it can be inferred that the case was heard at least three times. Earlier, in 83, Aquilius had acted as an arbiter in settling a debt owed by C. Quinctius to P. Scapula (*Quinct.* 17); for Aquilius' close relation with the Scapulae, see above at note 10.

[36] On this lawsuit, see U. von Lübtow, *Eranion G.S. Maridakis* vol. I (1963) 196-201; A. Watson, *Obligations* 32-36; M. Kaser, *Über Verbotsgesetze und Verbotswidrige Geschäfte im Römischen Recht* (1977) 80-86.

The Jurists

through stipulation (the *stipulatio Aquiliana*),[37] and also with a testamentary clause covering the testator's posthumous grandchildren by a son who predeceases him (*postumi Aquiliani*).[38] But far and away his most important contribution was the wording of the *actio doli*, introduced into the Praetor's Edict on his proposal.[39] Aquilius is the last of the great cautelary jurists.[40]

All this relentless and diffuse activity was sufficient to win Aquilius a praetorship (together with Cicero) in 66; Aquilius was allotted the court for criminal *ambitus*,[41] and so presumably presided at the trial of the Consuls Elect for 65.[42] But a year later he decided not to run for the consulate of 63. Cicero, a potential rival, noted Aquilius' withdrawal with irony and evident satisfaction: Aquilius had alleged poor health and "that dominion of his in the courts" (*Att.* 1.1.1: *illud suum regnum iudicial*.[43] The setback seems to have affected Aquilius deeply. After 65 B.C. he virtually disappears from view, apart from a casual reference in a Ciceronian letter of 56 (*Att.* 4.12), and another in a speech of the same year (*Balb.* 45). It is true that Cicero's attention had long since turned away from the courts of private law. But there is other evidence. A strange and somewhat garbled notice in Pomponius' *Enchiridion* (D.

[37] Florent. D. 46.4.18.1. Cf. F. Sturm, *Stipulatio Aquiliana* (1972); M. Kaser, *SZ* 90 (1973) 346-358.

[38] Scaevola, D. 28.2.29 pr.-2; Africanus, D. 28.6.33.1. See A. Watson, *Succession* 31-32.

[39] Cic. *Off.* 3.60; *Nat. Deor.* 3.74. See U. von Lübtow, (cited n.36) 183-201. Since the dramatic date of the *Nat. Deor.* is ca. 76, the reception into the Edict antedates Aquilius' praetorship by at least a decade. (Despite Pease's commentary *ad loc.*, anachronism is not likely.) For a different view, see A. Watson, *Law Making* 72-75, with further bibliography.

[40] A. Pernice, *Labeo* vol. I (1873) 3; Klebs and Jörs, *RE* s.v. "Aquilius" (1895) 327-330.

[41] Cic. *Cluent.* 147. Cf. *Off.* 3.60; *Top.* 32.

[42] On the trial, see esp. Cic. *Sulla* 11, 49-50, 81. Cic. *Cluent.* 147 refers to an *ambitus* trial in progress before Aquilius.

[43] Cicero's remarks are clearly not to be taken at face value; cf. D.R. Shackleton Bailey *ad loc.* In particular, *regnum iudiciale* does not have the strongly negative connotation of similar phrases in (e.g.) Cic. *Div. in Caec.* 24; 1 *Verr.* 35; 2 *Verr.* 2.77. In *Fam.* 9.18.1, Cicero refers to his own *regnum forense*.

C. Aquilius Gallus

1.2.2.43) states that he lived at Cercina, and that Ser. Sulpicius Rufus, while visiting him, was able to write *libri complures*. Cercina is a small island off the coast of Africa Proconsularis, in the lesser Syrtis bay. Some have thought that Aquilius retired there, perhaps out of consideration for his delicate health;[44] but more probably Cercina conceals some other name.[45] Salubrious places were not lacking in parts of the Roman world that were a good deal more accessible.

There is no sign that Aquilius and Cicero were particularly close. Indeed, Cicero's continual, somewhat stilted references to him as "my colleague and friend" (*Off.* 3.60 and *Top.* 32: *collega et familiaris meus*; cf. *Nat. Deor.* 3.74) suggest, if anything, the reverse.[46] So too does Aquilius' famous and often repeated answer when consulted about cases turning on questions of fact: "This case concerns not law but Cicero" (*Top.* 51: *nihil hoc ad ius; ad Ciceronem*). Aquilius' involvement in Caecina's dispute with Aebutius certainly antedated Cicero's own (cf. *Caec.* 95) and resulted perhaps from personal interest in the affairs of a wealthy and influential *eques*.[47] Nor is it entirely unfair to inquire whether Aquilius' later interpretation of the interdict was influenced by his relationship with Caecina.

Caecina's lawsuit offers a revealing glimpse of how cautelary jurisprudence operated within the judicial system of the late Republic. C. Aquilius had evidently submitted a *responsum* supporting at least some aspects of Cicero's interpretation of the interdict *de vi armata*, and an unknown jurist had done the same on behalf of Piso (*Caec.* 79). One curious and important fact that emerges from this passage is that the two *responsa*

---

[44] So B. Kübler, *SZ* 14 (1893) 79; P. Stein, *Regulae Iuris* (1966) 44. Cercina was suitable for exile: Tac. *Ann.* 1.53.4.

[45] Likeliest is Circeii, a favorite watering hole (Cic. *Att.* 12.19.1, 15.10) enrolled in the Pomptine tribe (*CIL* 10.6426, 6428); see above, note 6.

[46] But contrast *Top.* 51, after his death: *Gallus noster*.

[47] At a similar stage in his quarrel with Fannius, Q. Roscius had also sought legal help (Cic. *Rosc. Com.* 56). Roscius had been made an *eques* by Sulla: C. Nicolet, *Ordre* vol. II 1003-1004.

The Jurists

were anonymous when brought before the court;[48] for Aquilius' authorship became known only when Piso attacked him.[49] It does not appear that such *responsa* were authenticated, or that they relied for credibility upon the reputation of their authors. In response to Piso's attack on Aquilius, Cicero first reads the opening words of the *responsum* from Piso's jurist: "In whatever terms anything has been framed and stated" (79: *Quibus quidque verbis actum pronuntiatum sit*).[50] The *responsum* obviously went on to support Piso's literal interpretation of *deiectio*. Cicero then recounts a conversation that he had with the person he supposes to be Piso's jurist. Under Cicero's informal questioning, the jurist clings to the literal wording of the interdict, but also suggests a novel interpretation of it: Aebutius must lose this case because he "thrust out" Caecina, if not from the Fulcinian farm itself, then at least from the road or the neighboring farm (79-80).

How seriously should this "conversation" be taken? Cicero's discussion at 79-85 is clearly intended to drive Piso's literal interpretation *ad absurdum*. Further, the argument supposedly offered by Piso's jurist is patently bogus. The proceedings *in iure* had revolved around a specific piece of property, the Fulcinian farm. After Dolabella's issuance of the interdict *de vi armata*, Aebutius "asserted that he had restored" Caecina to

---

[48] It is hard to know whether this was normal practice even in the Republic. On the form of submission, see Pompon. D. 1.2.2.49: "ante tempora Augusti . . . neque responsa utique signata dabant [*scil*. iurisconsulti], sed plerumque iudicibus ipsi scribebant, aut testabantur qui illos consulebant." See P. Jörs, *Rechtsw.* 230 n.2.

[49] This much seems certain, though the text is corrupt. The crucial sentence reads, in the paradosis: "Illud autem miror, cur [*or* cum] vos aliquid contra me sentire dicatis, cum eum auctorem vos pro me appelletis, nostrum [*or* vestrum] nominetis." D.R. Shackleton Bailey, *Harv. St. Class. Phil.* 83 (1979) 240, proposes: "Illud autem miror, cur meum auctorem vos pro me appellatis, vestrum, quem vos aliquid contra me sentire dicatis [dicitis?], <non> nominetis." F.L. Keller, *Sem.* 507-508, records similar early suggestions. Emendation along these lines seems more plausible than the larger restoration proposed by W. Stroh, *Taxis* 88 n.29. See also Chapter III, note 107.

[50] The manuscripts have *omnibus quidque*; but *quibus* can be restored on the basis of 85 (*quibus verbis Praetor interdixerit*). At the end of 79, Cicero summarizes the view of this jurist: "a verbo autem posse recedi non arbitrabatur."

the place from which he had been thrust out (23: *Restituisse se dixit*).[51] This answer, though oddly worded, really means two things: *either* Aebutius admits having "thrust out" Caecina from a place, but claims to have restored him there already, *or* Aebutius denies having "thrust out" Caecina from a place, and in this sense claims to have restored to him all that was owed. In *Caec.* 80, the anonymous jurist argues that Aebutius is committed to the first alternative, since 1) "he admits that Caecina was thrust out from some place" (*fatetur aliquo ex loco deiectum esse Caecinam*, obviously a reference to the *confessio* of 3, 24, 104), and 2) "he claimed to have restored him" (*se restituisse dixit*). From these premises "it follows that Aebutius must lose his *sponsio*" (*necesse est male fecerit sponsionem*).

But this conclusion hardly follows, since the *sponsio* clearly concerned not "some place," but rather a specific piece of property whose value had to be estimated *in iure* by the plaintiff.[52] Therefore, at least by the time of the *sponsio*, the plaintiff was committed to claiming a specific property; and the *formula* he subjoined for restoration of this property if he prevailed (Gaius 4.165) must surely have confirmed his commitment.[53] Finally, although a defendant to an interdict *de vi* did not still have to possess the contested property at the time of the trial,[54] it is scarcely likely that for a recuperatory interdict he was not at least required to have sought to hold possession previously. In sum, the argument at *Caec.* 79-85 is not serious.

Indeed, Cicero himself allows that this argument is "more sophistical than my normal pleading" (85: *versutius quam mea consuetudo defendendi*). No jurist could have been serious in proposing such an argument. Yet that is not quite the same thing

---

[51] *Restituere* is used also at 55, 60, 80, 82, 92. On what follows see Chapter II, note 64.

[52] Or so it seems: Chapter II, at note 84.

[53] As Cicero recognizes (*Caec.* 83). Gaius 4.154 states that the interdict *de vi* is given "si ex possessione vi deiectus sit"; but Just. *Inst.* 4.15.6, which derives directly from Gaius, adds "fundi vel aedium" after "possessione," and these words, which restrict use of the interdict to specified immovables, may have fallen out of Gaius' text.

[54] So, at least, Ulpian, (69 *ad Ed.*) D. 43.16.1.42, 43.17.3.10; and Paul, (24 *ad Ed.*) D. 43.16.7.

as saying that the dialogue in sections 79-80 is itself a "fiction" or that the jurist is only a "caricature."[55] Cicero is quite right in saying that the argument does not sound like his own. What it sounds like is a joke spun out in a conversation between friends, a conversation that Cicero now reports with suitable coloring in order to emphasize for one last time the pitfalls of literal interpretation (83-84). On the other hand, the joke has a decided "juristic" quality; it plays on what was emerging in the trial as an obvious and fundamental defect in the interdict's wording. There is not the slightest reason to believe that Cicero did not in fact obtain this argument from Piso's jurist, whose identity would surely have been known to him in any case, just as Aquilius' was known to Piso.

Who is *Ignotus*? There can be no certainty. By the early 60's, the students of Q. Mucius the Pontifex had begun to yield before a new generation, whom they had helped train. Three names stand out.[56] The first is P. Orbius, Praetor in 65 and then Governor of Asia (Cic. *Flacc.* 76, 79); he was a student of T. Juventius (*Brut.* 178-179). The second is A. Cascellius, a Quaestor at least by 73,[57] who in the interests of

---

[55] Contrast W. Stroh, *Taxis* 88 n.29; and cf. A. Boulanger, *Discours* vol. VII 126 n.2. It should be observed that Cicero does not attack this jurist directly. On this passage, I regret lacking access to O. Behrends, *Die Fraus Legis* (Göttinger Rechtsw. Studien 121, 1982); but see U. Manthe, *Gnomon* 56 (1984) 143-145.

[56] Also possible is Q. Cornelius Maximus, Trebatius Testa's teacher (*Fam.* 7.8.2, 17.3; cf. Pompon. D. 1.2.2.45), cited by Alfenus (D. 33.7.16.1). D.R. Shackleton Bailey, *Cicero's Letters to Atticus* vol. I (1965) 297-298, identifies him with Q. Cornelius, Cicero's acquaintance (*Att.* 1.12.1; *Fam.* 5.6.1) and a *pontifex minor* in 69 and 57 (*MRR*)—hence, probably an *eques*, cf. G.J. Szemler, *RE* Suppb. XV s.v. "Pontifex" (1978) 338-339.

[57] Cf. *FIRA* vol. I no. 36, line 13 (*Senatusconsultum de Oropiis*); he is there described as "the son," which apparently means that his father was also in the Senate. The father is probably Cascellius the famous *praediator* of the 90's (Cic. *Balb.* 45; Val. Max. 8.12.1); cf. E. Bormann, *Festschrift O. Hirschfeld* (1903) 432. The Cascellii presumably entered the Senate under Sulla. Notwithstanding T.R.S. Broughton, *MRR* Supp. p. 14, the son did not hold a praetorship. Cf. W. Kunkel, *Herkunft*² 26 n.55; A. Rodger, *CQ* 22 (1972) 135-138. Also R. Syme, *SZ* 97 (1980) 104; contrast N. Horsfall, *Historia* 23 (1974) 254. He is undoubtedly the originator of the *iudicium Cascellianum*.

C. Aquilius Gallus

jurisprudence disdained higher office; he was an *auditor* of Volcacius.[58] The third is Ser. Sulpicius Rufus, Praetor in 65 and Consul finally in 51, the foremost Republican jurist after Q. Mucius. By a good deal, he is the likeliest to have been *Ignotus*.

Ser. Sulpicius Rufus[59] (called Servius by later jurists) came of a patrician family that by his father's time had slipped to equestrian rank (Cic. *Mur.* 16). A year younger than Cicero, Servius had studied with him from boyhood (*Fam.* 4.3.3; *Brut.* 151). As Cicero recounts in the *Brutus* (151), Servius came to law rather late; he was still thinking of oratory in 78 when he joined Cicero on an educational trip to Rhodes, but soon thereafter he opted for law, allegedly out of fear that he could not surpass his friend in eloquence.[60] But Pomponius recounts a story, perhaps derived from Servius' own writings,[61] that suggests his doubts about oratory began somewhat earlier (D. 1.2.2.43): after Servius had repeatedly consulted Q. Mucius on a point of law, and failed to understand the answer, Scaevola scolded him for not knowing law, something that was base in a patrician and a noble and an orator. In the event, it

[58] Pompon. D. 1.2.2.45; cf. note 26. The opinions of Cascellius reported in the *Digest* seem to stem mainly from Trebatius and Labeo: O. Lenel, *Pal.* vol. I 107.

[59] Cf. F. Münzer and B. Kübler, *RE* s.v. "Sulpicius" (1931) 851-860; P. Meloni, *Servio Sulpicio Rufo e i Suoi Tempi* (Ann. Fac. Litt. et Fil. Cagliari 13, 1946) 67-245, esp. 72-121. On his juristic abilities, see M. Bretone, *Tecniche* 75-87; the more negative assessment by O. Behrends, (cited n.70) 269-281, is hardly convincing.

[60] Servius' eloquence is praised by both Cicero (*Brut.* 150-151, 155) and Quintilian (10.1.116, 5.4, 7.30; 12.3.9, 10.11), as well as by Pomponius (D. 1.2.2.43). His speech on behalf of Aufidia is widely cited (Festus p. 140 L; Quintil. 4.2.106, 10.1.22). The case, dating probably to 45 or 44, concerned an inheritance: R. Hanslik, *RE* s.v. "Valerius" (1955) 137. The theme of an orator turning jurist out of despair is a commonplace: Cic. *Mur.* 29; Quintil. 12.3.9, 11.

[61] D. Nörr, in *ANRW* vol. II.15 (1976) 529, suggests this is an apocryphal school story; in any case, it has been improved in the retelling. B. Schmidlin, in *ANRW ibid.* 102-104, takes the story more seriously; cf. also P. Meloni, (cited n.59) 77. The Augur had the same opinion as his cousin: Cic. *de Or.* 1.167.

The Jurists

was only after Q. Mucius' death that Servius turned definitively to law. He took instruction with two of Scaevola's students, L. Lucilius Balbus and Aquilius (Cic. *Brut.* 154; Pompon. D. 1.2.2.43).[62] Servius was a swift learner. Cicero (*Mur.* 19, 21-22) pictures him, soon after his quaestorship in 75, already hard at work in the routine of jurisprudence: giving responses, preparing documents, advising clients on legal procedures, and even beginning to teach.[63]

The case for supposing Servius to be *Ignotus* can be outlined as follows: his close friendship with Cicero may help to explain his "conversation" in *Caec.* 79-80 as well as his apparent reluctance to be publicly identified with the defendant;[64] because of his high reputation, Piso would have consulted him by preference; the view *Ignotus* takes of the interdict *de vi armata* foreshadows the classical view in some respects (as we shall see below); and his willingness to contradict Aquilius Gallus is entirely in character.[65] Admittedly, the case is less than conclusive.

During the more than half a century between 95 and 39 B.C., Servius was the only jurist to be elected Consul (for 51); and it did not come to him easily. His first try for election in 63 had failed, and a second try in 59 (Cic. *Att.* 2.5.2) seems to have been aborted even before its announcement. Between 62 and 51 Servius all but disappears from Cicero's letters, and

[62] Pomponius: "institutus a Balbo Lucilio, instructus autem maxime a Gallo Aquilio." This means that Lucilius Balbus gave him a theoretical introduction, while Aquilius introduced him into practice. Cf. D. Liebs, in *ANRW* vol. II.15 (1976) 224. The lessons with Balbus may well date from the 80's, when Servius still intended an oratorical career.

[63] Cf. Pompon. D. 1.2.2.44, with F. Casavola, in *La Critica del Testo* vol. I (1971) 153-163, on his numerous students. On Cic. *Mur.* 19, see A. Bürge, *Die Juristenkomik in Ciceros Rede pro Murena* (1975) 71-82.

[64] Cicero (*Mur.* 9) notes with some surprise Servius' willingness to give *responsa* even to the enemies of his friends (*adversariis amicorum tuorum*); but for Servius this was doubtless a matter of professional ethics. See Chapter V, at note 126.

[65] See Labeo, D. 32.29.1; Javolenus, D. 40.7.39 pr.; Ulpian, D. 43.24.7.4. Servius' rivalry with Aquilius is explicitly attested by Cic. *Brut.* 154. Servius also attacked various views of Q. Mucius; fragments in Lenel, *Pal.* vol. II 323. See also P. Stein, *Fs. F. Wieacker* (1978) 174-184.

it may be that he did much of his voluminous writing in this period.[66] After his failure to win the consulate in 63, Servius joined M. Porcius Cato in prosecuting Licinius Murena, the Consul Elect. Cicero, clearly preoccupied with the unfolding Catilinarian affair, defended Murena with a lighthearted and successful speech, in which he patiently explained to Servius why cautelary jurisprudence is, compared with oratory or a military career, a poor basis for political success (*Mur.* 19-30, esp. 23 ff.). The speech should of course not be taken too seriously.[67] But in any case Cicero plainly believed that knowledge of law was a rapidly declining source of social and political prestige (*Off.* 2.65-66), clearly lagging far behind oratory (*Mur.* 29; *Orat.* 141; *Brut.* 151; *Leg.* 1.14). For Cicero, the case of Servius proved that knowledge of law must be combined with oratory if one wished to obtain the consulate (*Brut.* 155).

Cicero's views, though they are evidently motivated by a desire to elevate the status of orators, cannot simply be brushed aside; the absence of jurists from the consular *Fasti* of the late Republic speaks all too clearly. In this tumultuous era, the courts of private law offered too narrow a field for constructing the alliances required to win the consulship. The prestige of cautelary jurisprudence was a thing of the past.

THE HERITAGE OF Q. MUCIUS SCAEVOLA

There survives only one narrative account of the rise of Roman jurisprudence: a passage from Pomponius' *Enchiridion*, a treatise written perhaps around A.D. 130-140;[68] the passage was inserted by the compilers of the *Digest* in title 1.2: "On the Origins of Law and of All the Magistracies, and on the

---

[66] So P. Stein, (cited n.44) 44.

[67] This is the modern view. See A. Bürge, (cited n.63); D. Nörr, *Rechtskritik* 84-85. But A. Michel, in *Hommages K. Kumeniecki* (1975) 180-195, takes some of the speech more seriously. Cicero's *Ninth Philippic*, delivered after Servius' death in 43, is virtually a funeral laudation. On the *pro Murena*, see now C. Cantegrit-Moatti, *RH* 61 (1983) 515-530.

[68] D. Nörr, (cited n. 61) 513-516, with much earlier bibliography.

The Jurists

Juristic Tradition."[69] This long passage is badly preserved, and in parts is almost unreadable owing to abbreviation and textual corruption. Yet its immense historical importance can now be considered to be beyond question. What emerges from this work is Pomponius' belief that, around the middle of the second century B.C., Roman jurisprudence was profoundly transformed by the efforts of three men: M.' Manilius (cos. 149), M. Junius Brutus (pr. 142), and P. Mucius Scaevola (cos. 133). In some sense or another, they "established the civil law" (D. 1.2.2.39: *fundaverunt ius civile*). In the next generation, Q. Mucius P.f. Scaevola (the Pontifex) "first formed the civil law, organizing it by categories in eighteen books" (41: *ius civile primus constituit generatim in libros decem et octo redigendo*). Pomponius then traces the course of this tradition downward from Q. Mucius to his students and to his students' students (42 ff.).

Pomponius' laconic, almost lapidary phrases give little clue as to just what he thinks happened during this "revolution." Further, the work of these jurists survives only in a scattering of fragments, from which it is hardly possible to derive an accurate picture of their activity; indeed, there is no clear evidence that the "founders" themselves understood the significance of what they were about, much less that any of them had a deeper or more general view of their "revolution."[70] The present section is intended to suggest the major characteristics of the "revolution," using mainly evidence drawn from the fragments of Q. Mucius; my broad strokes are not, however, a formal history of this "revolution," since such a thing can hardly be written. In the final section of this chapter, I try to describe the larger implications of the "revolution."

[69] *De Origine Iuris et Omnium Magistratuum et Successione Prudentium.* This title corresponds to the three sections of the quoted passage from Pomponius: the origin and development of law (D. 1.2.2 pr.-12); the names and origin of the magistracies (13-34); the list of those who professed the *iuris civilis scientia* (35-83).

[70] So already F. Schulz, *Legal Science* 38. On Q. Mucius, see F. Horak, *SZ* 95 (1978) 402-421, reviewing O. Behrends, *Die Wissenschaftslehre im Zivilrecht des Q. Mucius Scaevola Pontifex* (Nachr. Akad. Wiss. Gött., Phil.-Hist. Kl. 7, 1976); also A. Schiavone, *Nascita*, and M. Bretone, in *Lineam.* 381-383.

The Heritage of Scaevola

By 150 B.C. the craft of the Roman *iurisconsulti* was already centuries old; its origins lay in the collegiate activities of the Pontifices, and the jurisconsults had not yet entirely freed themselves from this background.[71] But very gradually there had arisen, in place of the earlier pontifical jurisprudence, a secular jurisprudence wedded to the patronage system whereby the Roman aristocracy maintained its control of Roman society. Patrons who were skilled in the law (and often in public speaking as well) gave advice to petitioners in the tacit expectation of future social and political support. For reasons that are not entirely clear, Roman courts had been accustomed to accept pontifical pronouncements as authoritative on private law; and the secular jurisconsults of the third and second centuries B.C. had inherited that authority. The jurisconsults passed on their expertise from generation to generation, through a kind of personal apprenticeship that endured well into the Empire. This is the system of cautelary jurisprudence whose gradual decline I described in the preceding section.

However, in the second half of the second century B.C., the Roman jurisconsults had been forced to confront developments that threatened the stability of the *ius civile*, and thereby also their own independent authority as oracles of the law. The first of these developments was the increasing importance of the flexible formulary procedure and the accelerating pace of change in the Praetor's Edict, together with the decline of the archaic and highly formalistic *legis actio* system based (at least ultimately) on statute.[72] The *lex Aebutia*, dating probably from around the middle of the second century, gave public sanction to this development, at any rate in some areas.[73] The second development was the rise of rhetorical advocacy based

[71] On early Roman *iurisconsulti*, see F. Schulz, *Legal History* 5-37; on the lingering influence of pontifical jurisprudence, W. Kunkel, *Herkunft* 45-49. On pontifical jurisprudence, see B. Schmidlin, *TR* 38 (1970) 367-387; G. Nocera, *Iurisprudentia* (1973), with O. Behrends, *SZ* 92 (1975) 308-314; M. Bretone, in *Lineam.* 323-330. On the subsequent "laicization," cf. *ibid.* 331-336.

[72] See A. Watson, *Law Making* 31-62.

[73] Gaius 4.30; Gellius, *NA* 16.10.8. See M. Kaser, *RZ* 114-115; A.A. Schiller, *Mechanisms* 404-410, with further literature.

The Jurists

on Greek models; for the relativistic framework of rhetorical advocacy increased the uncertainty of judicial decisions by providing numerous alternatives for construing not only evidence but even received law.[74] Both of these developments rapidly shifted public attention toward the praetorian judicial system as the primary arena for the shaping of private law.

It is the jurisconsults' response to these two developments that constitutes Pomponius' "revolution." The response was slow in developing and did not become entirely clear until Q. Mucius, though the seeds were planted earlier. The essence of the response was to increase the intellectual content of law and to bound it more adequately against disruptive influences on the judicial system. This response took three forms, described below.

Expansion and Reorganization of Legal Materials

Early second-century jurists were still preoccupied with the Twelve Tables as the cornerstone of the *ius civile*.[75] The evolution away from this cornerstone[76] was painfully slow. But the "founders," in the middle of the century, began to experiment with new literary forms: collections of *responsa*, which surely reflected contemporary concerns more accurately than did the old-fashioned commentaries on the Twelve Tables, and even collections of the elaborate clauses used in conveyancing.[77] Only the writings of Q. Mucius' father may have

[74] See Chapter III, at notes 109-110. It is said that jurists' responses and rulings were "frequently" upset by orators: Cic. *Mur.* 29 (*saepe*); cf. *Orat.* 141.

[75] On Sex. Aelius Paetus' *Tripertita*, see recently F. D'Ippolito, (cited n.32) 53-70; R.A. Bauman, *Lawyers* 139-148. L. Acilius also produced a commentary on the Twelve Tables (Cic. *Leg.* 2.59) and he can be dated to ca. 200-150; cf. Pompon. D. 1.2.2.38, with Cic. *Lael.* 6. Cicero, who as a boy had been forced to learn the Twelve Tables by heart, laments the passing of the custom: *Leg.* 2.9, 59.

[76] Cicero, *Leg.* 1.17, notes the jurists' turn from the Twelve Tables to the Praetor's Edict.

[77] Brutus' three books *de Iure Civili*, in dialogue form (Cic. *de Or.* 2.223-224), were perhaps used as a framework for presenting *responsa*. The experiment was not repeated. On the other juristic work of the "founders," see A. Watson, *Law Making* 137-141; A. Schiavone, *Nascita* 79-83; S. Tondo, *Iura*

The Heritage of Scaevola

explored beyond this immediate casuistic typology, into larger questions arising from the organic unity and autonomy of the *ius civile.*[78]

Q. Mucius' commentary on the *ius civile,* while it no longer employs the Twelve Tables as its framework, is still heavily influenced by their content—often to the detriment of its own organization.[79] Thus, it ignores important innovations introduced through the Edict except where they can be directly related to the content of the Twelve Tables and other statutes, and by consequence it presents the misleading image of a *ius civile* still largely directed toward serving a small agrarian community. The quickening commerce of the Roman dominion, its dealings with money and credit, are almost entirely neglected.[80] Yet we are told that in conversation Q. Mucius was wont to stress the fundamental importance for Roman law of the concept *bona fides* and the actions *ex fide bona* (Cic. *Off.* 3.70).[81] Likewise his commentary apparently ignored numerous topics crucial to upper-class social life, such as marriage and divorce, dowry, *cura,* and the institution of slavery. Finally, the law of procedure was also not treated, though the need for such a treatment must have been obvious by this time.

While Q. Mucius' *Ius Civile* must have seemed in many

---

30 (1979) 36-51, esp. 50-51, with further bibliography; M. Bretone, in *Lineam.* 339-341. The views of the "founders" probably survived mainly in the writings of Q. Mucius; see Cic. *Fam.* 7.22 and Gellius, *NA* 17.7.3, with A. Watson, 138-139.

[78] See F. Bona, *SDHI* 39 (1973) 425-480; A. Schiavone, *Nascita* 83-86. I lack access to A. Guarino, *La Coerenza di Publio Mucio* (1981); but cf. O. Behrends, *SZ* 100 (1983) 458-484.

[79] It is not easy to reconstruct this chaotic work, as is shown by the wide difference in two recent attempts: A. Watson, *Law Making* 143-158, and D. Liebs, (cited n.62) 223. See also F. Wieacker, *Iura* 20 (1969) 466-467. E. Rawson, *PBSR* 46 (1978) 12-34 (esp. 24-29), tries to set Q. Mucius' work in the literary context of its time. On Q. Mucius' *Horoi* (which I accept as genuine), see now B. Schmidlin, (cited n.61) 106-111.

[80] F.P. Bremer, *Iurisprudentia Antehadriana* (1896) 51; A. Schiavone, *Nascita* 116-118; F. Horak, (cited n.70) 418.

[81] On this passage see below, at note 93. There is a clear reflection of this view in *Top.* 65-66.

respects anachronistic even to its author, its "civilistic" system remained an important model for juristic writing well into the Empire.[82] Q. Mucius had at least reached out to embrace some crucial praetorian creations, such as the actions on sale and partnership and the possessory interdicts. Further, he had sought to integrate these new materials into the traditional statutory material of the *ius civile*, instead of holding them apart. Some measure of Scaevola's success can be had from Cicero's *Brutus*: when Cicero argues that Servius is a better jurist than Q. Mucius, his interlocutor at first expresses disbelief (151-152). Cicero is willing to concede to Q. Mucius a great familiarity with law (152: *magnum usum*), but little *ars*; Cicero longs for still greater systematization of law, which he believes to find in the writings of Servius.[83] Whether or not Cicero is correct, Servius is at least the first jurist to avoid the "civilistic" system in favor of a new system based directly on the Praetor's Edict: the "praetorian" system.[84]

Increasing Emphasis on Analytical Jurisprudence

Q. Mucius' efforts at system building may have led to mixed results, but his contribution in the area of analytical jurisprudence is incontestable even from the scattered fragments. The techniques he employs are not unique to law itself; they display an obvious kinship with other analytically organized fields. But they transformed the face of law by providing a method for manipulating legal materials from within. The examples below are intended to illustrate this transformation.

Q. Mucius clearly recognized the importance of legal definitions.[85] Cicero, quoting his definition of *gentiles* (*Top.* 29),[86] also suggests that Q. Mucius was renowned for this characteristic; and definition often appears as a basis for argument

[82] See A. Schiavone, *Nascita* 88-91.

[83] See below, at notes 129-133.

[84] But see below, at notes 131-133.

[85] Cf. R. Martini, *Le Definizioni dei Giuristi Romani* (1966) 90-99; B. Schmidlin, *Rechtsregeln* 186-197. Aquilius Gallus was also an expert at definition: Cic. *Off.* 3.60; *Top.* 32.

[86] See A. Watson, *Persons* 100-101.

The Heritage of Scaevola

in other fragments: e.g., D. 9.2.31 (Paul), where he uses a definition of *culpa* in order to establish a tree trimmer's liability for dropping a branch on a passing slave,[87] or D. 17.2.30 (Paul, = Gaius 3.149), where he uses an implied definition of *societas* to rule out a partnership in which the partners take varying shares in profit and loss.[88] Such definitions, it should be stressed, are highly normative, in that they become a basis for applying or not applying pertinent law to specific cases. Thus, Q. Mucius' careful definition of *penus*, "provisions" (Gell. *NA* 4.1.17),[89] provides him grounds for not including certain items in a legacy of *penus* (Ulpian, D. 33.9.3.9); and his definition of *argentum factum*, "wrought silver" (Ulpian, D. 34.2.27 pr.), is used for similar purposes (Ulpian, D. 34.2.19.9).

Closely related to this process of normative definition is Q. Mucius' strong reliance on "categories" (*genera*) of legal institutions that are related but not identical.[90] He discerned five *genera* of tutelage (Gaius 1.188)[91] and also discussed various *genera* of possession, including possession on a magistrate's order to preserve property (Paul, D. 41.2.3.23).[92] Such *genera* served as a foundation for larger legal concepts. Thus, as Cicero notes (*Off.* 3.70), Q. Mucius grouped all the various ac-

---

[87] A. Watson, *Obligations* 238-239. There seems no reason to suppose the definition is interpolated, though it is the earliest text to describe a *culpa* standard for Aquilian liability. So also O. Behrends, (cited n.70) 291-292; D. Pugsley, *TR* 50 (1982) 11-12.

[88] See F. Bona, *Studi sulla Società Consensuale* (1973) 26-29; M. Kaser, *SDHI* 16 (1975) 312-315; A. Schiavone, *Nascita* 142-143. Somewhat differently, F. Horak, *Rationes* 158-165.

[89] See Ulpian, D. 33.9.3 pr., 6. Cf. R. Astolfi, *Studi sull'Oggetto dei Legati* vol. II (1969) 81-83 and, on *argentum factum*, 156-158.

[90] Cf. the famous *tria genera deorum* (August. *Civ. Dei* 4.27), with R.A. Bauman, *Lawyers* 351-361. On the meaning of *genera*, see A. Schiavone, *Nascita* 101-104. Against O. Behrends, (cited n.70) 285-304, it is doubtful that Q. Mucius used *genera* in a specifically Stoic sense. See M. Talamanca, in *La Filosofia Greca e il Diritto Romano* vol. II (1977) 211-213, with the review by B. Schmidlin, *Iura* 29 (1978) 175-187.

[91] See A. Watson, *Persons* 130; but also M. Talamanca, (cited n.90) 229-239.

[92] Unfortunately, the nature of the *genera* in this text is less than clear; see A. Watson, *Property* 49.

The Jurists

tions in which the words *ex fide bona* appeared, and argued that in all of them the *iudex* should on principle be given the greatest latitude to consider the parties' reciprocal duties.[93] But *genera* could also be used to separate ostensibly similar legal acts. Thus, against earlier authority, Q. Mucius clearly distinguished between mancipation as a source of personal obligation (*nexum*) and mancipation as a means for transferring ownership (Varro, *LL* 7.105).[94] All this classificatory activity reaches a kind of acme in the remarkable "symmetry principle," whereby contractual obligation is dissolved in the same manner it is contracted: *re, litteris, consensu*.[95] Q. Mucius' strict stance favoring privity of contract is also coupled with a list of different forms for contracting obligation (Q. Mucius, D. 50.17.73.4).[96]

Q. Mucius also begins to deploy loose canons for interpretation. Through definition, he discovers examples of equivalent wording in wills (Ulpian, D. 28.5.35.3)[97] and conveyances (Pomponius, D. 18.1.66.2).[98] He explores the effects of including or omitting a guarantee of title in conveyances (Celsus, D. 18.1.59; Venuleius, D. 21.2.75).[99] Nonsensical clauses in wills should be treated as if unwritten (Q. Mucius, D.

[93] See A. Schiavone, *Nascita* 144-149.

[94] See O. Behrends, *RIDA³* 21 (1974) 156-173; A. Watson, *XII Tables* 111-113; A. Magdelain, *RIDA³* 28 (1981) 129-131; S. Tondo, (cited n.77) 40-43.

[95] Pompon. (4 *ad Q. Muc.*) D. 46.3.80; the attribution to Q. Mucius is likely. On the fragment, see C.A. Cannata, in *Fg. von Lübtow* (1970) 431-455, esp 439 ff.; A. Schiavone, *Nascita* 123-137. On the principle, B. Schmidlin, *Rechtsregeln* 74-79; D. Nörr, *SZ* 89 (1972) 59-60, with further bibliography.

[96] See B. Schmidlin, *Rechtsregeln* 70-73; D. Nörr, (cited n.95) 56-59.

[97] See A. Watson, *Succession* 143-144, where the further conclusions drawn by Q. Mucius are also discussed; also H.J. Wieling, *Testamentsauslegung im Römischen Recht* (1972) 29-30.

[98] Cf. Q. Mucius, D. 50.16.241. Both texts concern the definition and meaning of *ruta et caesa* (roughly, detachables). While Aquilius eventually held that the express exclusion of such things from a sale was superfluous (Ulpian, D. 19.1.17.6), for Q. Mucius this seems to be untrue; cf. A. Watson, *Obligations* 95. See also M. Marrone, *St. Volterra* vol. I 213-223.

[99] See A. Watson, *Obligations* 78-81.

50.17.73.3).[100] He begins to elucidate the difficult links between a testator's intent and the words in which this intent is expressed (e.g., Pomponius, D. 34.2.33, 34.1-2);[101] and in cases of genuine ambiguity he opens the door to an interpretation based on public policy (Ulpian, D. 7.8.4.1).[102] Similar expansive techniques are applied in interpreting statutes (Gell. NA 17.7.1-3)[103] and the Praetor's Edict (Ulpian, D. 43.24.5.8; Q. Mucius, D. 50.17.73.2).[104]

A modern lawyer will find nothing unusual in all this activity. But there is simply no evidence that any human being, let alone any Roman, had ever previously worked with such sustained effort on the materials of a secular legal system. Q. Mucius' achievement as a jurist probably lay less in the realm of "grand theoretical system" than in his salutary concentration on the legal meaning of the particular. His intensity marked a quantum leap in legal science. It is in this sense that he "established" the *ius civile*. Through his students, his methods passed into the generation of Cicero.

The Hypothetical Case

The problem that remained[105] was to find a way to link this new legal science to the hurly-burly of the courts, while at the same time preserving its autonomy as a discipline. Part of the answer lay in avoiding the contingency of particular lawsuits. Cicero (*de Or.* 2.142) complains that jurists in the middle of the second century still routinely recorded their *responsa* under the names of petitioners, as though it were the parties

---

[100] See F. Horak, *Rationes* 123-126; A. Schiavone, *Nascita* 39-40.

[101] See A. Watson, *Succession* 87-88, 91; H.J. Wieling, (cited n.97) 37-38, 46-47, 130-131. See also Ulpian, D. 28.5.35.3.

[102] See A. Watson, *Property* 219-220; H.J. Wieling, (cited n.97) 29.

[103] See A. Watson, *Property* 24-25.

[104] See A. Watson, *Property* 226, 222-223 (respectively). With the latter text, cf. Ulpian, D. 43.24.1.5 (citing Q. Mucius); see B. Vonglis, *Lettre* 67-68.

[105] With this section, cf. L. Vacca, *Contributo allo Studio del Metodo Casuistico* (1976) 103 ff. Also especially F. Wieacker, *Recht*[2] 139-148, esp. 140-141 on casuistry; F. Horak, *Rationes* 31-32. On B. Schmidlin, *Rechtsregeln* 143-160, see D. Nörr, (cited n.95) 77 n.80.

The Jurists

and not the circumstances that had produced the need for legal clarification.[106] But second-century jurists may already have been finding a way out of this dilemma. At another place (*Fin.* 1.12), Cicero recounts a discussion among the three "founders" as to whether it was true that the offspring of a slave woman should count as *fructus* and therefore belong to a usufructuary rather than to her owner; Brutus held that it was untrue (a view that prevailed in later law: Ulpian, D. 7.1.68 pr.), while P. Scaevola and Manilius held the opposite.[107] What is interesting about this debate is that it develops not in relation to some specific and actually impending case, but rather in relation to a hypothetical case,[108] one that has been sundered from any particular social background, simplified to remove all its extraneous circumstances, and then presented for discussion. On the other hand, the hypothetical case is still recognizably a legal case; the three "founders" were not speaking of *fructus* as an abstract legal institution, nor were they discussing the general social and economic problem raised by slave children, even though both these broader topics were rather obviously inherent in their discussion.

In Q. Mucius' writings this technique emerges fully developed, though not yet with its classical form and elegance.[109] The hypothetical case is so characteristic of later Roman juristic casuistry that its unusual form and its importance are not always realized; in particular, it has little or nothing to do with Anglo-American "case law." Above all, cases in Roman

[106] On P. Mucius Scaevola, see R.A. Bauman, *RIDA*³ 25 (1978) 223-245, who rightly emphasizes his frequent involvement in specific, often politically charged cases. On the role played by jurists in the Gracchan crisis, see O. Behrends, in *Symposion F. Wieacker* (1980) 25-121, esp. 64-70, with R.A. Bauman, *Lawyers* 245-290; but I am not convinced.

[107] See M. Kaser, *SZ* 75 (1958) 156 ff.; A. Watson, *Property* 214-216. On Brutus' reasoning, F. Horak, *Rationes* 235.

[108] By "hypothetical case," I mean the presentation of an abbreviated statement of facts to which a rule is then applied by way of illustration. No emphasis is laid on the actuality of the events described, and it is understood that the same rule might apply to other, similar situations.

[109] Much of what follows is inspired by R. von Jhering, *Geist des Römischen Rechts* vol. II.2 (5th ed. 1898) 334 ff.

juristic writings normally omit most references to contingent circumstances, even when it can be presumed that an actual case underlies the jurist's decision. For example, there can be little doubt that Q. Mucius' decision in D. 40.7.29.1[110] is based on an actual *responsum*. A certain *paterfamilias* has died, leaving a will that names an heir and also frees the slave Andronicus if he pays 20 to the heir. The testamentary heir takes possession of the estate and Andronicus pays him 20. But then the validity of the will is challenged by the heir-upon-intestacy, who loses the judgment. Andronicus inquires about the pertinence of this lawsuit to his own freedom. Q. Mucius responds that the outcome is pertinent, but that if the verdict had gone the other way, Andronicus would still be a slave.[111] What remains of the original *responsum* is this: the somewhat disjointed and repetitious narrative of the petitioner; the insertion of legally irrelevant details (e.g., that the testamentary heir is in possession); the petitioner's inability to phrase his question exactly (is his conditional freedom dependent on the will's validity?); and Q. Mucius' not entirely elegant attempt to put him on the right track.

On the other hand, the testator has been reduced to an anonymous *paterfamilias*, as often in Q. Mucius' hypotheti-

---

[110] Pomponius, (18 *ad Q. Muc.*) D. 40.7.29.1: "Quintus Mucius scribit: Pater familias in testamento scripserat 'si Andronicus servus meus heredi meo dederit decem [*Bas.* viginti], liber esto.' Deinde de his bonis coeperat controversia esse: qui se lege heredem aiebat esse, is eam hereditatem ad se pertinere dicebat, alter, qui hereditatem possidebat, aiebat testamento se heredem esse. Secundum eum sententia dicta erat, qui testamento se aiebat se heredem esse. Deinde Andronicus quaerebat, si ipsi viginti dedisset, quoniam secundum eum sententia dicta est, futurusne esset liber an nihil videatur sententia, qua vicit, ad eam rem valere? <Respondit valere.> Quapropter si viginti heredi scripto dedisset et res contra possessorem iudicata esset, illum in servitute fore." In the first sentence, *decem* is corrected to *viginti* on the basis of the *Basilica* scholia (BS 2907 Schelt.). The context requires Lenel's addition of *respondit valere*; the compilers presumably struck out Q. Mucius' response.

[111] On this text, see H.J. Wolff, *Tulane Law Review* 33 (1958/1959) 534-539; G. Impallomeni, *Le Manomissioni Mortis Causa* (1963) 17-20; A. Watson, *Persons* 201-203.

cals.[112] The two contesting heirs are also unnamed; the nature and seriousness of the alleged problem with the will are not discussed; we are given no account of how and why Andronicus paid the 20; and we are provided neither the means to determine the size of the estate nor the date or location of the events described. Even the slave's name, Andronicus, need not be genuine, since elsewhere Q. Mucius deploys, apparently for the first time, the repertory of "John Doe" nomenclature that would become familiar in later juristic writings.[113] Andronicus has become a lay figure with a "timeless" legal problem; the boundaries between real life (as reflected in *responsa*) and the purely hypothetical problems of legal science have been deliberately obscured.[114]

Andronicus may yet be a genuine person. But is this true also of the tree trimmer who flings down a branch on an unsuspecting passerby (Paul, D. 9.2.31); or the man who, by beating his neighbor's pregnant mare after it strays onto his field, causes it to abort (Pomponius, D. 9.2.39 pr.); or the testator who elaborately provides for the maintenance of his children (Pomponius, D. 33.1.7)? In an entirely singular fragment, Q. Mucius discusses a certain Senator of his acquaintance who likes to dress up in women's clothing; what would this Senator intend if in his will he were to legate his women's dinner gowns (Pomponius, D. 34.2.33)? The problem is loosely drawn from observation and conjecture about real life, but is intended solely to illustrate the relation between a testator's intent and his words.[115]

[112] See Pompon. D. 34.2.10, 34 pr.; Ulpian, D. 28.5.35.3; Gell. NA 4.1.17.

[113] The slave Stichus (D. 33.1.7; 40.7.39 pr.); the free Romans Titius (D. 46.3.81.1), Titia (D. 32.29.1), and Attius (D. 40.7.39 pr.). These texts paraphrase Q. Mucius, so it is not quite certain that he himself deployed these lay figures; and Andronicus is not used as a slave name by later jurists.

[114] So too in later jurists. Cf. F. Schulz, *Legal Science* 224: "It is not always possible to distinguish between problems suggested by the writer's own speculations and those propounded to him by others. . . . A collection entitled *Responsa* . . . included questions suggested by speculation as well as those occurring in practice." A glance at preserved fragments confirms this. See also B. Schmidlin, *Rechtsregeln* 150-158.

[115] See A. Watson, *Succession* 87-88; A. Wacke, *ANRW* vol. II.13 (1980)

As this text illustrates, the hypothetical cases in juristic writings serve a large number of purposes;[116] they range from entirely plausible and everyday situations to which rules can be straightforwardly applied, to farfetched "limiting cases" through which highly theoretical propositions can be elucidated. The one common characteristic they share is that their purpose is always to clarify law,[117] and for this reason a legal principle or rule (usually a new one) is always involved in their solution; the case thus implies a capacity to generalize beyond the case. Gellius (*NA* 6.15.1-2) illustrates this quality: Brutus had ruled that a person who borrowed a draught animal and then used it for other than the agreed purpose, or who drove it farther than had been agreed upon, was liable for theft (*furtum*). Q. Mucius then generalized this rule for all property held under contractual bailment, whether for safeguard or for use. By a fortunate circumstance, we probably know the actual case that led to Brutus' ruling: a man was condemned for theft because he borrowed a horse to drive to Aricia and drove beyond Aricia to its further slope (Val. Max. 8.2.4).[118] There is an evident difference in level of generalization between the actual case, Brutus' hypothetical restatement and solution of it, and Q. Mucius' broad rule.

While Q. Mucius is therefore not averse in principle to generalization, nonetheless he usually avoids it in his casuistic fragments. His writings, like those of the classical jurists after him, "are casuistic in a peculiar way. They do not—as in a modern commentary—illustrate abstract principles by means of true or fictitious cases; rather does the work consist of a

---

567-568; B. Albanese, in *Fg. von Lübtow* (1980) 155-161; and R. Astolfi, *Labeo* 17 (1971) 33-39, for the further development of this problem in later sources.

[116] Cicero, *Top.* 45, may imply that they were also used in legal education. This seems to have been an innovation of Servius; see F. Schulz, *Legal Science* 91 (with n.8); F. Casavola, (cited n.63) 157-161. On the Cicero passage, cf. R. Bertau, *Latomus* 39 (1980) 395. On examples in Gaius, see M. Fuhrmann, *Das Systematische Lehrbuch* (1960) 117.

[117] More particularly, the law administered within the Roman judicial system. It must be stressed that Roman jurisprudence is always oriented toward the actually functioning judicial system at Rome, and hence is "biased" by Rome's legal culture; cf. Chapter II, at notes 102-107.

[118] See F. Schulz, *Principles* 50; also P. Stein, (cited n.44) 45-46.

series of cases in which the legal rule occurs, but is not abstracted from them in a formula. The authors make no theoretical deduction from the series of cases; they confine themselves to the 'merely paratactic association of the analogy.' "[119] Cicero often remarks on the difficulties such casuistry created for those lacking a legal training.[120] Indeed, juristic casuistry was clearly intended for consumption not by novices, but by those who could be expected to grasp principles and central issues without their being explicitly pointed out, i.e. by other jurists; it is they who gained from the "active co-operation which is produced by . . . concealment of a legal principle."[121]

Emphasis on hypothetical casuistry was a critical step forward in the development of Roman legal science. If we speak in the broadest terms, Q. Mucius was faced with three interrelated problems: first, how to raise the intellectual content and authority of the *ius civile* as expounded by the jurists; second, how to defend the *ius civile*[122] from the disintegrative influences of the rapidly evolving Praetor's Edict and of rhetorical advocacy within the courts; third, how to give the jurists a firm basis from which to exert and increase their own influence on courts, without at the same time inextricably enmeshing them in the conduct of actual cases.[123] Further, his strategy had to be devised within the stringent limitations imposed by the fact that "the jurists possessed a comprehensive and expert knowledge of law," while "no one else had even a remotely comparable grasp of the subject."[124] Thus, the jurists were not only the propounders of law, but also its professional critics.

[119] F. Schulz, *Principles* 51-52, citing M. Weber, *Wirtschaft und Gesellschaft* (4th ed. 1956) 396.

[120] Cic. *de Or.* 1.190, 2.142; *Brut.* 152.

[121] F. Schulz, *Principles* 65.

[122] This expression, while it may seem too strong, comes from Cicero: *Orat.* 141; cf. *Brut.* 155 (of Servius). On Q. Mucius' anger concerning orators' ignorance of law, see Pompon. D. 1.2.2.43 (with note 61, above).

[123] Cicero, *de Or.* 2.142, sees the last problem clearly: if every actual case must be treated as legally unique, then the internal complexity of law will become intolerable.

[124] A.A. Schiller, *An American Experience in Roman Law* (1971) 153.

Within these limitations, Q. Mucius' strategy was complex and subtle. His efforts at systematization and at analytical jurisprudence speak largely for themselves; in these areas he opens a new chapter in legal history. But hypothetical casuistry was also important to him, in two separate senses. First, the "timeless" hypothetical case stood emphatically at one remove from the complexities of any actual case.[125] To this extent, emphasis on hypothetical casuistry helped to create a substitute for a law-finding appellate court system in which legal issues are abstracted from courts of first instance and then debated and decided. Andronicus' problem, first addressed to Q. Mucius,[126] was still being discussed centuries later, by Labeo, and then by Aristo and Pomponius, with results that eventually reversed Q. Mucius' decision (Pomponius, D. 40.7.29.1). This is a good example of juristic controversy conducted at a level that is "well bounded" with respect to the Praetor's court.

Second, hypothetical casuistry also helps to relieve the tensions that appear in any legal system which combines in a single person the roles of law finder, doctrine builder, and legal critic. I will discuss this problem more fully in the final section of this chapter;[127] for now it suffices to state the obvious. Namely, concentration on isolated hypothetical cases deters the inherent striving of legal science toward systematic dogmatism, by keeping law firmly oriented to concrete legal relationships with which doctrine is always obliged to deal. Already in Q. Mucius' writings there emerges an avoidance of grand system, an avoidance that will also characterize later Roman jurisprudence except in introductory texts.[128]

[125] On the "illusion of timelessness" in Roman juristic sources, see B.W. Frier, *LTIR* 197, 207, 216. The consequent difficulties for legal sociology are remarked by A. Wacke, *ANRW* vol. II.13 (1980) 566-567.

[126] Above, at notes 110-114.

[127] At notes 195-196.

[128] See, e.g., M. Fuhrmann, (cited n.116) 186-188. On the absence of system in Roman jurisprudence, see K. Ayrter, in *St. A. Biscardi* vol. I (1982) 9-21. The essentially external relationship of "system" to basic processes of legal thinking is discussed in an illuminating passage by M. Weber, (cited n.119) 395-396.

The Jurists

In his *de Oratore*, Cicero advocates (through the *persona* of L. Crassus) that Roman jurisprudence move away from a casuistic model and toward grand system; but Cicero already reckons with the jurists' negative reaction to this proposal.[129] In the end, he is willing to settle for a treatise that will at least make comprehensible to orators the main lines of Roman private law; this is certain to have been the thrust of Cicero's lost monograph *de Iure Civili in Artem Redigendo*.[130] Cicero's highly laudatory remarks on Servius (*Brut.* 152-155) strongly suggest that Servius supported at least this much of Cicero's broader program.[131] In this regard, it is significant that Servius' two-book commentary on the Praetor's Edict, the first work of its kind, was addressed to the orator Marcus Brutus (Pomponius, D. 1.2.2.44), and that the book had such slight impact on later jurists.[132] Servius' book was perhaps designed to fulfill the need, perceived by Cicero, for introductory handbooks usable by orators. On the other hand, these treatises by Cicero and Servius also bear some relationship to contemporary efforts (all of them ultimately unsuccessful) at codifying Roman private law.[133]

[129] See recently F. Bona, *SDHI* 46 (1980) 296-351, with extensive bibliography; add M. Herberger, *Dogmatik* (1981) 46-54. Bona rightly stresses (p. 343 ff.) the cool and evasive reply that Q. Scaevola the Augur gives to Crassus' grand schemes: *de Or.* 1.204. (Cf. Cic. *Att.* 4.16.3 on Scaevola's role in book 1 of the *de Oratore*.) Cicero frequently describes casuistry as the hallmark of the jurist: e.g., *Mur.* 19; *de Or.* 1.212; *Off.* 2.65; *Orat.* 141; *Top.* 44-45. I incline to agree with B. Schmidlin, *Rechtsregeln* 167-173, that Cicero never entirely abandoned his belief in legal systematization; the *Topica* are in this regard highly important. On the relationship Cicero saw between philosophy and jurisprudence, cf. J. Mancal, *Zum Begriff der Philosophie bei M. Tullius Cicero* (1982) 178-179.

[130] See F. Bona, (cited n.129) 366-382, who summarizes earlier views at pp. 282-296. See esp. M. Villey, *Recherches sur la Littératur Didactique du Droit Romain* (1945) 15 ff.

[131] F. Bona, (cited n.129) 351-366, tries to limit Cicero's praise to Servius' use of dialectic in responses; but this view is plainly too narrow.

[132] The sole definite fragment (Ulpian, D. 14.3.5.1) concerns a relatively simple point, the definition of *institor*.

[133] See F. D'Ippolito, (cited n.32) 93-116, with further literature; and below, Chapter VI, at notes 105-108. As A. Guarino, *ANRW* vol. II.13 (1980)

Q. Mucius may well have seemed to his contemporaries an almost wholly isolated figure, alone in his understanding of Roman law and of how it would develop. The story is a dramatic one: a narrow channel of juristic tradition, passing from Q. Mucius to his students, and then widening under the influence of Ser. Sulpicius Rufus, until it finally emerges as the great river of classical Roman law. Perhaps the story is a bit too dramatic. It may do some injustice to Q. Mucius' valued forerunners, the preceding generation of the "founders." We cannot know. But Q. Mucius is undeniably the earliest jurist to have significant impact on the juristic tradition of Rome. Though modern scholars may exaggerate his contribution, it is unlikely that the distortion is great.

Mindful of the intellectual debt that he and other late Republican jurists owed, A. Cascellius bequeathed his estate to the grandson of Q. Mucius, *in illius honorem* (Pompon. D.1.2.2.45). This story may perhaps be doubted, but the truth for which it stands is unassailable. Q. Mucius is the father of Roman legal science and of the Western legal tradition. He is the inventor of the legal profession.

THE "CORRECT" INTERPRETATION OF THE INTERDICT *de Vi Armata*

The *pro Caecina* was delivered during an era in which Roman jurists were striving to establish their independent authority. Probably the last private oration delivered by Cicero, it is also, doubtless coincidentally, the only one of his speeches that mentions juristic *responsa* in a judicial context.[134] Although Piso had argued that judges need not defer to the authority of jurists (*Caec.* 65, 67, 79), he nonetheless produced a *responsum* from an anonymous jurist upholding his initial

---

71-72, suggests, Servius' commentary *ad Ed.*, along with the much larger one of his student Ofilius (Pompon. D. 1.2.2.44), reflect the increasing stability of the Edict.

[134] Cicero's client Q. Roscius had however consulted a jurist; see note 47. Cic. *Caec.* 65, 67, alludes to *responsa* used in earlier trials that Cicero had witnessed.

The Jurists

interpretation of the interdict *de vi armata*; Cicero reads the opening words from this *responsum* (79). It is possible that Piso also obtained a *responsum*, whether from the same or a different jurist, upholding his "fallback position" (90-91); but if so, Cicero does not mention this. As for Cicero himself, he readily concedes that Aquilius Gallus is the authority for his attack on Piso's initial position (77, 79); it is probable that Cicero also had presented to the *recuperatores* an anonymous *responsum* obtained from Aquilius. On the other hand, Cicero does not explicitly rely on a *responsum* in refuting Piso's "fallback position" (90-93).

Piso appears to have developed his "fallback position" in his second speech, in response to Cicero's criticism of his initial interpretation of the interdict *de vi armata*.[135] Piso had initially held that the interdict applied only to physical removal from a place, not also to prohibition of entry (cf. esp. *Caec.* 66). Cicero objected that if *deiectio* does not, at least in some cases, include preventing a person from entering property, then Piso himself will be unable to use this interdict should an armed gang prevent him from returning to his own house (35-39, 89). To counter this argument, Piso revised his position, now arguing that "a person who possesses can be thrust out, but a non-possessor cannot be; accordingly, if I am thrust out of your house, I have no claim to recover, but if you yourself are [thrust out of your house], you have a claim."[136] In other words, the plaintiff under the interdict must have possessed at the time of the *deiectio*. Since the interdict *de vi armata* made no express reference to possession, Piso must have relied on an interpretation of the word *deiecisti* in the interdict.

Cicero's reply to this argument has been perhaps the foremost source of controversy in modern treatments of the *pro Caecina*. Cicero relies on a comparison between the interdict

---

[135] For a reconstruction of the first two hearings, see Chapter III, under subhead "The Earlier Speeches."

[136] *Caec.* 90, of Piso: "eum deici posse qui tum possideat; qui non possideat, nullo modo posse; itaque, si ego sim a tuis aedibus deiectus, restitui non oportere, si ipse sis, oportere."

The Interdict *de Vi Armata*

de vi and the interdict *de vi armata*, the texts of which are here set out synoptically with italics indicating divergence:

INTERDICT *de Vi*:	INTERDICT *de Vi Armata*:
Unde tu aut familia aut procurator tuus	Unde tu aut familia aut procurator tuus
illum *aut familiam aut procuratorem illius*	illum
in hoc anno	
vi deiecisti,	vi *hominibus coactis armatisve* deiecisti,
cum ille possideret, quod nec vi nec clam nec precario a te possideret,	
<eo restituas>.	eo restituas.

The interdict *de vi armata* had been introduced on the model of the interdict *de vi* two years before Caecina's lawsuit, in 71 B.C.[137] In the *pro Caecina*, Cicero argues that, because of their close relationship, differences in wording between the two interdicts must be considered deliberate and significant. He stresses two differences in particular. The first involves the type of violence covered. The interdict *de vi* concerns only "everyday violence" (92: *vi cotidiana*), while the interdict *de vi armata*, through its addition of the words *hominibus coactis armatisve*, concerns violence aggravated by the use of weapons and mobs (92-93). The second difference involves the defenses available to the defendant. In the interdict *de vi*, the words *cum ille possideret* require the plaintiff to have been in possession at the time of the *deiectio* (91-92); further, the words *quod nec vi nec clam nec precario a te possideret* require that his possession also be faultless as against the defendant (92). These two express requirements burden the plaintiff and protect the de-

[137] On the date see Chapter II, at notes 48-49.

The Jurists

fendant (93). (The limitation of the interdict *de vi* to one year has the same effect, but Cicero forgoes this obvious point.)

By contrast, the interdict *de vi armata*, governing aggravated violence, omits these express provisions. The omission, so Cicero argues, must be deliberate. Hence the plaintiff under the interdict *de vi armata* need not have have possessed, much less faultlessly possessed, at the time of the *deiectio* (93).

Cicero's argument thus has two heads: first, the difference in level of violence which the two interdicts envisage is related to the inclusion of the "defenses" in the interdict *de vi*; second, the complex clause establishing these "defenses" must be read as two independent requirements, namely both possession and "faultless" possession. From these two points Cicero reaches the conclusion that possession is not required of the plaintiff by the interdict *de vi armata*.

Cicero does not attribute this argument to a jurist; and in fact its direct source has long been known.[138] In the *pro Tullio*, delivered in 71,[139] Cicero argues that the wording of the *formula* under which Tullius' lawsuit was brought must be considered significant especially in its omissions (*Tull.* 38-43). He then adds an example illustrating this principle of interpretation (44-46):[140]

---

[138] E. Costa, *Orazioni* 97-100; *Cicerone Giur.* 128-129. The point was also noticed by H. Bögli, *Rede* 53-54, who suggested that the *pro Tullio* passage was a later addition reflecting the *pro Caecina*—a desperate suggestion.

[139] For the date see Chapter II, at note 39.

[140] *Tull.* 44-46: "Fuit illud interdictum apud maiores nostros de vi quod hodie quoque est: 'Unde tu aut familia aut procurator tuus illum aut familiam aut procuratorem illius in hoc anno vi deiecisti.' Deinde additur illius iam hoc causa quicum agitur: 'cum ille possideret,' et hoc amplius: 'quod nec vi nec clam nec precario possideret.' [45] Multa dantur ei qui vi alterum detrusisse dicitur; quorum si unum quodlibet probare iudici potuerit, etiam si confessus erit se vi deiecisse, vincat necesse est vel non possedisse eum qui deiectus sit, vel vi ab se possedisse, vel clam, vel precario. Ei qui de vi confessus esset tot defensiones tamen ad causam obtinendam maiores reliquerunt. [46] Age illud alterum interdictum consideremus, quod item nunc est constitutum propter eandem iniquitatem temporum nimiamque hominum <licentiam>. . . ."

Our ancestors had an interdict *de vi* that still survives today: *Unde tu aut familia aut procurator tuus illum aut familiam aut procuratorem illius in hoc anno vi deiecisti*. Then these words are added, for the defendant's benefit: *cum ille possideret*; and then these: *quod nec vi nec clam nec precario <a te> possideret*. [45] Many lines of defense are provided the person alleged to have driven out someone else by force. If he can prove any of these to the judge, either that the person thrust out had not possessed, or that he possessed by force or by stealth or on grant from himself, then he must prevail even if he admits having thrust him out by force. When someone admits using force, our ancestors still left him many arguments for winning his case. [46] Next, examine the second interdict, now also established owing to the same unsettled conditions and men's excessive [license]. . . .[141]

Although the manuscript breaks off just as Cicero is about to discuss the interdict *de vi armata*, it is obvious that his argument here is identical to that in the *pro Caecina*. Above all, Cicero clearly distinguishes the plaintiff's possession from his faultless possession, as two separate requirements under the interdict *de vi* (44-45); and he relates these requirements to the two interdicts' difference in purpose.

The appearance of this argument in the *pro Tullio* is illuminating; for in that speech the argument is developed in an excursus irrelevant to Cicero's central case. Thus we can categorically exclude the possibility, often raised by modern scholars,[142] that Cicero's argument in *Caec.* 90-93 is a mere rhetorical trick devised with the exigencies of the present case

---

[141] The word *licentiam* is restored from *Tull.* 8.

[142] E.g., H.J. Roby, *Private Law*, vol. II 523-524; A. D'Ors, *Defensa* 46; A. Watson, *Property* 89; G. Nicosia, *Deiectio* 45-51; W. Stroh, *Taxis* 82-83. Typical is Roby, 524: "Cicero adroitly in the interest of his client seized on the apparent difference between the wording of the two interdicts, and gave an independence and an importance to the clause [*viz.*, 'cum ille possideret'] which it was never intended to have." So already T. Mommsen, *Gesammelte Schriften* vol. III (1907) 563. None of these authors observed the *pro Tullio* passage. See also Chapter III, notes 42, 58.

The Jurists

in mind. It is especially significant that Cicero knew this argument already in 71 B.C., the year when the interdict *de vi armata* was first placed in the Edict—though whether Cicero devised the argument himself or obtained it from others is uncertain. In any case, if Cicero uses the same argument also in 69, it is surely because he thought the argument to be correct. Likewise, if (as seems likely) Piso advanced his "fallback position" only tentatively after the weaknesses in his initial position had been exposed, it is not unreasonable to suppose that he too was aware of the counter-argument Cicero would employ, and that he too thought it a strong one.

The apparent ease and confidence with which Cicero disposes of Piso's "fallback position" has deeply troubled modern scholars. For there is no doubt that Roman jurists later uphold a concept of *deiectio* identical to Piso's "fallback position." That is, they interpret the word *deiecisti* to mean that the plaintiff had to have possession at the time of the *deiectio*.[143] For example, Cicero (*Caec.* 90) says of Piso, "you deny that a person who does not possess can be thrust out" (*eum qui non possideat negas deici posse*); nearly three centuries later Ulpian writes, "nor is a person understood to be thrust out unless he possesses" (*nec alius deici visus est quam qui possidet*).[144] In this respect, classical jurists recognize no distinction between the interdicts *de vi* and *de vi armata*, and so they reject Cicero's argument based on the different wording of the two interdicts. On the other hand, later jurists tacitly accept Cicero's view that *deiectio* includes prohibiting entry;[145] and they likewise accept that *terror armorum*, fear of armed force, is enough to constitute *vis armata*.[146]

Since the earliest of these juristic sources dates more than two centuries after Caecina's lawsuit, a problem arises. Was

---

[143] See Gaius 4.154; Ulpian, (69 *ad Ed.*) D. 43.16.1.1, 9, 23-24, 26; Paul, *Sent.* 5.6.4, 7. On these texts, see G. Nicosia, *Deiectio* 7-22.

[144] Ulpian, (69 *ad Ed.*) D. 43.16.1.23. The coincidence in wording was noted by Lenel, *EP*3 464.

[145] Ulpian, (69 *ad Ed.*) D. 43.16.1.24, 3.8.

[146] Ulpian, (69 *ad Ed.*) D. 43.16.3.5. On the other hand, unlike Cicero they require physical (not just psychological) terror; cf. Chapter III, note 77.

Piso's view also "correct," at any rate from a juristic perspective, in the late Republic? Did *deiectio* already imply dispossession? Was Cicero's interpretation of the interdict *de vi armata* demonstrably wrong in 69 B.C.?

The leading modern authority[147] considers it "possible, and indeed likely, that in Cicero's time a technical concept of *deiectio*, with the specific meaning of dispossession, had already been isolated. But it cannot be excluded that the terms *deicere* and *deiectio* were also used in a more generic sense, and hence that the full consequence had not yet been drawn that possession was necessarily presupposed whenever *deicere* and *deiectio* were mentioned. For this reason Cicero could maintain, albeit wrongly, that the *deiectio* covered by the interdict *de vi armata* did not presuppose possession by the person expelled." This measured view nonetheless seems to me essentially misleading.

The problem obviously arises from the strange wording of the interdict *de vi*, a wording which undoubtedly reflects an accretive process whereby clause had been laid on clause without sufficient regard for overall sense.[148] The interdict begins with a flourish: "Whence you (or your household or procurator) have in the past year thrust out this man (or his household or procurator), . . ." Already the first clause probably contains accretions, since the verb *deiecisti* reflects only the subject "you" and not the following words (in parentheses).[149] The interdict then adds some qualifications: first, "when he possessed"; then, "what he possessed neither by force nor by stealth nor on grant from you, . . ." Cicero (*Tull.* 44-45; *Caec.* 91-93) reads these two clauses separately, as constituting two independent requirements: first, the plaintiff's possession;

[147] G. Nicosia, *Deiectio* 59 (my translation).

[148] See esp. H.J. Roby, *Private Law* vol. II 524. The general use of the *exceptio vitiosae possessionis* in this and other interdicts is discussed by L. Labrunna, *Vim Fieri Veto* (1971) 160-167.

[149] Neither the *familia* nor the procurator of either party is mentioned in the version given by the late-second-century *lex agraria* (quoted just below). Contrast the Hadrianic interdict, as reconstructed by Lenel, *EP*³ 465: "Unde in hoc anno tu illum vi deiecisti aut familia tua deiecit. . . ."

The Jurists

then, his faultless possession. By contrast, classical jurists obviously took them to constitute a unit (the *exceptio vitiosae possessionis* requiring faultless possession at the time of *deiectio*), and most modern scholars support this view.[150]

From a purely grammatical standpoint, both views can be defended.[151] But it is not possible to suppose that a technical concept of *deiectio* as "dispossession" could have been formed on the basis of the interdict *de vi* alone, since such a concept would not have been necessary when the plaintiff's possession was already required elsewhere in the interdict. In this connection, the version of the interdict's wording given by the late second-century *lex agraria* is crucial:[152]

> [Sei quis eorum, quorum age]r s(upra) s(criptus) est, ex possessione vi eiectus est, quod eius is quei eiectus est possederit, quod neque vi neque clam neque precario possederit ab eo, quei eum ea possessione vi eiec[erit . . .]

In English:

> If one of those persons whose land was described above has been forcibly thrust out of possession from land that the person who was thrust out possessed, which he possessed neither by force nor by stealth nor on grant from the person who forcibly thrust him out of this possession . . .

On the one hand, it is true that the *lex* requires the plaintiff's prior possession already with the words *ex possessione*, so that the succeeding clause is awkward if read as a completely independent requirement of possession.[153] On the other hand,

---

[150] See G. Nicosia, *Deiectio* 48-49.

[151] *Contra*: H. Bögli, *Rede* 48-53. *Possidere* is often used in a "quasi-absolute" sense, where an object of possession is easily supplied from context; see just *Caec.* 90 (three times).

[152] *FIRA* vol. I no. 8, line 18. This law dates from 111 B.C. The quoted provision provides relief if those assigned land under the *lex* are forcibly dispossessed; the wording is modeled on the interdict *de vi*. See Chapter II, at note 42.

[153] H.J. Roby, *Private Law* vol. II 523-524; H. Bögli, *Rede* 48-49; P. Koschaker, *SZ* 28 (1908) 453-454; G. Nicosia, *Deiectio* 49 n.120. The verbose draftsmanship of the *lex agraria* vitiates this argument, however.

it is equally plain that the words *eiectus est* are not yet considered sufficient in themselves to establish this requirement;[154] and when the words *ex possessione* were dropped from the first clause of the interdict *de vi* (if indeed they were ever in it), the requirement of possession could still be readily derived from the *exceptio*—as indeed Cicero does in the *pro Tullio* and *pro Caecina*.

A generation after the *lex agraria*, a passage in the *Rhetorica ad Herennium* (4.40), dating from the mid-80's, describes a plaintiff's case under the interdict *de vi*. The plaintiff is attempting to prove that he has been forcibly thrust out from his farm. But instead of straightforwardly asserting his prior faultless possession and forcible dispossession, he uses a much more circuitous route: he first proves his ownership (*istum fundum nostrum fuisse*), then shows that the defendant has no countervailing right (the farm was not standing vacant, nor was it usucapted, nor had it been sold or bequeathed by the plaintiff). "Wherefore," reasons the plaintiff, "it remains that you forcibly thrust me out of my farm" (*Relinquitur ergo ut me vi de meo fundo deieceres*). The plaintiff's proof freely intermingles ownership and possession, and even property and obligation rights; most of his points are irrelevant in classical Roman law. This passage, which reflects courtroom practice in the period just before the rise of the Roman jurists, not only contains no trace of a developed doctrine of *deiectio*, it also all but ignores juristic categories in favor of purely equitable arguments.

What possible motive was there for "isolating" an extended concept of *deiectio* so long as no such concept was required for interpreting the interdict *de vi*? But the situation changed when the interdict *de vi armata* was introduced in 71. Since this interdict omits the entire *exceptio vitiosae possessionis*, the plaintiff's possession, if it was to be found in the interdict's wording, had to be derived from the verb *deiecisti*; thus, a broader concept of *deiectio* was required.

[154] So even Gaius 4.154: "Reciperandae possessionis causa solet interdictum dari, si quis ex possessione vi deiectus sit."

The Jurists

However, construction of this broader concept was not automatic; it depended on recognition of the underlying problem with the interdict *de vi armata*, and thus upon either sustained juristic reflection or pertinent cases. Caecina's lawsuit in 69 displays clearly the delay in constructing the extended concept. Both responding jurists (Aquilius and *Ignotus*) initially fastened on a purely physical concept of *deiectio*: did the plaintiff have to be on the property at the time of the *deiectio*, or not?[155] Neither jurist's *responsum* involved the plaintiff's possession; both jurists discussed only his physical presence, including presumably not only his praetorian possession (whether just or unjust),[156] but also his detention (e.g., as a lessee or usufructuary) and perhaps even his mere causeless presence on the land. *Ignotus* required such a presence; Aquilius did not. Only with Piso's "fallback position" did the issue of praetorian possession arrive belatedly on the scene; and Cicero countered this new position by repeating his argument from the *pro Tullio* virtually word for word.

Furthermore, it is by no means evident that praetorian possession should have been required for the interdict *de vi armata*. To take just an obvious case, such a requirement denied standing to a usufructuary; this problem was so severe that a specially constructed interdict had to be devised to handle it.[157] An alternative view was at least possible, that the victim of armed force need have only a "recognized" property interest; such a view might even have given standing to a tenant driven out by a third party's armed men.[158] I see no clear reason why the classical Roman view with regard to the interdicts *unde vi* is preferable to this alternative (which in one

[155] See esp. *Caec.* 79 (of *Ignotus*): "non posse probari quemquam esse deiectum nisi ex quo loco in quo fuisset." Aquilius' opposing view emerges from 64-65, 77.

[156] Cf. Ulpian, (69 *ad Ed.*) D. 43.16.1.9, as reconstructed by G. Nicosia, *Deiectio* 14-22.

[157] Lenel, *EP*³ 468-469; cf. G. Nicosia, *Deiectio* 59-68, on classical texts discussing the *deiectio* of a usufructuary. By contrast, the *superficiarius*, who also lacked praetorian possession (M. Kaser, *RPR*² vol. II 456), nonetheless could use the interdict *de vi*: Ulpian, (69 *ad Ed.*) D. 43.16.1.5.

[158] On the tenant's position, see just B.W. Frier, *LTIR* 64-68.

form or another all modern legal systems have preferred). To be sure, Caecina's claim to the Fulcinian farm might still have been insufficient to give him standing even under this alternative view.[159] Yet Caecina may have believed in good faith that he owned the Fulcinian farm (through inheritance from his wife) and also that he had possessed it (through his visit). Cicero's arguments in sections 94-95 do not "prove" that Caecina possessed the farm, but they can provide reasons for assuming his good faith. For example, the *deductio* Caecina arranged with Aebutius (20, 95) strongly suggests that both men acknowledged the controversy between them.

We are invited to choose between Piso's interpretation (the interdictal plaintiff *de vi armata* must have possessed) and Cicero's (no possession is required). We are further told that Cicero's interpretation means "putting (or restoring!) into possession any casual intruders who have been threatened with a pike or sword by the farmer or his servants on a lonely holding."[160] But this outcome is absurd, "not at all in harmony with the good sense and practical character either of Roman legislation or of the praetor's action."[161] Therefore Cicero's interpretation must be rejected, and Piso's accepted—or so we are told. Naturally, we cannot know how Cicero would have answered this argument. But he might have replied that rejection of Piso's position does not necessarily mean eliminating all requirements for standing as a plaintiff. We have a wide spectrum of possibilities for interpreting *deiecisti*, and no preexisting law guides us; we can draw the line where we wish. We must test the sense of Piso's narrow interpretation against the case before us, against Caecina's case, and not against

[159] Here and in the following paragraph, I am thinking mainly of F.L. Keller's theory about an *umbra possessionis*: *Sem.* 376-389. Mommsen's refutation of this view, (cited n.142) 561-563, though mainly dogmatic, is widely accepted; see G. Nicosia, *Deiectio* 54 n.130. But even if Keller's view is "wrong," it is both deeper and more interesting than the usual view. In any case, W. Stroh's extremely harsh tone toward Cicero (*Taxis* 82-84) is unjustified.

[160] H.J. Roby, *Private Law* vol. II 525, drawing on an example raised by Mommsen, (cited n.142) 563; see also A. Ubbelohde, *Die Besitzklagen* vol. I (1896) 170, who however also accepts Keller's view (above, note 159).

[161] H.J. Roby, *Private Law* vol. II 525.

some hypothetical "limiting case."[162] If Caecina could reasonably have believed he was possessor of the Fulcinian farm (even though a court might someday rule against his possession), can he then use the interdict against someone who uses armed force to bar his entry? After all, Caecina was no "casual intruder." He and Aebutius did not meet as strangers on the Tarquinian plain.

If a technical concept of *deiectio* as dispossession existed already by 69 B.C., it could not have been constructed except on the basis of the recently disused *detrudere* interdict.[163] Cicero himself admits the historical relationship between the *detrudere* interdict and the interdict *de vi armata*, to the extent of using *detrudere* to interpret *deicere* (*Caec.* 49); elsewhere he employs *detrudere* and *deicere* as synonyms (*Tull.* 29, 45). Since the *detrudere* interdict also lacked explicit reference to the plaintiff's possession, its interpretation presented problems similar to those of the interdict *de vi armata*. To be sure, we know nothing of how the *detrudere* interdict was interpreted in this respect.[164] But the verb *detrudere* was also used in another section of the Edict, one governing praetorian *missio in possessionem* by creditors (Cic. *Quinct.* 84);[165] and this section was applied, at least eventually, not only to unpossessed things like a usufruct, but even to unpossessable things like an outstanding debt.[166]

In sum, there is no reason whatsoever to believe, and much reason to doubt, that a clear technical concept of *deiectio* as dispossession had been "isolated" before Caecina's lawsuit. Such a concept was not yet needed; there is no sign that it already existed, and considerable evidence that it did not. For the rest, we have grounds to query whether such a concept was

[162] Similar objections can also be raised against Cicero's argument concerning Piso's home (*Caec.* 35-39, 89).

[163] On which see Chapter II, at notes 45-47.

[164] The *detrudere* interdict also requires the defendant's *dolus malus* (cf. *Tull.* 29-30), which complicates interpretation somewhat.

[165] Lenel, *EP*[3] 423.

[166] See Ulpian, (61 *ad Ed.*) D. 42.5.8 pr., (69 *ad Ed.*) D. 50.16.49. Cf. M. Kaser, *RZ* 302-305, esp. 304 n.41.

even desirable. Later jurists would have held that Piso's "fall-back position" was the "correct" interpretation of the interdict *de vi armata*, and that Cicero's rejection of this interpretation was "wrong." But nothing indicates that Cicero or any of his contemporaries knew Cicero's view to be "wrong," or that they yet recognized any indisputably "correct" way to interpret the interdict's ambiguous wording. Finally, even had late Republican jurists been able to arrive at a unanimous interpretation of the interdict, this fact would not necessarily have been decisive within the judicial system of 69 B.C.

In our own century, Cicero's argument in favor of his client has found few defenders among legal historians.[167] To my mind, however, the central issue in the *pro Caecina* is not whether Cicero was "correct" (who cares?), but rather whether we have in fact any reliable criterion for evaluating Cicero's argument apart from the logic of the speech itself. I fear we do not. Late Republican sources paint a discouraging picture of indefiniteness and insecurity in the judicial system of Rome: the procedural forms of the Edict shifted constantly; rhetorical advocacy remained supreme in harsh adversary trials; broad social commitment to minimum standards of formal justice was still lacking; public ignorance of law was widespread; the judicial system was still passive; and, at the margin of this pandemonium, a handful of jurists struggled to establish a place for their tenuous legal science. The picture is not bright, nor does it offer much room for modern scholarly dogmatism.

If in the end we do not simply abandon the search for a *ius certum* in Ciceronian Rome, this is perhaps only because of one remarkable fact: by the end of Cicero's career as a civil advocate, legal professionals were beginning to exercise a small but detectable influence on the conduct of trials. Rome's jurists may have affected only slightly the progress and outcome of Caecina's lawsuit; but nonetheless they did participate in it, and through their work they were beginning already to construct the standards by which it could at last be evaluated, albeit only in hindsight.

[167] Cf. G. Nicosia, *Deiectio* 52 n.127.

The Jurists

In the preceding sections, we have seen how the elite group of Roman legal experts gradually transformed themselves during the first half of the first century B.C.—from externally oriented cautelary jurisconsults into internally oriented jurists—as part of an effort to reconstitute their discipline on a more intellectual and hence more influential basis. But we have also seen how painfully slowly the jurists progressed in implementing their program within the judicial system of contemporary Rome.

Yet it would be wrong to end this chapter on so pessimistic a note; for the future belonged to the jurists. In the present section I want to describe, on a rather more abstract level, what it was the jurists were offering to Rome. In subsequent chapters and in my conclusion, I try to explain why the jurists' program ultimately succeeded, despite its somewhat unpromising start.

In the *pro Caecina*, Cicero expresses outrage over Piso's attack on the authority of the jurists in general (*Caec.* 65, 67) and on that of Aquilius in particular (77). In rebutting Piso's attack, Cicero delivers a long and passionate eulogy of the *ius civile* and of the jurists (65-78). Despite its overtly rhetorical tone and purpose, the passage is a major document in the evolution of the Roman judicial system toward its early classical form.

Cicero begins by distinguishing three "levels" of law, with progressively greater degrees of fallibility and contingency. The first and highest level is the *ius civile* itself: an apparently independent body of rules and institutions that together constitute "the bonds of social welfare and life" (70: *vincula . . . utilitatis vitaeque communis*).[168] These rules, knit together by an

---

[168] On *utilitas communis* see Chapter III, at note 76. Cicero obviously thinks of private law as mainly non-statutory; but he probably sees the *ius civile* as analogous to statute in criminal law, cf. *Cluent.* 146: "Hoc enim vinculum est huius dignitatis, qua fruimur in re publica, hoc fundamentum libertatis, hic fons aequitatis: mens et animus et consilium et sententia civitatis posita est in legibus." Cf. *Rep.* 1.49: "Quare cum lex sit civilis societatis vinculum, ius

intelligible intellectual structure (78: *iuris civilis rationem*), offer the sole reliable basis for determining rights to ownership and general legal interrelationships (70), and for then protecting these rights "against a third party's influence" (74: *contra alicuius gratiam*). Cicero thinks here mainly of the secure tenure and devolution of property:[169] boundaries, possessory relationships, servitudes, usucapion, and testamentary succession (74). Law is the incorruptible guarantor of such rights; and as such, *ex hypothesi*, influence cannot bend it, nor personal power break it, nor wealth corrupt it (73). In this sense the *ius civile* is removed and set apart from ordinary political and social life; it is autonomous.[170] Further, between citizens it is neutral, "uniform among all and identical for everyone" (70: *aequabile inter omnes atque unum omnibus*). This autonomous *ius civile* is a great inheritance (74), which Romans should defend as diligently as they defend property itself (75).

The jurists constitute the second level of law, intermediate between the incorruptible *ius civile* and the judicial system. They are the "interpreters of law" (70: *interpretes iuris*), whose prerogative it is to "rule" on law (68, 69: *statuere*). At several points Cicero suggests that their *auctoritas* is bound up with that of the *ius civile* itself; an attack on them must inevitably be an attack on law as well (67, 70), and their attacker thus "weakens statute and law" (70: *leges ac iura labefactat*). Aquilius Gallus is in this respect the ideal jurist, whose *ingenium, labor,*

---

autem legis aequale, quo iure societas civium teneri potest, cum par non sit condicio civium? Si enim pecunias aequari non placet, si ingenia omnium paria esse non possunt, iura certe paria debent esse eorum inter se qui sunt cives in eadem re publica. quid est enim civitas nisi iuris societas civium?" Here the transition from *lex* to *ius* is clear, as is the nature of the *ius* envisaged by Cicero. On *aequabilitas* ("equality of treatment") as the end of law, see *de Or.* 1.188, with M. Herberger, (cited n.129) 53-54.

[169] In later works (esp. *Off.* 1.23, 2.78), Cicero adds security of contract to this list: M. Villey, in *Das Neue Cicerobild* (ed. K. Büchner, 1971) 259-303, esp. 292 ff. The jurist's importance in this area is emphasized by Cicero, *Top.* 65.

[170] Cicero later integrates this view into his theory of the state; see, with bibliography, H.P. Kohns, *Gymnasium* 81 (1974) 485-498, esp. 494-495 on Cic. *Off.* 2.73-74, 78; F. Cancelli, in *Studi G. Donatuti* vol. I (1973) 211-235.

and *fides* are constantly available to the Roman people (77-78); he is so skilled that both his knowledge of civil law and his goodness seem innate, and he never separates legal science from *aequitas* (78).[171] Yet there are also "stupid men" (*stultis hominibus*) who should not be considered jurists when they make rulings "that ought not to be applied as law" (68: *quod non oporteat iudicari*). Likewise, even skilled jurists may disagree with one another; but if so, either opinion is good law, as the *causa Curiana* showed (69). Cicero thus plainly believes it is possible for jurists to make rulings that are not law, just as it is possible for judges to reach verdicts that are law despite the opposition of jurists (69).

The third and most fallible level of law comprises the courts themselves. Cicero asserts that judges must decide in accord with *responsa* that correctly declare the law (68); to this extent, the *ius civile* binds courts (70: *vincula . . . iudiciorum*). Naturally, this does not mean unchallenged domination by jurists; judges may also determine that a jurist's opinion is wrong and is not law, or they may choose between conflicting juristic opinions (69). But Cicero carefully distinguishes this position from the view, which he describes as common among advocates, that "the jurists need not be followed, nor the *ius civile* always prevail in trials" (67: *nec iuris consultis concedi nec ius civile in causis semper valere oportere*; cf. *Mur.* 29). On the contrary, while Cicero readily admits the fallibility of judicial fact finding (false witnesses and evidence are common, or the judge may be bribed: *Caec.* 71), he holds that even a corrupt judge will not dare to decide against recognized rules of law (72-73). The sanction against such misbehavior is, to be sure, entirely moral: general public censure resulting from fear that legal rules will weaken (69) and that legal insecurity will then increase (73, 76). Nonetheless, this weight of public opinion generally suf-

[171] As this description suggests, Cicero is not committed to a view that the *ius civile* is unchanging. Cf. Cic. *Leg.* 1.40, 42-43, on desirable changes in law; *Off.* 3.58-71, with D. Nörr, *Rechtskritik* 42-43, on the development of *dolus* doctrine; *Top.* 66, on the juristic elaboration of fiduciary relationships. In *de Or.* 1.193, the Twelve Tables and other outdated laws are praised only as a "mirror of antiquity" (*antiquitatis effigies*).

fices to ensure that corrupting influences are unable to break the rule of law within the courts (72).

This passage from the *pro Caecina* has not attracted much scholarly notice, apparently because it seems to have little to do with the lawsuit's central issue and so has not been closely read.[172] The importance of the passage lies in two fundamental propositions: 1) private law's central function is to preserve the long-term material security of the existing social order, and for this reason its rules must be insulated from transient social and political influences; 2) the jurists, interposed between the *ius civile* and the courts, are uniquely empowered to make authoritative statements regarding the substance of the *ius civile*, and their statements are presumptively binding on private judges. Further, Cicero clearly sees a link between these two propositions; the *ius civile* is unable to fulfill its central function unless the *responsa* of jurists are authoritative within courts. This link is surely to be found not in the simple existence of jurists (for there are also "stupid men" who falsely claim to be jurists, *Caec.* 68), but rather in the qualities of the best jurists: their justice, skill, and maintenance of a balance between the *iuris civilis ratio* and *aequitas* (78).

What is the origin of the ideas in this passage? The first of Cicero's propositions, regarding the central function of private law, recurs often in later writings,[173] but never is found, so

[172] For instance, J.M. Kelly, *Litigation* 32-33, states that Cicero's "disquisition rests on a not very realistic distinction between issues of fact (which can be wrongly resolved if a witness is dishonest or a judge unfair) and issues of law (which depend on known rules, and cannot be perverted)." The summary is less than accurate. E. Fraenkel, *Hermes* 60 (1925) 436, describes this section as a maneuver whereby Cicero attempts "die Aufmerksamkeit der Auhörer von der juristisch bedenklichen Situation seines Klientes abzuziehen." This is exaggerated; see Chapter V, at notes 90-96. A. Magdelain, *RHD* 28 (1950) 166-168, is exceptional in recognizing the importance of the *pro Caecina* passage.

[173] Cf. H.P. Kohns, (cited n.170); also Chapter III, at notes 74-76. The idea that private property is inviolable first clearly emerges in the debates of second-century Stoics, which may have affected the Gracchan crisis; cf. R.A. Bauman, *Lawyers* 249-255, with bibliography. Cicero carries the idea one step further. On Q. Mucius' possible Stoicism, see Bauman, 351-361.

The Jurists

far as I know, in any source prior to the *pro Caecina*; it may have originated in the Middle Stoa. Cicero's second proposition bears more than a striking resemblance to later juristic theories on the authority of juristic *responsa* within trials;[174] in particular, it foreshadows Pomponius' famous description of the *proprium ius civile*, "which is unwritten and rests solely on the interpretation of jurists" (*quod sine scripto in sola prudentium interpretatione consistit*).[175] It hardly strains belief to suppose that the idea was first expressly articulated by late Republican jurists, perhaps by Q. Mucius. In any case, the proposition is quite alien to the rhetorical tradition. No source earlier than the *pro Caecina* proposes that juristic *responsa* were presumptively binding on judges.

However, it is not Cicero's propositions taken separately, but rather their collocation, that commands attention. Cicero's eulogy of the *ius civile* is the earliest clear enunciation of the theory of "autonomous law"—a theory that not only became the guiding ethos of classical Roman law, but also is perhaps the single most important Roman contribution to the Western legal tradition.[176] "Autonomous law" is less a systematic doctrine of law than a loose bundle of characteristically juxtaposed ideas, which together constitute a sort of "ideal type."[177] Among these ideas are

[174] See Gaius 1.7: "Responsa prudentium sunt sententiae et opiniones eorum quibus permissum est iura condere: quorum animum si in unum sententiae concurrunt, id quod sentiunt legis vicem optinet; si vero dissentiunt, iudici licet quam velit sententiam sequi. idque rescripto divi Hadriani significatur." For a summary of modern discussion on this difficult passage, see A.A. Schiller, *Mechanisms* 297-306. See recently S. Tondo, (cited n.77) 65-77, who notes (pp. 68-69) the connection of the *ius respondendi* with the *pro Caecina*.

[175] Pompon. (*Ench.*) D. 1.2.2.12, cf. 5; on which see M. Bretone, *Tecniche* 128-135.

[176] See, e.g., E. Bodenheimer, *Jurisprudence* (2d ed. 1974) 192-194. On the Roman achievement, see esp. M. Bretone, *Tecniche* 137-142; also A. Schiavone, *Nascita* 118-144.

[177] This paragraph relies heavily on P. Nonet and P. Selznick, *Law and Society in Transition* (1978), esp. 16, 53-72. I have somewhat rephrased their points. Cf. H.J. Berman, *Law and Revolution: The Formation of the Western Legal Tradition* (1983) 7-10.

1) strong separation of law from politics, and a consequent emphasis on the independence of the judicial system from political influence as well as on the division between legislative and judicial functions of government;

2) a conception of law as a self-consistent body of rules that are applied in individual cases and that, because of their existence, both limit the discretion of the judicial system and help to prevent it from intruding into politics;

3) an emphasis on procedural regularity and fairness (formal justice) as the primary end and competence of a judicial system; and

4) a belief that "fidelity to law" means primarily obedience to established rules of positive law and, likewise, a conviction that changes in law (at any rate, major changes) must be channeled through the political process.

The doctrine of "autonomous law" thus aims to provide a coherent account of the legal profession's particular expertise (it is concerned, as Cicero puts it, with the *iuris civilis ratio*), while simultaneously describing the general social limits of that expertise. Although many elements of "autonomous law" are already present in Cicero's discussion, a fully developed ideology is a much later phenomenon associated above all with the nineteenth century.[178]

By contrast, in the twentieth century the ideology of "autonomous law" has been subjected to almost uninterrupted attack from numerous quarters. The most interesting of this criticism concerns the external social functions of "autonomous law." As one scholar has recently explained it,[179] the

[178] Especially in the writings of A.V. Dicey, *Introduction to the Study of the Law of the Constitution* (8th ed. 1915, repr. 1982), esp. part II ("The Rule of Law"); see the discussion in D. Lyons, *Ethics and the Rule of Law* (1984) 194-208. For a summary of modern assaults on the "autonomy of law," see J. Stone, *Social Dimensions of Law and Justice* (1966) 470-545. The concept of formal justice is assessed critically by D. Lyons, *Cornell Law Review* 58 (1973) 833-861.

[179] G. Teubner, *Law and Society Review* 17 (1982/1983) 414-415, whose references (to Luhmann, Habermas, and Duncan Kennedy) I have omitted. For

The Jurists

justification of autonomous law "lies in its contribution to individualism." Autonomous law "restricts itself to the definition of abstract spheres of action for the autonomous pursuit of private interests. In doing so, it guarantees a framework within which substantive value judgments are made by private actors. Thus 'formalities' facilitate private ordering." Autonomous law "develops its own system rationality insofar as it establishes spheres for the autonomous activity and fixed boundaries for the action of private actors. Thus, it contributes to the mobilization and allocation of natural resources, which is a necessary concomitant of a developed market economy." While on the one hand this ideology of law provides an "adequate legal forum for the functional differentiation of an autonomous economic system,"[180] it also serves to legitimize what it creates. "A logically formal legal order appears to be a neutral and autonomous source of normative guidance, and this very neutrality forms one basis for the claims of political systems . . . to legitimate authority."[181]

It is, I think, essentially this position for which Cicero pleads in the *pro Caecina*, though he would not of course have expressed his views in such modern terms. Cicero's reason for accepting juristic opinions as authoritative sources of law, and thus for resisting the prevalent rhetorical relativism, is that doing so will increase trust in private law and insulate the judicial system (at least partially[182]) from contemporary social and political pressures; and legal security will, in turn, be an important guarantor of the existing social order. Thus: "Wherefore you should guard this public inheritance of law, which you have received from your ancestors, no less scrupulously than the personal inheritance of your wealth; and

a conservative defense of the rule of law, see D.M. Davis, *Acta Juridica* (1981) 65-81.

[180] G. Teubner, (cited n.179) 415, citing N. Luhmann, *Gesellschaftsstruktur und Semantik* vol. II (1981) 80. Cf. W. Simshäuser, in *Festschrift für H. Coing* (1982) 329-361: ownership is "absolute" in Roman private law, but limited through numerous duties imposed by public law.

[181] D.M. Trubek, *Law and Society Review* 11 (1977) 529.

[182] On judicial corruption see Chapter V, at notes 61-62.

you should do so not merely because these things are protected by the *ius civile*, but also because a lost inheritance is
one person's misfortune, while law cannot be lost without great
misfortune to us all."[183]

This is the tacit bargain that Q. Mucius and his students
offered to the Romans: increased security in private law in
exchange for the greater prestige of legal experts. Nor can it
be doubted that the late Republican jurists had already committed themselves to at least an incipient version of "autonomous law." Their rule orientation is obvious even from our
meager sources. Further, despite their internal disagreements
with one another, the jurists assume that there must be only
one correct solution to questions of law.[184] They also assume
that this solution is discoverable through jurisprudence alone—
a view that provoked ridicule from laymen when jurists relied
on the opinions of earlier jurists.[185] Finally, at least with the
earlier jurists, there is a clear tendency to justify decisions
mainly through internal argument (subsumption or probability), rather than through appeal to external social values such
as *aequitas* or *utilitas*; this tendency must be partially responsible for the widespread, and somewhat misleading, impression among laymen that the jurists were politically and socially conservative as a group.[186]

---

[183] Cic. *Caec.* 75: "Quapropter non minus diligenter ea quae a maioribus
accepistis, publica patrimonia iuris quam privata rei vestrae retinere debetis,
non solum quod haec iure civili saepta sunt verum etiam quod patrimonium
unius incommodo dimittetur, ius amitti non potest sine magno incommodo
civitatis." E. Fraenkel, (cited n.172) 440, read *privata* for *privatae* of the manuscripts.

[184] See A.B. Schwarz, in *Fs. Schulz* vol. II 209-211.

[185] See, e.g., Cic. *de Or.* 1.239-240 (with Chapter III, note 137). On arguments from authority in Republican jurists, see F. Horak, *Rationes* 71-74, 102-
115; and more generally F. Schulz, *Principles* 183-186; D. Nörr, *Rechtskritik*
85, 141-143. On "traditionalism," see D. Nörr, *Fs. Flume* vol. I (1978) 153-
190; *Bull.* 23 (1981) 9-33.

[186] F. Horak, *Rationes*, discusses internal argument in jurists up to Labeo (a
projected second volume will consider external argument). F. Wieacker, *SZ*
94 (1977) 1-42, studies the rise of "overtly evaluative jurisprudence" during
the Empire. Lay attacks on juristic conservatism are discussed by F. Schulz,
Principles 83-87; D. Nörr, *Rechtskritik* 60-61, 141-146.

The Jurists

The law of the jurists remained faithful to their tacit bargain; its liberal temper has long been renowned. The science of the jurists "presupposed the play of free and equal units transferring property, making contracts, committing wrongs, intermarrying, each an emperor in his own household and an equal citizen in his external relations."[187] That is to say, the jurists did not question, on any fundamental level, the existing distribution of social resources within the Roman community, nor did they analyze the effects of this distribution on the practical operation of their legal rules and institutions, nor did they systematically attempt to redress this distribution or to alleviate its consequences.[188] The formal equality of Romans before the law became a shield behind which the mercantile economy of Rome could operate with greater confidence.[189]

However, in several respects the problem of "autonomous law" is more complex than the presentation above suggests. First of all, it needs to be stressed, ever and again, that the juristic program did not quickly prevail within the late Republican judicial system; as we have seen, that system remained theoretically capable of operating entirely without reliance on juristic opinion. Advocates still generally regarded juristic opinions with considerable skepticism, if not outright

[187] T. Honoré, *Tribonian* (1978) 35. See F. Schulz, *Principles* 146-158, who rightly emphasizes "the liberal nature of Roman private law" and adds: "it is not superfluous to stress the fact that none of the characteristic legal institutions of modern capitalism are derived from Roman law" (p. 158). However, against Honoré (p. 35), there is nothing specifically "conservative" or "republican" about Roman private law even in the Empire. This common historical fallacy is exposed by, among others, S.N. Eisenstadt, *The Political Systems of Empires* (1963) 98-99; see also Chapter VII, at notes 31-38, below. On the political attitudes of the jurists, see D. Nörr, *Rechtskritik* 54-56; and below, note 197.

[188] B.W. Frier, *LTIR* 208; cf. L. Lombardi, *Saggio* 29-30. Contrast M. Finley, *Politics in the Ancient World* (1983) 7: "of course the 'mould' of Roman law, as of every other legal system examined by historians, was an instrument and a reflection of society and therefore of social inequality." This view as it stands is too generalized to be of value; a subtler and more differentiated position is required.

[189] See recently J.H. D'Arms, *Commerce and Social Standing in Ancient Rome* (1981). See also Chapter VII, at notes 21-23.

contempt;[190] and social or political considerations still exercised unabated influence on the conduct of private trials.[191] Juristic theories of "autonomous law" can be regarded, in this respect, mainly as a manifestation of professional aggressiveness in securing influence for the jurists within the judicial system; certainly "autonomous law" had not yet become the ethos of the judicial system itself.

Second, while the juristic program avowedly sought "legal security," the early days of Roman legal science nonetheless provided an extraordinary opportunity to organize large sections of private law for the first time. The jurists did not hesitate to exploit this opportunity in order to reform law. Doubtless it is an exaggeration to call this period an "heroic age of creative genius and daring pioneers";[192] but the Republican jurists' achievement, taken in its sum, was undeniably considerable. Their achievement lay in the liberation of Roman private law from its stultifying archaic formalism, in the ascendancy of the quasi-ethical principle *bona fides*, and in the creation of a juristic method for managing legal materials.[193] Above all, what has commanded the admiration of all posterity is the concentration and frugality of the symbols and mechanisms they established for legal expression: frugality in the fundamental principles of law (*fraus, dolus, fides, libertas, potestas*, and especially *bona fides*); frugality in the elements of procedural law as established in the Edict and then elaborated in juristic writings (the formulary system); and frugality in reducing the most diverse legal relationships to a small repertory of basic forms (ownership, possession, obligation, condition, and so on).[194]

Third, whether by intuition or design, the Republican jurists created a jurisprudential tradition that was generally averse

[190] See Chapter III, at notes 105-108.

[191] See Chapter II, at notes 91-107; Chapter III, at notes 27-28, 122-124.

[192] F. Schulz, *Legal Science* 99.

[193] W. Kunkel, *Römisches Privatrecht* (1935) 23-24; cf. F. Pringsheim, *Gesammelte Abhandlungen* vol. I (1961) 70-75; F. Wieacker, *Recht*² 173-175, to whom my succeeding sentence is also indebted. P. Jörs, *Rechtsw.* 1-14, is still important.

[194] See F. Schulz, *Principles* 66-77. Rudolph von Jhering was the first to emphasize this point.

The Jurists

to grand system, and hence continuously susceptible to change. I suggested above[195] that this phenomenon was largely a practical response to a situation in which the legal profession had not yet been differentiated into its characteristic modern roles: legal draftsmen, trial lawyers, judges at both trial and appellate levels, professional teachers, systematic writers, internal critics, and so on. In the late Republic the jurists had professional duties in most of these areas, and legal experts were in any case otherwise absent. Juggling these multiple roles required a considerable measure of self-restraint if law was to retain its internal balance; this may be partially responsible for the surface blandness of most juristic writing.[196] Nonetheless, jurists' law rarely disintegrated, either then or later, into sterile abstraction; more usually it remained in reasonably close contact with the functioning judicial system, from which it continued to draw much of its pragmatic inspiration.[197]

In the end, there is no reason to doubt that the Roman jurists early encountered one of the great paradoxes of "autonomous" legal thinking: that the quest for legal security through jurisprudence, far from producing simplicity and dogmatic narrowness, instead makes possible the reverse, an increase both in law's complexity and in its tolerance of uncertainty. "The function of doctrine . . . lies . . . not in chaining the intellect, but rather in the exact reverse, the increase of freedom in manipulating experience and texts. Dogmatic conceptualism makes it possible to hold one's distance at just the point where society anticipates commitment. . . . In the case of legal doctrine, what is involved is the increase of uncertainties that are compatible with two central requirements of the legal system: the binding force of legal norms and the duty to decide in legal disputes."[198] This increase in uncertainty and analyt-

[195] At notes 125-126.

[196] See B.W. Frier, *LTIR* 196-197. On juristic personalities, see recently A.A. Schiller, *Mechanisms* 308-311; F. Casavola, *Giuristi Adrianei* (1980) 97-103. The views of F. Schulz, *Principles* 106-108, are now widely rejected.

[197] B.W. Frier, *LTIR* 203, cf. 206-212. See Pompon. D. 1.2.2.13 ("constare non potest ius, nisi sit aliquis iuris peritus, per quem possit cottidie in melius produci"), with L. Lombardi, *Saggio* 5-11; D. Nörr, (cited n.61) 596-597. Also *idem, Bull.* 23 (1981) 9-33, on the "idea of progress" in the jurists.

[198] N. Luhmann, *Rechtssystem und Rechtsdogmatik* (1974) 16-17 (my transla-

ical complexity, made possible by the professional intellec-
tualization of law, in turn generates a substantial increase in
law's capacity as an instrument of social control. By and large
the paradox is still with us today.[199] The success of the jurists
in exploiting this capacity remains, to be sure, a moot issue.[200]

During the last century before our era, the civil government
of Rome (magistrates, assemblies, and Senate) gradually surrendered much of its direct, day-to-day control of private legal norms to an extra-constitutional body of "legal experts."[201]
It did not of course surrender its ultimate sovereignty, its claim
to control the substance and procedure of Roman private law.
The central court remained in the charge of the Urban Praetor; and statutes (in the widest sense) still were both a possible
way to alter law and a way that was sometimes exercised.[202]
But in practice the private law of Rome became largely subject to determination by the jurists. Operating within the traditional framework of civil and praetorian procedure, the jurists were successful in elaborating the law of Rome on a new
and more rational basis. Under their influence, private law
acquired a measure of independence and "autonomy" from
the central political structure of Rome. Indeed, perhaps at no
point in the long tradition of Western law has the "autonomy"
of law verged so nearly on the absolute as in this, its earliest
period.

For all the febrile brilliance of its civic organization, classical Greece had not obtained this; nor had the Hellenistic world,
where social and political conditions were perhaps even more
favorable to law's emergence as an autonomous discipline.[203]

---

tion). Luhmann cites R. Lautmann, *Justiz: Die Stille Gewalt* (1972) 143 ff. See
also P. Selznick, in *International Encyclopedia of the Social Sciences* vol. IX, s.v.
"Law: The Sociology of Law" (1968) 58, of Common Law.

[199] See, e.g., K. Llewellyn, *The Common Law Tradition* (1960) 11-18.

[200] My own view is perhaps more optimistic than that of most Romanists.

[201] T. Mommsen, *Gesammelte Schriften* vol. VII (1909) 212: "Die ganze
Weisheit der römischen Rechtsetzung bestand ja darin, dass man den Juristen
gestattete selbst die Gesetze zu machen und zu ändern." Mommsen's *Staatsrecht* thus has no index entry for "Juristen."

[202] F. Schulz, *Principles* 6-18.

[203] See H.J. Wolff, *Opuscula Diversa* (1974) 81-103. M. Lavency, *Aspects de*

The Jurists

The Greek "failure" has no straightforward explanation. Perhaps it suffices to say that circumstances were never exactly right,[204] and that, unless circumstances were right, no ancient state was prepared to surrender so great a measure of control over the interpersonal dealings of its subjects. In any case, the Greek "failure" is all the more startling because, as Cicero observes (*de Or.* 1.187), the basic modes of legal thinking, whereby legal materials are intellectualized, are not fundamentally different from those underlying the "sciences" of music, geometry, literature, linguistics, or oratory—all areas extensively cultivated by the Greeks.[205]

But the long-term social importance of the law's autonomy was immense. "The emergence of a separate and functionally specialized legal system has enormous consequences not only for law itself but also for other sectors of society. . . . The development of a separate legal system not only ensures a degree of rationality and independence in the application of norms, but also provides legal 'instruments' necessary for the functional and structural differentiation of society as a whole. . . . At least during a specific historical stage in the evolution of society, the emergence of a functionally specific legal system appears to possess special significance as an achievement of social evolution: it is a condition for all further social evolution."[206] "Autonomous law" enables and protects the unfolding of a more complexly organized society. While much of this potential remained unrealized in the Roman world, it is a major part of the legacy Rome left to the modern age.

---

la Logographie Judiciaire Attique (1964) 96-122, has some interesting observations on proto-jurisprudence among Athenian speechwriters.

[204] In Chapter VII, I have tried to suggest why circumstances may have been "exactly right" in late Republican Rome.

[205] On the methodology Roman jurisprudence shared with other "logical arts" (even medicine), see now M. Herberger, (cited n.129) 46-76, 106-120. As to philosophic influence on Roman legal reasoning, F. Wieacker, *Iura* 20 (1969) 448-477, says all that is worth saying; O. Behrends, *RHD* 55 (1977) 7-33, still reckons with heavy influence, unnecessarily in my view.

[206] N. Luhmann, *The Differentiation of Society* (trans. S. Holmes and C. Larmore, 1982) 127-130.

V

The *Recuperatores*

iudicis est semper
in causis verum sequi
—Cicero

THROUGHOUT his speech for Caecina, Cicero appeals to the
panel of judges simply as *recuperatores*; the vocative occurs
twenty-two times, or slightly more than once every five chapters. But Cicero does not address any of the *recuperatores* by
name, nor does he attempt to praise them either individually
or as a group, beyond calling them *prudentissimi homines* (40)
on whose *fides* and *religio* Caecina rests his case (103). Cicero's
tone is always restrained and respectful, even a little distant.
Cicero remonstrates with the *recuperatores* for having delayed
their decision (6), for not having believed the defendant's own
witnesses (31), and for allowing the defense to say such ex-
travagant things in a court of law (74); he begs them to listen
carefully to his argument (86). But he also stresses that the
final decision is theirs alone.[1] Cicero's direct addresses to the
recuperatores also punctuate the stages in his speech. He habit-
ually calls on the court when he begins a new section of the
speech: the *narratio* (10), the consideration of the defendant's
witnesses (23), the argument on *verba* (86), the evaluation of
Piso's "fallback position" on the interdict (90), the consideration *extra causam* of Caecina's possession (94), and the *conclusio*

---

[1] E.g., *Caec.* 23: "Hac de sponsione vobis iudicandum est"; 77: "vos sta-
tuite, recuperatores."

(103). At the start of the argument on *res*, a formal *partitio* (32) serves much the same purpose.[2]

The likeliest explanation for Cicero's courteous tone is that this was part of courtroom etiquette; for the *pro Tullio* is similar in respecting the anonymity and impersonality of the *recuperatores*. By contrast, the *pro Quinctio* and *pro Roscio Comoedo* were each delivered to a single *iudex*: C. Aquilius Gallus and C. Calpurnius Piso, respectively. Not only does Cicero repeatedly name both men, he also lavishes explicit praise on them (e.g., *Quinct.* 5, 10; *Rosc. Com.* 7). Cicero even names the members of their *consilia*, the *adsessores* or *advocati*. In the suit brought against Quinctius, there is the jurist L. Lucilius Balbus (*Quinct.* 53-54), the *nobilis* M. Claudius Marcellus (54), and a certain P. Quinctilius (54).[3] In the suit against Q. Roscius, Cicero names only M. Perperna (*Rosc. Com.* 3, 22), probably the Consul of 92 and Censor of 86, who had earlier been *iudex* in a suit described by Cicero (*de Or.* 2.262). The rest of the *consilium* is unknown doubtless only because so much of the speech is missing; but Cicero does not hesitate to praise them "for their outstanding distinction" (*Rosc. Com.* 15: *propter eximium splendorem*). Likewise, the *consilium* judging Quinctius comprises "the most select men in Rome" (*Quinct.* 5: *viris lectissimis civitatis*). The difference from the *pro Tullio* and *pro Caecina* is apparent and striking.

This difference is largely explained through history. At Rome, most private suits were heard by a single judge, the *iudex privatus* or *arbiter*.[4] But a small and somewhat heterogeneous class of suits was heard instead by a panel of *recuperatores*, "recoverers," who sat as a kind of jury.[5] The origins of

---

[2] Only the abrupt opening of the argument on Volaterran citizenship (95) lacks any explicit address to the *recuperatores*—perhaps another sign of this segment's later insertion. See Chapter III, at notes 6-10, 67-68.

[3] On Balbus see Chapter IV, note 26. Marcellus is perhaps the Aedile of 91 (*MRR*). P. Quinctilius is likely to be the Varus praised in Cic. *Cluent.* 53; but *contra* H. Gundel, *RE* s.v. "Quinctilius" (1963) 398, there is no reason to think him a jurist.

[4] See M. Kaser, *RZ* 41-44, 138-142. On J.M. Kelly, *Judicature* 112-133, see O. Behrends, *SZ* 94 (1977) 447-456, with whom I substantially agree.

[5] On *recuperatores*, see esp. Y. Bongert, in *Varia: Études de Droit Romain*

the recuperatorial trial are largely unknowable, though scholars usually assume, perhaps correctly, that it began in the arbitration of "international" disputes.[6] However, by the late Republic recuperatorial trials were used also in private law for a variety of cases that were deemed to have particular urgency or social importance. In the 70's, two of the praetorian innovations against wanton violence (the *iudicium de vi coactis armatisque hominibus* of 76 and the interdict *de vi armata* of 71)[7] made use of *recuperatores* as judges. The "social urgency" of these actions presumably helps to explain Cicero's respectful address toward the *recuperatores*.

In the first section of this chapter, I reconstruct the external form of Caecina's lawsuit before the *recuperatores*. In the second I consider how late Republican judges arrived at their verdicts; the third section discusses the nature and purpose of the verdict in Roman trials, and then tries to determine the outcome of Caecina's lawsuit.

THE COURT OF THE *Recuperatores*

During the late Republic, private lawsuits were usually decided by members of Rome's upper classes, who were chosen for this role because of their status.[8] Prior experience with law was not considered necessary or even desirable,[9] though

---

(Publ. Inst. Droit Rom. Paris 9, 1952) 99-266; B. Schmidlin, *Rekup.*, with the reviews by M. Kaser, *SZ* 81 (1964) 377-388, and G. Pugliese, *Iura* 15 (1964) 399-412; G. Pugliese, *Processo* vol. II.1 194-215; J.M. Kelly, *Judicature* 40-70 (with caution). On other specialized multi-member courts (the *centumviri*, the *Xviri stlitibus iudicandis*), see M. Kaser, *RZ* 37-41.

[6] Cf. M. Kaser, *RZ* 142-145, based primarily on B. Schmidlin, *Rekup.* 3-44. This view is vigorously contested by J.M. Kelly, *Judicature* 40-47, on whom see O. Behrends, (cited n.4) 460-462.

[7] On the introduction of these actions, see Chapter II at notes 35-49; on the use of *recuperatores* in them, B. Schmidlin, *Rekup.* 45-51.

[8] See P. Collinet, in *Rec. F. Gény* vol. I 25-26, for a list of known Republican judges; however, this list is incomplete and somewhat inaccurate.

[9] See J.P. Dawson, *A History of Lay Judges* (1960) 15-30, esp. 27 ff. On the Roman evolution toward professional judges, see M. Kaser, *Österr. Zeitschr. f. Öffentl. Recht* 19 (1969) 381-391.

The *Recuperatores*

in fact jurists sometimes served as judges in more complex cases.[10] In most private trials the parties were free to settle on any judge acceptable both to them and to the Praetor; but parties seem normally to have selected judges from an *album* drawn up by the Urban Praetor at the outset of his term (cf. Cic. *Cluent.* 121). Since this *album* was also used for criminal trials having major political implications, the criteria for selection had become a sensitive political issue by the late Republic. Sulla's legislation had limited the "jury class" to the Senate. However, in 70 B.C., just one year before Caecina's lawsuit, the *lex Aurelia*[11] had instituted a reform whereby the *album* was to comprise three *decuriae*, one each to be drawn from the Senate, the equestrian order, and a third group called *tribuni aerarii*; the status of this last group was apparently defined by wealth alone, but all three groups represented only the uppermost strata of Roman society. Our sources indicate that the Urban Praetor divided the jurors listed in his *album* among the various praetorian courts, both private and criminal, with the result that the list of potential private judges was undoubtedly much smaller than the *album* itself.[12]

The procedure for selecting *recuperatores* varied in important respects from the usual model. Details are sketchy, and con-

---

[10] P. Mucius Scaevola: *Rhet. ad Herenn.* 2.19, cf. 1.24. C. Flavius Fimbria (on whom, Chapter IV, at note 13): Cic. *Off.* 3.77, whence Val. Max. 7.2.4, apparently a non-judicial arbitration. C. Aquilius Gallus: Chapter IV, at notes 35-36.

[11] On which, H. Bruhns, *Chiron* 10 (1980) 263-272, with much bibliography; see also C. Nicolet, *Ordre* vol. I 573-613; T.P. Wiseman, *Historia* 19 (1970) 67-83. Probably the most lucid account of the late Republican *album iudicum* is W. Kunkel, *RE* s.v. "quaestio" (1963) 749, based mainly on J. Lengle, *SZ* 53 (1933) 275 ff.; 290 ff.; see also G. Pugliese, *Processo* vol. II.1 221-227; on the *recuperatores* and the *album*, see esp. J. Stroux, *Eine Gerichtsreform des Kaiser Claudius* (1929) 19-39.

[12] See in general G. Pugliese, *Processo* vol. II.1 215-227; M. Kaser, *RZ* 138-142; O. Behrends, *Die Römische Geschworenenverfassung* (1970) 54-64; all with further literature. On Behrends, see in general M. Lemosse, *Labeo* 17 (1971) 193-198. On a special list for private trials, see esp. Gell. *NA* 14.2.1: "a Praetoribus lectus in iudices sum, ut iudicia quae appellantur privata susciperem."

siderable reconstruction is required;[13] but the following is approximately correct. Out of the larger pool of potential private judges in the *album*, the Praetor selected by lot a smaller initial panel, probably numbering eleven. Then the parties were allowed to eliminate judges alternately, one named by the plaintiff and one by the defendant, up to a maximum of four pairs. The final panel of *recuperatores* was thus usually three in number, though one panel of five is known.[14] In any case, an odd number seems to have been preferred, apparently to avoid ties. Nothing comparable to a modern *voir dire* (a judicial examination of the fitness of jurors) is attested, and the selection process apparently depended on the likelihood that the potential jurors would already be familiar to the litigants or their representatives. The members of a recuperatorial panel were thus drawn only out of the pool of the "jury class" established by the *album*; the parties had no freedom to name non-members of the "jury class" to judge their case. Sortition was used to obtain from this pool a spectrum of potential judges; the parties then narrowed this spectrum by rejecting individuals who, from their respective viewpoints, lay at its extremes, until a group at the "center" of the spectrum was isolated.

The *recuperatores*, once selected, sat as a panel of equals; there is no evidence that they chose a foreman to preside over the ensuing trial.[15] Those selected were, as it seems, under a public obligation to serve without pay, unless they could offer a valid excuse for not doing so.[16]

[13] The major source is the *lex agraria* (*FIRA* vol. I, no. 8), lines 37-39. For other sources and discussion, see Y. Bongert, (cited n.5) 223-225; B. Schmidlin, *Rekup.* 123-126; M. Kaser, *RZ* 142-145.

[14] Panels of three *recuperatores*: Livy 26.48.8; Cic. 2 *Verr.* 3.30, 54, 137; *Flacc.* 40. Five: Livy 43.2.3. There is no Republican evidence for private trials in Rome.

[15] Cicero does not address such a foreman in either the *pro Tullio* or the *pro Caecina*; this is strong evidence against M. Kaser's assumption, *RZ* 274, that *recuperatores* chose a foreman.

[16] See M. Kaser, *RZ* 9, 142; O. Behrends, (cited n.12) 118-119. And of older literature, esp. M. Wlassak, *Der Judikationsbefehl der Römischen Prozesse* (1921) 27-29; J. Mazeaud, *La Nomination du Judex Unus* (1933) 81-87.

The *Recuperatores*

The method for selecting *recuperatores* bears resemblance to that used in obtaining a criminal jury,[17] an evident reflection of the sense of public urgency attending recuperatorial trials. Other details of recuperatorial procedure also reflect this urgency. Above all, the *recuperatores* were supposed to move speedily to a verdict.[18] Inscriptions describing recuperatorial procedure in non-private trials enjoin that the panel of *recuperatores* must be formed within a short time (ten days) after the plaintiff's claim is first raised, and that a verdict must then be rendered shortly thereafter (twenty or thirty days).[19] We know from Cicero (*Tull.* 10; cf. *Div. in Caec.* 56) that recuperatorial procedure in private trials was also swifter than normal procedure, though it is not certain that private *recuperatores* had any time limit for reaching a verdict.[20] Certainly they were not prevented from re-hearing trials that seemed to them uncertain, as the *pro Tullio* (6) and the *pro Caecina* show. Perhaps, however, they operated under a swifter timetable for the initial and subsequent hearings.

Finally, it is likely that the Praetor gave to the two parties the right to summon involuntary witnesses, while at the same time limiting the total number of witnesses they could present. Provisions of this nature are widely attested on inscriptions; usually they allow for a maximum of ten or twenty witnesses apiece.[21] Again, it is not certain that this official summoning of witnesses was also available in private trials;

[17] See B. Schmidlin, *Rekup.* 124, citing J. Lengle, (cited n.11) 274-296.

[18] It is usually supposed that recuperatorial trials lay outside the *actus rerum*, and hence could be held without regard to normal scheduling of trials. See B. Schmidlin, *Rekup.* 132-133, with literature; but also O. Behrends, (cited n.12) 92 n.5, 97.

[19] Formation of panel: the *lex agraria* (cited n.13), line 37; cf. Dion. Hal. 6.95.2. Rendering of verdict: *lex Urson.* (*FIRA* vol. I, no. 21), sec. 95 (twenty days); *SC Calvis.* (*FIRA* vol. I, no. 68), lines 133-134 (thirty days).

[20] See Y. Bongert, (cited n.5) 238-240; B. Schmidlin, *Rekup.* 130-133; G. Pugliese, *Processo* vol. II.1 212-214; O. Behrends, (cited n.12) 91-97, who also emphasizes that swift procedure was intended to discourage bribery of judges.

[21] Ten witnesses: *lex Julia agraria* (*FIRA* vol. I, no. 12), sec. 5; *edictum Venafrum* (*FIRA* vol. I, no. 67), line 67; cf. Valerius Probus, 5.8. Twenty: *lex Urson.* (cited n.19), sec. 95. The *SC Calvis.* (cited n.19), lines 137-140, provides for five witnesses each in private trials, ten each in public trials.

but in the *pro Caecina* Cicero notes rather emphatically that the defense summoned exactly ten witnesses (28: Fidiculanius Falcula testified *decimo loco*), strongly implying that ten was the upper limit on the number of witnesses. If this was so, then perhaps the parties were also empowered to summon involuntary witnesses, although there is no sign that any of Aebutius' witnesses (*Caec.* 24-30) testified involuntarily.[22] In this respect as well, the recuperatorial procedure apparently contained elements of criminal procedure.[23]

Despite this accelerated and slightly abbreviated procedure, in most outward respects recuperatorial trials probably differed very little from normal trials before a single *iudex*.[24] If the *recuperatores* in Caecina's lawsuit were not present during the initial proceedings before the Praetor, it was necessary to summon them, and thus to delay their formal installation until a later date.[25] At this time the Praetor would formally "grant" (*dare*) *recuperatores*, and order them to give a judgment on the three *formulae* prepared by the parties *in iure* (*iubere iudicare*).[26] From this time onward the *recuperatores* took charge of the trial.

Soon after their installation, the *recuperatores* met with the two parties in order to set a place and date for the trial.[27] Either at this time or perhaps even earlier *in iure*, the judges took an oath, the exact wording of which is not preserved.[28] According to Justinian (C. 3.1.14 pr.; A.D. 530), it was common knowledge that "judges of old" (*antiquos iudices*) had al-

[22] See B. Schmidlin, *Rekup.* 126-130; J.M. Kelly, *Judicature* 59-61.

[23] See, e.g., the *lex Acilia* (*FIRA* vol. I, no. 7), lines 32-33.

[24] See in general M. Kaser, *RZ* 272-284. The argument of J.M. Kelly, *Judicature* 57-70, that the *recuperatores* had power to enforce their own judgments, is not persuasive.

[25] See at note 19, above.

[26] See just M. Kaser, *RZ* 222-224.

[27] M. Kaser, *RZ* 274.

[28] See M. Kaser, *RZ* 273; O. Behrends, (cited n.12) 15-16; and, of earlier literature, esp. M.A. von Bethmann-Hollweg, *Civilprozess* vol. I 67 n.29, vol. II 586-587. For the meaning of *iurare in leges*, see J. Bleicken, *Lex Publica* (1975) 226-231. The origin of the oath is unknown. As Behrends, p. 16 n.64, argues, judges probably took a second oath when rendering their verdict; see Quintil. 5.6.4.

ways sworn to decide cases "in accord with truth and respect for the laws" (*cum veritate et legum observatione*).[29] In the *de Officiis* (3.43-44), Cicero evaluates the ethical content of the judge's oath. *Fides* to the oath required the judge to lay aside any personal feelings of friendship or animosity with the parties. To be sure, a judge might prefer that the case of his friend be correct (43: *veram*). But his verdict had to correspond with the truth of the case as he saw it, and both litigants were obliged to respect this fact. The most a judge could do was to arrange the hearings for a time his friends found convenient, "to the extent that law permits" (43: *quoad per leges liceat*). At this preliminary hearing, the judges probably also received a brief and provisional statement of the allegations that would be made by either party (*coniectio causae*).[30]

In accord with a very old tradition, private lawsuits were heard in the open Forum, out-of-doors and before the public.[31] However, by the late Republic the spatial limitations of the Forum and the inconvenience of extended hearings beneath the elements had led to the holding of at least some trials indoors—perhaps most usually in the large basilicas beside the Forum, although even private homes were used on occasion.[32] Nonetheless, trials remained public in principle. Cicero (*Caec.* 28) notes the presence of the *populus* at the first

[29] Words from this oath are apparently quoted by Cicero, *Acad. Pr.* 2.146: the judge swears to decide "ex sui animi sententia," and accepts liability "si sciens falleret." See also Cic. *Inv.* 1.48, 2.132; Quintil. 5.6.4.

[30] So M.A. von Bethmann-Hollweg, *Civilprozess* vol. II 586. Most scholars suppose that such statements were unnecessary in formulary procedure: e.g., M. Wlassak, *RE* s.v. "coniectio" (1900) 882-884; so recently O. Behrends, *SZ* 92 (1975) 162-185. But a *formula* is too brief to be of much help as a summary of the issue; and for an apparent reference to introductory statements, cf. Macrob. *Sat.* 3.16.16 ("quorum negotium est narrant").

[31] M.A. von Bethmann-Hollweg, *Civilprozess* vol. I 75; M. Kaser, *RZ* 9, 147, 274. The determined assault on this doctrine by J.M. Kelly, *Judicature* 103-111, seems unsuccessful; see O. Behrends, (cited n.4) 450-453. Cicero, *de Or.* 1.173, makes it certain that most important *iudicia privata* were heard openly in the Forum (*in Foro*); see also Cic. *Nat. Deor.* 3.74.

[32] On private houses, see Vitruv. 6.5.2: such houses require very large *atria*, obviously to accommodate crowds. On basilicas, the earliest evidence for private trials is apparently Seneca, *Dial.* 5.33.2.

hearing of Caecina's lawsuit, as well as their derisive reaction to the testimony of Fidiculanius Falcula.

Outwardly, the private court somewhat resembled the simple court of the Praetor, except that (as it seems) there was no tribunal and the judges sat on benches at the same level as the parties.[33] The judges also had no staff members to assist them in handling the case. Whether or not the judges had any previous experience with law, they usually summoned a *consilium* of advisors (*adsessores* or *advocati*) to help them in reaching a verdict; at least by the end of the Republic, jurists were often included in these *consilia* (Cic. *Top.* 65).[34] There is, however, no evidence that multi-member panels of judges (such as *recuperatores*) also relied on help from *consilia*; nor does Cicero mention in the *pro Tullio* or *pro Caecina* that juristic advice independent of that provided by the parties was available to the *recuperatores*, despite the heavily legal character of these two speeches. At this early date it was in any case still probably uncommon for judges to seek juristic advice independently of the parties.

The hearing of the case was conducted by the judges themselves, according to an etiquette that was largely customary.[35] The broad framework of the trial—the cause of action, the plaintiff, and the defendant—had of course been determined

[33] Except for the centumviral court, tribunals are not mentioned for private trials: E. Weiss, *RE* s.v. "tribunal" (1937) 2429-2430. Gellius, *NA* 14.2.11, indicates that a *iudex* sat on the *subsellia*; cf. also Quintil. 11.3.156.

[34] On *consilia* see above, at note 3; M. Kaser, *RZ* 142; and, of earlier literature, esp. H.F. Hitzig, *Die Assessoren der Römischen Magistrate und Richter* (1893) 9-10, 15, 22-23. As is apparent from Val. Max. 8.2.2, judges gained social prestige from the eminence of members of their *consilia*; cf. W. Kunkel, *SZ* 72 (1955) 468-469. Aquilius Gallus is the first *iudex* known to have used a jurist as an *adsessor* (cf. n.3), and it may be that the jurists themselves fostered this practice; but it still does not appear among the typical activities of a jurist in, e.g., Cic. *Mur.* 19, 21-22. Hitzig (p. 22) doubted that *recuperatores* had a *consilium*, probably rightly.

[35] M. Kaser, *SZ* 59 (1939) 97-98 and *RZ* 275; A. Steinwenter, *SZ* 65 (1947) 88-92. A judge's conduct of a private trial is satirically described in a second-century B.C. speech quoted by Macrob. *Sat.* 3.16.15-16. The judge ordered parties to speak: Quintil. 11.3.156. In the early Empire, judges often relied on procedural handbooks prepared by jurists: Gell. *NA* 14.2.1, 20, with Steinwenter, p. 87 n.60.

The *Recuperatores*

earlier through the *formulae* the judges had been appointed to decide. The proceedings were almost entirely oral, and no official transcript was kept.[36] The hearing began with long speeches delivered first by the advocate for the plaintiff, then by the advocate for the defendant. In the Republic these speeches were in principle continuous; judges did not interrupt them with questions, nor did the opposing advocate raise objections.[37] Further, advocates firmly resisted external attempts to limit the amount of time they could speak (Cic. *Quinct.* 33), though excessively long speeches were a source of resentment (*Quinct.* 34; *Tull.* 6).

It requires about two hours to read the *pro Caecina* aloud at a steady and deliberate pace; but if the *narratio* (10-23) and the argument on Caecina's citizenship (95-102) are omitted,[38] about one and a half hours are needed. In one standard edition the *pro Caecina* occupies thirty-six pages of text. In that same edition Cicero's other private orations, all fragmentarily preserved, take thirty-one pages for the *pro Quinctio*, seventeen for the *pro Roscio Comoedo*, and thirteen for the *pro Tullio*; all these speeches look to have been originally about the same length as the *pro Caecina*.[39] If the *pro Caecina* is taken as the norm for late Republican private orations, then delivery of speeches by the two sides would have required about three to four hours in all. Orators delivered their speeches while standing, to a seated court.[40] The constrained circumstances

[36] M. Kaser, *RZ* 274 n.19.

[37] On the speeches, see M.A. von Bethmann-Hollweg, *Civilprozess* vol. II 590-593. Cicero's published speeches are the main evidence; but see also Tac. *Dial.* 19.5-20.2, 38. Witty interjections, however, were common: e.g., Cic. *de Or.* 2.216 ff. During the Empire, presentation of a party's case was sometimes divided among several orators (Quintil. 6.4.6-7; 12.3.6-7); Cic. *Caec.* 35 indicates that this may have occurred also in the Republic (and cf. *Quinct.* 80; Tac. *Dial.* 38.1). Parties could also change orators between hearings (*Quinct.* 3).

[38] See Chapter III, at notes 67-68.

[39] The *pro Quinctio* is complete except for an extended portion of the argument and the beginning of the *peroratio* after 85; the *pro Roscio Comoedo* lacks *exordium*, *narratio*, and *peroratio*, as well as the beginning and end of the argument; the *pro Tullio* is lacunose throughout.

[40] Quintil. 11.3.156. Cf. Cic. *Rosc. Am.* 60; A. Checchini, *Scritti Giuridici e*

of private trials obviously did not lend themselves to lofty flights of rhetoric; except in the centumviral court, speeches were normally addressed only to one or at the most a handful of judges, and hence had a more matter-of-fact tone.[41] But the *pro Caecina* shows how a skilled orator could expand the context by constructing mock dialogues with the defendant (48-49), his advocate (36-38, 64, 82-84, 89-91), his jurist (79-80), and even with the spectators at large (e.g., 30).

The gathering and presentation of physical evidence[42] were left to the initiative of individual parties. Documents were used rather sparingly; in the *pro Caecina*, Cicero refers to none except the *tabulae* of the *argentarius* Phormio (17). He gives no hint that the various wills (11, 12, 17) were produced in court, though he describes their contents. Caesennia's account books had allegedly been stolen by the defendant (17); the tenant farmer's accounts are mentioned only in passing (94). No procedure was used for authentication of documents, and Cicero admits that forged documents were not uncommon (71).[43] The *responsa* of jurists (79) were handled in a similarly casual fashion; normally those who consulted the jurists simply reported the result,[44] though jurists also sent unsealed *responsa* to judges (Pompon. D. 1.2.2.49). Documentary evidence of all types, including even depositions by absent witnesses (Cic. *Rosc. Com.* 43), was usually presented to the court during the advocates' speech, without formalities and as the occasion arose.[45]

After the two advocates had spoken, witnesses were pre-

Storico-Giuridici vol. II (1958) 132-134, 154. For other points of courtroom etiquette, see Chapter II, at note 60.

[41] See, e.g., Cic. *Orat.* 72; *Opt. Gen. Orat.* 10; *Fam.* 9.21.1. The difference in tone between the centumviral court and the *iudicium privatum* is remarked by Pliny, *Ep.* 6.33.9.

[42] See esp. G. Pugliese, *Jus* 11 (1960) 404-421. On documents: *ibid.* 416-419; M. Kaser, *RZ* 283-284. The Romans had no process for discovery, but cf. Lenel, *EP*³ 59-64, on *editio*. On rhetorical theories of proof, see F. Gnoli, in *Seminario Romanististico Gardesano* (1976) 127-137.

[43] See M. Kaser, *RZ* 284 n.69; cf. Cic. *Nat. Deor.* 3.74, *Off.* 3.73-74 (forged wills).

[44] As it seems, without naming the jurists: Chapter IV, at notes 48-49.

[45] See M. Kaser, *RZ* 276.

sented.[46] The defense in Caecina's lawsuit had ten witnesses (*Caec.* 24-31); if the plaintiff produced an equal number, and if the average length of the witnesses' testimony was just fifteen minutes, the examination and cross-examination of witnesses would have lasted five hours. The amount of time devoted to witnesses must have considerably mitigated the effect of the opening orations. Witnesses testified under oath (*Caec.* 25, 28; *Rosc. Com.* 44-46), and there was a criminal penalty for perjury.[47] After completing their direct testimony, they were cross-examined by the opposing advocate (*Caec.* 28). Aebutius did not testify on his own behalf, and indeed litigants seem generally not to have done so in private trials (cf. *Rosc. Com.* 45); their testimony was, so to speak, embedded in the speeches of their respective advocates.[48]

When the two sides had completed their arguments and presentation of witnesses, the two advocates probably engaged in a brief exchange of argument about the case (*altercatio*).[49] Quintilian (6.4.7) gives the earliest certain evidence for *altercationes* in private trials; but the custom was probably an old one. The *altercatio* had a question-and-answer format between advocates, and was used to impress both positive and negative points on the judge (*ibid.* 2, 5).

Throughout the hearing, the advocates observed no limits on what could or could not be produced as evidence. General

---

[46] M.A. von Bethmann-Hollweg, *Civilprozess* vol. II 597-599; M. Kaser, *RZ* 281-283. On techniques for examining and cross-examining witnesses, see Quintil. 5.7.3-32. By the late Republic, examination of witnesses probably followed the set speeches from both sides; but see *ibid.* 25. The Romans' heavy reliance on testimony from witnesses probably affected judicial accuracy adversely. See E.F. Loftus, *Eyewitness Testimony* (1979), whose results are controversial; cf. the debate in *American Psychologist* 38 (1983) 550-577.

[47] M. Kaser, *RZ* 283 n.64. Cic. *Rosc. Com.* 46 ff. suggests that this sanction was not taken too seriously.

[48] See M.A. von Bethmann-Hollweg, *Civilprozess* vol. II 594-597; G. Pugliese, (cited n.42) 415-416; M. Kaser, *RZ* 280-281. But Cic. *Rosc. Com.* 42 may raise the possibility of a litigant testifying.

[49] On which, Quintil. 6.4, with Kipp, *RE* s.v. "altercatio" (1894) 1692-1693. Cicero occasionally mentions orators skilled in *altercatio* (e.g., *Brut.* 159, 173).

report and hearsay (*rumores*) were freely admissible,[50] as, for example, Aebutius' alleged mandate from Caesennia (*Caec.* 15-17) or Falcula's acceptance of a bribe (28-30). Likewise, only the orator's sense of propriety restrained his use of vituperation and innuendo (Cic. *Tull.* 5; Quintil. 12.9.8-13), though to be sure nothing in the *pro Caecina* quite equals Cicero's scathing description of the plaintiff in an earlier suit (*Rosc. Com.* 20).

The first hearing of Caecina's lawsuit is likely to have lasted some eight to ten hours, not counting intermissions. Most scholars presume that, under the influence of rhetoric, the archaic rule requiring that private trials be concluded within one day had long since fallen into abeyance.[51] L. Quinctius, Cicero's opponent in Tullius' lawsuit, is described as having spoken until sunset at the first hearing (*Tull.* 6)—something that Republican audiences are said to have enjoyed (Tac. *Dial.* 19.2), though Cicero plainly felt differently.[52] Yet the defendant's witnesses had already testified by the time of the second hearing (*Tull.* 1-2, 24-25). This presumably means that the first hearing was held on two separate days, doubtless on two consecutive days.

Rather different is the complete re-hearing of the case, where the judge or judges are unable to reach a verdict at a hearing. This was extremely common.[53] At the conclusion of a hearing, the single *iudex* withdrew with his *consilium* in order to consider the verdict;[54] a roughly parallel procedure must have been followed by the *recuperatores*. Presumably it was in their discussion together that the *recuperatores* reached a consensus to re-hear Caecina's lawsuit (*Caec.* 9: *prolato iudicio*), owing to

[50] See *Rhet. ad Herenn.* 2.9 and Quintil. 5.3; with G. Pugliese, (cited n.42) 419-420.

[51] E.g., M.A. von Bethmann-Hollweg, *Civilprozess* vol. II 591-592; M. Kaser, *RZ* 274.

[52] In the trial of Quinctius, by contrast, Cicero's opponent accused him of filibustering and tried unsuccessfully to persuade the Praetor to set a time limit on speeches (*Quinct.* 33).

[53] See Chapter III, at note 4.

[54] Macrob. *Sat.* 3.16.15 (*eunt in consilium*); Cic. *Quinct.* 34.

what Cicero terms *dubitatio in iudicando* (4) and an inability to reach "clarity" (31: *quid liqueret*).[55] In *iudicia privata*, re-hearing a case could extend to the representation of former witnesses or even the presentation of new ones (Cic. *Quinct.* 58, 75); in recuperatorial procedure, because of the limitation on the number of witnesses, this was presumably not possible.[56] In the *pro Caecina*, Cicero makes it quite clear that the *recuperatores* themselves were responsible for the delay in decision (4-9, 31). The extent of the interval between hearings is uncertain; but Cicero, who took up Quinctius' case after it had been abandoned by another advocate (*Quinct.* 3), plainly had sufficient time to work up the case afresh.

Perhaps the most extraordinary aspect of late Republican trials is what has been aptly called the "passivity" of the judge.[57] Although he presided over the trial, he was essentially only a silent spectator to the presentation of argument and evidence by the two parties. No knowledge of law was presumed of him.[58] He asked no questions of the parties, their advocates, or the witnesses; in principle, he allowed the adversary proceedings to develop more or less according to the wishes of the parties, without intervening to assert opinions of his own. In theory, at any rate, "the judge is bound to the facts and the evidence that the parties present."[59] As Tacitus (*Dial.* 38)

[55] *Proferre iudicium* is used also for adjournment of a private trial at Cic. 2 *Verr.* 2.75. Gellius, *NA* 14.2.11 (cf. 2), uses the phrase *diffindere diem* for such an adjournment; this phrase was also used in a rather different sense (postponement owing to illness), cf. Festus p. 336 L (= *XII Tab.* 2.2) and Ulpian, D. 2.11.2.3. On adjournments in recuperatorial trials, see Y. Bongert, (cited n.5) 239-240.

[56] See above, at note 21. In *Tull.* 1-2, 24, Cicero looks back to the testimony of witnesses at the first hearing of Tullius' lawsuit; this is clearest in 24 (e.g., "quae mei testes non dicunt, quia non viderunt nec sciunt, ea dicit ipse adversarius," where the *confessio* obviously occurred in the first hearing, cf. 1: "confessus est").

[57] Cf. M. Lemosse, *Cognitio* (1944) 166-170; and 175-180, on the *recuperatores*.

[58] See L. de Sarlo, *Riv. di Dir. Proc. Civ.* 16 (1939) 281-284.

[59] L. Wenger, *Institutionen des Römischen Zivilprozessrechts* (1925) 192 (my translation); cf. M. Kaser, *RZ* 8. F. Sturm, *RIDA*³ 9 (1962) 377-381, argues against this view.

observed, it was their passivity that ensured the dominance of rhetorical advocacy within late Republican courts.

As we shall see below, this model of judicial passivity did not entirely correspond to reality; judges found ways to influence the course of trials even without directly participating in them. But the formal ideals of the Roman judicial system[60] are nonetheless important for what they say about its sources of legitimacy: the impartiality of the judge or judges; the dominance of the parties in shaping the trial; the judges' discretion in evaluating cases; the heavily oral nature and emphatic publicity of hearings; and their relative efficiency. These ideals were as characteristic of recuperatorial procedure as of *iudicia privata*. Legitimacy was achieved through stark orientation to individual cases, not through implementation of other system values such as consistency, accuracy, or "social justice" of verdicts. Both sides were allowed to "have their say," and then a neutral third party decided the winner.

It is not difficult to undermine the legitimacy of the Roman judicial system, above all by appealing to values other than those the Roman system preferred and elevated. In any case, it seems clear that so simple and forthright an arbitrational model could not easily withstand the stresses produced, in the late Republic, by the rapid demoralization of the upper classes. In the *pro Caecina*, Cicero speaks openly of the "unworthy judge" (71: *iudici . . . improbo*) who can be bribed to give a wrong judgment (72); and popular literature suggests not only that improper influences on Roman judges were thought to be common, but also that cynicism about the judicial system was widespread.[61] Nor do the sanctions against misbehaving judges

---

[60] See M. Kaser, *RZ* 6-8; and Chapter VI, below, under subhead "Legitimation through Procedure."

[61] For sources, see J.M. Kelly, *Litigation* 31-68. On Macrob. *Sat.* 3.16.14-16, see O. Behrends, (cited n.12) 56 n.24. On the other hand, some sources indicate continued faith in the old system: e.g., Hor. *Sat.* 1.4.122-124 (the *iudex* as a model for personal conduct); Ovid, *Tristia* 2.93-96 (pride in having judged fairly), with E.J. Kenney, *Yale Cl. Stud.* 12 (1969) 246-249. C. Nicolet, *The World of the Citizen in Republican Rome* (trans. P.S. Falla, 1980) 340, is rightly doubtful that judicial corruption was as widespread as our sources sometimes suggest.

seem to have been particularly effective, doubtless because proof was very difficult when judges remained so passive during trials.[62] But in the end, the Roman judicial system was probably threatened far more by the widening maldistribution of social resources; a modern observer might well feel that late Republican judges decided not which side was right, but rather (as Balzac would put it) which side had the better lawyer.

Nonetheless, even when the Roman judicial system is regarded in its "ideal" form, it raised certain further obstacles to the efficacy of law. These obstacles are the subject of the two following sections.

RELATING RULES TO CASES: THE CAPABILITIES OF LAW (II)

The Praetor's order to the *recuperatores* in Caecina's lawsuit essentially required them to organize a hearing, to listen to both sides, and then to reach a verdict concerning the issue described in the *formulae* for the trial.[63] But the Praetor's order did not prescribe the manner in which they were to reach their verdict, and in particular it said nothing as to the criteria on which the verdict should be based. Even the burden of proof was not legally distributed between the two parties, although custom, in accord with common sense, required that the plaintiff establish the nature of and basis for his claim and, likewise, that the defendant prove any defenses raised to this claim.[64] No legally determined burden of proof was pre-

---

[62] See J.M. Kelly, *Litigation* 102-117, esp. 116-117. On the *iudex qui litem suam fecit*, see recently D.N. MacCormick, *Acta Juridica* (1977) 149-165 and *ANRW* vol. II.14 (1982) 3-28, both with further bibliography; A. D'Ors, *SDHI* 48 (1982) 368-394.

[63] M. Kaser, *RZ* 9, 222-224. On the *formulae* see Chapter II, at note 84; on the form of the verdict, below at notes 103-105.

[64] See esp. G. Pugliese, *RIDA*³ 3 (1956) 349-422; further literature in M. Kaser, *RZ* 278-280. So also, broadly speaking, in rhetorical writings: Cic. *Part. Orat.* 102; Ps.-Quintil. 312 ("Cum res sine teste esset, iudicio victus petitor," etc.). A. Wacke, *TR* 37 (1969) 369-414, is a complex but highly interesting study of this theme.

scribed because, with very few exceptions, the verdict was neither reviewable nor appealable.[65] The judge was pretty much left to his own devices in assessing the evidence, and both his assessment and his verdict were matters largely between him and his conscience.

Judges must often have felt ill at ease with their wide-ranging discretion. More than two centuries after Caecina's lawsuit, Aulus Gellius describes how as a *iudex* he had agonized over a relatively simple case (*NA* 14.2).[66] The plaintiff, a man of impeccable reputation, claimed money he had allegedly lent to the defendant, a notorious scoundrel; but the plaintiff had no proof of the debt's existence beyond his own word (4-8). Gellius, who at the time of this trial had no experience as a *iudex*, expresses anger that he could find no handbooks describing, in at least general terms, how to handle such a situation (2-3); even classical law resolutely declined to provide instructions of this kind.[67] Gellius' *consilium*, men with considerable experience in trials, advised him to absolve the defendant because of the absence of evidence against him (9). But Gellius thought them unduly hasty (9-10),[68] and therefore he adjourned the trial so that he could talk things over with a philosopher friend (11). The philosopher, laying more weight on the relative character of the parties, advised Gellius to find for the plaintiff (21-23). But Gellius felt himself unable to render a verdict based on character and not on evidence (to do so, he says, would be considered presumptuous and self-

[65] On the verdict, see the following section.

[66] On this passage, see esp. P. de Francisci, *Helikon* 1 (1961) 591-604. There is no reason to suppose the case is fictitious (cf. *ibid.* 595-596). Gellius' account of a judge's behavior is in any event unique; see also P. Garnsey, *Social Status and Legal Privilege* (1970) 210-211.

[67] Cf. Ulpian, (5 *Off. Proc.*) D. 5.1.79.1: "iudicibus de iure dubitantibus proconsules respondere solent; de facto consulentibus non debent consilium impertire." Hadrian was equally reluctant (Callistr. D. 22.5.3). See esp. A. Steinwenter, (cited n.35) 87-88; M. Kaser, *RZ* 8-9, 274-276.

[68] As P. de Francisci, (cited n.66) 598, observes, Gellius was partially moved by the likelihood that the plaintiff, if he lost, would be subjected to a charge of *calumnia* (cf. Gell. *NA* 14.2.8, with Chapter II, at note 83).

important for a young man), and in the end he simply reported *non liquet* (24-25).

The quandary in which Gellius found himself may not have been totally dissimilar to that into which the *recuperatores* of Caecina's lawsuit had fallen, at any rate if they accepted Cicero's evaluation of the relative characters of plaintiff and defendant; in his *peroratio* Cicero invites the *recuperatores* to consider this aspect of the trial (*Caec.* 103), something that was indeed well-nigh traditional in Roman lawsuits.[69] Caecina had originally built his claim on his ownership and possession of the Fulcinian farm.[70] However, in the course of the trial it had emerged that his proof for these claims was, to say the least, extremely weak, and he was obliged to shift his ground. Yet despite the failure of Caecina's original case, the *recuperatores* showed themselves reluctant to decide against him. In one respect, though, the position of the *recuperatores* was far different from that of Gellius. Gellius's case raised no substantive legal problem; but had it done so, then Gellius, as he himself elsewhere states (*NA* 12.13.3, cf. 5), would unhesitatingly have accepted as binding on him the opinions of jurists in his *consilium*. The *recuperatores* in Caecina's case had no such easy refuge. In this respect, a sea change divided the Ciceronian from the Antonine court.

Legal determination of a case rests largely on a process of typification: the elements of the case are reduced to legally meaningful patterns which permit the application of rules.[71] Typification helps the judge both to understand the circumstances of the case (its relative particularity as well as its extensiveness in time and space) and to determine its meaning. The task is necessary, and yet supremely difficult if it is to

---

[69] See Gell. *NA* 14.2.26 (= Cato the Elder, frg. 206 Malc.²). Cicero, to be sure, admits that the issue of character is *extra iudicium*. Arguments from *fama* are examined by Cic. *Part. Orat.* 34-35; Quintil. 5.3, cf. 5.10.23-31. In *Rosc. Com.* 20, Cicero urges the judge to observe the plaintiff's eyelashes.

[70] See Chapter III, at notes 30-40.

[71] On what follows, see chap. 3 of R. Lempert and J. Sanders, *Desert, Disputes, and Distribution: A Social Science Perspective on Law and the Legal System* (forthcoming).

be accomplished both efficiently and fairly. Like the members of Aulus Gellius' *consilium*, experienced judges are "outside observers" heavily conditioned by the repetitiveness of their previous decision making and by their desire to control the future behavior of the litigants and others; hence they often incline to a rather shallow case logic, one that stresses the objective social meaning of the case by narrowly typifying it and confining the extensiveness of its circumstances. But Gellius, whether through naiveté or simple humanity, was drawn into a different and deeper case logic that more nearly approximated that of the litigants; for them, an account of the events that produced the trial had to be more wide-ranging (hence less typical) and interpenetrated by the meaning that they themselves each assigned to the dispute.[72] Gellius' *consilium* treated the character of the litigants as irrelevant to the issue at hand; but Gellius could not see it that way.

Rhetorical advocacy was not in principle irreconcilable with judicial typification, yet in various ways it hindered judges from arriving at any independent understanding of cases. In the first place, strong forms of adversary procedure, with their combative format, are in any event not well suited to facilitating the disinterested reconstruction of a case.[73] Second, control of typification lay mainly in the hands of the advocates themselves, whose views as to the uniqueness and extensiveness of cases were largely determined by the immediate desire to persuade rather than by the broader purposes of the judicial system.[74] For Cicero, Caecina's lawsuit begins with events far in the past—the property relations of a couple both of

[72]See E.E. Jones and R.E. Nisbett, in *Attribution: Perceiving the Causes of Behavior* (ed. Jones, 1972) 79-94; e.g., 73: "Actors tend to attribute the causes of their behavior to stimuli inherent in the situation, while observers tend to attribute behavior to stable dispositions of the actor." For an empirical study of judicial typification, see R. Lautmann, *Justiz: Die Stille Gewalt* (1972), esp. 143-155.

[73] See the thoughtful comments of M. Damaska, *Pennsylvania Law Review* 123 (1975) 1083-1106.

[74] See Quintilian's interesting remarks (12.8) on the nature of a case. Especially in his later rhetorical writings, Cicero tends to reject this view; see Chapter VI, at note 101.

The *Recuperatores*

whom are now dead (*Caec.* 10-11)—while the final confrontation between Caecina and Aebutius, and their subsequent lawsuit, are taken as manifestations of the universal and ceaseless struggle between *ius* and *vis*, between the spirit and the letter of the law.[75] It is not so much that Cicero is "wrong" in this view, as that his case might well seem less appealing on a narrower construction of the facts; yet the *recuperatores* are given no clear indication as to how they should determine between a broader and a narrower construction. Third, Cicero offers his case as a "global view," which the *recuperatores* are invited to compare and contrast with the "global view" that Piso offers.[76] Both sides posit that one view or the other must yield the better solution to the lawsuit. Neither entertains the notion of a third alternative emerging out of their conflict.

Cicero believed that this was as it should be. In his *de Republica* (1.59) he remarks, quite in passing, that the *bonus iudex* ought to be swayed more by force of argument than by evidence of witnesses. In the *de Oratore* (2.178) he suggests that persuasion occurs mainly through the hearer's "mental impulse or emotion" (*impetu . . . animi et perturbatione*) in favor of the speaker, rather than through his "judgment or consideration" (*iudicio aut consilio*); "for men judge far more issues on the basis of hate or love or desire or rage or sorrow or joy or hope or fear or delusion or some other mental emotion, than on the basis of truth or principle or some legal norm or the *formula* for the trial or statutory law."[77] This extraordinarily candid passage sheds considerable light on the administration of justice during the late Republic. As Cicero goes on to ob-

[75] See Chapter III, under subhead "Cicero's Strategy in the *pro Caecina*."
[76] See Chapter III, at notes 121-124.
[77] Cic. *de Or.* 2.178: "plura enim multo homines iudicant odio aut amore aut cupiditate aut iracundia aut dolore aut laetitia aut spe aut timore aut errore aut aliqua permotione mentis quam veritate aut praescripto aut iuris norma aliqua aut iudici formula aut legibus." Cf. Cic. *de Or.* 1.60, 2.201; *Brut.* 317, 322; *Orat.* 97; Quintil. 5.7.33 and, generally, 6.2. On ancient reactions to Cicero's emotionalism, see M.L. Clarke, *Rhetoric at Rome* (1963) 78-79, citing esp. Quintil. 8.3.4.

Relating Rules to Cases

serve (2.187), an emotional *iudex* is much more easily manip-
ulated by the orator than one who is "neutral and unpredis-
posed" (*integer quietusque*); but eloquence, like a good general,
can ultimately "capture" (*capere*) even judges of the latter sort.
Such imagery of siegecraft, common in rhetorical writings,
reflects the passive role traditionally assigned to Roman judges.

However, there is good evidence that late Republican judges,
themselves usually men of considerable political and social experience, chafed under the narrowness of this passive role.[78]
The philosopher whom Aulus Gellius consulted had recently
read a book, *On the Duties of a Judge*, by the late Republican
jurist Aelius Tubero (*NA* 14.2.20); evidently on the basis of
this perusal,[79] the philosopher lists four ways whereby a judge
can assume a more active role in conducting a trial. First, the
judge may take advantage of his prior knowledge regarding
the matter at issue, rather than limiting himself to what the
parties prove (14); there seems to be no legal barrier to his
doing so. Second, he may temporarily put off his role as judge,
and undertake private consultation with the parties in order
to mediate their quarrel (15); there is good evidence that judges
assumed such an activist role during the late Republic.[80] Third,
within the trial itself the judge may become actively inquisitorial, directing questions to a party about points at issue even
if the other party has failed to raise them; but this course
seems to have been frowned upon as representing abandon-
ment of judicial neutrality (16). Fourth, the judge can at least

[78] On the independence of Roman judges, see M. Lemosse, (cited n.57)
158-166.
[79] So, rightly, P. de Francisci, (cited n.66) 600-601. On this work, see also
A. dell'Oro, *I Libri de Officio nella Giurisprudenza Romana* (1960) 8-9. It is not
entirely certain that this work is to be ascribed to the late Republican jurist,
rather than to his second-century antecedent; in favor of the latter view, see
G. Broggini, *Iudex Arbiterve* (1957) 219 n.8. For further discussion of the
constant confusion between the two Tuberones, see M. Bretone, *Iura* 27
(1976) 72-74, with further bibliography.
[80] In 100 B.C. C. Marius, as *iudex*, intervened outside of court when C.
Titinius, who was being sued by his ex-wife for return of her dowry, asserted
her inchastity: Plut. *Marius* 38.5; Val. Max. 8.2.3, implying that Marius'
conduct was excessive.

try to guide the course of the trial by making occasional summaries of the issues at stake and indicating his own reactions to the argument as it progresses (17).[81] This sort of intervention was also controversial; activist judges preferred it as a means to improve their understanding of disputes (18), while more passive judges held that it risked upsetting the neutrality of the proceedings by exposing the judge's reaction prematurely, before all argument was in (19).

Two points are especially important about this discussion. First, if we may properly speak of an "ethos" among judges,[82] it is plain from this passage that by the late Republic discussion of the "ethos" had evolved well beyond the simple principles of "truth and neutrality" articulated by Cicero (*Off.* 3.43-44), and had penetrated to core ambiguities in the role of the judge. Second, it is also clear that a judge was legally free to pursue an activist course if he wished to, the main restraint on such conduct being social. Further, the trend was toward activism and intervention. As Tacitus remarks (*Dial.* 19.5-20.2, 39.3), by the early Empire judges had become so prone to interrupt and so eager to hurry proceedings along that protracted speeches of the Ciceronian type—the *pro Caecina* is even mentioned as an example—were no longer feasible. Pliny the Younger (*Ep.* 6.33.9) also regards such intervention as highly characteristic of *iudicia privata*;[83] and Quintilian notes the demand by judges for "credibility of presentation, not mere show" (10.1.32: *non speciem expositionis, sed fidem*).

The reason why the issues raised above are so important is that the Ciceronian judge was asked to rule not just on his

[81] Ca. 60 B.C. a plaintiff abandoned a trial when the *iudex* indicated he would give an adverse judgment: Cic. *Flacc.* 50. Advocates fairly hung on any sign of the judge's reaction, even facial expressions: Quintil. 6.2.7, 4.19.

[82] See for instance O. Behrends, (cited n.12) 11-12, 202; also G. Broggini, *Coniectanea* (1966) 314-315. The notion of an *officium iudicis* appears already in Cic. *Inv.* 2.125; the sources deserve a major re-study.

[83] He contrasts the centumviral court, where the size of panels made intervention by individual judges unfeasible. Hence this court became the last refuge of unfettered rhetorical advocacy; cf. *Ep.* 6.12.2 (*harena mea*). On the centumviral court, see also Cic. *de Or.* 1.173; *Brut.* 197; Martial, 6.38.5; Tac. *Dial.* 38.2; Pliny, *Ep.* 2.14.4 ff., 6.33.3; Suet. *Gram.* 30.

understanding of the case before him, but also on the law that applied to it. In the *peroratio* of his speech for Caecina (103-104), Cicero urges the *recuperatores* to consider the following issues: the relative character of the litigants; the defendant's *confessio* that he had used armed force against Caecina; the defendant's attempt to justify his actions through literal interpretation, rather than through *aequitas*, and the demonstrated failure of this attempt; the weighty authority (104: *auctoritatem sapientissimorum hominum*) backing Caecina's case;[84] and the facts, not technically relevant, that Caecina both possessed and owned the Fulcinian farm.

The problem with this heterogeneous "laundry list" is that it presents the *recuperatores* with no procedural theory for making a decision, no clear way to determine the linkage between law and the instant case. Both law and facts are left to their deliberation. Take, for example, the issue of the plaintiff's prior possession.[85] At least by the second hearing of Caecina's lawsuit, Piso had asserted that a plaintiff under the interdict *de vi armata* had to possess (*Caec.* 90-91); Cicero rejects this position (90-93), and yet offers a proof *extra causam* that Caecina had possessed (94-95). What is the status of this proof? If Piso is correct in asserting that the interdict requires plaintiff's possession, then the factual issue must also be admitted and decided; but if Cicero is correct in rejecting Piso's view, then the proof is irrelevant. In theory, at any rate, the issue of law must be decided first, and then the issue of fact if it is relevant.

Yet this neat compartmentalization is not so easily accomplished in practice. The existence or no of the disputed legal rule is crucial to the understanding of a case such as Caecina's, in that it instructs a judge on whether or not to pay attention to the dispute over the fact of Caecina's possession. Yet a Roman judge, confronted with the disputed circumstances of a single case, will also have found it impossible to know whether

[84] Evidently Cicero is claiming the support of *Ignotus*, on the basis of *Caec.* 80-85.

[85] My discussion here takes up from that in Chapter IV, at notes 157-159.

the disputed rule was or was not a proper one in circumstances other than the immediately present ones. Even if he used the instant case as his guide in determining the rule, he could still not escape from an evaluation of the facts of the case prior to a determination of the law. While this dilemma is more or less endemic to all judicial procedure, it is considerably exacerbated when not even some threshold level of certainty as to prevailing law is possible.

This dilemma manifests itself most immediately, I think, in the propensity of late Republican judges to re-hear trials when legal issues arose. Cicero complains bitterly about this tendency, which, so he argues, obstructs just retribution for wrongdoing (*Caec.* 6-7). In Cicero's (naturally quite biased) view, the defendant has successfully gambled that, by brazenly confessing his use of armed force and then defending its legality, he would provide the judges with "a reason for deliberation and a legitimate hesitancy and scruple in deciding" (4: *causam deliberandi et iudicandi iustam moram ac religionem*); the focus of the trial would then shift from Aebutius' wickedness to a point of law (4). Cicero, as an orator, expresses doubts about his ability to handle such a theme (5). Indeed, he is convinced (6: *ego mihi sic persuadeo*) that the "real" reason for the two adjournments is not "owing to the ambiguous and doubtful purport of the law" (*propter iuris obscuram dubiamque rationem*), but rather because the *recuperatores* are loath to condemn the defendant in so weighty a case (6-7). Yet Cicero also admits that "hesitancy on law" (9: *iuris dubitatio*) may after all be responsible for the delay.

Of course, none of this can be taken at face value. The whole tenor of the *pro Caecina* makes clear that, in Cicero's opinion, the trial now hinged on the meaning of the interdict.[86] If Cicero nonetheless advances a different reason for the adjournments, surely his reasons are tactical: the *recuperatores*, in considering the "legal issue," must not forget the enormity of Aebutius' alleged deed. But there is no reason to

[86] Let me quote, once again, Cic. *Orat.* 102: "Tota mihi causa pro Caecina de verbis interdicti fuit."

doubt that Cicero, in wheeling to focus on the interdict's interpretation, thought he was following the wishes of the *recuperatores*.

What I am arguing is that late Republican judges, confronted by a pervasive climate of legal insecurity, began to use adjournment as a means to force advocates into narrowing and tightening their debate. Adjournment, coupled perhaps with a summary indication of their desires expressed in or out of court,[87] doubtless sufficed. A measure of confirmation comes from Cicero's earliest oration, the *pro Quinctio* of 81 B.C. Cicero took up that case after it had been several times adjourned and Quinctius' first advocate had withdrawn (3). Although Cicero tries to expound the case afresh, he does promise at the outset of his *argumentum* to deal with issues about which the judge wishes to hear (35: *quibus de rebus auditurus sis*), thus implying some form of communication from the *iudex*.[88] The *iudex* was the jurist Aquilius Gallus, and the issues he was interested in were doubtless mainly legal.[89] Likewise, the second hearing of Tullius' lawsuit went off on highly technical points of interpretation; so too, as it seems, did the case of the woman from Arretium (*Caec.* 97).

If frequent adjournments and re-hearings forced advocates into the uncomfortable position of arguing technical legal questions, the most promising way out was to upgrade the legal value of juristic opinions on law. This is the purport of Cicero's famous statement in praise of the *ius civile* (*Caec.* 65-78),[90] a passage that has often been condemned as irrelevant to the purpose of the *pro Caecina*.[91] Cicero, with the eminent

[87] The possibility of such communication is clearly raised by *Caec.* 8 ("Ac si qui mihi hoc iudex recuperatorve dicat," etc.).

[88] So, rightly, M. Kaser, *RZ* 275 n.29.

[89] The scholarly fate of the *pro Quinctio* has been broadly similar to that of the *pro Caecina*: scholars have widely argued that Quinctius' case was hopeless: e.g., T.E. Kinsey, *Pro P. Quinctio Oratio* (1971) 5-6. If this is so, why did Aquilius (a jurist!) have such difficulty in reaching a verdict? More fair and accurate are H.J. Roby, *Private Law* vol. II 485, and G. Broggini, (cited n.82) 318-325.

[90] On this passage see Chapter IV, at notes 168-175.

[91] See Chapter IV, note 172 (E. Fraenkel). W. Stroh, *Taxis* 97, describes

authority of Aquilius Gallus behind him (79), and even a
measure of claimed backing from the defendant's jurist (79-
85), unhesitatingly demands that judges regard juristic *responsa*
as *prima facie* binding statements of law (70). Yet Cicero also
presents in full his own arguments on the proper interpretation of the interdict *de vi armata*, doubtless because he realizes
that the principle of juristic authority he is arguing has been
widely contested (cf. esp. 67); even Cicero concedes that some
juristic opinions may falsely state the law (68). Nonetheless,
his argument on juristic authority provides what must have
seemed an attractive solution to the dilemma confronting late
Republican judges: if they were in doubt as to the law, they
could short-circuit protracted judicial argument by accepting
jurists' *responsa* as binding unless proved otherwise.

This logic gradually won acceptance among late Republican
judges.[92] The increasing influence of jurists on trials flowed
through three distinct channels: litigants made judicial use of
juristic *responsa* as binding statements of law;[93] judges themselves solicited juristic *responsa* to assist their deliberations;[94]
and jurists were summoned into the *consilia* of judges, as advisors on technical legal questions.[95] By the end of Cicero's
life the jurists were ubiquitous in the courts. As Cicero writes:
"Private trials involving important matters seem to me to rely
on the expertise of jurists. They are frequently present, are
invited into *consilia*, and furnish weapons to careful orators
who seek their skill."[96] Cicero chooses his words carefully,

the passage as "die akrobatischsten Verdrehungen, die Cicero in dieser Rede
leistet."

[92] To some extent, this acceptance may also stem from other implications
of Cicero's argument; see Chapter VII.

[93] First attested in the *pro Caecina*; see above. Cf. Pompon. D. 1.2.2.49:
"ante tempora Augusti . . . responsa . . . testabantur qui illos consulebant."
Cic. *de Or.* 1.242 and *Top.* 65 (the jurists supply "weapons" to orators) probably refer to the same practice.

[94] Pompon. D. 1.2.2.49: "iudicibus ipsi scribebant."

[95] Cic. *Top.* 65; cf. note 34, above.

[96] Cic. *Top.* 65: "Privata enim iudicia maximarum quidem rerum in iuris
consultorum mihi videntur esse prudentia. Nam et adsunt multum et adhi-
bentur in consilia et patronis diligentibus ad eorum prudentiam confugienti-
bus hastas ministrant."

and they are not free of equivocation. But the central point is clear.

The presence of jurists in trials is important, but not enough.[97] It is impossible to locate the evolutionary moment when Roman judges generally stopped determining law for themselves—the moment when they ceased treating juristic *responsa* as advisory and began regarding them as effectively declarative of law. At this moment the jurists were no longer mere "expert witnesses" as to the law, but instead the law's determiners. The evolutionary moment may even lie beyond the end of the Republic; but if so, not far beyond. All but impenetrable mystery surrounds Augustus' and Tiberius' grant to selected jurists of a *ius publice respondendi ex auctoritate Principis*.[98] But the motive of the Emperors is unmistakable: "to increase the authority of law" (Pomponius, D. 1.2.2.49: *ut maior iuris auctoritas habeatur*). This motive implies that the "authority" of law had not hitherto been completely decisive in private trials, and that the "authority" of law was broadly identified with the authority of the jurists as expressed in *responsa*.

The imperial intervention, which marks the final act in the transformation of the Roman judicial system into its early classical form, implies acceptance at the political level of Cic-

[97] This point is crucial. Contrast H.F. Hitzig, (cited n.34) 15: "Im allgemeinen war, da ja factisch mit dem Ausspruch des Consiliums gewöhnlich das Urteil gegeben war, der Einfluss des Consiliums ein sehr grosser"; and F. Schulz, *Legal Science* 52: "A *iudex*, once the law had begun to shed its primitive simplicity, could hardly dispense with professional advice, unless indeed he happened to be himself a jurist. There is clear evidence that in Cicero's day *iudices* normally took jurists into their *consilia*," citing Cic. *Top.* 65. In fact, Cicero says rather less. But no source ever states that *consilia* decided cases themselves, and the distinction in roles emerges clearly in, e.g., Fronto, *ad M. Caes.* 4.13.1 (p. 68 van den Hout), reporting a friend: "facile esse ait oscitantem iudici assidere, ceterum quidem iudicare praeclarum opus."

[98] See A.A. Schiller, *Mechanisms* 298-302, for a summary of the major scholarship; and Chapter VII, below, at note 31. The issue of divergent *responsa* (i.e. juristic difference of opinion) is not crucial so long as the *iudex* must accept one of the opinions as dispositive of law, a point seen already by Cicero, *Caec.* 69; contrast L. Wenger, (cited n.59) 109-110. The text of D. 1.2.2.49 is sound as it stands, and should not be changed to *iuris <consultorum> auctoritas*, which is trivial; contrast S. Tondo, *Iura* 30 (1979) 69.

ero's logic in the *pro Caecina*. What startled Tacitus, as he
looked back on Republican advocacy, was not just the length
of Cicero's orations for Tullius and Caecina, but also their
legalism: "Who now will endure those huge tomes on defenses
and formulas?" (*Dial.* 20.1: *Quis de exceptione et formula perpetie-
tur illa immensa volumina . . .?*) By Tacitus' time the revolution
was long since over.

The consequences of the revolution should not be overestimated. Judging remained an exceedingly onerous task, as
Aulus Gellius was eventually to discover. Even stripped of its
independent role in determining legal rules, the Roman court,
operating under the formulary procedure, remained an imperfect instrument of justice, especially as regards its capacity
to analyze cases accurately. Further, even in the area of law,
large amounts of discretion were deliberately reserved to the
iudex in evaluating and judging cases; his discretion was especially wide in all trials *ex fide bona*, as Quintus Mucius had
already observed (Cic. *Off.* 3.70), but not small in other cases.
The exercise of this discretion often required him to decide
lower-order questions of law.[99] Further, the whole difficult
chore of linking rules to cases remained the prerogative of the
judge. It is hyperbolic to claim that the imperial grant of the
ius respondendi dramatically limited "the sovereignty of [the
judge's] critical spirit, the independence of his judgment."[100]
Such reduction of independence as it did effect came probably
as a welcome relief.

From the viewpoint of litigants, the judicial system of the
late Republic can be generally characterized as cheap but also
inaccurate. The cost of litigating was essentially confined to
the parties' outlays in presenting their cases;[101] the social costs

[99] In Roman law, a *quaestio iuris*, as opposed to a *quaestio facti* (e.g., Ulpian,
D. 5.1.79.1), is more narrowly defined than in modern law; cf. M. Kaser,
RZ 272-273.

[100] *Contra* H. Lévy-Bruhl, *RH* 5 (1926) 5-28, at 28 (my translation).

[101] See F. Schulz, *Principles* 242; and Chapter I, above, at notes 75-82,
where it is also observed that these costs were nonetheless prohibitive for
many litigants. Note that the successful litigant did not normally recover his

of running the judicial system were low, and were absorbed by distributing the burden of judging among unpaid and non-professional members of the upper classes. The inaccuracy of judicial proceedings stemmed, in the main, from identical sources. A judicial system that is both cheap and inaccurate tends to increase the volume of litigation, while at the same time it diminishes the overall social effectiveness of and respect for law.[102] The reason for this curious result is that such a system encourages both judicial risk taking by potential litigants and cynicism about the decisions the system reaches. So long as Rome was unwilling to increase its public commitment to justice through material subvention and political support, this would remain a fundamental problem of its judicial system. The rise of the Roman jurists, while it helped to allay the problem, did not finally eliminate it.

DECIDING CASES: THE PROBLEM OF LEGAL INDETERMINACY

As a result of the proceedings *in iure*, the *recuperatores* in Caecina's case received three *formulae* for decision.[103] The first ordered the *recuperatores* to determine whether the defendant owed the plaintiff a stipulated amount (*sponsio*) for having contravened the Edict by not restoring the property in question. The second *formula* ordered them to determine whether the plaintiff owed the defendant this same amount because the defendant had *not* contravened the Edict. The third ordered them to award the plaintiff the value of the property in question if the plaintiff won his suit and the defendant failed to restore the property. These *formulae* were decided as a unit: either a verdict for the plaintiff, Caecina, in which case the verdict ran Yes/No/Yes, or a verdict for the defendant, Aebutius, in which case the verdict ran No/Yes/No. Verdicts

---

procedural costs: M. Kaser, *RZ* 283; this reduces law's effectiveness, cf. G. Tullock, *Trials on Trial* (1980) 105-118.

[102] See, for a demonstration, G. Tullock, (cited n.101) 75-76.

[103] See Gaius, 4.165; also Chapter II, at note 84.

deviating from this pattern were void.[104] The *recuperatores* were thus settling the question of the Fulcinian farm indirectly, by making a series of monetary awards determined through the *formulae* (*condemnatio pecuniaria*).[105]

Judges in private lawsuits had a legal duty to return a verdict,[106] and could escape this duty only by taking an oath that the case was insoluble (*non liquere*).[107] The three or more *recuperatores* in Caecina's lawsuit reached their verdicts (*sententiae*) separately; the judgment of the court (*iudicatum*) was obtained by an absolute majority vote.[108] While the precise mechanics of this voting process are poorly known, the reasons for having a multi-judge panel decide a case in this way are reasonably clear. First, the weight and legitimacy of the verdict were increased by the broader participation in reaching it. Second, the probable accuracy of the verdict was also increased. For example, if there was a .8 probability that the hearing of a given case before a single *iudex* would produce a "correct" judgment, there was approximately a .9 probability that the same case would result in a "correct" verdict when heard before a three-member panel of *recuperatores*.[109] Thus,

---

[104] "Yes" is *condemno*; "No" is *absolvo*. Cf. M. Kaser, *RZ* 284-285.

[105] This is one of the central features of Roman civil procedure; cf. M. Kaser, *RZ* 286-287.

[106] On the verdict, see esp. B. Biondi, *Scritti Giuridici* vol. II (1965) 435-517. *Sententia* is the "verdict"; *iudicatum* is the verdict's "content" (Biondi, 440-444). Further literature in M. Kaser, *RZ* 284-285.

[107] Gellius, *NA* 14.2.25; Ulpian, D. 4.8.13.4; M. Kaser, *RZ* 284. A *recuperator* could also take such an oath: Paul, D. 42.1.36. If for this reason no verdict was reached, the case could be reassigned by the Praetor: M. Kaser, *RZ* 271-272.

[108] So, e.g., the *lex agraria* (cited n.13), lines 38-39; the *SC Calv.* (cited n.19), line 144; Celsus, D. 42.1.39; Pompon. D. 4.8.18; M. Kaser, *RZ* 285. Paul, D. 42.1.36, apparently indicates that an absolute majority was required (cf. Celsus, D. 42.1.39); but, in D. 42.1.38 pr., Paul discusses tie votes, perhaps in cases with even numbers of *recuperatores*. A tie meant victory for the defendant except in *causae liberales*.

[109] Probability of a unanimous "correct" verdict is .512 (= .8 x .8 x .8); probability of a 2-1 majority "correct" verdict is .384 (= 3 x .8 x .8 x .2). Therefore, probability of a "correct" verdict is .896. A five-member panel increases this probability to about .942. If, however, the accuracy of a single

about half of the cases that would be "wrongly" decided by a single *iudex* would be "correctly" decided by a panel of three *recuperatores*. Both legitimacy and accuracy were important, since recuperatorial trials were thought to have an urgent social character.[110]

Judges were required to announce their verdicts orally, though they probably also supplied written copies to the litigants.[111] The verdict, though its exact form was not prescribed, nonetheless was usually a straightforward response to the question or questions raised in the Praetor's charge.[112] With one exception, there is no evidence from the later Republic or the early Empire that either oral or written explanations ever accompanied verdicts delivered under the formulary system.[113] If, as a result of a verdict, one side or the other was adjudged, the verdict created a judicial debt (*obligatio iudicati*) that was then actionable through the law governing execution of judgments;[114] such judicial debts might arise either absolutely (e.g., if Caecina or Aebutius lost his *sponsio*) or only upon failure of a condition (e.g., if Aebutius was adjudged to pay the value of the Fulcinian farm after not restoring it to Caecina). In principle, verdicts under the formulary

---

iudex was lower (say, .7), then the improvement under *recuperatores* would be more modest (three members: .784; five members: .837). These computations are very rough, since "wrong" verdicts may have depended most often on other factors, such as inequality of litigants' advocates. There is a good discussion of method in D. Kaye, *Connecticut Law Review* 13 (1980) 1-15.

[110] Above, at notes 5-7.

[111] Announcement of the verdict is *pronuntiatio*: G. Wesener, *RE* Suppb. IX s.v. (1962) 1241-1246. Pap. Mich. III 159 (ca. A.D. 41-42; = *FIRA* 3.64) is an excellent example of the written record of a verdict. On the customary form of verdicts, see Cic. *Acad. Pr.* 2.146; *Fin.* 2.36. To the best of our knowledge, no official record of the verdict was kept, nor was a copy sent to the Praetor.

[112] In this sense, the verdict did the minimum required by the *formula*.

[113] See K. Visky, *RIDA*³ 19 (1972) 735-759. For the exception, see below at note 119.

[114] For details, see B. Biondi, (cited n.106) 477-478, 486-488; M. Kaser, *RZ* 289-317. Nonetheless, Cic. *Rosc. Com.* 42-43 indicates that a *iudex* might witness fulfillment of a judgment.

procedure were not appealable, and they could be set aside only under very limited circumstances.[115]

The absence of a justificatory verdict is one of the most decisive differences between Roman and modern procedural law. The immediate reason for not requiring Roman judges to render a justification was doubtless that non-professional judges (like modern juries) found it hard to write a verdict which both determined factual issues and presented the norms that had been applied to these facts. But modern scholars have looked for a deeper explanation. For instance, it has been argued that[116]

> the *formula* given by the Praetor, through which the dispute came to the judge, was essentially an obligatory directive in which both the main lines of the judicial procedure and the tasks of the judge were specified. The judge was obliged to stick closely to the directive given in the *formula*; he was bound to it. The *formula* also prescribed the content of the verdict, since in it the legal question to be decided by the judge was exhaustively established. The judge's duty was to decide the dispute according to alternatively established conditions; i.e., the verdict was basically already present in the *formula*, albeit in an alternative form. An extended justification, one that reached not only the facts but also the legal norms applied, was unnecessary even in a complex situation, especially since there was no appeal. If someone thereafter undertook a new action on the same object of suit, the defense of a decided suit (*exceptio rei iudicatae*) was available, by consequence of which it could easily be determined whether the disputed circumstance had already formed the basis of a trial and a judicial decision.

This overly sanguine view is plausible only when judicial issues are narrowly confined to determination of fact: e.g., what did Aebutius do in preventing Caecina from entering

---

[115] M. Kaser, *RZ* 289-290; also W. Litewski, *RIDA³* 12 (1965) 347-436 and 13 (1966) 231-323.

[116] K. Visky, (cited n.113) 756-757 (my translation).

the Fulcinian farm? But the hearing of Caecina's lawsuit reached well beyond the narrowly factual, into questions of law concerning which the *formulae* themselves gave not a clue:[117] for instance, did Aebutius' actions constitute *vis hominibus coactis armatisve* within the meaning of the interdict *de vi armata*? The *recuperatores* listened to extensive argument from the advocates on this and many other questions of law, as well as on numerous tangential issues (such as the relative character of the litigants); indeed, they listened to such argument on three distinct occasions. Yet their final verdicts almost certainly gave no indication as to what of this argument had persuaded them, not even what they had found relevant in forming their decisions. The consequence was that their verdicts had only the barest minimum of educative value. Their judgment quieted the dispute between Caecina and Aebutius by awarding possession of the Fulcinian farm plus the value of the winner's *sponsio*. But the judgment did not inform either the litigants themselves or third parties as to the legal characterization of the events leading up to the lawsuit. Further, it offered no guarantee of consistency and conformity to law, nor did it supply the incentive to thoughtfulness a judge has when he "must dredge up the reasons that were persuasive to him and place them in writing on his own responsibility."[118]

To be sure, Cicero does not hesitate to urge the *recuperatores* repeatedly that they not set an evil precedent by deciding for Aebutius (*Caec.* 5, 38-40, 75-77). In general, advocates in the late Republic seized on principles that had allegedly been established, "once and for all," in earlier lawsuits. Cicero's use of the case of the woman from Arretium (*Caec.* 97) is a good example of the technique. Yet Cicero's report of this verdict and the reasons for it is pure hearsay; he is unable to produce

[117] This is conceded by, e.g., H. Lévy-Bruhl, (cited n.100) 28. See also G. Broggini, (cited n.82) 305-329; M. Kaser, *RZ* 273: "Wo immer die Formel dem Richter eine Ermessensfreiheit einräumt, bedeutet die Ausfüllung dieses Spielraums die Entscheidung von Rechtsfragen. Das zeigen am sinnfälligsten die *bonae fidei iudicia*, es gilt aber vielfach auch sonst."

[118] J.P. Dawson, *The Oracles of the Law* (1968) 88. F.M. Coffin, *The Ways of a Judge* (1980), has recently depicted this process with extraordinary candor.

The *Recuperatores*

any written verdict to confirm his allegations, and there is little sign that the earlier trial had in fact established the principle he deduces. In the early first century B.C., one judge had experimented by appending to his verdict a brief declaration of law.[119] This modest experiment, though never to our knowledge repeated, is an important signpost pointing to a road the Roman judicial system did not take: judge-made law.

Although unreasoned and unappealable verdicts had obvious drawbacks, they also had certain advantages. They permitted the widespread participation of untrained laymen in the judicial process, thus avoiding a specialized judiciary while retaining a broader social legitimacy for the decision-making process.[120] Further, unreasoned decisions, both quick and dispositive, left little room for prolonged ambiguity or uncertainty as to the outcome of trials. Nor did such verdicts expose the community to the divisiveness which a written evaluation of individual conduct might cause; winners and losers could each discover their own explanations for the judge's enigmatic *sententia*. The late Republican judicial system, careless not only in the accuracy of its fact finding but also in its law finding, remitted most troublesome questions of fact and law to a kind of "black box," the *iudex*. Indeed, it was widely

---

[119] Cicero, *Off.* 3.66, quotes this declaration, in a case concerning a seller's concealment of a public prohibition against construction on an urban lot; the judge (M. Porcius Cato, father of Uticensis, dead ca. 95-91) ruled that "cum in vendendo rem eam scisset et non pronuntiasset, emptori damnum praestari oportere." The rule of law is left implicit; see A. Watson, *Obligations* 87-88. Cicero draws legal conclusions from this verdict, in *Off.* 3.67, and shows that other advocates had done the same. P. Collinet, (cited n.8) 28, sees a reasoned judicial opinion also in Javolen. D. 24.3.66 pr. (the *sententia* of P. Mucius on Licinia's dowry); but this is likely to be a juristic *responsum*, see R.A. Bauman, *RIDA*³ 25 (1978) 238-245, with bibliography. On the force of precedent in late Republican law, see Chapter III at notes 101-104.

[120] J.P. Dawson, (cited n.118) 106: "The constant exposure to lay opinion surely helped to produce a painless adjustment between ancient rules and emerging needs in a time of drastic change in Roman society." *Idem*, (cited n.9) 289: "The Roman *iudex*, chosen by the praetor with party consent, and the gentry employed by the English Chancery as court-appointed arbitrators, may not have been for the litigants men of their own kind, but at least they were in some degree men of their own choice."

expected that a *iudex* would exercise a rough-hewn equity, deviating from dictates of law where justice or changing community *mores* required.[121]

All in all, "when one measures the gain against the effort involved, it seems plain enough why judicial reporting of verdicts was not worth the effort. Each *iudex* was appointed to serve only in a particular case. Some might have been called on frequently; when called on it was their duty to serve, for the office of *iudex* was a public office which could be declined only for valid reasons. But for men of affairs, on whose time and energy there were many demands, service as *iudex* was a burden that had to be distributed and that many sought to escape. Without some continuity of tenure there was little chance to develop expertise.... Why should the Romans have erected monuments to these thousands of men—men of distinction though they were—who came and went on short-term service, with powers that were often limited, and who were so greatly trusted that they were put under no compulsion to explain their decisions?"[122]

The outcome of Caecina's lawsuit is unknown. Yet there is one fairly good reason to suppose that Caecina prevailed over Aebutius. Not only did Cicero publish his speech *pro Caecina*, he also pointed to it with pride more than two decades later, as an example of the "plain style" of oratory (*Orat.* 102). Cicero's point in the *Orator* is that a public speaker must command a variety of speaking styles suitable for different types of argument; his point is considerably strengthened if he had won with all the speeches he refers to. And in fact he did support the winning side in all the other speeches: the *pro lege Manilia* of 66, representing the "middle style"; the *pro Rabirio Perduellionis Reo* of 63, representing the "grand style"; and (103) the *Verrines* of 70, the *pro Cluentio* of 66, and the *pro Cornelio* of 65, representing the "mixed style." The reasonable inference is that he was probably victorious in Caecina's lawsuit as well.

---

[121] So Cic. *Caec.* 65; and see generally Chapter III, at notes 79-86.
[122] J.P. Dawson, (cited n.118) 103 (footnote omitted).

Other evidence, though much less secure, points to the same conclusion. First, Cicero continued to enjoy the favor of the Caecinae, and Caecina's son still speaks of Cicero as a *patronus* (*Fam.* 6.7.4).[123] Second, at some point evidently prior to his election to the consulate, Cicero had rendered the Volaterrans a "great boon" for which they later repaid him with electoral support (*Fam.* 13.4.1: *magno . . . beneficio*); this boon may plausibly be identified with Cicero's defense of their citizenship (*Caec.* 95-102) in a successful trial.[124] Third, Cicero's description of Piso's slow-wittedness in argument (*Brut.* 239) is perhaps based on their sole known face-to-face encounter[125] and, if so, would argue that Piso did not evade the traps Cicero laid for him in the *pro Caecina*. Fourth, if the unnamed jurist consulted by Piso (*Caec.* 79) can be identified with Ser. Sulpicius Rufus,[126] then additional color is lent to Cicero's description of Servius in the *pro Murena* (9) as a man who lent aid to the enemies of his friends and resented being on the losing side; in any case, Cicero's remark, intended to rebut the charge that he is ungrateful in opposing Servius now (*Mur.* 7-9), has a personal ring to it, a settling of old scores.

This evidence is all quite circumstantial, but has sufficed to persuade most scholars that Caecina won his case.[127] Many have conceded the victory grudgingly: "if Caecina won the trial, then eloquence scored a deplorable triumph over good law."[128] But those scholars who have been critical of Cicero's argument in the *pro Caecina*, especially of his interpretation of

[123] See Chapter I, note 48 and at note 82.
[124] See Chapter III, at notes 20-22, with note 20.
[125] See Chapter III, at notes 23-24.
[126] See Chapter IV, at notes 64-65 (but "the case is less than conclusive").
[127] However, H.J. Roby, *Private Law* vol. II 535, was unconvinced that Caecina won. A. D'Ors, *Defensa* 52, suggests that Aebutius won.
[128] Mommsen, *Gesammelte Schriften* vol. III (1907) 563 (my translation), reviewing F.L. Keller, *Sem.* Cf., e.g., J. Kappeyne van de Coppelo, *Drei Abhandlungen zum Römischen Staats- und Privatrecht* (1891) 149: "Piso hat vor dem Richterstuhl der Wissenschaft den Prozess gewonnen." Similarly, H. Bögli, *Rede* 57. Such concentration on the results of a single trial seems to me rather perverse.

the interdict *de vi armata*, have not always explained why they believe that a verdict favorable to Caecina would be a miscarriage of justice. Their complaints often seem more accurately directed against Rome's strong adversary system itself, rather than against Cicero's conduct of Caecina's case.[129] Within the context of an adversary system, Cicero could not ethically have abandoned his client merely because points of the client's case were weak or failed of proof.[130] In any event, as we have seen in earlier chapters, there is no credible evidence of any kind that Cicero's argument for Caecina was consciously duplicitous, or that Cicero substantially misrepresented to the *recuperatores* either the facts or the law.[131] Since we know nothing of Piso's reply to Cicero's speech, it is not possible to determine whether the court "should" have found for Aebutius.

Of course, it is possible to argue instead that Rome's adversary system was itself inherently unjust and corrupt. But is this any more than a glib historical judgment imposing the values of modern Continental jurisprudence on a distant and alien culture? Strong adversary systems of procedure hinge on what has been called "the principle of procedural justice," according to which "there is an inherent value or legitimacy to the judicial proceeding (and to a more qualified extent, the entire legal system) which makes it possible for a lawyer to

---

[129] See C.J. Classen, *Rh. Mus.* 122 (1979) 278-302, esp. 299-300.

[130] See Amer. Bar Assn., *Model Code of Professional Responsibility* (1982) EC 7-1: "The duty of a lawyer, both to his client and to the legal system, is to represent his client zealously within the bounds of the law"; and EC 7-3: "While serving as advocate, a lawyer should resolve in favor of his client doubts as to the bounds of the law." See also EC 7-4: "The advocate may urge any permissible construction of law favorable to his client, without regard to his professional opinion as to the likelihood that the construction will ultimately prevail. His conduct is within the bounds of law, and therefore permissible, if the position taken is supported by a good faith argument for an extension, modification, or reversal of law."

[131] See especially Chapter IV, under subhead "The 'Correct' Interpretation of the Interdict *de Vi Armata*."

justify specific actions without reference to the consequences they are likely to promote."[132] Within such an adversary system, the lawyer is before all the partisan representative of his client, and he must remain within the boundaries of this role regardless of whether his doing so will assist the discovery of truth; although the goal of truth may legitimate the entire procedural system and inform its design, it does not in itself determine specific ethical decisions by lawyers. Continental scholars, inured to the different values of inquisitorial procedure, might well be surprised by the tenacity and articulateness of those who defend strong adversary systems.[133]

Finally, what was the likely consequence of a verdict for Caecina or Aebutius? No matter which side won, it is not probable that the loser pursued further his claim to the farm (for example, in a suit on ownership). As plaintiff, the loser would have had the burden of proof in such a lawsuit, plus the additional burden of having lost in the previous interdictal trial; the earlier trial, though technically irrelevant, would certainly have been recalled prejudicially in a second lawsuit. Therefore the verdict of the *recuperatores* in Caecina's lawsuit was doubtless effectively dispositive of the Fulcinian farm; and Cicero's assertion that his client would press his claim even if he should lose the present trial (*Caec.* 75-76) was only a bluff. If Aebutius in fact lost, then he paid an extremely heavy price for his use of armed men in defending the perimeters of the Fulcinian farm. Whether that price was too heavy would appear to depend on one's evaluation of the gravity of his act.

[132] H. Simon, *Wisconsin Law Review* 29 (1978) 38. See also Chapter III, at notes 111-119.

[133] See, e.g., M.H. Freedman, *Lawyers Ethics in an Adversary System* (1975); G.C. Hazard, *Ethics in the Practice of Law* (1978). I admit that I am not persuaded by their arguments, for reasons given by B.R. Gross, *Loyola Law Review* 26 (1980) 525-565; and see the excellent essays in *The Good Lawyer: Lawyers' Roles and Lawyers' Ethics* (ed. D. Luban, 1983). But the truth-discovering capacity of inquisitorial procedure is, I would venture to guess, overrated.

VI

The *Corona*

et vagus auditor adsuevit exigere
laetitiam et pulchritudinem orationis
—Tacitus

CICERO, in cross-examining Fidiculanius Falcula, the witness for the defendant, inquired of him how far his farm was from Rome. The witness replied, "Nearly 50,000," meaning 50,000 paces or 50 Roman miles. At this point "the crowd gleefully cried out, 'The very amount!' " (*Caec.* 28: *populus cum risu adclamavit ipsa esse*). As Cicero explains, they remembered that Falcula's farm was allegedly purchased with HS 50,000 of bribe money he had received as a judge in a criminal trial of 74.[1] The spontaneous outburst from the gallery so disconcerted Falcula that he declined to repeat his answer.

The urban masses of the late Republic reveled in listening to the back-and-forth of rhetorical advocacy, the joy and beauty of it (Tac. *Dial.* 20.3). A good orator could always attract to the edges of the court a circle of onlookers called the *corona* (literally, "crown").[2] In turn, orators responded to the atmosphere of expectancy that large crowds created. Cicero (*Brut.* 289-290) describes the orator's pleasure when the court is crowded with persons come to hear him speak: the onlookers

---

[1] The alleged bribe exceeded HS 40,000 (Cic. *Cluent.* 74, 104); on the text of *Caec.* 28, see F.L. Keller, *Sem.* 457 n.99.

[2] Cf. J. Carcopino, *Daily Life in Ancient Rome* (trans. E.O. Lorimer, 1940) 187-191. Crowds often contained aspiring young orators (Cic. *de Or.* 1.173), as well as semi-professional *cognitores* like Aebutius (Chapter II, at notes 73-78) and jurists (Chapter IV, at note 34).

hush as the orator rises, and when he speaks they cry out their agreement or approval, laugh or weep as he plays on their emotions, and viewers from afar mistakenly suppose that some great actor is giving a performance.[3]

It is hard to read such a description without a sense of nostalgia for what we have lost through our submission to modern mass media. We can no longer feel the simple delight that Romans derived from well-turned thoughts and carefully balanced phrases. We therefore easily ignore the subtler aspect of this intimate relation between speaker and hearer. Rhetoric was for the Romans a means of communication, a device for transmitting news of law outward into society.[4] In this sense, the *corona* stands for the force of public opinion in the conduct of private trials.

In the previous five chapters I have followed Caecina's lawsuit from its origin to its verdict, as the lawsuit was experienced by the various participants: the litigants and their advocates, the jurists, the Urban Praetor and the judges. By this means I have tried to depict what a private lawsuit was like during the years when Cicero spoke as a private advocate. In the present chapter I largely turn aside from Caecina's lawsuit, and begin to tie together the diverse threads of my argument. First, I describe how the Ciceronian judicial system, despite its extremely crude character, was nonetheless able to attain a measure of legitimacy; in the second section I broadly outline the evolution of the judicial system during the last decades of the Republic, as jurists' law gradually acquired greater weight in lawsuits.

LEGITIMATION THROUGH PROCEDURE

It has been estimated, to be sure on the basis of infirm evidence, that in about one-eighth of all cases American juries

---

[3] Compare the description of Hortensius in Cic. *Brut.* 322 (*in fine*); also Chapter V, at note 77, on Cicero.

[4] The importance of such communication is rightly stressed by N. Luhmann, (cited below n.7) 121-123.

render "incorrect" verdicts;[5] that is, from the viewpoint of a disinterested and reasonable observer, these juries either fail "correctly" to evaluate the facts of the case or fail "correctly" to apply the law as it is put to them by the judge. If this gloomy estimate is anywhere near accurate, it has important implications for the late Republican judicial system. For, compared with a modern American jury, the judge of a late Republican trial was far more exposed to sources of potential error, even if he struggled conscientiously to arrive at a "correct" verdict. I have described these sources of error at length in preceding chapters; they include the dominance of rhetorical advocacy within a strong adversary system of procedure, the inadequacy of judicial evidence taking, the relative weakness of authoritative law finding in the judicial context, and the highly passive role that tradition assigned to the Roman judge. It is likely that a Roman judge's verdict was much more often inaccurate than that of an American jury. Indeed, the Ciceronian court could be not unfairly described as a fundamentally irrational proceeding cloaked in the trappings of superficial rationality.

How could such a judicial system ever generate legitimacy, a conviction on the part of some or most members of Roman society that it was "right and proper for [them] to accept and obey the authorities and to abide by the requirements of the regime"?[6] How could such a system create "a generalized predisposition, within certain limits of tolerance, to submit to decisions that have as of yet no determined content"?[7] Legit-

[5] G. Tullock, *Trials on Trial* (1980) 31-33. Some support may be gleaned from a recent study of English criminal juries by J. Baldwin and M. McConville, *Jury Trials* (1979). For a discussion of jury effectiveness under different conditions, see R. Hastie *et al.*, *Inside the Jury* (1983), esp. 227-240, with much bibliography.

[6] D. Easton, *A Systems Analysis of Political Life* (1965) 278.

[7] N. Luhmann, *Legitimation durch Verfahren* (2d ed. 1975) 28 (my translation). This book has deeply influenced the following pages. Luhmann's definition does not mean that litigants are necessarily content with actual decisions affecting them. Such contentment is rarely achieved, cf. M. Lerner and L.A. Whitehead, in *Justice and Social Interaction* (ed. G. Mikula, 1980) 219-254; but that is hardly crucial to the existence of legitimacy. The attack on

imacy means, in essence, that the system is generally granted
the benefit of advance doubts; although future judicial decisions may not always be "correct," those who will be affected
by them are nonetheless willing, for whatever reason, to accept such decisions as premises for their own behavior, and
to adjust their expectations accordingly. It goes without saying that the predisposition to accept decisions can be quite
variously motivated within any given historical society; reasons for acceptance may range from unthinking acquiescence
in a traditional regime to enthusiastic belief in the present
moral validity of that regime. Nor need approval be shared
by all, or even most, members of a society in order for a
regime to enjoy some stability of existence. In a pre-modern
society like Rome, the extent of normative integration among
dominant groups was undoubtedly a far more important influence on overall continuity than, for instance, a majoritarian
"consensus" of the modern type.[8] Yet even in such a society
some minimum level of popular approval was surely required
if the regime was to function effectively without unceasing
resort to force.

A private judicial system, because it relies on outside individuals to bring disputes before it, is perhaps unusually sensitive in the matter of legitimacy. A long record of evidently
capricious verdicts, or a pattern of unpredictability in decision
making, can finally undermine the general approval on which
a private judicial system depends. Yet despite persistent criticism on these counts, there is little evidence that the late
Republican judicial system faced a "crisis of legitimacy," or
even widespread disillusionment. If the numerous laws reshaping the "jury class" are left to one side as mainly concerning the criminal courts,[9] the only major piece of late Republican legislation reforming private procedure was the *lex*

the concept of legitimacy by A. Hyde, *Wisconsin Law Review* (1983) 379-426,
rests on a misunderstanding of this point that is common in American legal
writing.

[8] A. Giddens, *Central Problems in Social Theory* (1979) 101-103; *A Contemporary Critique of Historical Materialism* (1981) 103-104.

[9] See Chapter V, at notes 11-12.

Cornelia of 67, which sought to curb excessive praetorian discretion in granting trials.[10] Even the Augustan judiciary laws, though they effected widesweeping reforms, did little to alter the fundamental lines of the formulary procedure.[11] Augustus' aim was mainly to eliminate vestiges of archaic procedure, and by and large he strengthened the dominance of formulary procedure in private law. To be sure, reform of private procedure could hardly have been a high priority in the crowded legislative agenda of the late Republic; yet the absence of any widespread reform movement, or even of calls for major reform, suggests a reasonably high level of general acceptance of the private judicial system, despite its obvious deficiencies. What was the source of this legitimacy?

It is helpful to distinguish two levels of legitimation: acceptance of the grounds for decisions and acceptance of the decisions themselves.[12] If for the moment acceptance of the grounds for decisions is narrowly defined as general approval of the rules of Roman private law as developed by the jurists, then it is fairly clear that Roman private law commanded broad support during the late Republic, at any rate among the upper classes whose testimony survives.[13] Private law was recognized as an important part of Rome's cultural patrimony, reaching back to the Twelve Tables (e.g., Cic. *de Or.* 1.193-198); and it was also seen as the concrete embodiment of those equitable standards upon which present social interrelationships were constructed (e.g., *ibid.* 188). Cicero dwells on both themes in the *pro Caecina* (e.g., 70, 74-75), obviously in the expectation that neither theme will provoke derision from his

[10] See Chapter II, at notes 96-101, and below at notes 87-96. On the abortive movement to codify private law in the 50's and 40's, see below at notes 105-108. On the *lex Pompeia*, see note 98.

[11] See M. Wlassak, *Römische Prozessgesetze* vol. I (1888) 173-276; P.F. Girard, *SZ* 34 (1913) 295-372; G. Pugliese, *Processo* vol. II.1 65-73; M. Kaser, *RZ* 115-116, with further literature; N. Palazzolo, *Processo Civile e Politica Giudiziaria* (1980) 16-29.

[12] N. Luhmann, (cited n.7) 31.

[13] This is the main conclusion emerging from D. Nörr, *Rechtskritik* 151-153.

audience.[14] Criticism of this or that area or rule of law, while widespread, was also largely internalized, part of the process whereby a body of positive law is perpetually renewed. Admittedly, criticism of the jurists themselves is much more common; their supposed pretentiousness, pedantry, and conservatism are all often attacked, but in terms that imply more a lighthearted disdain for the "lawyer class" than any deep-seated animosity.[15]

The matter is quite otherwise when we turn to the judicial system. Skepticism was all but inevitable with regard to both the competence of judicial fact finding and the accuracy of judicial application of law. Obviously there is no inherent contradiction in approving a body of legal norms and principles while at the same time rejecting judicial decisions supposedly made under those norms; for instance, one may argue that judges do not correctly apply the law, or that they render verdicts on the basis of false interpretation or erroneous assumptions of fact.[16] In such cases, general approval of legal rules may nonetheless "overflow" to legitimate individual judicial decisions, at any rate up to a point. But the gap between law and the judicial system was very wide in the Ciceronian court. If Roman private courts nonetheless retained some measure of generalized public support, the explanation must lie elsewhere than in its faithful execution of the juristic program. The most likely explanation is that the procedure of private law, despite all its manifold shortcomings, was in the end a net contributor to the judicial system's legitimacy.

Lawyers usually think of civil procedure as a "conduit" for channeling disputes toward their proper judicial resolution in a verdict; *ubi ius, ibi remedium.*[17] However, within any judicial

[14] See Chapter IV, at notes 168-170.
[15] D. Nörr, *Rechtskritik* 83-87.
[16] N. Luhmann, (cited n.7) 31.
[17] F. James, *Civil Procedure* (1965) 1-2: "the rules of substantive law govern the rights and duties of men in their ordinary relations with each other or the body politic, while procedural rules govern the means whereby these rights may be maintained or redressed when they have been violated, or when their violation has been threatened."

system the intricacies of procedure have numerous other functions as well.[18] Procedure helps to establish boundaries between courts and their social environment, and thus acts to confirm the identity and differentiation of courts; at the same time, it provides courts with a cohesive internal organization of their own, an autonomous structure through which disputes are processed. Procedure, with its traditional roles and role playing (litigants, advocates, witnesses, judges, and so on), allows patterned recurrent interaction of individuals within a constricted system of social contact; such symbolic interaction defines a sphere of "allowable conflict," in relation to which individuals are encouraged to act and indeed must act if they wish to be successful. But through their participation, no matter how grudging, individuals lose or see diminished their capacity for independent criticism. By means of this ceremonial interplay, judicial procedure achieves much of its capacity to instruct; individuals must, for a time, alter or reinterpret their conduct in the light of judicial norms and proceedings. Because of the principle of publicity,[19] even outsiders are drawn into and bound by the ritual of justice being visibly administered. Finally, judicial procedure induces loyalty to its own internal values by organizing and coordinating responsibility to reach decisions on a cooperative basis.

The tacit premise of procedural justice is that the "correctness" of judicial decisions is, to a large extent, a question of how decisions are arrived at, rather than only an intrinsic property of the decisions themselves. Though this premise has often been attacked,[20] procedural justice remains a highly popular attribute of courts; litigants are aggrieved if they are not allowed at least to present their side of the case fully be-

---

[18] On what follows, see N. Luhmann, (cited n.7) 35-135. Luhmann's argument produced considerable controversy in Germany, to which Luhmann replies in the foreword to the second edition, pp. 1-3.

[19] See Chapter V, at notes 31-32.

[20] E.g., by Plato, *Gorgias* 471e-427a. So also, e.g., P.G. Keilmansegg, *Politische Vierteljahresschrift* 12 (1971) 367-401, and R. Zippelius, in *Festschrift K. Larenz* (1973) 293-304; both attacking Luhmann.

The *Corona*

fore the verdict is reached.[21] Since it can hardly be anticipated
that the binding force of judicial decisions will alone absorb
all dissatisfaction, reaction must be prepared by a process that
anticipates, narrows, and disposes of criticism at whatever level.
One function of procedure is precisely to narrow dissatisfaction, to disperse and absorb protests; if a litigant has been
heard, he may not be any happier with an adverse verdict,
but his possible grounds for criticizing the verdict must shift
in order to be credible. This is true so long as the outcome is
uncertain; for if the outcome is known in advance, then the
motive for cooperation is lost. To this extent, uncertainty of
outcome is the engine of judicial procedure.[22]

The late Republican judicial system is characterized by two
especially prominent strategies for achieving procedural legitimacy. The first strategy is alluded to in the *exordium* of the
pro Caecina, where Cicero remonstrates with the *recuperatores*
over their failure to reach a verdict in two earlier hearings.[23]
All private trials, says Cicero, are instituted for one of two
purposes: "either to settle disputes or to punish misdeeds" (6:
*aut distrahendarum controversiarum aut puniendorum maleficiorum
causa*). As an example of the first type, Cicero gives the action
based on failure to fulfill a stipulation; as examples of the second type, he adduces actions based on fraud in fiduciary relationships such as tutelage or partnership (7). The first type
is less serious, says Cicero, because it has little potential for
general social harm; indeed, such disputes are frequently en-
trusted to a "domestic arbiter" outside the judicial setting (6:
disceptatore domestico).[24] The second type, however, concerns

[21] On the Roman principle that both sides must be heard, see M. Kaser,
RZ 9; for the sensitivity of Roman judges on this point, see Chapter V, at
note 81.

[22] N. Luhmann, (cited n.7) 116. On behavioral changes by Roman litigants, see Chapter I, paragraph after note 72.

[23] See Chapter V, in the paragraph before note 86.

[24] Cf. Cic. *Rosc. Com.* 15, on which G. Broggini, *Iudex Arbiterve* (1957) 210-
218. On private arbitration, K.H. Ziegler, *Das Private Schiedsgericht* (1971).
On negotiated settlement (esp. "out of court"), bibliography in M. Kaser,
RPR² I 642-643 and II 606-607; add J.M. Kelly, *Litigation* 132-152, and P.
Garnsey, *Social Status and Legal Privilege* (1970) 195-197.

much weightier matters, and so demands "not the unpaid services of a friend, but the severity and force of a judge" (7: *non honorariam operam amici, sed severitatem iudicis ac vim*).[25] Caecina's lawsuit, argues Cicero, is a clear case of the second type, and therefore its decision should not be delayed.

Cicero's dichotomy between dispute settlement and punishment of wrongdoing seems rather forced, but can probably be understood as describing a spectrum along which most private actions are to be arrayed: from those that are highly arbitrational (such as the action for dividing an inheritance, *actio familiae eriscundae*) to those that have a quasi-penal character (such as the action on theft, *actio furti*). Yet even in the most purely arbitrational suits the state retains some interest in the quieting of disputes, although it may be rather indifferent as to the outcome; and in suits such as those over unfulfilled stipulations, substantially greater social interests are involved (e.g., the security of promises for future performance).[26] To be sure, as one moves along the spectrum, the role of sanction becomes ever more overt, signifying the state's aggressive intent to repress conduct of the type alleged. Yet, even in such extreme situations, the state retains a residual interest in seeing disputes quieted before they become disruptive. In the third hearing of Caecina's lawsuit, Cicero flamboyantly describes the central issue as one of "punishing" Aebutius for his antisocial use of armed violence; but Cicero's presentation deliberately obscures the underlying dispute between the litigants over property rights to the Fulcinian farm.

Although most Romans doubtless recognized the existence of this spectrum, the late Republican judicial system is strongly characterized by its effort to handle almost all private lawsuits through a consensual model of procedure akin to domestic arbitration. The consensual model may have little or nothing to do with the institutional origin of the formulary procedure,

[25] Cf. Cic. *Rosc. Com.* 24-25. The suits listed by Cicero all involve *infamia* for the convicted defendant. See M. Kaser, *RZ* 213-214; also A. Watson, *TR* 31 (1963) 76-85.
[26] On legal protection of this social interest, see B.W. Frier, *LTIR* 186-187.

or with its "real nature";[27] but it is crucially relevant to the perceived ethos of late Republican civil procedure, which is dominated by the notion that the parties themselves, with the aid and assistance of the Praetor, define the issue between them, select a judge to determine the issue, submit their respective cases for the judge's unappealable determination, and then themselves supervise the verdict's enforcement.[28] References to this model are numerous in late Republican literature; for example, the right of the parties to define the issue between them is emphasized by Cicero in the *pro Caecina* (8). In a famous passage of the *pro Cluentio* (120) Cicero stresses the tradition that parties agree on a *iudex* in all civil cases; and the preeminence of the parties in conducting the trial was secured by the traditional passivity of the judge.[29] The consensual model suffered ostensible inroads only in isolated cases and to a limited extent—as in the modified procedure for choosing *recuperatores*.[30]

The explanation for the Roman emphasis on a consensual model of judicial procedure is rooted in the very nature of courts. Consider, for example, the following discussion:[31]

The basic social logic, or perceived legitimacy, of courts rests on the mutual consent of two persons in conflict to refer that conflict to a third for resolution. This basic logic is threatened by the substitution of office and law for mutual consent, both because one of the two parties may perceive the third as the ally of his enemy and because a third interest, that of the regime, is introduced. Even within the

[27] See above all the discussion in M. Kaser, *RZ* 19-21, 109-114. Modern Romanists have come round to rejecting Moriz Wlassak's famous theory that the formulary procedure was contract-like in origin; see esp. G. Broggini, (cited n.24). Also see the survey in O. Behrends, *Die Römische Geschworenenverfassung* (1970) 48-49; W. Selb, in *Fs. Flume* 799-204.

[28] See L. Wenger, *Institutionen des Römischen Zivilprozessrechts* (1925) 192-193; M. Kaser, *RZ* 8.

[29] See Chapter V, at notes 57-59. On *Cluent.* 120, see J.M. Kelly, *Judicature* 126-128.

[30] See Chapter V, at notes 13-14.

[31] M. Shapiro, *Courts: A Comparative and Political Analysis* (1981) 36-37.

Legitimation through Procedure

realm of judicial conflict resolutions, no rigid prototype of court is applicable to the real world. Along one dimension we find a continuum of go-betweens—mediator, arbitrator, judge—in which most of those officials we normally label judges engage in a great deal of mediation and arbitration. Along another dimension we discover that most triadic conflict resolvers are deeply embedded in the general political machinery of their regimes and that the administrator or general big man as judge is far more typical than the holder of a separable judicial office. When we move from courts as conflict resolvers to courts as social controllers, their social logic and their independence is even further undercut. For in this realm, while proceeding in the guise of triadic conflict resolver, courts clearly operate to impose outside interests on the parties. Finally, in the realm of judicial lawmaking, courts move furthest from their social logic and the conventional prototype because the rules they apply in the resolution of conflicts between two parties are neither directly consented to by the parties nor "preexisting." Instead, they are created by the third in the course of the conflict resolution itself. Thus, while the triadic mode of conflict resolution is nearly universal, courts remain problematical in the sense that considerable social tension invariably exists between their fundamental claims to legitimacy and their actual operations.

From this perspective, judicial systems are characterized by a perpetual tension between their "social logic" (the "triadic conflict" of plaintiff, defendant, and third-party arbiter) and the broader roles arbiters play within the apparatus of government (social control, even law making). The transition from the elemental "social logic" of primitive courts to more complexly motivated judicial systems is accomplished above all through "the substitution of office and law for mutual consent": the creation of a professional judiciary, and the imposition on parties of preexisting or even newly created norms. Yet in almost all courts of almost all times, elements of their basic "social logic" remain as visible and usually significant

245

parts of civil procedure; the parties are not normally obliged
to litigate, they retain extensive control of the presentation of
their own cases, and the resolution of their dispute may involve its submission to a "lawless jury" of their peers rather
than to a professional judge. The widespread survival of this
"social logic" even in modern courts is undoubtedly tied to its
undiminished popularity, and hence its ability to serve as a
source of legitimacy.

The Ciceronian judicial system was still closely wedded to
the elemental "social logic" of courts. The institutionalization
of the judiciary had not progressed beyond isolation of a "jury
class," to which, however, parties were not obliged to confine
themselves in choosing a *iudex*; and, by and large, party will
remained theoretically uppermost in the framing and conduct
of trials. The Urban Praetor's *imperium* was regarded mainly
as a device of last resort against contumacious litigants.[32]
Though it was widely recognized that social control played a
major role in the formation of the Praetor's Edict and in the
granting of trials, this purpose was masked behind the pervasive consensual model of procedure, which extended even
to most suits having a quasi-penal character. As for law, Cicero's confident proclamation of its preeminence in civil
adjudication[33] is plainly premature, though it foreshadows an
impending change in the judicial system. The Ciceronian judicial system's apparent hesitancy to substitute "office and law"
for mutual consent is obviously related to its quest for legitimacy despite its perceptible deficiencies.

If the consensual model of procedure was the Ciceronian
court's first strategy for generating legitimacy, the second
strategy was the strong adversary system of rhetorical advocacy. Here, too, an ostensible source of weakness for the court
became, when viewed in a different light, a source of strength.[34]
Rhetoric re-worked the dull stuff of private disputes into ceremonial drama. Presentation of cases occurred principally

[32] G. Pugliese, *Processo* 118-124; M. Kaser, *RZ* 132-135.
[33] *Caec.* 65, on which see Chapter IV, at notes 168-172.
[34] See esp. Chapter III, at notes 64-66, 120-128.

through the elaborately prescribed etiquette of formal orations, with their articulated format (*exordium, narratio, argumentum, peroratio*) and elegantly contrived commonplaces. The power of this etiquette derived in part from the familiar artifice of its stock motifs repetitiously employed, and in part from the endless novelty of the cases in which it was applied. The art of rhetoric sought to reduce the universe of possible argumentation to a standard repertory of those arguments that could predictably command support within the community values of the ancient world. In doing this, it transformed disputes into a sort of chivalrous combat in which the disputants, despite their conflict, were still overtly united in their subscription to the common stock of values.[35] Even while rhetoric conceded the futility of seeking a definitive resolution to any human conflict, it suggested that—simply because of this ultimate relativism—each conflict must be carefully contained, lest the corporate structure of society fragment and dissolve. The limitations of rhetorical advocacy as a substitute for law have, I trust, become apparent in this book. Nonetheless, rhetoric contributed substantially to the endurance of pluralism in ancient societies, and its contribution to the legitimacy of the Ciceronian judicial system also should not be underestimated.

Beyond the ceremonial significance of rhetoric, the strong adversary system of civil procedure itself had an undoubted positive impact.[36] It has recently been argued that "an important key to understanding the effectiveness of the adversary system may be found in two of its properties. The adversary system seems to require (a) the maintenance of a high degree

[35] See L.A. Coser, *The Functions of Social Conflict* (1956), esp. chap. 7, "Conflict—The Unifier" (pp. 121-137).

[36] J.H. Skolnick, *Journal of Conflict Resolution* 11 (1967) 52-70, at 52-53, rightly remarks on the similarity between adversary litigation and sporting events. In each, "*Procedure* is as important as *outcome*," and each "may . . . be viewed as resting upon an assumption of genuine conflict," according to which players must try to win. This is why the adversary system is undermined by charges of explicit or implicit collusion between opposing advocates (e.g., in plea bargaining).

of control over its process by the disputants and, at the same time, (b) a high degree of regulated contentiousness between the disputants themselves. In other words, the disputants have a common interest in limiting the control of the decision maker, while engaging in competitive pursuit of their opposed self-interests."[37] Psychological experiments conducted in the United States, Britain, and the Continent strongly support the proposition that the adversary procedure produces a high level of psychological satisfaction among participants and onlookers alike—a level considerably higher than that produced by any tested variant of inquisitorial procedure.[38] Participants as well as onlookers attach particular importance to the non-intervention and "passivity" of the judge, these qualities being construed as signs of his impartiality.[39]

Although in all situations respondents prefer an adversary procedure to its alternatives, they especially prefer it in certain types of situations.[40] Three variables increase the likelihood that people will prefer an adversary procedure in which a third party does not control dispute settlement: if the envisaged outcomes of their dispute are correspondent (i.e., it is not desired that one party will win and the other lose, in a zero-sum outcome); if no clear-cut standards are available for determining their dispute; and if they are not under time pressure to obtain a solution. When all three of these variables are strongly present, parties prefer to delegate less control to dispute resolvers, so they retain the leisure to discuss issues at length; through discussion and negotiation they can develop surrogate standards for settling their differences. If their out-

[37] J. Thibaut and L. Walker, *Procedural Justice: A Psychological Analysis* (1975) 119, with a survey of psychological literature on pp. 142-143.

[38] *Ibid.* 119-121, summarizing results on pp. 88-96.

[39] *Ibid.* 120-121, summarizing results on pp. 97-116. See also the interesting discussion by T. Eckhoff, *Scandinavian Studies in Law* 9 (1965) 11-48, esp. 40 ff.

[40] On what follows, see J. Thibaut and L. Walker, (cited n.37) 14-16. The demand for procedural justice remains by far the most important single factor in shaping popular opinions of courts: A. Sarat, *Law and Society Review* 11 (1977) 440-441. So too, litigants' attitudes toward trials are strongly determined by "perceived fairness": T.R. Tyler, *ibid.* 18 (1984) 51-74.

comes are correspondent, the role of the judge is essentially the "friendly" one of recognizing the "correct" solution; if their outcomes are non-correspondent, then their interests are more sharply opposed and they will tend to acknowledge that a higher degree of third-party control is required. This distinction roughly corresponds to Cicero's dichotomy between the "domestic arbiter," who offers "the unpaid help of a friend" in resolving smaller matters, and the *iudex*, who must judge weightier matters with "severity and force"; but the distinction is now examined from the viewpoint of the parties themselves, not from that of the state.

As to the other two variables that lead to a preference among disputants for adversary procedure, we may ignore for present purposes the press of time in dispute resolution.[41] But the remaining factor, namely the absence of clear and agreed-upon standards for dispute settlement, is obviously crucial in explaining why the consensual model of the formulary procedure found favor in the late Republic. Legal insecurity, the uncertainty surrounding legal norms and their application, was beyond any doubt the most pervasive feature of the Ciceronian court. Statute had dwindled to form but a small part of private law; the Praetor's Edict determined law only indirectly, through its actions and *formulae*; and the authority of the jurists was not yet widely acknowledged as dispositive of law. In the absence of clearly defined legal norms, the litigants were allowed to participate in devising *ad hoc* standards for resolving their differences;[42] and the judicial system, by allowing this participation, generated and clung to a measure of legitimacy. All major features of the Ciceronian judicial system—the long, uninterrupted speeches from either side, the parties' examination and cross-examination of witnesses,

[41] Cicero acknowledges this variable mainly from the social standpoint that certain especially heinous disputes should be quickly settled: *Tull.* 10; *Div. in Caecil.* 56; *Caec.* 6-7. On the slowness of Roman civil procedure, see J.M. Kelly, *Litigation* 118-131, with literature.

[42] While it may seem odd to express it this way, the shifting positions of Cicero and Piso during the hearings of Caecina's lawsuit (Chapter III, under subhead "The Earlier Speeches") can be seen as a form of negotiation.

the terse interchange of the *altercatio*, the passivity of the judge, the failure to justify decisions, even the frequent re-hearings of cases—find at least part of their justification in the striving of the system to achieve legitimacy, albeit on a basis quite different from what modern lawyers would think of as "legal."

Procedural justice may seem to some (as it does to me) only a pale shadow of justice itself.[43] Yet it continues to play an important part in modern law as well, more so than is usually admitted. "Every attempt to legitimize that does not rely directly on the power of legal norms to persuade and motivate, must in the end depend on extra-legal mechanisms. This is the case also for legitimation through procedure. How else can the leap be made from the fact that a party has been heard, to the fact that he accepts an unfavorable decision? Time and again the expectation that procedure will legitimize breaks open the juristic cosmos."[44]

To be sure, the efficacy of procedural legitimation within the late Republican judicial system may not have been especially high. Above all, it is hard to believe that any society could secure abiding legitimacy for its judicial system on the basis of procedure alone—regardless of the quality and content of judicial decisions—unless that society either was highly unstable or possessed very elaborate safeguards and complementary institutions in every sphere of social life.[45] But the late Republic was not highly institutionalized, and its instability, though real, should not be exaggerated.[46] For the rest, it is less than clear that this form of legitimation was very

[43] See however R.S. Summers, *Cornell Law Review* 60 (1974/1975) 1-52; J.R. Lucas, *On Justice* (1980) 72-98.

[44] N. Luhmann, (cited n.7) 79 (my translation). Cf. T. Parsons, *Societies: Evolutionary and Comparative Perspectives* (1966) 27: "Only on the basis of procedural primacy can the system cope with a wide variety of changing circumstances and types of cases without prior commitment to specific solutions."

[45] See N. Luhmann, (cited n.7) 29.

[46] On the surprising degree of stability of the governing elite, despite political troubles, see E. Gruen, *Last Generation*, esp. 498-507.

successful. Such evidence as there is (it has not been exhaustively collected) suggests widespread indifference or apathy
toward private courts, coupled with considerable personal
aversion to being drawn into litigation.[47] If these attitudes,
which are admittedly common in many societies,[48] nonetheless precipitated no strong movement toward legislative reform of civil procedure, the reason may be that the pathway
to reform was not yet entirely clear, and that far more urgent
matters weighed on the minds of late Republican politicians.
The Ciceronian judicial system apparently held its ground,
but little more.

The perceptible fluidity of law in the Ciceronian court is
likely to have produced a sort of legal entropy, in which the
outcome of lawsuits became increasingly unpredictable and
"lawless." One scholar has recently argued that a strong adversary system of procedure must necessarily tend to such
entropy in the absence of determined countervailing measures.[49] Legal entropy was perhaps not especially dangerous in
itself, so long as the governing elite remained relatively homogeneous and integrated in its social and cultural values; but
as the elite became more diverse in its membership, and as its
stock of shared values dwindled, the threat posed by entropy
grew more present.

As we shall see in the following section, during the last
decades of the Republic Romans began to reverse the process
of judicial entropy, and they did so largely without the aid of
legislation; they did not abandon the Ciceronian model, but
they did slowly modify it from within so that verdicts took
greater effective account of juristic opinions on law. It is this
deliberate reversal of entropy that ushered in the rise of the
Roman jurists. In order to understand the phenomenon, we
must concentrate fixedly on two questions: first, what sorts of
Romans found it in their material interests to check and re-

[47] See J.M. Kelly, *Judicature* 97-102; B.W. Frier, *LTIR* 48-50.
[48] Compare the general unpopularity of American courts: Law Enforcement Assistance Administration, *Public Images of Courts* (1977).
[49] A. D'Amato, *California Law Review* 71 (1983) 1-55.

verse the prevailing insecurity of law[50] and, second, what practical steps were they able to take in achieving their goal?

ON THE ROAD TO CLASSICAL ROMAN LAW

As has often been observed, the last several decades of the Roman Republic marked the low-water point of juristic prestige within the Roman governing elite. This fact is at first sight disquieting, particularly when the late Republic is juxtaposed with the periods on either side of it. In the second century B.C., jurisconsults had been remarkably successful in using law as a basis for building political support; predominantly the members of noble families, they had advanced in an almost gapless line to the consulate. The first century of the Empire saw the resumption of juristic prestige and a new line of jurists as Consuls, although both phenomena were mainly attributable to imperial patronage.[51]

The contrast between these eras and the later Republic is sharp.[52] For almost two generations, between 95 and 39 B.C., the sole jurist known to have won the consulate was Ser. Sulpicius Rufus, elected only after a bitter defeat in 63 and a wait of eleven years;[53] Servius is the butt of Cicero's observations in the *pro Murena* that jurisprudence is a poor route to the consulate, a theme Cicero frequently sounds in other works

---

[50] The argument I use here and in the succeeding section is based on a form of the "Bad Man" analysis proposed by O.W. Holmes, *Harvard Law Review* 10 (1897) 457-478, esp. 459-461; for a discussion, see W. Twining, *Cornell Law Review* 58 (1972/1973) 275-303. Such analysis involves looking at the judicial system from the viewpoint of an essentially amoral person who in planning his conduct wishes to know the practical implications of various actions he may take. Under what circumstances will such a person prefer that general judicial predictability be greater, and therefore that the legal consequences of his actions be easier to determine in advance, even if the results may not be always in his immediate favor?

[51] On the second century B.C., see W. Kunkel, *Herkunft*[2] 41-44; on the early Empire, *ibid.* 272-281.

[52] The decline in the social status of jurists is recognized explicitly by Cicero, *Off.* 2.65, on which see W. Kunkel, *Herkunft*[2] 38-40 and 367. On P. Frezza, *AG* 142 (1952) 174-176, see L. Lombardi, *Saggio* 48 n.80.

[53] See Chapter IV, at notes 66-67.

as well. Political failure was the repeated fate of jurists throughout this period. Aquilius Gallus chose not to place himself in candidacy for the consulate, alleging ill health and the press of legal duties (Cic. *Att.* 1.1.1). At least Gallus won the praetorship; his contemporary A. Cascellius reached only the quaestorship and "declined to go further" (Pompon. D. 1.2.2.45: *nec ultra proficere voluit*), and A. Ofilius "deliberately remained an equestrian" (*ibid.* 44: *in equestri ordine perseveravit*). The record is redolent with political failure and honorable excuses, which need not be taken at face value.[54]

First century jurists are only rarely men of direct senatorial descent.[55] The family traditions that had once produced great lines of aristocratic jurisconsults (the Aelii Paeti, Porcii Catones, and Mucii Scaevolae) now failed. In the late Republic the jurists came from humbler backgrounds. The preponderance and the best of them were equestrian by birth, their status defined by wealth and recognition but not by office.[56] Perhaps still more significant is that a large number of these jurists came not from Rome but from the municipalities of peninsular Italy. To be sure, Italian origin can be established

[54] To be sure, *equites* not infrequently claimed a deliberate decision not to pursue political careers; cf. J.H. D'Arms, *Commerce and Social Standing* (1981) 111-114. On *otium equestre* see below, at note 76.

[55] The chief exception, Q. Aelius Tubero, came from a prominent praetorian family: W. Kunkel, *Herkunft*[2] 37. Volcatius (or better Volcacius), the teacher of A. Cascellius, is called a *nobilis* by Pliny, *NH* 8.144. Despite W. Kunkel, *Herkunft*[2] 20-21, he may be a near relative of L. Volcacius Tullus (cos. 66), also of senatorial descent. Cf. Cic. *Planc.* 51 with P.A. Brunt, *JRS* 72 (1982) 1-17, at 9; but also T.P. Wiseman, *New Men* 276. The jurist is perhaps L. Volcacius, trib. pl. ca. 68 (*ILLRP* 465a).

[56] On defining equestrian status, see below at notes 66-68. The following jurists are definitely equestrian or of equestrian origin: P. Alfenus Varus (Pompon. D. 1.2.2.44); C. Aquilius Gallus (Pliny, *NH* 17.2); A. Ofilius (Pompon. 44); Ser. Sulpicius Rufus (Cic. *Mur.* 16); C. Trebatius Testa (Porphyr. *ad Hor. Sat.* 2.1.1); and C. Visellius Varro (son of an *eques*, Cic. *de Or.* 1.191). See further Chapter IV: note 56 on Q. Cornelius, note 57 on A. Cascellius; also notes 65 and 86, below. W. Kunkel, *Herkunft*[2] 50-53, conjectures equestrian status for several other jurists. However, it is misleading to call these men "equestrian jurists," since most pursued senatorial careers (below, at note 65). See also M. Bretone, in *Lineam.* 383-384.

The *Corona*

only in a handful of cases: Alfenus Varus, allegedly from the Latin colony at Cremona (Porphyr. *ad Hor. Sat.* 1.3.130);[57] C. Trebatius Testa, from Velia in Lucania (Cic. *Fam.* 7.20.1); L. Valerius, from Apulia (Cic. *Fam.* 1.10); Pacuvius Antistius Labeo, from Samnium;[58] and A. Ofilius, from Oscan Campania.[59] Yet the names of numerous other jurists suggest similar backgrounds.[60]

How should we explain the "falling off" of the jurists' status in the late Republic? The most prominent theory[61] advances two explanations: first, legal expertise was undervalued owing to chaotic political conditions, which made demagogic oratory a more promising avenue to political success; second, because the aristocracy was both decimated by civil war and morally exhausted, legal science fell by default to the equestrian class. These two theories explain only the obvious absence of interest in legal science among the Roman aristocracy, and do not attempt to explain why a career in law became attractive to members of the equestrian class. Further, the second explanation is not plausible; the aristocracy of the late Republic is, if anything, rather alarmingly vibrant, and hardly so depleted or demoralized as to have ceded whole fields of its traditional strength through mere default.[62]

The first explanation, however, rings true, at least if put in a slightly modified form. Doubtless, as Cicero maintains in the *pro Murena* (25), oratory offered late Republican politicians

[57] See T.P. Wiseman, *New Men* 211. See however E. Fraenkel, *Horace* (1957) 89–90, who challenges the scholion.

[58] On Labeo (father of the renowned Augustan jurist), see W. Kunkel, *Herkunft*[2] 32–34 (Saepinum or Ligures Baebiani).

[59] C. Nicolet, *Ordre* vol. II 963–964; but see M. Frederiksen, *PBSR* 27 (1956) 119.

[60] W. Kunkel, *Herkunft*[2] 53–56. A. Cascellius apparently came from Latin Sora: T.P. Wiseman, *New Men* 222.

[61] W. Kunkel, *Herkunft*[2] 58–59.

[62] See note 46 and, e.g., R. Syme, *Sallust* (1964) 16: "The fashion persists of condemning and deploring the last epoch of the Roman Republic. It was turbulent, corrupt, immoral. And some speak of decadence. On the contrary, it was an era of liberty, vitality—and innovation. . . . Roman life was coming to feel to the full the liberating effects of empire and prosperity."

a surer means of acquiring the consulate than the less flam-
boyant discipline of law (so also *Brut.* 155); and this flowering
of oratory was obviously linked to the general instability of
the late Republic.[63] Further, within the private judicial system, the acquisition of legal expertise had become a far more
formidable task after Q. Mucius succeeded in increasing the
breadth and complexity of the field; but the contemporary
ascendancy of orators in private trials diminished the tangible
benefits to be had from learning law. In the second century,
jurisconsults had given legal advice to clients in exchange for
the tacit promise of future political support.[64] Such patronage
depended on a delicate balance of effort and reward: the jurisconsults were by birth mainly men of social prestige in their
own right; however casually they acquired their knowledge of
law, their pronouncements were authoritative by virtue of their
source and at first were apparently accepted without much
question. All this changed with the ascendancy of orators in
the judicial system. Cautelary jurisprudence did not disappear
in the late Republic; but it now became more or less ancillary
to legal science, while the influence of juristic *auctoritas* within
the judicial system was sharply restricted by the successful
attacks of orators. The consequence of all these developments
was a precipitous decline in law's attractiveness for young
aristocrats.

Into their place came men of somewhat lower social status,
for whom, perhaps, even the diminished personal rewards of
legal expertise were yet considerable. Most of the so-called
equestrian jurists pursued senatorial careers with some success.[65] It is reasonable to assume that they perceived legal

[63] So esp. Tacitus, *Dial.* 36-41 (Maternus' speech).
[64] See Chapter IV, at notes 5, 11-14, 71.
[65] Of the "equestrian jurists" in note 56 above, only Ofilius, Trebatius, and
Cornelius remained equestrian. Alfenus Varus was Consul in 39; Aquilius
Gallus, Praetor in 66. Cascellius was Quaestor at least by 73; Servius was
Praetor in 65 and Consul in 51; and Visellius Varro was Curule Aedile prob-
ably in 59. (See *MRR* for sources.) In addition, P. Orbius was Praetor in 65
(*MRR*). Senatorial careers seem likely also for Volcacius (see note 55) and for
L. Lucilius Balbus and T. Juventius (W. Kunkel, *Herkunft*[2] 21-23). Orbius,
Lucilius, and Juventius probably came of equestrian stock. On the law as a

expertise as an aid to their political careers, despite the fact that the consulate remained normally beyond their reach. Diminished returns on investment attracted only marginal investors.

So the theory runs, compact and persuasive. Yet, a different view is also possible, one that stresses not the political opportunities that legal expertise continued indirectly to provide, but rather the attractions of private law itself to the sort of person who took up this field. There is ample room to argue that the jurists of the late Republic were jurists by design, not just by default. This argument, if it is correct, has a major implication: for the first time in history, law and legal values had become integral to the structuring of society.

The title of *eques*, granted by Censors or Roman magistrates, implies no homogeneity of origin, fortune, or way of life; it means only two things: that its holder has an estate of HS400,000 and that he has been registered in the censorial list of *equites*.[66] The title "defines only an aristocracy of fact, based on something other than electoral suffrage. The great mass of *equites* content themselves with leisure, doubtless living on revenue from their estates. A small minority use the prestige and connections that it implies, in a society of status where the *elogium* is king, in order to devote themselves to activities for which it gives vocation: public contracting, the courts, but also military adventure, judicial and political eloquence, and, a little later, intellectual pursuits. But it is the title of *eques* that is basic, not these activities." Especially in the decades following the Social War of 91-89, the *equites* are recruited not just from Rome but from every corner of peninsular Italy. Their numbers grow steadily, from about 2,400 in 130 B.C. to more than 5,000 under Augustus.[67] They form

path to political success in the late Republic, see T.P. Wiseman, *New Men* 118-120.

[66] On what follows, see C. Nicolet, *Ordre* vol. I, esp. 457-464. The quotation is from p. 459 (my translation). On the definition of *equites* in the late Republic, see also T.P. Wiseman, *Historia* 19 (1970) 67-83 and *New Men* 67-69; E. Badian, *Publicans and Sinners* (1972) 82-85; F. Càssola and L. Lombardi, in *Lineam.* 350-351.

[67] C. Nicolet, *Ordre* vol. I 113-123.

an Italian elite, a sort of artificial "third estate" linking the magistral aristocracy of the Senate to the masses of Roman citizens throughout Italy.[68] Openings in the senatorial aristocracy are normally filled by members of this upwardly mobile group, though few of them reach the highest offices of the state.

The appeal of law and legal science to men of this rank lay, I would suggest, on two levels: their interest in the substantive law that began to emerge with the reforms of Q. Mucius and their general desire for an increase in legal security. The first point is obvious enough[69] and requires no protracted discussion; in Chapter IV I discussed at length the achievement of late Republican jurists in creating a law of markedly liberal temper, freed from archaism and oriented to the needs of commerce.[70] These qualities strongly correlate with the interests of a plutocracy, many of whose members were actively engaged in commerce.[71] To be sure, by no means all equestrians were directly involved in banking or trade or public contracting; but many derived their wealth from these sources, and not a few remained engaged in such affairs throughout their lives, unrestricted by the cultural and legal taboos that bound the senatorial order.[72] Further, the *equites*, though not a class defined by economic position, commonly perceived and reacted as a group to questions affecting their *dignitas*, their political influence and social rank.[73]

The second point, their desire for legal security, is more

[68] So Pliny, *NH* 33.34 ("tertium corpus").

[69] L. Lombardi, *Saggio* 48-53, who however overplays "il legame della giurisprudenza con la democrazia politica" (p. 53).

[70] Chapter IV, at notes 187-189 and 192-194.

[71] C. Nicolet, *Ordre* vol. I 357-379; see also I. Shatzman, *Senatorial Wealth and Roman Politics* (1975) 99-104; J.H. D'Arms, (cited n.54) 31-39; and note 77, below.

[72] Even in the case of Senators the force of these taboos has been doubted; see, e.g., J.H. D'Arms, (cited n.54) 31-39. Economic interests of late Republican Senators are canvassed by T.P. Wiseman, *New Men* 191-202; cf. I. Shatzman, (cited n.71); H. Schneider, *Wirtschaft und Politik* (1974).

[73] See, e.g., C. Nicolet, *Ordre* vol. I 382-386 (esp. 385) on the part played by the *equites* in the crisis of 66-61 B.C. Cf. W.V. Harris, *Imperialism* 93-101, on the role of commercial interests in Roman expansion.

difficult. Quite apart from the merits of the jurists' law, the *equites* are likely to have taken a keen interest in increasing the security of private law within the judicial system,[74] and this for three interrelated reasons. First, to the extent that private trials are decided through application of recognized legal norms, a defense is provided against their determination through non-legal standards, such as the wealth or influence of the parties—a circumstance that outsiders must always find fearful. Second, the notion of an autonomous and non-political private law serves somewhat to insulate the sphere of private interrelationships (family, property, contract, succession) from disruption caused by transitory political developments; private law defines a protected sphere where the interests of the state are in theory minimal or non-existent. Since the *equites* by definition abstained from direct participation in the magistral aristocracy, they had an urgent interest in defining such a protected area. Third, legal security is of particular importance to those who are involved in commerce, since trade emphatically requires a capacity to minimize risk in planning for the future.[75]

Admittedly, it is one thing to argue that the *equites* "ought" to have held views such as these, or that they are "likely" to have held them; it is another thing to prove that they did commonly hold them. The *equites* themselves produced no great intellectual spokesman to articulate their ideology; and the implications for law of *otium equestre*, the deliberate abstention

[74] With what follows, cf. M. Weber, *Wirtschaft und Gesellschaft* (4th ed. 1956) 470: "Ihnen werden alle diejenigen politischen und ökonomischen Interessenten zufallen, welchen die Stetigkeit und Kalkulierbarkeit des Rechtsganzes wichtig sein muss, also speziell die Träger rationaler ökonomischen und politischen Dauerbetriebe. Vor allem den ersten wird die formale und zugleich rationale Justiz als Garantie der 'Freiheit' gelten, eben desjenigen Gutes, welches theokratische oder patriarchal-autoritäre ebenso wie unter Umständen demokratische, jedenfalls alle ideologisch an materialer Gerechtigkeit interessenten Mächte verwerfen müssen. Diesen allen ist nicht mit formaler, sondern mit 'Kadijustiz' gedient. Die Volksjustiz in der unmittelbaren attischen Demokratie z.B. war eine solche in hohem Masse." See also A. Kronman, *Max Weber* (1983) 92-95, for a lucid exposition of this passage.

[75] See M. Weber, (cited n.74) 94, on the relation between formally rational justice and economic development.

from magistral office in favor of concentration on personal affairs,[76] remain largely tacit, though totally compatible with the thesis outlined above. Furthermore, views such as these, or portions of them, are certain to have had some attraction beyond the immediate perimeter of the equestrian order. The economic and social position of the *equites* was broadly similar to that of the senatorial aristocracy; the division between them was one of rank, not class.[77] But rank counted for a great deal in an intensely status-conscious society such as Rome. It would at least occasion no surprise if the equestrians, a large number of whom had municipal origins, were markedly more sensitive than their superiors on the issue of legal security. Indeed, late Republican judicial speeches provide most of our more vivid evidence for social prejudice among the Roman upper classes; Cicero's vituperative attack on the Tarquinian landowners who testified for Aebutius (*Caec.* 24-27) is a comparatively mild example.

Yet Cicero's *pro Caecina* also provides the clearest and earliest statement of a new ideal: the famous *laus iuris civilis* (65-78).[78] The speech was delivered in 69, the year after the *lex Aurelia* had, through an artful compromise, re-defined the "jury class" so that its majority comprised non-senatorial men whose status was defined by wealth.[79] The law was directed mainly

[76] See C. Nicolet, *Ordre* vol. I 699-722, based esp. on Cic. *Cluent.* 153-154 and *Rab. Post.* 16-17; also J.H. D'Arms, (cited n.54) 60-61, 113-116. Note Sallust, *Hist.* 1.55.9 M, of the *equites*: "illa quies et otium cum libertate."

[77] Historians have generally admitted this since the appearance of P.A. Brunt's essay in *Second International Conference of Economic History* vol. I (1965) 117-149, repr. in *The Crisis of the Roman Republic* (ed. R. Seager, 1969) 83-115. See, e.g., M.I. Finley, *The Ancient Economy* (1973) 49-50; I. Shatzman, (cited n.71) 177-212; G.E.M. de Ste. Croix, *The Class Struggle in the Ancient Greek World* (1981) 41-42, 338-340. But most scholars still insist on the relatively greater direct involvement of *equites* in commerce; see note 71.

[78] See Chapter IV, at notes 168-172.

[79] See Chapter V, at notes 11-12. Modern scholars, who generally play down the differences between Senators and *equites*, have not found it easy to explain the persistence with which the *equites* demanded control of the "jury class"; see, e.g., C. Nicolet, *Ordre* vol. I 625-630. I. Shatzman, (cited n.71) 212, argues: "The principal explanation of the Equites' frame of mind is that they wanted public recognition of their social importance." This appears to trivialize the question.

The *Corona*

toward control of the criminal courts, but its implications for private law cannot be entirely ignored: the original panel of *recuperatores*, drawn by lot from the *album* of private judges, undoubtedly contained a non-senatorial majority.[80] Caecina, himself an *eques*,[81] is described to the *recuperatores* as "having always hoped for the approval of you and men like you" (*Caec.* 103: *se probatum vobis vestrique similibus semper voluit*). It is to this jury that Cicero addresses his theory of law, arguing that private law must be autonomous if society is to remain stable, and that attainment of this ideal requires judges to accept the pronouncements of jurists as *prima facie* binding statements of law.

To be sure, Cicero is not just tailoring his remarks to his audience; similar statements on legal autonomy are scattered throughout his later writings, and his eventual theory of the state reserves a prominent place for the autonomy of private law.[82] Yet it is not unfair to suppose that Cicero, in this early speech, still functioned as a spokesman for equestrian values. He was himself the son of a Roman *eques* from Arpinum, and a nephew of another, the jurist C. Visellius Aculeo.[83] Through his father's connections in Rome, the young Cicero had first been put in contact with the Mucii Scaevolae, from whom he absorbed many of his later values.[84] While in his later life Cicero, as a Senator and ex-Consul, remained somewhat aloof from the equestrians,[85] he maintained lively and amicable relations with many jurists of equestrian origin.[86]

[80] On the selection procedure see Chapter V, at notes 13-14.
[81] Chapter I, note 50. C. Nicolet, *Ordre* vol. II 813-814, uses this passage to prove Caecina's equestrian status.
[82] H.P. Kohns, *Gymnasium* 81 (1974) 485-498.
[83] On the two men, see G. Nicolet, *Ordre* vol. II 1056-1057 and 1078-1079, respectively. On Aculeo as a jurist see Chapter IV, note 22.
[84] Cic. *Leg.* 1.13; *Brut.* 306; *Lael.* 1. See T.N. Mitchell, *Cicero: The Ascending Years* (1979) 4-6, 12-13, 44-45.
[85] C. Nicolet, *Ordre* vol. I 673-698. In the 60's, however, Cicero cultivated them unceasingly: I. Shatzman, (cited n.71) 178-185; T.N. Mitchell, (cited n.84) 100-105.
[86] Besides Aquilius and Servius, Cicero had especially close relations with his protégé C. Trebatius Testa, for whom he wrote the *Topica*. Note also his

In the years after Cicero left the civil bar (and in part doubtless because he left it), the new ideal gradually took hold in the Roman judicial system. With one major exception, the process was not one of "great events" or of "history," but rather a slow process of virtually unconscious change through recurrent social practice.[87] The one exception is the *lex Cornelia* of 67, which limited the Praetor's free exercise of discretion in granting trials.[88] C. Cornelius, the plebeian Tribune who proposed and carried this and several other laws in 67, seems to have aimed at consolidating and extending the legislative program introduced by Pompey in 70; Cornelius probably enjoyed at least tacit support from Pompey.[89] Cornelius' legislation had three identifiable aims: to curb the corrupt administration of provinces by senatorial Governors, to accommodate some broad popular demands, and to enhance the position of the new citizens. It has been argued that the *lex Cornelia de iurisdictione* was aimed mainly at provincial Governors;[90] but that is hardly plausible in view of Cicero's defense of the law through examples drawn from the Urban Praetor's court (Ascon. p. 74 C). The likelier hypothesis is that the law aimed to protect especially the new citizens against arbitrary decisions *in iure*.

The law was highly unpopular in the Senate, though no one dared oppose it openly (Ascon. p. 59 C; cf. Dio 36.40.1-2); its supporters therefore came from outside the Senate, most

---

friendly ties to his cousin C. Visellius Varro (Cic. *Brut.* 264), the Apulian jurist L. Valerius (*Fam.* 1.10, 3.1.3), and Precianus (*Fam.* 7.8.2), from whom he probably inherited (*Fam.* 14.5.2; *Att.* 6.9.2). All three were probably equestrian, at least in origin. One might add Q. Haterius, apparently a jurist (*Fam.* 9.18.3) though he is omitted by W. Kunkel, *Herkunft*[2]; he was a Senator, but doubtless of equestrian origin.

[87] See A. Giddens, *Central Problems in Social Theory* (1979) 198-233.

[88] See Chapter II, at notes 92-97.

[89] See, e.g., W. McDonald, *CQ* 23 (1929) 196-208; R. Seager, in *Hommages à M. Renard* vol. II (1969) 680-686; A. Ward, *TAPhA* 101 (1970) 554-556; E. Gruen, *Last Generation* 262-265; M. Griffin, *JRS* 63 (1973) 203-211; A.M. Giomaro, *St. Urbinati* 43 (1974/1975) 307-311. T.N. Mitchell, (cited n.84) 160-161, denies this, unconvincingly.

[90] M. Griffin, (cited n.89) 208.

The *Corona*

probably from among the *equites*. The principal opponent of all Cornelius' legislation was the redoubtable C. Calpurnius Piso,[91] while Cicero valiantly defended the legislation when Cornelius was charged with *maiestas* two years later. Thus the antagonists from Caecina's lawsuit were once more divided. The consequence of the law, perhaps an unintended one,[92] was both to curb the pace of innovations in the Edict and to shift responsibility for them. The jurists began to assume greater prominence in proposing edictal changes. The *actio doli*, introduced at the suggestion of Aquilius Gallus, was probably in the Edict already in 76.[93] Other late Republican innovations bear the names of jurists: the *actio Serviana*, governing security for debt and named probably for Servius; the *iudicium Cascellianum*, against contumacious defendants of possessory interdicts, named for A. Cascellius.[94] The increasing stability of the Edict in the later Republic made it feasible for the first time to base commentaries on its text; the first of these appeared, as it seems, in the reign of Julius Caesar, from the pens of Servius and (at far greater length) his pupil Ofilius.[95] Although the Edict eventually ossified, jurists continued to recommend changes in its text until well into the Empire.[96]

We are less well informed with regard to changes in the *apud iudicem* stage of trials; but here too, as it seems, the balance gradually tipped away from the orators. The *lex Aurelia*, in ending senatorial control of the "jury class," had granted majority control to the *equites* and their allies; and while in most trials it remained possible for parties to choose a *iudex* from outside the *album*, still it is likely that after 70 B.C. judges were increasingly of non-senatorial origin.[97] Perhaps as a con-

[91] *Ibid.* 203, 210. On Piso's politics see Chapter III, at notes 23-24.

[92] See A. Metro, *Iura* 20 (1969) 500-524 and *La 'Denegatio Actionis'* (1972) 145-150. See also Chapter II, at notes 100-101.

[93] See Chapter IV, note 39.

[94] On the *actio Serviana*, see recently M. Kaser, *Studien zum Römischen Pfandrecht* (1981) 8, 145, with bibliography. On the *iudicium Cascellianum*, see A. Rodger, *CQ* 22 (1972) 135-138.

[95] Pompon. D. 1.2.2.44; see Chapter IV, at notes 84, 131-133.

[96] B. Vonglis, *Lettre* 184; and Chapter IV, note 133.

[97] See Chapter V, at notes 11-12.

sequence of this change, *iudices* seem increasingly to have taken an activist role in conducting trials, checking the once unrestricted eloquence of orators and forcing them to address the issues.[98]

Orators responded to the change by reining in their lush modes of address. In the last decade of his life Cicero was confronted by the overt hostility of younger "Atticist" orators, who professed their "preference for a plainer style with a high value assigned to purity of diction and avoidance of amplification."[99] The terser style was at least in part a response to the changing taste of judges (Tac. *Dial.* 19.5). Two passages of Cicero imply that this new style was especially successful in private trials.[100] Judges seem at last to have wearied of rhetorical melodramatics applied to the ordinary stuff of private law. Finally, it is worth noting Cicero's pleas, often repeated during the final decade of his life, for a rapprochement between orators and jurists.[101] In an important and unjustly neglected passage of his *de Oratore* (2.133-143), Cicero urges orators to avoid purely case-oriented argument and instead to subordinate cases to the "abstract issues" defined by law and legal science. Unless this is done, argues Cicero, every case will require totally fresh discussion (137), and the result-

[98] See Tac. *Dial.* 19.5-20.2; and generally Chapter V, at notes 78-83. Admittedly this change cannot be precisely dated. It is not known whether the *lex Pompeia* of 52, which limited length of speeches in criminal trials (Cic. *Brut.* 324; Tac. *Dial.* 38.2), also restricted oratory in private trials; see M. Kaser, *RZ* 274 n.26.

[99] G. Kennedy, *The Art of Rhetoric in the Roman World* (1972) 239-246, at 239, with further bibliography; see also W. Kroll, *RE* Suppb. VII s.v. "Rhetorik" (1958) 1105-1108. See esp. Cic. *Opt. Gen.* 12, of the Atticists: "intellegentiam ponunt in audiendi fastidio neque eos quicquam excelsum magnificumque delectat." On early imperial developments see J. Fairweather, *Seneca the Elder* (1981) 243-303, esp. 259.

[100] Cic. *Opt. Gen.* 10 and *Orat.* 72; cf. *Fam.* 9.21.1.

[101] See Chapter IV, at notes 129-133. On Cic. *de Or.* 2.142, see F. Bona, *SDHI* 46 (1980) 303-304. On the philosophical background of the passage, see W. Kroll, (cited n.99) 1085-1089 and 1101-1105; but I would take the passage far more seriously than Kroll does. Cf. also Cic. *Brut.* 322 (*in fine*), *Orat.* 46 (with Sandys), *Q. Fr.* 3.3.4. The underlying principle is discussed in N. Luhmann, *Rechtssoziologie* vol. I (1972) 178-179.

ing infinitude of cases (140: *quot homines tot causae*) is something
greatly to be feared. All in all, our sources give the impression
that oratory was rapidly adjusting to a new reality.

There is some evidence that jurists encouraged both activism on the part of judges and rule-oriented argumentation by
advocates.[102] In both cases, as the jurists doubtless realized,
the likely consequence was an increase in the prominence of
law within the judicial system; in any event, this result was
gradually achieved. An important passage from Cicero's *Topica*, written in the last year of the orator's life, provides not
only the earliest evidence for frequent juristic presence in *consilia*, but also a strong suggestion that private trials were increasingly hinging on judicial opinions.[103] As Cicero continues: "In all suits containing the words *ex fide bona*, or where
conduct must be honest *ut inter bonos*, and especially in judgment on dowry where the principle is *aequius melius*, the jurists should be on hand. It is they who defined fraud and good
faith and equity, the legal duties between partner and partner,
manager and principal, mandator and mandatary, husband and
wife."[104] Cicero clearly implies that jurists' law had come to
determine broad areas of law that were previously discretionary. In short, our meager sources indicate that the tide was
turning in favor of the jurists even before the beginning of the
Empire.

In the last years of the Republic, the movement toward

[102] The evidence is Aelius Tubero's *de Officio Iudicis* (discussed in Chapter
V, at note 79) and Servius' introduction to praetorian law, evidently intended
for orators (cf. Chapter IV, at notes 131-133).

[103] Cic. *Top.* 65, discussed in Chapter V, at notes 92-96. Cic. *Fam.* 7.21
(44 B.C.) discusses a juristic dispute over an apparently erroneous ruling by
the Urban Praetor (cf. A. Watson, *Succession* 73-75); the jurists seem to have
the situation well in hand.

[104] Cic. *Top.* 66: "In omnibus igitur eis iudiciis, in quibus ex fide bona est
additum, ubi vero etiam ut inter bonos bene agier oportet, in primisque in
arbitrio rei uxoriae, in quo est quod eius aequius melius, parati eis esse debent. Illi dolum malum, illi fidem bonam, illi aequum bonum, illi quid so-
cium socio, quid eum qui negotia aliena curasset ei cuius ea negotia fuissent,
quid eum qui mandasset, eumve cui mandatum esset, alterum alteri praestare
oportet, quid virum uxori, quid uxorem viro tradiderunt."

Toward Classical Roman Law

legal security reached its apogee in the unsuccessful drive for codification of the *ius civile*.[105] Probably during his third consulate in 52, Pompey entertained a plan for collecting and publishing all valid statutes; but this plan failed because of widespread opposition (Isid. *Etym.* 5.1.5), presumably from Pompey's aristocratic allies in the Senate.[106] Julius Caesar, during the final years of his reign, revived Pompey's plan, and added to it a project for codifying the *ius civile*; however Caesar's assassination in 44 prevented fulfillment of the program (Suet. *Caes.* 44.2; Isid. *Etym.* 5.1.5). It appears that A. Ofilius, an equestrian jurist with close ties to Caesar (Pompon. D. 1.2.2.44), was to have been mainly responsible for executing the program.[107] Some have thought that Caesar's program, "like other of his later measures, only shows how strongly he had become influenced by the spirit of Hellenism";[108] but while so premature a codification would doubtless not have been in the best interests of private law, the drive to codify is itself entirely consistent with the temper of the late Republic.

It is of course a great pity that we have so few direct sources after 69 B.C. and, therefore, cannot follow the exact evolution of private judicial procedure in the late Republic. That this evolution occurred is hard to doubt; but we learn of it only by accident, through stray remarks or related events. Nor is there much doubt that the social origins of the movement for legal security can be found in the equestrian order, which provided so many of the late Republican jurists; the interests

[105] On autocratic attempts to reform private law, see A. Watson, *Law Making* 95-100. See also Chapter IV, above, at note 133.

[106] On the plan, see esp. E. Pólay, *Acta Antiqua* 13 (1965) 85-95. Pólay's argument that the opponents were supporters of Caesar (pp. 94-95) is hardly convincing. F. Schulz, *Legal Science* 61, argues that such schemes died because they "received no support from the lawyers"; a doubtful proposition.

[107] See esp. E. Pólay, *Iura* 16 (1965) 27-51 (48-50 on Ofilius); F. D'Ippolito, *I Giuristi e la Città* (1978) 93-116; both with further literature. It is odd that neither attempt at codification is mentioned by contemporary sources; but the sincerity of these efforts cannot be doubted, cf. Z. Yavetz, *Julius Caesar and His Public Image* (1983) 176.

[108] F. Schulz, *Principles* 7; cf. *Legal Science* 61. Also E. Pólay, (cited n.107) 47.

of this order were directly served by the propagation of the new ideal.

In any case, the movement toward legal security in the late Republic did not seek to subject rhetorical advocacy to the dominance of legal science; rather, it aimed to redress the balance between the two disciplines within the judicial system or (more precisely) to reconstruct this balance on a new and far more sophisticated plane. Rhetoric was harnessed and made to play a more responsible role. For centuries still to come, the anarchic impulses of rhetorical advocacy were crucial to the judicial system; they established a buffer between abstract jurists' law and the infinite variety of actual cases.[109] The classical Roman jurists showed great sensitivity on this point, refusing to compromise the large discretionary area defined by the *officium iudicis*.[110] Historical legal systems have found many ways of reconciling "law as logic" with "law as experience." The Roman way is, however, not the least happy of classical Roman law's accomplishments.[111]

The heirs of Q. Mucius could look back on the last century of the Republic with considerable satisfaction. The relatively uncontested preeminence of orators within the judicial system lasted only about two generations (ca. 125-50 B.C.). For the jurists, this period was transitional, a prelude to classicism.[112]

[109] The enduring appeal to judges of arguments based on *aequitas* is stressed by Quintil. 7.1.63. It is impossible to speculate on the extent to which imperial jurists also drew their ideas from courtroom argument; but one may note, for example, the similarity in argument between Ps.-Quint. *Decl. Mai.* 13 (property rights in bees during their flight from hives) and Celsus' treatment of this issue in *Coll.* 12.7.10, on which see B.W. Frier, *Class. Journ.* 78 (1983) 105-114.

[110] See M. Kaser, *RZ* 268 ff., esp. 274 ("Der Hergang der Verhandlung war nur zum geringsten Teil rechtlich geregelt"). In any case, it is doubtful the jurists held "the [false] belief that the meaning of all legal rules is fixed and predetermined before any concrete questions of their application arise"; cf. H.L.A. Hart, *Essays in Jurisprudence and Philosophy* (1983) 269, discussing Jhering.

[111] B.W. Frier, *LTIR* 196-219.

[112] There is no point in pursuing the endless debate about whether late Republican jurists qualify to be called "classical," since this is largely a matter

In the second century, the substance of the *ius civile* had been narrow and archaic; the practice of law was mainly cautelary, still amateurish and tentative, and practitioners viewed law primarily as an avenue to political advancement. But the ascendancy of the orators had eventually galvanized the jurists, who, at long last, looked inward to their craft. Q. Mucius and his students successfully sought to reorganize law on a broader and more socially adequate basis, to intellectualize its substance, and to justify the rule of law not through tradition, but through the coherence and adequacy of its norms; these efforts represent the historical foundation of the legal profession. By good fortune, important segments of the Roman upper classes found it in their interests to champion the jurists, and so the jurists' revolution took hold.

Caecina's lawsuit, tried in 69 B.C., still participated in the older tradition of rhetorical advocacy; and yet, in certain respects, it anticipated the coming change. The *pro Caecina* ought to symbolize for scholars not the abject perversion of law by rhetoric,[113] but rather the ambiguous and fluctuating relationship between two competing disciplines during the transitional period of Roman law. Cicero and Piso, as they explored the meaning of the interdict *de vi armata*, threw up idea after idea with seemingly gleeful prodigality. One of these ideas for interpretation was advanced perhaps not quite seriously and, in any case, is not likely to have carried the day in 69; but the idea nonetheless became orthodoxy among the classical jurists.[114] This indirect and selective flow of legal ideas from judicial oratory into law is perhaps the one crucial aspect of the transitional period, the real basis of Roman law's growth into maturity. By contrast, had an advocate in the first cen-

---

of definition; see F. Wieacker, *Recht*² 168-185. My analysis tends to focus on the position of the jurists within the judicial system.

[113] See Chapter V, at notes 127-131.

[114] Chapter IV, at notes 143-146. H.J. Roby, *Private Law* vol. II 521, suggests that classical jurists picked up their interpretation of the interdict *de vi armata* from Cicero's speech; this may be dubious, but cf. D. Nörr, in *Ciceroniana* 3 (1978) 111 ff., on the jurists' knowledge of Cicero.

tury A.D. argued with the abandon of a Cicero or a Piso, the impatient *iudex* would have gaveled him to order and insisted that he "stick to the subject" (Tac. *Dial.* 19.5-20.2). For, in the meantime, "the subject" had been narrowed in the interests of law.

VII

Conclusion:
The Professionalization of Law

> What lawyers love above all things is an ordered life, and
> authority is the greatest guarantee of order. Moreover, one must
> not forget that although they value liberty, they generally
> rate legality as far more precious; they are less afraid of tyranny
> than of arbitrariness, and provided that it is the lawgiver himself
> who is responsible for taking away men's independence,
> they are more or less content.
> —Alexis de Tocqueville

ONCE LAW had been successfully transformed into an intellectual discipline under the control of professionals, the new form
of law became effectively irresistible. The profession of law
has survived (and in most circumstances prospered) under the
most astonishing array of social and economic conditions, and
under almost every imaginable type of monarchy, despotism,
aristocracy, and democracy; even the modern socialist states,
whose founders often proclaimed their contempt for law, have
learned to rely on the flexible repertory of legal thinking. After
two millennia, it is hard even to conceive of a political society
without law and lawyers. Such a society would have to be
either utopian or barbarous, but in any case exceedingly primitive.

Yet this attitude is really only the result of successful cultural conditioning over centuries. Classical Greece and the
Hellenistic states, though not primitive societies by any ra-

Conclusion

tional gauge, had constitutions and statutes and regulations, courts and judges and juries, but neither intellectually organized law nor lawyering as a profession.[1]

Why, therefore, was it the later Roman Republic that brought forth a legal science? No one, I think, will deny the brilliance, vision, and energy of the great jurists of that age, men such as Q. Mucius and Servius. Without the continuous commitment of such men, the "struggle for law" would surely have come to naught, swallowed up in the ceaseless turmoil that preceded the founding of the Empire. But the genius of a few great men hardly seems a sufficient answer to our question. The seed that these jurists sowed did not fall on sterile ground. Why was that so?

The judicial system of the later Roman Republic might appear, at first glance, most unpromising for the juristic enterprise. As Roscoe Pound observed, "One can but marvel how the Roman law of Cicero's time, with its crude enforcing agencies, its crude methods of reviewing decisions, its crude methods of instructing tribunals as to the law, could ever have maintained itself, much less have developed into a law of the world. It could not have done so, indeed, except among a disciplined, homogeneous people, zealous to know the law and to obey it."[2] Yet Pound's solution, which predicates among the Romans a deep cultural drive to law, seems frail and paradoxical when juxtaposed with the tumultuous history of the late Republic. The Romans of this era were hardly characterized by moral discipline or social homogeneity, much less by any perceptible predisposition to discover and observe the law. On the contrary, the late Republic is an unsettled and creative era, a time of swift economic growth, social disharmony, political ferment, and widespread skepticism about inherited ways

[1] H.J. Wolff, *Opuscula Diversa* (1974) 81-103. On the Greek achievement in law, see *ibid.* 1-14; on the Greek failure to develop jurisprudence, M. Talamanca, *Il Diritto in Grecia e a Roma* (1981) 19-32, with the review of A. Maffi, *Quad. di Storia* 9 (1983) 245-262.

[2] R. Pound, *Ethics* 27 (1916) 150. To account for the jurists' rise by invoking the "legal spirit" of the Romans is basically to rephrase the question.

Conclusion

of doing and believing.[3] Is it possible to find the "fertile earth" of law not in the innate discipline, homogeneity, and lawfulness of the late Roman Republic, but rather in the very opposite qualities: in unrest, conflict, and uncertainty?

It may clarify the problem to examine it on a more abstract, "systemic" level.[4] Already in Classical Greece, legal norms were generally regarded from what we may call a "positivist perspective"; that is, the Greeks generally and consciously recognized that legal norms are human creations, and hence that we as humans may claim the inalienable right to discover, formulate, interpret, modify, change, or multiply them. The Greeks also understood that application of law would predictably set off clarification and even criticism of law; and when this dynamic process ceased being considered something fearful, it became a source of strength for law, since the very alterability of law was turned into the foundation of its endurance and validity. These Greek viewpoints, a hard-won historical achievement, serve to indicate the final acceptance in principle of autonomous law as an integral part of statecraft.[5]

Otherwise, apart from its pioneering discussions on the philosophy of law, the Greek world seems to have got no further. In the later Roman Republic the next decisive step was taken. This step involved not just substantive law (though here too the late Republican contribution was considerable),

[3] See just C. Meier, *Res Publica Amissa* (1966) 301-306; and above, Chapter VI, note 62. E. Gruen, *Last Generation* 498-507, paints a rather more optimistic picture.

[4] The theory that follows is drawn from N. Luhmann, "The Autonomy of the Legal System," in *The Differentiation of Society* (trans. S. Holmes and C. Larmore, 1982) 122-137, at 122-127. The essay originally appeared in *Rechtstheorie* 7 (1976) 121-135. On legal positivism in the ancient world, see D. Nörr, *Rechtskritik* 21-40; on Greek positivism, J. Triantaphyllopoulos, in *Symposion 1971* (1975) 23-66, with literature. The societal evolution toward increasing complexity of legal institutions is explored by R.D. Schwartz and J.C. Miller, *American Journal of Sociology* 70 (1964) 159-169, and H. Wimberly, *ibid.* 79 (1973) 78-83; their findings make it clear that professionalization of law has nothing to do with the introduction of courts or counsel.

[5] N. Luhmann, (cited n.4) 124.

Conclusion

but also the way in which law itself was handled. At the fringes of the Roman judicial system there emerged a group of legal professionals, the jurists. This group was largely self-recruited through informal modes of legal education; its membership was determined by recognition from the group itself and from without. The jurists began to study and manipulate the materials of private law in a disciplined, rational fashion: they enunciated and organized existing legal rules in a convincing presentation, they discovered and described the systemic boundaries and internal articulation of private law, they deduced fundamental principles and concepts of law, and they applied these principles and concepts in the coherent development of new legal rules and institutions. Through their efforts, the intellectual content and social capacity of private law were markedly increased; and soon the discipline of law also became all but inaccessible to those not specially trained in it. To this extent, law was "professionalized" by being transformed into a self-consciously autonomous field of study.

The development was crowned with historical success. Part of the reason for the jurists' success can be found in the internal organization of the Roman judicial system. That system, emphatically non-bureaucratic, relied on the nominally gratuitous services of annual magistrates and of lay judges casually enlisted from the upper classes; such persons necessarily lacked the expertise, experience, and incentive required to master law's intricacies. Likewise, the orators, educated in the long-established traditions of Greek rhetoric, were far too case-oriented to serve as a lawyer class. On the other hand, the patronal system of the third- and second-century jurisconsults had accustomed Romans to the notion of legal experts operating outside the formal boundaries of the judicial system and serving as a self-reproducing repository of legal knowledge. In addition, most Roman trials were heard before a single *iudex* or a relatively small panel, not before the huge juries that characterized Attic law. For this reason the Roman judge could not seek refuge in masses of co-judges, but was more directly accountable (in a moral if not a legal sense) for his verdict, and hence was more inclined to submit to popular

272

will as to how his verdict should be formed. What the organization of the judicial system helps to explain, therefore, is why the professionalization of law at Rome took the ultimate form of a non-judicial jurists' law (rather than, for instance, a judge-made law) and, also, why the Roman judicial system itself long remained largely immune to professionalization.

What cannot be explained by such analysis, however, is why jurists' law had such profound impact on the Roman judicial system. The reasons for this impact must be sought in external factors, and of these one was undoubtedly of cardinal importance: the dramatic increase in the number of citizens. In 91-88, many of the non-citizen Italian allies of Rome had risen in revolt against the narrowly based suzerainty of the capital; though their armies were defeated, the allies forced Rome to make statutory grants of citizenship that eventually embraced all Italy south of the Appennines. The Censors of 86/85, who evidently failed to include many new citizens, registered only 463,000 adult males; but those of 70/69 reported 910,000, a virtual doubling. These figures suggest that Rome's citizenry grew from about 1.5 million in 90 B.C. to about 3 million in 70 B.C.; and all or nearly all of this increase is attributable to the enfranchisement of the new citizens.[6] Rome's citizen body, by ancient standards large to begin with, now became immense.

The great majority of Roman citizens, whether old or new, probably had, to be sure, little or no access to the Urban Praetor's court. But the number of those in the "upper classes" (those with the means to bring or resist suits) also undoubtedly grew, if perhaps less dramatically.[7] At least 1,600 *equites*

---

[6] See P.A. Brunt, *Italian Manpower* (1971) 91-99 and 121-130. Brunt's figures, which are often thought too low, at least give some notion of the increase. L. Lombardi, *Saggio* 51, also stresses the importance for jurisprudence of the extensions of citizenship.

[7] A good portion of the Italian upper classes were already citizens before 90 B.C.; cf. T.P. Wiseman, *New Men* 17-19, 24-32. As K.-P. Johne, *Gnomon* 55 (1983) 139-140, remarks (in reviewing my *LTIR*), my use of the term "upper classes" is a bit untraditional in that I do not confine it to the status elite. I believe that the Roman "litigating class" was determined mainly by

Conclusion

are alleged to have perished during Sulla's brief and savage *dominatio*, 82-81; and Sulla adlected a further 300 *equites* to fill the Senate's depleted ranks. Yet the post-Sullan *equester ordo* seems, if anything, much larger than the pre-Sullan one, and this increase was certainly a result of massive recruitment from the cities and towns of Italy.[8] Although the old noble families of Rome still clung stubbornly to the consulate and to control of the state, it was nonetheless these "new men" who set the tone of the late Republic; they are the emergent Italian aristocracy that would ascend to power in the early Empire.[9] The senatorial and equestrian orders, together with their family members, must have numbered at least 20,000 persons in the late Republic. Beneath their ranks, a large and heterogeneous group of the more or less upwardly mobile rounded out the "upper classes": municipal notables, the *ordo* of freedmen, Italian shippers and merchants, the more successful practitioners of the liberal arts, and so on.[10] All told, the "upper classes" of the late Republic could easily have numbered around 150,000-200,000 persons—still only about 5-7% of the population, admittedly, and widely dispersed through peninsular Italy and the Roman dominions.

---

relative control of social goods (especially wealth), not just by status; the "litigating class" is thus somewhat larger than the status elite.

[8] See C. Nicolet, *Ordre* vol. I 116-123, who examines the contradictory sources.

[9] R. Syme, *The Roman Revolution* (1939). E.g., p. 355: "The class of knights, indeed, is the cardinal factor in the whole social, military and political structure of the New State" created by Augustus. And pp. 359-360: "Augustus was eager to provide for further recruitment and admission to the Senate of the flower of Italy, good opulent men from the colonies and *municipia*. They were the backbone of Augustus' faction, the prime agents in the plebiscite of all Italy." (Syme refers to the speech of Claudius, *ILS* 212 col. ii, line 1 ff.) On the numbers of the upper classes, see R. MacMullen, *Roman Social Relations* (1974) 88-89. On the *equites* in the Empire, see now P.A. Brunt, *JRS* 73 (1983) 42-75, esp. 43-44.

[10] Cf. C. Nicolet, *Les Structures de l'Italie Romaine* (1977) 202-204; and, for the Empire, P. Huttunen, *The Social Strata in the Imperial City of Rome* (1974) 189-191. On the *municipales*, see esp. T.P. Wiseman, *New Men* 33-94; on freedmen, S. Treggiari, *Roman Freedmen during the Late Republic* (1969); on merchants, J. Hatzfeld, *Les Trafiquants Italiens* (1919). See now also the essays in *Les "Bourgeoisies" Municipales Italiennes aux IIe e Ier Siecles av. J.-C.* (1983).

This spectrum of the "upper classes" closely resembles the spectrum of litigants in Cicero's lawsuits during his years before the civil bar, 81-69 B.C.[11] From the senatorial order, Cicero represented Titinia, the wife of C. Aurelius Cotta (Cos. 75), in a suit probably dating to the early 70's (Cic. *Brut.* 217); in around 70 B.C. he was asked to speak for Q. Mucius Orestinus (trib. pl. 64) in an *actio furti* that was settled out of court (Ascon. p. 86 C). Cicero's equestrian clients are the actor Q. Roscius Gallus—who had received equestrian status from Sulla (Macrob. *Sat.* 2.10; cf. Cic. *Rosc. Com.* 17) and whose family came from Lanuvium (Cic. *Div.* 1.79)—and A. Caecina from Volaterrae; the defendant in Orestinus' lawsuit was to have been L. Fufius Calenus, undoubtedly at least an *eques.*[12]

The other known litigants in Cicero's trials are typically members of the mainly urbanized "middle classes." Cicero's client M. Tullius came from a family that had possessed an estate in Thurii for at least a generation (*Tull.* 14); Tullius himself apparently lived in Rome and ran the estate through his procurator (17). P. Quinctius, an elderly member of a distinguished but relatively poor Latin family residing in Rome (*Quinct.* 2, 85-86, 99), was married to the sister of the equestrian actor Roscius (77-78). Sex. Naevius, who sued Quinctius, was a Roman banker (11, 25) with influential ties to Rome's nobility (47, 93); connected to Quinctius by marriage (16), he had joined with Quinctius' brother in a ranching venture in Narbonese Gaul (11-12, 28), one aspect of which involved selling slaves (24). P. Fabius, the defendant in Tullius' lawsuit, had obtained a small fortune while serving under a consular in Asia (*Tull.* 14-15, 19); in partnership with the *vir optimus* Cn. Acerronius (16), he later used this money to purchase a Thurian estate from the Senator C. Claudius (14). Sex. Aebutius is described as a social parasite living off his legal representation of wealthy Roman women (*Caec.* 14); yet he too was plainly better connected than Cicero cared to ad-

[11] The plaintiff and defendant in the trial of the Arretine woman (Cic. *Caec.* 97) are unknown, though of some status to judge from their advocates. Ser. Naevius, the defendant in Titinia's lawsuit, is otherwise unknown.

[12] C. Nicolet, *Ordre* vol. II 885 n.3; he is the brother of a moneyer ca. 70.

Conclusion

mit. Finally, C. Fannius Chaerea, who sued Roscius, was a freedman, if we may judge from his cognomen and the abuse Cicero heaps upon him (*Rosc. Com.* 20-21); he had earlier entered into a partnership with Roscius to exploit the acting talents of his slave Panurgus (27-29).

Cicero's clients and their opponents may be taken as broadly defining the spectrum of Rome's "litigating class." Since Cicero chose his cases were a cut above average; but no evidence gants in these cases were a cut above average; but no evidence suggests that the disparity is very great. Thus, the spectrum of litigants in trials handled by C. Verres (Cic. 2 *Verr.* 1.104-127, 2.21) includes several members of the senatorial and equestrian orders, as well as freedmen (1.123, 127), *municipales* (1.127), and a catchall category of the *plebs Romana* (122-123). Likewise, numerous anecdotes about Republican private disputes, collected by Valerius Maximus (7.7-8, 8.2), entirely corroborate this general pattern and, in addition, provide some choice examples of the *plebs Romana*: Genucius, a eunuch in the service of Magna Mater (7.7.6), and the wealthy *leno* Vecillus (7.7.7), both non-suited in seeking inheritances.

On the other hand, at least during the Republic, large sectors of society are not attested as litigating in Rome: yeomen farmers and peasants; free farm workers, skilled and unskilled; carriers by land and sea; craftsmen and small-scale merchants; the urban proletariat; skilled and unskilled laborers in production and service jobs; and others. Such persons undoubtedly constituted the vast majority of the population. Rome's "litigating class," though it evidently extended somewhat below the threshold of the political elite, nonetheless had definite limits. At Rome it was already a sign of status to have sued or been sued.

The enfranchisement of the Italians considerably enlarged the size of Rome's "litigating class." Simply because of the larger number of people now served by the Urban Praetor's court, the immediate consequence is certain to have been a significant jump in the number of suits brought at Rome, and hence a strain on the non-bureaucratic judicial system. Further, the enfranchisement broadened and diversified the "liti-

Conclusion

gating class," by bringing into it individuals from widely scattered areas of Italy who were not bound by the common moral values of the Roman aristocracy. The result was a sharp rise in the "social density" of late Republican society, with predictable consequences: "An increase in social density will tend to produce an increase in social interaction, and hence an increase in the number of disputes. Unless the number of dispute institutions expands proportionately, each will have to handle more disputes; increasing caseload is an important factor in bureaucratizing an institution. . . . Functional specialization . . . is another response to increased caseloads; cases, like widgets, can be processed more efficiently if they, or their elements, are treated as being identical."[13] But Rome's judicial system was constitutionally unable either to replicate itself or to bureaucratize. My argument is that the Romans therefore eased the burden of an increased caseload by relying more and more on the jurists as external specialists "empowered" to make authoritative pronouncements on law. Through acceptance of juristic opinions the judicial system was able to increase the speed at which it handled cases, using rules to limit the issues examined in lawsuits.

From this viewpoint, the rise of the Roman jurists was in part a systemic response to the demands of an increased caseload. While this hypothesis is fairly likely to be correct, little direct evidence supports it; only rarely do late Republican authors imply that the volume of private cases was getting out of control, and their complaints are vague as to the causes (e.g., Cic. *de Or.* 2.140). Yet even a relatively simple case required preparation of speeches by the two advocates, plus at least a full day's commitment from a *iudex*, the members of his *consilium*, the advocates and *cognitores*, and the witnesses— all of whom were not directly compensated for their time. Against the background of an increased caseload, it is easy to understand the resentment of protracted speeches (*Quinct.* 33-

[13] R.L. Abel, "A Comparative Theory of Dispute Institutions in Society," *Law and Society Review* 8 (1974) 217-348, at 287-288 (footnotes omitted). See also C. Kluckhohn, "The Moral Order in an Expanding Society," in *City Invincible* (ed. C. Kraeling and R. Adams, 1960) 320.

34; *Tull.* 6), the dislike of multiple hearings (*Caec.* 6-7), and the tendency of judges to intervene more frequently in trials.[14] The *lex Aurelia* of 70 not only reformed the composition of the "jury class," it also at least doubled its effective size;[15] if we assume that the number of judges allocated to private trials grew more or less proportionally (there is no evidence for this), then the burden of an increasing caseload may simply have been distributed among a larger number of judges—and of course the parties could also look for a *iudex* outside the Praetor's *album*. Likewise, the corps of orators may also have expanded to meet the demand.

But even if the Ciceronian judicial system did rise to the challenge in this fashion, it still cannot have escaped altogether the implications of the increasing caseload that enfranchisement produced. The newly enfranchised, many of whom had not previously encountered Roman private law, are certain to have been more rule-oriented in their understanding of law than were the old citizens for whom it was familiar. Further, as more cases were processed and decided, any apparent discrepancies from case to case became more glaring; for trials were more readily juxtaposed with one another, and invidious contrasts more easily drawn. The consequence, as we saw in Chapter VI, was a movement for uniformity at least in the application of law in private trials; and the main proponents of uniformity appear to have been members of the equestrian order, acting in a broad sense as representatives of the newly enfranchised and abetted by jurists of mainly

[14] See Chapter V, at notes 82-83. On the volume of late Republican lawsuits, see perhaps Cic. 2 *Verr.* 1.125, where Cicero points to "many hundreds" (*sescenta*) of decisions made by Verres and then overruled; cf. *ibid.* 119. This order of magnitude seems right, in any case. For instance, if each Urban Praetor devoted the equivalent of 100 eight-hour days (a third of his term) to judicial decisions, and if decisions took an average of thirty minutes, he could make 1,600 decisions per year.

[15] On the lowest estimate (that of Mommsen), the "jury class" increased from 600 Senators, under Sulla's legislation, to 900 under the *lex Aurelia*. However, the first figure was effectively much lower, since many Senators were unavailable for judicial duties in any given year; and the second figure may be too low. For a discussion, C. Nicolet, *Ordre* vol. I 611-613.

equestrian origin.[16] It is this group to whom we may attribute the controversial demands to limit the Urban Praetor's discretion and to codify the civil law, and more generally the effort to elevate the role of jurists' law in private trials.

It is probably not amiss, therefore, to describe the mass enfranchisement of the Italians, and the subsequent increase in the judicial caseload, as the direct "precipitant" for the rise of the Roman jurists within the Roman judicial system.[17] Yet, from a slightly different perspective, this chain of events takes on a different meaning. The Italian enfranchisement was itself a response to the demands of Rome's allies for a share in Roman political life; behind these demands lay a generalized sentiment favoring the equality of citizens before the law.[18] Seen in this larger context, the rise of the Roman jurists may be regarded as one part of the intricate recursive process whereby Roman citizenship was finally sundered from its historical roots in the Roman city-state and re-defined on a national basis.[19] The integrative power of the city-state receded, and was replaced in part by the integrative power of shared law. Thus,

[16] See Chapter VI, under subhead "On the Road to Classical Roman Law"; also K. Hopkins, *Conquerors and Slaves* (1978) 85-87. On the close ties of *equites* with Italian municipalities, see C. Nicolet, *Ordre* vol. I 387-415.

[17] On the concept of a "precipitant" in relation to social change, see R.M. MacIver, *Social Causation* (1942) 163-164, 169-172, 177-178.

[18] On the legalism of the *municipales*, see already A.H.M. Jones, *JRS* 41 (1951) 112-119, at 112. On the Social War, see also P.A. Brunt, *JRS* 55 (1965) 90-109. (E.g., 104: "Our sources insist on the allies' demand for justice and equality.") There is a survey of modern views in A.N. Sherwin-White, *The Roman Citizenship* (2d ed. 1973) 134-145, who rightly observes that the allies' purposes in revolting should be kept distinct from their reasons for revolting. However, I would not discount the view of E. Gabba, *Republican Rome: The Army and the Allies* (trans. P.J. Cuff, 1976) 70-96, that the allies were at least partly influenced by economic considerations.

[19] See Cic. *Leg.* 2.5, with A.N. Sherwin-White, (cited n.18) 150-155 and 165-173. With my general point, cf. J.K. Lieberman, *The Litigious Society* (1981) 186: "Litigiousness is not a legal but a social phenomenon. It is born of a breakdown in community, a breakdown that exacerbates and is exacerbated by the growth of law." On the rising tide of litigation in the early Empire, see J. Carcopino, *Daily Life in Ancient Rome* (trans. E.O. Lorimer, 1940) 186-187.

Conclusion

it is entirely possible that one leading late Republican jurist was in fact the grandson of a rebel Samnite commander in the Social War.[20]

In this sense, it is possible to argue that, while the increased caseload appears to be a decisive factor in the rise of the jurists, in fact Rome's judicial system was ripe for change, and enfranchisement did not so much cause as trigger the transformation. Attitudes toward private law were changing; and the new citizens were not the only cause. A huge surge of commerce had followed in the wake of Rome's expanding empire; the upper classes of Italy had enjoyed a general rise in their personal wealth, derived from this commerce and from other opportunities imperialism had created.[21] Late Republican authors commonly describe these phenomena as causing the decline of "morality," by which they intend particularly the morality of the upper classes.[22] But it is perhaps more accurate to say that commerce and wealth helped break down the stifling mechanical solidarity of Rome, by encouraging segmented, instrumental social relationships and more individualistic social values. Increased commerce and wealth undoubtedly contributed their share to the rising volume of litigation; and the transitory, non-affectual relationships they promoted will have led to a preference among disputants for "a dispute process in which factual inquiry is severely restricted in scope" and "the outcome is certain and predictable."[23] Law substituted for the waning power of purely social constraint on disputes. Indeed, this point is potentially of much broader application; for instance, Servius' monograph on dowry (Gell. NA 4.3-4; Nerat. D. 12.4.8) is not unreasonably con-

[20] C. Trebatius Testa, from Velia in Lucania (Cic. Fam. 7.20.1). E.T. Salmon, Samnium and the Samnites (1967) 357 n.4, suggests that he may be descended from the Trebatius in App. BC 1.52.228.

[21] On trade, see just K. Hopkins, JRS 70 (1980) 101-125, esp. 105-112; and idem in Trade in the Ancient Economy (ed. P. Garnsey et al., 1983) xiv-xxi. On the increase in personal wealth, see W. Kroll, Die Kultur der Ciceronischen Zeit vol. I (1933) 88-120; I. Shatzman, Senatorial Wealth and Roman Politics (1975) 104-108, 143-147.

[22] See just D.C. Earl, The Political Thought of Sallust (1966), esp. 41-59.

[23] R.L. Abel, (cited n.13) 294. Compare Chapter I, above, at notes 93 and 100-101.

Conclusion

nected with the increasing complexity and instability of Roman marriage patterns, a "decay" upon which the lawyers feasted.

Finally, there is the political restlessness and instability of the late Republic—a factor not easy to evaluate, but certainly omnipresent in the background. In the Ciceronian court the boundaries between law and politics were still quite porous, and political issues or influences not infrequently intruded overtly upon judicial deliberations.[24] The jurists, by contrast, promoted a view that sharply divided private from public law, and so sought to secure an area of formal autonomy for private law;[25] this is the view that Cicero extols in the *pro Caecina* (65-78), and it seems slowly to have carried the day. The new ideology can be seen at work, for instance, in Cicero's denunciation of Caesar's debt relief measures in 49-48; Cicero argues that it is contrary to the very nature of the State to interfere with existing patterns of property holding (*Off.* 2.72-85). Caesar, for his part, stresses in his memoirs those aspects of his debt program that did not constitute a redistribution (*BC* 3.1.2),[26] while distancing himself from more radical initiatives (3.21.1-2). The ideology of autonomous private law, though ultimately impotent in the face of revolutionary movements such as those that produced the proscriptions of 43, was nonetheless powerful in more normal circumstances; it is certain to have encouraged more rule-oriented decision making.

Broadly speaking, the rise of the Roman jurists may thus

[24] See esp. Chapter II, at notes 27-28.

[25] F. Schulz, *Principles* 26-33. Cf. R. Syme, (cited n.9) 513, speaking of Augustus: "There is something more important than political liberty; and political rights are a means, not an end in themselves. That end is security of life and property: it could not be guaranteed by the constitution of Republican Rome. . . . The New State might be called monarchy, or by any other name. That did not matter. *Personal rights and private status need not depend upon the form of government.*" (Emphasis mine.) For all Syme's irony, the point is crucial.

[26] See the interesting analysis of this passage in A. Bürge, *SZ* 99 (1982) 128-157, at 135-136. On the debt crisis, see esp. M. Frederiksen, *JRS* 56 (1966) 128-141, and Z. Yavetz, *Julius Caesar and His Public Image* (1983) 132-137, 150 (partially inaccurate); both have further bibliography.

be attributed to three external factors: the enfranchisement of the Italians (perhaps the most important factor); the increase in commerce and personal wealth during the late Republic; and the political instability of the era. These external factors produced demands upon the internal structure of the Roman judicial system, which in practice could satisfy the demands only through a gradual upgrading of the weight accorded to jurists' pronouncements on law. Most of the change probably occurred on the micro-scale, as new patterns of judicial conduct emerged and were reinforced through social acceptance; hence the evidence for the change is mainly indirect and circumstantial, though rather conclusive. In general, so I would argue, the increasing scale and complexity of late Republican society made it desirable (though not necessarily inevitable) that law become differentiated at a higher and more deliberate level than in earlier Mediterranean societies; and the presence of the jurists at the margins of the Roman judicial system made it possible for this to occur. The factors that caused the rise of the Roman jurists are thus broadly similar to those that created and shaped the Principate.

One implication of my argument is that the rise of the jurists depended less on the specific content or rational interrelationship of the norms the jurists developed than it did on the fact of the jurists' professional presence, and on the opportunities for legal security their presence seemed to provide. To some extent this proposition is true. In societies where law is strongly differentiated from its social context, it is not rare for laymen to be more concerned with what law is than with how it was obtained or what its purposes are; inside broad limits of tolerance, and provided only that legal norms do not severely inhibit social or economic development, laymen are prepared to accept legal norms as simply the rules of the game, and to cope with the consequences as best they can.[27] On the other hand, Roman law had emerged from its

[27] See the comments of R.L. Abel, *Michigan Law Review* 80 (1982) 785-809, on A. Watson, *Society and Legal Change* (1976), esp. chaps. 2-4 on Roman law. A. Sarat, *Law and Society Review* 11 (1977) 438, summarizing the results of numerous surveys, notes: "What they do demonstrate is that courts are not particularly visible or salient to the American people." Indeed, these surveys

Conclusion

long struggle with rhetorical advocacy in a far more flexible and socially appealing form; in many areas the jurists had developed doctrines that at least accommodated upper-class moral values and that, on occasion, could even command intellectual respect, as Cicero's discussion of the *dolus* doctrine on sale (*Off.* 3.65-71) clearly shows.[28] The greater breadth of late Republican law undoubtedly removed one potential obstacle to the rise of the jurists. But already by the late Republic, private law had probably obtained a sufficient degree of overall social adequacy—to be sure, not in itself an especially great accomplishment. The specific content of Roman legal norms is thus probably more relevant to evaluating the social purpose and effects of Roman law than to understanding the sources of its legitimacy.

In any event it is more than doubtful that legal science itself ever served as an important basis for rallying support among the law-affected population, either in the late Republic or later. To most Romans, it appears, the ways of the jurist remained largely mysterious and were thus the frequent object of uncomprehending humor, even derision.[29] The role played by formal legal science was primarily internal: it served first to distinguish jurists from non-jurists, and then to facilitate communication among jurists as they enunciated and developed norms. The Roman jurists, like the practitioners of Common Law in a much later time, shared a highly technical, proce-

---

support the hypothesis that "the widespread public ignorance of what courts do and how they operate should enhance their support" (p. 439). By and large, familiarity breeds contempt.

[28] See D. Nörr, *Rechtskritik* 42-43. In any case, Max Weber's belief that law can obtain legitimacy through the formal rationality of its rules is deeply problematic; see T. Parsons, in *Max Weber: The Theory of Social and Political Organization* (repr. 1966) 68-71. Also P.M. Blau, *American Political Science Review* 57 (1963) 305-316; D. Easton, *A Systems Analysis of Political Life* (1965) 301 with n.7; N. Luhmann, *Legitimation durch Verfahren* (2d ed. 1975) 28-31. Weber's theory is recently expounded by A.T. Kronman, *Max Weber* (1983) 45-47.

[29] D. Nörr, *Rechtskritik* 83-87; also 136-141 on juristic "attempts at legitimation" (largely perfunctory). On the widening gulf between jurists and laymen, see M. Bretone, in *Diritto e Potere nella Storia Europea* vol. I (1983) 73-92.

Conclusion

dure-oriented competence. This competence involved not just knowledge of prevailing norms, but also experience and judgmental capacity in the operative potential of legal concepts, understanding of the possibilities for conduct and argumentation in juristic disputes, and skill in the practical channels available for achieving certain legal effects—in short, mastery of that aspect of a system of norms which is most emphatically "open" and rich in alternatives.[30] Their mastery lifted law above the comprehension of laymen, while simultaneously creating new responsibilities for the jurists in the development of legal norms.

The broad advance of the jurists continued undiminished into the early Empire, and the Julio-Claudians confirmed and consolidated past tendencies. Probably under Augustus, selected jurists were first granted the *ius respondendi*; though the sources are extremely murky, they suggest that this right lent imperial authority to *responsa* used in lawsuits, thereby making them preferable to other sources as statements of law in this context.[31] On the other hand, possession of the right appears to have had little if any impact on the internal organization of legal science itself, and so the *ius respondendi* is doubtless better regarded as a means both to increase the authority of law (so explicitly Pomponius, D. 1.2.2.49) and to institutionalize imperial patronage through selective preferment of jurists. Similar policies underlie the promotion of selected jurists to the consulate.[32] The Augustan judiciary laws mainly completed

[30] See N. Luhmann, *Rechtssoziologie* vol. I (1972) 179-180, whom I paraphrase; cf. also Chapter IV, above, at notes 122-128.

[31] See Chapter IV, at notes 173-175; Chapter V, at note 98. One crucial side-effect of the increasing solidity of the jurist's position was the much greater freedom jurists began to exercise in manipulating the law; Pomponius (D. 1.2.2.47) seems to regard the Augustan jurist Antistius Labeo as the major innovator in this respect. I would venture to recognize this greater freedom as the basic difference between classical jurists and their late Republican predecessors; cf. Chapter VI, note 112. Somewhat differently, D. Nörr, *Bull.* 23 (1981) 9-33.

[32] See W. Kunkel, *Herkunft*[2] 272-281, who to my mind overstates the social distinction between late Republican and early imperial jurists by concentrating on the consulate.

Conclusion

the conversion of the judicial system to formulary procedure by eliminating most archaic survivals.[33]

By and large, the autonomy of private law, though it stood in apparent contradiction to the centralist aspirations of the Caesars, nonetheless occupied a considerable place in early imperial statecraft.[34] This contradiction is easily explained. The Caesars had a highly ambivalent relationship to the aristocracy of their empire; the regime existed as an onslaught against the traditional aristocracy, yet depended on the aristocracy for legitimacy and help in governance. For the Roman Empire, as for all pre-modern bureaucratic empires, "persistence was a matter of constant, restless bureaucratic manipulation of that dilemma: the derogation of aristocratic privilege checked by the understanding that the regime's own legitimacy was tied to the legitimacy of aristocratic privilege; the encouragement of urban and commercial groups off-set by the alienation or extinction of those groups as the regimes extracted the resources which were the lifeblood of their existence. To the extent that they persisted their history was a history of endless movement in pursuit of immobility."[35]

The power of the Caesars rested first and foremost on their control of the army, second on the legitimation of their au-

[33] See Chapter VI, at note 11, with bibliography.

[34] Apart from legislation (on which see F. Schulz, *Principles* 10-12), the early Empire saw little intervention by the government in private law; overt intervention was highly unpopular (see, e.g., Sen. *Apoc.* 12.2 with Suet. *Claud.* 14) but increasingly common, cf. F. Millar, *The Emperor in the Roman World* (1977) 528-537. The major early imperial innovation was *cognitio extra ordinem*: M. Kaser, *RZ* 342-343, and in *Antologia Giuridica Romanistica e Antiquaria* vol. I (1968) 171-188; G.I. Luzzatto, in *St. Volterra* vol. II 665-757; I. Buti, in *ANRW* vol. II.14 (1982) 34-39, with further literature. An important parallel innovation was irregular appeal procedure: W. Litewski, in *ANRW ibid.* 60-96. See the survey in H.F. Jolowicz, *Historical Introduction to the Study of Roman Law* (3d ed. B. Nicholas, 1972) 395-401; also N. Palazzolo, *Processo Civile e Politica Giudiziaria* (1980) 16-49.

[35] P. Abrams, *Historical Sociology* (1982) 184-185, summarizing S.N. Eisenstadt, *The Political Systems of Empires* (1963). See also P. Anderson, *Passages from Antiquity to Feudalism* (1970) 74-75. As to the early Empire, see the recent study by A. Wallace-Hadrill, *JRS* 72 (1982) 32-48; and also K. Hopkins, (cited n.16) 93-95.

Conclusion

thority within the ruling elite, and only third (perhaps a distant third) on the formation of economic interdependence and prosperity within the Empire.[36] Pursuit of the third goal, and less directly pursuit of the second, required that they concede a degree of economic, social, and cultural differentiation outside the political sphere as well as the existence of resources not under direct governmental control.[37] Rome was the first bureaucratic empire to have pursued these goals (in part) by using "autonomous" private law as an instrument of social self-control;[38] Rome's success determined the pattern for most later imperial societies. A description of the Roman Empire's accomplishments in law lies, however, beyond the compass of this book.

The Caesars made use of "autonomous" private law, but they did not create it. Their ability to use private law depended on an earlier event: the rise of the jurists within the late Republican judicial system. The event, to be sure, passed virtually unnoticed in that creative but deeply troubled era when Romans were obsessed with, and for the last time freely debated, the larger questions of their collective destiny. In such bleak times the jurists had quietly but unswervingly pursued their own ambition. For the first time in history, a secular legal system was examined as a distinct and coherent body of knowledge: individual legal decisions, rules, and statutory enactments were considered objectively and were explained through reference to general principles and truths basic to the legal system as a whole. Law was finally sundered from the

[36] A. Giddens, *A Contemporary Critique of Historical Materialism* (1981) 103-104, on pre-modern imperial societies generally. See the good discussion in P. Petit, *Pax Romana* (trans. J. Willis, 1976) 125-152.

[37] See S.N. Eisenstadt, (cited n.35) 26-28; also pp. 98-99 on law, where the extent of the Roman achievement is understated.

[38] See B.W. Frier, *LTIR* 207-208, for a discussion of this concept. On social control, see M. Janowitz, *The Last Half-Century* (1978) 3: "Social control is . . . the obverse of coercive control. Social control refers to the capacity of a social group, including a whole society, to regulate itself. Self-regulation must imply a set of 'higher moral principles' beyond those of self-interest." On social control and the law, cf. *ibid*. 364-365; also K. Llewellyn, *Jurisprudence* (1960) 399-411.

Conclusion

elaborate apparatus of case-oriented rhetorical argument and was made over into an abstract body of norms, on the basis of which legal claims could in principle be scrutinized without special reference to the person of the claimant; gradually the participants in the Roman judicial system were persuaded to understand and use law in this way. All later legal development is ultimately based on this victory of the jurists. Yet it would be wrong to understand the jurists' victory solely as their personal triumph, and not as an achievement inextricably bound up with the social history of their time.

The circumstances in which law was professionalized at Rome turned out to have considerable importance for later legal history, especially that of Europe. Law was, in a sense, professionalized "from the top down": first at the level of analytical jurisprudence; only later within the judicial system itself. Although the early Empire saw the gradual differentiation of the legal profession into various sub-professions (legal teachers, trained judges and lawyers, notaries, and so on), the narrow circle of Roman jurists continued to dominate the profession until well into the third century A.D. The powerful historical example of the jurists later contributed to the peculiarly abstract and academic quality of Continental legal thinking. Likewise, the preoccupation of the jurists with private law, the original domain of their competence, was in part responsible for the long-enduring but somewhat artificial barrier between private and public law. Finally, Roman law's liberal temper, which was in origin primarily an aspect of its social function at Rome, in time became rather misleadingly identified with the existence and nature of law itself.

All these features are part of the price that history has exacted, and to a certain extent continues to exact, in exchange for the original professionalization of law—the last, but by no means the least estimable, of the gifts with which the failing Republic endowed the Roman Empire and subsequent ages.

Index of Passages Cited

I. CICERO

Index of Passages Cited

Index of Passages Cited

Index of Passages Cited

Index of Passages Cited

Index of Passages Cited

Index of Passages Cited

II. OTHER LITERARY AUTHORS

Index of Passages Cited

Index of Passages Cited

Index of Passages Cited

III. Legal Sources

Index of Passages Cited

Index of Passages Cited

General Index

accessibility of law, 76-78
account books, 32; of Caesennia,
    14, 16, 207; of Phormio, 16-17,
    108-109, 207; of tenant, 21-22,
    87, 106, 207
Acerronius, Cn., landowner, 79, 275
Acilius, L., jurist; comments on
    Twelve Tables, 158
Acilius Glabrio, M.' (cos. 67), 144
actio adversus nautas, 43
actio de dolo; introduction of, 93-94,
    148, 262. *See also dolus malus*
actio de pastu pecoris, 42
actio furti, 243. *See also furtum usus*
actio iniuriarum, 34, 68
actio in rem per sponsionem, 81-82, 85
actio mandati, 76. *See also* mandate
actio Publiciana, 51, 94
actio quod metus causa, 51-52. *See also*
    formula Octaviana
actio Serviana, 94, 262
actio vi bonorum raptorum, 52-53. *See*
    also iudicium de vi
actions *ex fide bona*; and Q. Mucius,
    159, 161-162, 224
adversary procedure; and legiti-
    macy, 246-250; and litigants, 30-
    31; and rhetoric, 131-134, 183,
    214-217, 233-234
advocates; attitudes of, toward ju-
    rists, 130-131, 134-137, 184, 186,
    192-193; and audiences, 207, 235-
    236; and *cognitores*, 67; decorum
    of, 62, 197-199, 206-209; domi-
    nance of, in private trials, 66, 96-
    97, 266-267; legal knowledge of,
    134-135; not lawyers, 135, 272.

See also agonistic law, orations,
    rhetoric
Aebutii, 86
Aebutius, Sex., defendant; access
    of, to advocates, 35, 102-103; ac-
    cess of, to jurists, 35; agrees to
    deductio, 23-24, 78-86, 89-90; and
    Caecina, 16, 20, 36-37; and Cae-
    sennia, 15-16, 35; challenges Cae-
    cina's citizenship, 20-21, 46, 97,
    101-103; claims to own Fulcinian
    farm, 22-23, 85, 106-107; as *cogni-
    tor*, 15, 66-67; as *defensor*, 38, 58,
    66; as heir to Caesennia, 3, 16; li-
    tigiousness of, 29-30, 38; pur-
    chases Fulcinian farm, 16-18,
    105, 109; repulses Caecina from
    Fulcinian farm, 24-26, 84, 86-88,
    107; resists interdict, 27, 63, 65,
    95; seizes Fulcinian farm, 22,
    109-110; social status of, 15, 28,
    35-36, 134, 275-276
Aelii Paeti; jurists, 253
Aelius Paetus, Sex. (cos. 198), ju-
    rist; comments on Twelve Ta-
    bles, 158
Aelius Tubero, Q. (tr. pl. 130?), ju-
    rist, 217
Aelius Tubero, Q. (sen.?), jurist,
    146; on duties of judges, 217-218,
    264
Aemilius Lepidus, M. (cos. 78); re-
    bellion of, 13, 52, 101
aequitas; in *pro Caecina*, 120-123; and
    criticism of Edict, 49-50; and ju-
    rists' law, 127, 186. *See also* jus-
    tice

xvi; social functions of, 188-190, 258, 281

banks; of Fidiculanius, 8; of Fulcinius, 7-11; of Phormio, 8, 16-17; Roman, 7-9, 257
bees; law of, 266
Billienus, C. (praet. ca. 107), jurist, 142
Blaesus, jurist, 146
bona fides; and jurists, 193, 264; and Q. Mucius, 159. *See also* actions *ex fide bona*
burden of proof, 85, 88, 125, 212-213, 234
Burrienus, P.(?); conduct of, as Urban Praetor, 74

Caecilius Metellus, L. (cos. 68); as Governor of Sicily, 46; conduct of, as Urban Praetor, 94; Edict of, 46, 53-56, 94
Caecilius Metellus, Q. (cos. 69); conduct of, as Urban Praetor, 74, 93; Edict of, 50, 93
Caecina, A., plaintiff; and Aebutius, 16, 20, 32, 36-39; arranges *deductio*, 23-24, 78-86, 89-90; and Cicero, 33, 102, 232; citizenship of, 20-21, 46, 97, 102-104, 109; consults Aquilius, 27, 67, 149; as heir to Caesennia, 3, 18-20; litigiousness of, 28-30, 38-39, 123; receives interdict, 27, 55, 62, 65, 94-95; repulsed from Fulcinian farm, 24-27, 86-88; seeks to divide Caesennia's estate, 22, 44; social status of, 18-19, 35-36, 39, 134, 260, 275; visits Fulcinian farm, 21-22, 105-107, 110, 113-114
Caecina, A., son of above, 18-19; and Cicero, 18-19, 33, 232
Caecina Largus, A. (cos. A.D. 13), 19

Caecina Largus, C. (cos. A.D. 42), 19
Caecina Severus, A. (cos. 1 B.C.), 19
Caecinae, 18-19
Caelius, L., landowner at Tarquinii; witness, 25-26, 107
Caesennia, from Tarquinii; account books of, 14, 16, 207; and Aebutius, 15-16; death and will of, 3, 16, 20, 105-106; dowry of, 7, 9-10, 13; leases Fulcinian farm, 12, 18, 29, 105-106; as legatee from son, 14-15; mandate of, to Aebutius, 17-18, 21, 105, 109; marries Caecina, 16, 18-20; marries Fulcinius, 7-8, 19; social status of, 4-5, 7-8; usufruct of, on Fulcinius' estate, 13-14, 17-18, 106, 109-110
Caesennii, 4-6
Caesennius, P.; as heir of M. Fulcinius (jr.), 14-17; testifies for Aebutius, 17, 108-109; tutor of Caesennia (?), 16
Caesius, T., jurist, 146
Calpurnius Piso, C. (cos. 67), 45; as advocate, 102-103, 134, 232; conduct of, as Urban Praetor, 74, 93-94; defends Aebutius, 35, 108-115; as *iudex*, 103, 198; political views of, 103-104, 262; rejects authority of jurists, 107, 136, 150, 171, 184; uses jurist, 112, 116, 123, 130, 149-150, 171-172
Calpurnius Piso Frugi, L. (praet. 74); intercedes against Verres, 73
Capua; citizenship of, 101
Cascellius, *praediator*, 152
Cascellius, A. (quaest. before 73), jurist; honors Q. Mucius, 171; and *iudicium Cascellianum*, 152, 262; legal education of, 145-146, 152-153, 253; political career of, 253, 255; social status of, 152, 253-254

General Index

Castellum Axia; Caecina at, 24, 28; site of, 5, 9-10
Castor, Temple of; near Praetor's court, 57, 59
casuistry, *see* hypothetical cases
causa Curiana, 135-137, 144, 186
census; and land registration, 17; and *lex Voconia*, 14-15; of 86/85 B.C., 14-17, 52, 273; of 70/69 B.C., 17, 46, 101, 273
centumviri, 199, 205; and oratory, 207, 218
centuria Populiana, 79, 81
Cercina, 149
Cicero, M. Tullius (cos. 63); on *aequitas*, 120-123; attitude of, to formal justice, 72-73, 121, 263-264; career of, as private advocate, 92-94, 126; criticizes Verres' Edict, 48-50; emotionalism of, 216; and *equites*, 259; and Etruria, 99, 102, 104, 232; and jurists, 260-261; on law, 118-120, 134-135; on law and jurists, 184-191, 259-260; on law as career, 155, 252-253; legal education of, 143-144, 260; legal knowledge of, 134; on persuasion, 216-217; on systematization of law, 170; on *vis*, 86, 118-119
  pro Caecina; agonistic law in, 133-134; argument of, 117-125; date of, 45-46; editing of, for publication, 21, 98, 100, 117, 198; legalism of, 224; length of, 206-207; organization of, 115-116; relation of, to earlier speeches, 114-115, 117, 214; reputation of, 126, 219; significance of, 267-268; as source, 3-4, 27-28, 108, 112-113; strategy of, 125-126; style of, 231; tone of, toward *recuperatores*, 197-199
  pro Quinctio, 221; background of, 9, 104; length of, 206; tone of, 198

  pro Roscio Comoedo; background of, 9; date of, 126-127; length of, 206; tone of, 198
  pro Tullio, 102; background of, 104; date of, 52; legalism of, 224; length of, 206; tone of, 198
  other speeches; *pro Cluentio*, 231; *pro Cornelio*, 75, 231; *pro Fonteio*, 102; *pro Lege Manilia*, 45, 231; *pro Muliere Arretina*, 99-100; *pro Murena*, 155; *Ninth Philippic*, 155; *pro Rabirio*, 231; *Second Catilinarian*, 13; *Verrines*, 48-49, 102, 231
Cinna, jurist, 146
Circeii; home of Aquilius Gallus (?), 141, 149
citizenship; and law, 279-280; and liberty, 100-101; of Volaterrans, 20-21, 97-104, 109, 116-129. *See also* enfranchisement of Italians, new citizens
Claudius, C. (sen.); landowner in Thurii, 275
Claudius Marcellus, M. (aed. 91?); serves on *cónsilium*, 192
clients, *see* patronage
Clodius Phormio, Sex.; as banker, 8; sells Fulcinius' estate, 16; testifies for Aebutius, 17, 108-109
codification of *ius civile*, 170, 239, 264-265
Coelius Valens, C., Tarquinian magistrate, 26
cognitio; before issuance of interdict, 65, 95; *extra ordinem*, 285
cognitores, 66-67, 235
Comitium; as site of Praetor's court, 58
commerce; and *equites*, 256-258; and law, 159, 258, 280-282
condemnatio pecuniaria, 226
condictio certae pecuniae, 93, 213
confessio; Piso's, 105, 110-111, 151; rhetorical use of, 108
coniectio causae, 204

General Index

consilium; of Caecina, 22-23, 26-28, 34, 79, 83, 90; of Caesennia, 15, 17; of *iudex*, 198, 205, 209, 213, 215, 222, 264; of Urban Praetor, 62, 65

constitutionality of statutes, 100-101, 103

consuetudo; and Praetor's court, 63-67, 74, 95; and Praetor's Edict, 50, 56-57; and trials, 205, 227. *See also* custom

consulate; and jurists, 142-143, 148, 154-155, 253-254; and Urban Praetors, 46-47, 72-73

Consuls; power of, over Urban Praetors, 74

contracts; and Q. Mucius, 162; security of, and law, 185

controversia ex scripto et sententia; in *causa Curiana*, 135-136; in *pro Caecina*, 120-125, 128-129

conveyancing, *see* mancipation

Coponius, M.; will of, 135

Cornelii Dolabellae, 44

Cornelius, C. (trib. pl. 67); proposes *lex Cornelia*, 73, 76, 261-262; prosecuted, 75, 262

Cornelius, Cn., freedman; estate of, 93

Cornelius Cinna, L. (cos. 87-84), 9

Cornelius Dolabella, Cn. (praet. 81); conduct of, as Urban Praetor, 74-75, 92

Cornelius Dolabella, L. (duumv. nav. 180-178), 44

Cornelius Dolabella, L. (praet. ca. 100), 44

Cornelius Dolabella, P. (praet. 69); gives action to divide estate, 22, 44, 94; as Governor of Asia, 45; grants interdict, 3, 27, 44, 63, 94-95; praetorship of (date), 45-46; social status of, 44

Cornelius Dolabella, P. (cos. 44), 46

Cornelius Lentulus Spinther, P.

(cos. 57); as Urban Praetor, 94

Cornelius Maximus, Q. (*eques*), jurist; identity of, 152; social status of, 253, 255; teaches Trebatius, 146, 152

Cornelius Scipio, P. (praet. ca. 93?); denied rights by Urban Praetor, 93

Cornelius Sisenna, L. (praet. 78); conduct of, as Urban Praetor, 75, 93

Cornelius Sulla, L. (cos. 88, 80), 9; and *equites*, 273-274; and Etruria, 13, 98-99; restricts Volaterran rights, 20, 97-104

corona, 235-236

corruption; of judges, 132, 186, 202, 211-212; of Urban Praetors, 48-49, 74-75; of witnesses, 208

culpa (negligence); defined by Q. Mucius, 161

cura (guardianship); and Q. Mucius, 159

Curius, M.'; as heir of Coponius, 135-136

custom; and *deductio*, 79-81, 83-85, 88-92; and law, 91-92, 127. *See also consuetudo*

debt crises, 9, 281

decemviri stlitibus iudicandis, magistral court, 99-100, 199

deductio quae moribus fit; arranged by Caecina, 23-24, 78-79, 107; arranged by Tullius, 79-84, 88; evidence for, 78-81; modern theories on, 81-83; purpose of, 83-90, 92

defensores, 38, 66

definition; in law, 160-161

deiectio, 56; classical view of, 176-177; in late Republic, 177-183; Piso's first view of, 110-114, 116-126, 172; Piso's second view of, 108, 112-114, 116-118, 124-126, 172

307

General Index

denuntiatio, 22-23, 85, 107
detrudere interdict; and possession,
182; relation of, to interdict *de vi
armata*, 56, 182; wording of, 54-
55
discretion, *see* judges, Praetor
divorce; law of, and Q. Mucius,
159
dolus malus; in *detrudere* interdict, 54-
55; development of, by jurists,
186, 283
dowry; law of, 280-281; and
Q. Mucius, 159; return of, 13,
217; use of, by husband, 9-10

Edict of Peregrine Praetor, 48, 51
Edict of Urban Praetor; character
of, 42-43, 56-57, 128-129; corrupt
influences on, 48-49; criticism of,
49-50; effect of, on *ius civile*, 157-
158, 168; fluidity of, 43, 44, 56-
57, 76, 183; Hadrianic redaction
of, 43, 54; interpreted by jurists,
163; juristic commentaries on, 76,
158, 170-171, 262; jurists' influence on, 90, 93-94, 148, 152, 262;
preparation of, 48
editio of evidence, 17, 207
enfranchisement of Italians; and
census, 52, 273; and Etruria, 4;
and law, 273-274, 276-280, 282.
See also citizenship, new citizens
equites; attitudes of, to law, 257-259,
265-266; and courts, 200, 259-
263; and jurists, 253, 255-256; as
litigants, 275-276; social status of,
256-257, 273-274
Etruria; and civil wars, 13; and
Sulla, 98-99
evidence, physical; in Caecina's
case, 207; forgery of, 186; and
hearsay, 87, 207-209; presentation
of, 33, 71, 207
exagogé, 81
exceptio vitiosae possessionis, 54-56, 67,

173-175, 178-179
exceptiones (demurrers), 63, 67-68, 95
exordium; of *pro Caecina*, 115, 118,
120, 242

Fabius, P., defendant in, 71; arranges *deductio*, 79-84, 88; social
status of, 275
Fabius Maximus Allobrogicus, Q.
(cos. 121); will of, not enforced,
74
Fannius Chaerea, C., plaintiff in,
73; acts as *cognitor*, 66; attacked
by Cicero, 209, 214; social status
of, 276; sues Q. Roscius, 93, 149
farms (*fundi*); size and price of, 11-
12, 36, 235. *See also* agriculture
Fidicolanius (freedman), 24
Fidiculanius, C. (freedman?), 8
Fidiculanius Falcula, C. (sen.); and
Aebutius, 35; bank of, 8; farm of,
11, 24, 235; prosecuted for bribery, 8, 132, 235; testifies for defendant, 24, 108, 132, 203, 235
fiducia, 9
Flavius, Q., Tarquinian landowner,
6
Flavius Fimbria, C. (cos. 104), jurist, 142; as *iudex*, 200
Flavius Priscus, jurist, 146
Fonteius, M. (praet. 75?); prosecuted, 102
formula arbitraria; in interdictal procedure, 69-70
formula Octaviana, 51-52, 93
formulae; in interdictal procedure,
69-70, 95-96, 225-226; in trials,
95-96, 203, 205-206, 212; and
verdicts, 225-229; in vindication,
85
formulary procedure, 95-96, 157,
274; consensual model of, 242-
246; in early Empire, 284-285. *See
also* procedure
Forum (Roman); and Praetor's

General Index

General Index

General Index

pontifical, 157; popular attitudes to, 191, 240, 283; role of, in Cicero's view, 184-191; social status of, 253-256; and systematization of law, 158-161, 169-170. *See also* law, legal science, profession, *responsa*

   influence of jurists; on Praetor's court, 73, 264; on Praetor's Edict, 90, 93-94, 148, 152, 262; on trials, 130-131, 149-150, 183, 221-225, 264

justice, formal; and *aequitas*, 121, 184-185; public attitudes to, 74-76, 183, 279; and Urban Praetor, 72-76; *See also aequitas*, legitimation

   procedural justice; and adversary system, 233-244; and legitimation, 241-242; limits of, 250-251

Juventius, T. (sen.?), jurist; career of, 255; legal education of, 145-146; teaches P. Orbius, 146, 152

lacus Juturnae, 57

law; and *aequitas*, 120-121, 123, 127; and analytical jurisprudence, 160-163, 191, 196; autonomy of, 184-196; codification of, 170, 239, 264-265, 279; and custom, 91-92, 127; and hypothetical cases, 163-169; legitimacy of, 239-240; liberalism of, 192, 257, 287; and litigiousness, 37-40, 279, 281; and politics, 104; popular attitudes to, 32, 91, 239-240, 250-251; and statutes, 184-185, 195; systematization of, 158-161, 169-171, 193-194. *See also* accessibility, autonomy, ignorance, insecurity, *ius*, jurists, justice, profession

lawyers; definition of, 67. *See also* jurists, profession

lease (*locatio conductio*); of farms, 13, 50-51; of Fulcinian farm, 12, 18,

21-22, 87, 105-106; and possession, 180

legal culture; and litigiousness, 76-78

legal profession, *see* profession

legal science, 155-171, 191-195; and legitimacy, 282-284. *See also* jurists, law, *responsa*

legatum partitionis, 14

legis actio sacramento in rem; and *deductio*, 81-82

legis actio system; decline of, 157

legitimation; defined, 237-238; of law and jurists, 239-240, 282-284; of legal system, 238-239; of Praetor's court, 62-63; of recuperatorial procedure, 226-227; of trials, 211-212, 240-251. *See also* justice, procedure

lex Aebutia (ca. 150), 157

lex agraria (111); and interdict *de vi*, 53, 178-179

lex Aquilia; action on, 42; and Q. Mucius, 161, 166

lex Aurelia (70); and jury class, 200, 259-260, 262, 278

lex Cincia (204); and pay for advocates, 33

lex Cornelia de iurisdictione (67), 51, 73, 75-76, 94, 238-239, 261-262

lex Lutatia de vi (78?), 52

lex Plaetoria, 62

lex Plautia de vi (70?), 52

lex Pompeia (52); limits speeches, 239, 263

lex Voconia (169), 49; circumvented, 14-15

liberty; loss of, 100-101

libido, 120

Licinia, wife of Ti. Gracchus; dowry of, 230

Licinius Crassus, L. (cos. 95); as advocate, 136, 143; on law and oratory, 135; legal knowledge of, 143; on system in law, 170

General Index

Licinius Crassus Dives, M. (cos. 70, 55), 52

Licinius Crassus Mucianus, P. (cos. 131), jurist; gives *responsa*, 137; legal knowledge of, 143

Licinius Lucullus, L. (cos. 74), 45

Licinius Murena, L. (cos. 62); praetorship of, 47, 94; prosecuted, 155

Licinius Sacerdos, C. (praet. 75); as Urban Praetor, 93

litigants; behavior of, 28-31, 240-242; and consensual model of procedure, 68, 211, 243-246; upper-class character of, 36, 63, 273-276

litigiousness; and development of law, 39-40; effect of, 277-279; factors affecting, 35-40; and insecurity of law, 32-33, 57, 224-225; social basis of, 40-41

Livius Drusus, M. (cos. 112); as Urban Praetor, 76

Lucilius Balbus, L. (sen.?), jurist; career of, 255; on *consilium*, 145, 198; legal education of, 145; teaches law, 154

Lucretius Vespillo, Q., civil advocate, 144

mancipation, 109, 158; of Fulcinian farm, 17; and Q. Mucius, 162

mandate, 264; to buy Fulcinian farm, 17. *See also actio mandati*

Manilius, M.' (cos. 149), jurist, 156, 164

Manlius Torquatus, L. (cos. 65), 46

Marcius Figulus, C. (praet. ca. 130), jurist, 142-143

Marius, C. (cos. 107, 104-100, 86), 9, 142; grandmother of, 8; as *iudex*, 217

marriage, 264, 280-281; *cum manu*, 7; law of, and Q. Mucius, 159

Memmius, P., Tarquinian landowner; as witness, 26, 107

Mithridates, king of Pontus, 9

Mucii Scaevolae; interest of, in law, 145, 253, 260

Mucius Orestinus, Q. (trib. pl. 64); contemplates suit, 94, 275

Mucius Scaevola, P. (cos. 133), jurist, 144, 156, 158-159, 164; gives *responsa*, 136, 230; as *iudex*, 200

Mucius Scaevola, Q. (cos. 117), jurist, 143-144; gives *responsa*, 136; on law and rhetoric, 135, 153, 170

Mucius Scaevola, Q. (cos. 95), jurist, 144-145; as advocate, 136-137, 144; on *bona fides*, 159, 161-162, 224; on functions of law, 188; on law and rhetoric, 135, 153, 168; and legal science, 140-141, 156, 158-171, 255, 257, 266-267, 270; reputation of, 144-145, 160, 171; teaches law, 144-146, 156, 163, 171; on *vis*, 131

Mummius, M. (praet. 70?), 46, 94

Naevius, Ser.; sued by Titinia, 93, 275

Naevius, Sex., plaintiff in, 81; receives irregular *sponsio*, 92; social status of, 275

narratio of *pro Caecina*, 115, 117

new citizens, 100, 274; and jurists, 253-254; and law, 259, 261; legalism of, 278-279. *See also* citizenship, enfranchisement of Italians

nexum; and Q. Mucius, 162

oaths; of judges, 203-204, 226; of witnesses, 208. *See also sacramentum*

Octavius, Cn. (cos. 76); conduct of, as Urban Praetor, 72, 93; Edict of, 51-52, 93

General Index

procedure, private (*cont.*)
and Q. Mucius, 159; and Praetor's discretion, 72-76; risks of, 68-72. *See also* adversary, advocates, formulary, judges, justice, legitimation, litigants, orations, trials

procuratores, 16; *ad litem*, 66

profession of law; defined, xiii, 271-272, 286-287; differentiation of, 168-169, 194, 287; success of, 269-270. *See also* jurists

property; security of, and law, 185, 187-188, 281

Publicius, Q. (praet. 67); and *actio Publiciana*, 51, 94

Publicius Gellius (?), jurist, 146

puteal Libonis, 58-59

Quinctilius (Varus?), P. (sen.?); on *consilium*, 198

Quinctius, L.; advocate for P. Fabius, 52, 209

Quinctius, P., defendant in 81 B.C., 92, 147; social status of, 275

Quinctius Scapula, P., 142, 147

Quintilian; praises *pro Caecina*, 63, 109, 126; on private trials, 218

quod quisque iuris, 51

rationality; and litigation, 31-34, 70-72

recuperatores in Caecina's lawsuit, 3, 27, 54, 95, 197-198; reasons of, for adjournment, 38-39, 114, 209-210, 214, 220-221; verdict of, 225-226, 231-234

recuperatorial procedure; equality of judges in, 201; no *consilium* in, 205; origins of, 198-199; and selection of judges, 200-202, 244; social urgency of, 199, 202; speed of, 202; witnesses in, 202-203

Regia; near Praetor's court, 57-59

registration of land, 17-18

re-hearing of cases, 96, 100, 209-210, 220-221

responsa of jurists; binding on judges, 130-131, 180, 187-188, 214, 260; collections of, 158, 163-164; form of, 130, 140, 149-150, 207; and hypothetical cases, 164-168; as means of patronage, 142-143, 149; and trials, 154, 171-172, 180, 187-188, 222, 264. *See also ius respondendi*, jurists

rhetoric; case orientation of, 131-132, 215-216, 272; decline of, 263-264, 266-267; effect of, on administration of law, 133-135; ethics of, 131-133; influence of, on substantive law, 137-138, 267-268; and interpretation of law, 122, 127-131; and jurists, 130-131; and legitimation, 246-247; relativism of, 131, 190. *See also* advocates, orations

Roscius Gallus, Q., defendant in 73 B.C.; consults jurist, 31, 149, 171; social status of, 275; sued by Fannius, 93; uses *cognitor*, 66

Rutilius, P., Tarquinian landowner; as witness, 26, 107

Rutilius Rufus, P. (cos. 105), 144

Sabinians, 146

Sacra Via, 57-58

sacramentum (judicial oath), 99-100

sale (*emptio venditio*); of dowry farm, 9-10; of Fulcinian farm, 11, 15-17; law of, 84, 230, 283; and Q. Mucius, 160

Salvius; as Urban Praetor in 76 (?), 50-51, 93

Scribonius Curio, C. (cos. 76); as advocate, 93

Scribonius Libo, L.; as Urban Praetor in 80 (?), 58, 92

self-help; in defending property, 25

General Index

General Index

trials (*cont.*)
210. *See also* procedure, recuperatorial procedure
tribunal of Urban Praetor, 57-59, 62-65
tribunes of plebs; curb Praetors, 9, 104
tribuni aerarii, 200
Tullia, Cicero's daughter, 46
Tullius, M., plaintiff in, 71; arranges *deductio*, 79-84, 88; granted *iudicium de vi armata*, 94; social status of, 275
Tullius Cicero, M., *see* Cicero
Tullius Cicero, Q. (praet. 62), 94
tutelage, 242; in Q. Mucius, 161; of women, 16
Twelve Tables, 158-159, 186, 239

Urban Praetor, *see* Praetor
usufruct, 164; of Fulcinius' estate, 13-14, 106, 109-110; and possession, 106, 180
utilitas communis, 119, 127, 184

vadimonium (bond for court appearance), 79
Valerius, L., jurist; and Cicero, 261; origins of, 254
Valerius Flaccus, L. (praet. 63), 94
Valerius Messalla Niger, M. (cos. 61), 94
Vecillus, pimp; denied *possessio bonorum*, 93, 276
verdict; accuracy of, 226-227, 236-237; basis of, 212-225; in Caecina's case, 231-234; effects of, 227-228, 234; form of, 225-228; not justificatory, 227-231; and oath of judges, 203-204; written, 227
Verres, C. (praet. 74); misconduct of, as Praetor, 63, 65, 72-73, 75, 93, 276, 278; prosecution of, 48, 94, 102
Edict of Verres; criticism of, 49-

50; innovations in, 49, 93; and will of Fulcinius (jr.), 14-15, 46, 49
Vesta, Temple of, 57, 59
Vetilius, C., Tarquinian magistrate, 25
Vetilius, P., Tarquinian landowner; as witness, 25, 107
via Aurelia, 4-5
via Cassia, 4-5, 10, 12
vindicatio, 68, 85, 234; *in libertatem*, 93, 99-101
violence; by followers of Sulla, 51-52; by slaves, 24-25, 52, 79-80, 108. *See also vis*
formalized violence; in *deductio*, 23, 80-81, 83, 86; in interdict *uti possidetis*, 82-83, 87, 127
vis (force); *armata*, 52-53, 55-56, 107, 111, 173-174, 176; Cicero's view of, 86, 118-120, 122-123, 131; and interdicts *unde vi*, 124, 172-175; and *ius*, 118-119, 133; and Praetor's Edict, 51-56, 86, 119. *See also* self-help, violence
Visellius Aculeo, C., jurist, 144, 260
Visellius Varro, C. (aed. 59?); career of, 255; and Cicero, 255; social status of, 253
Volaterrae; and Caecina, 13; citizenship of, 20-21, 97-103, 116, 129; gratitude of, to Cicero, 102, 232; resists Sulla, 13, 18-19
Volcacius, jurist; identity of, 253, 255; legal education of, 145-146; social status of, 253; teaches Cascellius, 146, 153, 253
Volcacius, C. (sen.?); denied rights by Praetor, 75, 92
Volcacius, L. (trib. pl. 68); identical with jurist above?, 253
Volcacius Tullus, L. (cos. 66), 253

wealth; and law, 159, 184-185, 187-

316

192, 212, 257, 280-282; and litigiousness, 31-33, 35-38, 40, 273-
274

wills; of Caesennia, 3, 20; and capacity to inherit, 49, 103, 106; as
evidence, 207; of freedmen, 49; of
Fulcinius, 13-14; of Fulcinius
(jr.), 14-15; interpreted by
Q. Mucius, 135-137, 162-163,
165-166, 169; invalidated, 127-
128; and litigiousness, 37-38, 153

witnesses; for Aebutius, 8, 24-26,
105, 108, 111, 134, 259; for Caecina, 17, 104-105; Cicero's view
of, 216; depositions by, 207; in
recuperatorial procedure, 202-
203; testimony of, 207-210; verac-
ity of, 186, 208

women; contractual capacity of,
127; as heirs, 14-15, 49; tutors of,
16, 127; wills of, 7

Bruce W. Frier is Professor of Classics at the University of Michigan, Ann Arbor, and the author of *Landlords and Tenants in Imperial Rome*, which won the 1983 Goodwin Award of Merit of the American Philological Association

Library of Congress Cataloging in Publication Data

Frier, Bruce W., 1943-
The rise of the Roman jurists.

Includes bibliographical references and indexes.
1. Lawyers (Roman Law) 2. Cicero, Marcus Tullius.
Pro Caecina. 3. Roman law. I. Title.

LAW   340.5'4'0924   84-42886
ISBN 0-691-03578-4 (alk. paper)